SOCIOCULTURAL PERSPECTIVES ON HUMAN LEARNING

AN INTRODUCTION TO EDUCATIONAL ANTHROPOLOGY

Judith Friedman Hansen
Indiana University

PRENTICE-HALL, INC., *Englewood Cliffs, New Jersey 07632*

Library of Congress Cataloging in Publication Data

Hansen, Judith Friedman.
   Sociocultural perspectives on human learning.

   Bibliography: p.
   Includes index.
   1.   Educational anthropology.   I. Title.
LB45.H36   370.19'3   78–16433
ISBN 0–13–821041–1

© *1979 by* PRENTICE-HALL, INC., *Englewood Cliffs, N.J. 07632*

PRINTED IN THE UNITED STATES OF AMERICA

10 9 8 7 6 5 4 3 2 1

PRENTICE-HALL INTERNATIONAL, INC., *London*
PRENTICE-HALL OF AUSTRALIA PTY. LIMITED, *Sydney*
PRENTICE-HALL OF CANADA, LTD., *Toronto*
PRENTICE-HALL OF INDIA PRIVATE LIMITED, *New Delhi*
PRENTICE-HALL OF JAPAN, INC., *Tokyo*
PRENTICE-HALL OF SOUTHEAST ASIA PTE. LTD., *Singapore*
WHITEHALL BOOKS LIMITED, *Wellington, New Zealand*

CONTENTS

PREFACE

The transmission of knowledge in human societies is a process both crucial and pervasive. Although all learning is individual, knowledge transmission is a social and cultural enterprise, inextricably part of human relationships. The structure of knowledge itself is conditioned by the social structure and cultural milieu of which it is an aspect. Thus learning and that which is learned cannot be understood apart from their sociocultural contexts. This is a fundamental premise of educational anthropology. It is also a vital factor in scientific inquiry itself.

In presenting sociocultural perspectives on human learning I have drawn heavily on my own discipline of anthropology, but contributions from other disciplines have also been incorporated. My aim has been to develop a synthetic framework for the study of knowledge transmission which does not bound the subject artificially by disciplinary fences. That anthropology has a vital contribution to make in combination with other perspectives is a basic assumption of the present work.

Most research on education and schooling in Western societies has been undertaken by educators and sociologists, although anthropological contributions are rapidly increasing. Cross-cultural comparison of knowledge transmission has often assumed a qualitative distinction between "complex," state-organized societies (typically Western) and "simpler" ones (typically Third World). The validity of this distinction as a dimension of contrast requires further examination. In the chapters which follow I will argue that this assumption obscures as much as it reveals, and that education in Western societies such as the U.S. can be understood adequately only in light of the range of educational forms and processes found cross-culturally.

This book represents an attempt to make a sociocultural perspective on knowledge transmission more accessible to students and practitioners in various disciplines. To accomplish this I have tried to (a) minimize jargon and emphasize clear definition and illustration of analytic concepts; (b) provide a synthetic framework within which existing studies may be systematically compared; and (c) present a sufficient range of examples from other societies and from within the U.S. that education in any society may be viewed more objectively.

Several premises underlie the perspective presented in this book. First, knowledge transmission presupposes knowledge construction; thus the processes of knowledge construction must be taken into account in analyzing transmission. Second, knowledge transmission in general, and education and schooling in particular, can be understood adequately only through *contextual* analysis. Third, educative processes are very complex phenomena that require multiple types of analysis for elucidation. Fourth, scientific inquiry itself is a culturally influenced mode of knowledge construction; thus it must be approached not only as a *tool* of inquiry but also as a topic in its own right.

The organization of the book reflects these premises. The first chapter suggests basic parameters for the study of knowing and learning as human phenomena, through a discussion of relevant concepts from several disciplines. In addition to a general outline of perception, cognition, and learning as socioculturally mediated processes, contributions from primate studies and cross-cultural research are discussed. The second chapter introduces the analytic concepts of education and schooling as forms of knowledge transmission and sketches the relationship between these phenomena and sociocultural context. The social distribution of knowledge in society and cultural assumptions and values regarding knowledge are discussed as aspects of that context. The third chapter has a dual focus. While scientific inquiry is an indispensable tool for the comparative study of education, it entails a set of assumptions and values about knowledge that influence in fundamental ways what we come to know about any subject. This chapter, therefore, is devoted both to an explication of the nature of scientific knowledge as a cultural construct and to discussion of its practical application in the study of education. Included here is a comparison of qualitative and quantitative methodological orientations. The fourth chapter continues this dual theme through comparative discussion of alternative analytic frameworks which may be applied in the study of education, including structural-functional, ecological, and sociopsychological perspectives. In this chapter, examples are taken primarily from U.S. schools, so that the analytic concepts presented can be grasped readily by reference to familiar sociocultural contexts. In both the third and fourth chapters I have argued that structure and process represent alternate faces of the same phenomena, differentiated largely by analytic vantage point and focus. The fifth and sixth chapters expand on this theme by focusing respectively on education-as-system and education-as-process. Following consideration of key issues in the analysis of educational systems, the fifth chapter presents two extended case studies of school systems, those of Ghana and Japan, examined in terms of historical development, system operation, and relationships to the larger sociocultural contexts in which each is embedded. The sixth chapter expands the focus to a variety of educative processes in addition to schooling. Here emphasis is laid on the complexity of interpersonal transactions which constitute educative process, highlighting the relationship among cognitive interpretive frameworks developed by both teachers and learners, behavioral strategies developed by both, media of transmission, and learning outcomes. The seventh chapter weaves together both structural and processual perspectives in an examination of continuity and change as functions of education. Following a discussion of education as a force for conservation and change, the final extended case study is presented. This example of the deliberate use of education in the service of change illustrates the complex interrelationship between educative process and sociocultural context and the interdependence of schooling and other forms of knowledge transmission. The final chapter summarizes the contribution that an anthropological perspective can make to the study of education and the premises on which my recommendations are based.

In writing this book, I have viewed my readers as fellow participants in an exploratory process. Each reader brings a unique set of background experiences which may be set against the analyses and examples presented in the following pages. To have drawn all the possible links among the diverse materials provided would have expanded the book beyond the limits allowed. Many of the same case studies have been used to illustrate different topics throughout the book; to facilitate reintegration of these materials by readers, each cultural group is listed in the index. Suggestions for further reading on specific issues have been provided as well, including reference to a wide variety of case studies. On each of the topics discussed, of course, there is a great deal more to be said. I have simply raised what appear to me to be key issues in the study of knowledge transmission. In some instances I have used chapter notes to indicate the direction that further analysis might take.

Many people have contributed to the creation of this book. Its conception is owed directly to Judith Preissle Goetz whose interest in anthropological approaches to research on education first sparked mine. Her detailed critical comments on several drafts were invaluable. John Singleton provided astute commentary and suggestions which markedly improved the final draft. Kent Maynard, William Baddeley, Charles Reafsnyder and Leonore T. Friedman made a number of insightful suggestions for improvement, as did anonymous reviewers. I am indebted to William Baddeley for the graphics of the figures in the third and fourth chapters and to Leonore T. Friedman for most of the typing. Rita K. Brown also provided much needed typing services. Stan Wakefield and Audrey Marshall provided editorial support. Finally, the completion of this book owes much to the support, encouragement, and intellectual stimulation of Gerald Berreman, James Spradley, and my students at Indiana University. For its weaknesses and flaws I alone am responsible.

JUDITH FRIEDMAN HANSEN

Indiana University

ONE

FOUNDATIONS OF HUMAN LEARNING

The problem of education in human societies has been tackled by many disciplines. Psychological investigations of learning processes, sociological studies of the operation of educational institutions, historical studies of the development of educational systems, and anthropological studies of the cultural matrix of knowledge transmission are among the most prominent contributions to our understanding of education as a human creation. Because the systematic transmission of knowledge is a basic requirement for the perpetuation of every culture and the organization of every human society, the combined efforts of all disciplines concerned with human behavior are crucial to our comprehension of how this transmission takes place.

Anthropology has a special role to play in this enterprise, for it has been concerned most directly with the comparative study of all human societies and cultures. While some degree of systematic education is common to all human societies, formal schooling is not. From an anthropological point of view, schooling thus is best understood within the larger comparative framework of educational institutions and processes which are found in a variety of societies. Modes of knowledge transmission other than schooling also differ widely. Only by cross-cultural comparison can we discern both the essential components of systematic knowledge transmission common to all societies and the distinctive features which differentiate groups.

The very structure of knowledge is conditioned by its sociocultural milieu.[1] Our ways of thinking, as well as what we know, reflect the particular kind

1

of education we have received. This has special relevance for the elucidation of educational process in multicultural groups; in what ways do variant modes of thinking and communicating affect knowledge transmission within such groups? Because researchers are also subject to the subtle effects of socioculturally conditioned knowledge, we must examine as well the relationship between our frameworks of scientific knowledge and our study of human realities. In what ways do our analytic perspectives influence our perception and understanding of each empirical case we examine?

Finally, because education always is embedded in a sociocultural milieu, anthropological analysis must take into account the relationship between education and other sociocultural events. This concern with the reciprocal influence of knowledge transmission and the larger context in which it takes place allows us to examine the way in which educational institutions and processes may encourage or retard change of particular types (cf. Bronfenbrenner 1976). In combination these characteristics of anthropological analysis provide a sound foundation for the interdisciplinary study of human education, and for the investigation of the role of education in the creation and solution of social problems.

In this chapter we begin with a discussion of the basic learning processes involved in knowledge transmission, drawing on a variety of disciplines for insight. In succeeding chapters conceptual and analytic tools useful in the study of education and ways in which cross–cultural comparison contributes to our understanding will be discussed.

knowing and learning

All knowledge transmission involves learning. In order to analyze education, it will be helpful to clarify what is entailed in both knowing and learning.

At birth humans are incomplete organisms in two respects. First, like other mammalian newborns, human infants are dependent on others for physical survival, since they are incapable of securing nutrition and protection by themselves. Human babies are even less mature physiologically and neurologically than other mammalian infants. More central to our concerns here is the fact that humans are born with less extensive genetic programs for behavior. Most other animals are equipped at birth with genetically transmitted "instincts" or programmed action patterns for dealing with many situations. For these animals, certain environmental conditions may be necessary to trigger these action patterns, but the amount of learning necessary for survival and competent adult behavior is relatively limited. Humans, in contrast, are dependent on an extensive and complex sort of learning. Without the long postnatal period of nurturing and of acquiring knowledge, a human would be incapable of even biological survival.

It has been said that we humans live in an "information gap." Between what our bodies tell us and what we have to know in order to cope effectively with our environment, there is a vacuum we must fill ourselves, and we fill it with information provided largely by the culture of the group into which we are born and in which we grow up. Our ideas, our values, our emotions, our behavior patterns, even our perceptions are all cultural products, in that they are constructed in response to our social experience from the tendencies, capacities, and dispositions with which we are born. Culture—all the knowledge learned and shared by members of a community—is an essential condition for human existence (Geertz 1973:33–54). Equally essential is a capacity for learning and what we might call a disposition to learn.

Culture provides a tool for organizing experience. Goodenough (1963:259) has defined culture as consisting of "standards for deciding what is, standards for deciding what can be, standards for deciding how one feels about it, standards for deciding what to do about it, and standards for deciding how to go about doing it." Culture aids the individual in organizing perception, processing information, and solving the problems which arise in daily life. The human capacity for learning and disposition to learn underlie the impact of standards held by others on the standards acquired by an individual growing up in a particular group. At the same time, variation in individual biographic experience, differences in biogenetic makeup, and inevitable vagaries of communication that render messages received different from messages sent, all contribute to heterogeneity within communities sharing many cultural standards. No culture is *totally* shared by all members of a group. Rather, as Goodenough (1971) has pointed out, each individual's stock of knowledge includes idiosyncratic and socially shared components. Moreover, even shared elements may be shared only with some other group members. In this respect every human group is multicultural.

The stock of knowledge on which an individual draws includes information about various domains of experience and about types of events, situations, objects, actors, and relationships. The general categories used by the individual to organize this mass of information usually reflect the assumptions, expectations, and beliefs prevalent in the community within which one was raised. Also part of one's knowledge repertoire are interpretive procedures for identifying which categories are pertinent for the processing of new information and relevance schemes for assessing their relationship to one's own interests and goals. As one interacts with one's environment and with other people, these interpretive processes are continually brought into play.

In daily life we typically assume that the actions of others, like our own, are motivated and purposeful, that others share with us a general set of assumptions and understandings, and that for these reasons the behavior of others is understandable and, to some extent, predictable. Our supposition of shared knowledge may be unwarranted, but as long as interaction proceeds in accord with our expectations and standards of reasonableness, we are unlikely to question it. Wallace (1970) has argued that cognitive sharing is unnecessary to social order. In a strict sense, all that is necessary is sufficient predictability in the overt behavior of others that we can coordinate our actions with theirs sufficiently to achieve our purposes. There need be no resemblance between the motivations, cognitive assumptions, or interpretations of one person and those of another for this to take place. All we need are "partial equivalence structures," working models of other people that effectively relate their behavior to given types of circumstances in a way that allows us roughly to predict their actions. We can then coordinate our own action with theirs in order to achieve given purposes. In this way, behavior is integrated across a social group or a society into a fairly reliable system.[2]

Wallace's insight is important for underscoring the leeway available in social organization for the individual variation which actually exists. However, it should not obscure the central importance of presumptive commonality in human social life. In our everyday lives as participants in a social world, we *assume* the existence of order and pattern, and seek to organize our perceptions in such a way as to discern it. We construct this order in the course of reflecting on our experience, picking out elements of pattern and regularity, using these to establish certain predictive hypotheses about the way things and people work, and orienting our own action by reference to these hypotheses. We look for typicality and construct implicit or explicit "typifications" against which we test and evaluate our ongoing experience. We assume that the actions of others, like our own, are meaningful, both to the other person and to ourselves, as well as oriented by motives and goals. And we assume that we can potentially understand or "know" not merely the overt behavior of others but also what generates it. We assume this whether or not in any strict sense it in fact is possible. That others with whom we interact are "like us" in various (though not all) respects, that we share a common world of experience and common bases for interpreting that experience, is a background premise of everyday life. This is crucial for comprehending the central part that interpretation plays in sociocultural life.

Our routine interpretations are based on the background premise of presumed commonality with others, commonality limited by personal differences in temperament, interests and goals, but nonetheless of significant scope. Individuals do not simply act out cultural scripts. Rather, using knowledge built up from unique and typical experiences filtered through cultural grids, personal orientation, and sets of relevances, we interact with our world. We interpret, reinterpret, and modify our interpretive schemes when our experiences fail to "make sense" within the interpretive "theory" we have been using.[3]

An individual's stock of knowledge is never equally developed in all areas. Some domains are more elaborated than others by virtue of the individual's personal interests and social roles; some are known only vaguely. Some elements of knowledge are explicit and subject to active test; others are tacit and taken for granted as part of the natural order. Rarely, if ever, is a person's total knowledge fully integrated or internally consistent. Much of one's knowledge is situational, specific to types of settings and tasks. Behavioral or cognitive strategies associated with one context may not be carried over to another context defined as unrelated. By the same token, an individual may have no difficulty behaving appropriately in settings marked by different cultural standards, as long as these settings remain separate.

Much cultural knowledge is encoded in language. As a coding system, a language allows its users to represent a vast array of unique experiences by a finite set of symbols. Such terms as "teacher" and "student," "work" and "play," "body" and "mind" represent conceptual categories to which particular phenomena are assigned as members of the general class. The category itself is an artifact of a specific set of assumptions, expectations, and values about the phenomenon in question. Those aspects of cultural knowledge which are linguistically encoded often reflect areas of experience which are central in the lives of language users. Yet, as Kimball (1974) has observed, the most fundamental assumptions of a society may not be linguistically encoded at all.

Verbal language is only one of several forms in which information is encoded. Body movement and orientation to others in space, for instance, can be powerful message carriers (cf. Bateson and Mead 1942, Hall 1966, Foerstel 1977), as can graphic and plastic images (cf. Forge 1967, 1970, Worth 1969, Worth and Adair 1972). The complexity and subtlety of human cultures are made possible by our ability to use multiple modes of encoding and decoding information and by our ability to integrate information diversely coded into generative syntheses of knowledge. As with other forms of cultural knowledge, language codes are shared only to a degree among users; individual differences in patterns of usage are as common as differences between codes used in separate language–communities. In both cases, that of linguistic codes and that of general cultural knowledge, individual repertoires often share sufficient features with one another that we can examine them collectively. For certain analytic purposes their commonality is more relevant than their variation.

The basis for the wide range of variation we find in and among sociocultural systems is the central role of learning in human maturation. To clarify the function of learning, we can think of it as a kind of information processing. It involves, first of all, *perception* of information which depends on the individual's perceptual capacities. For example, our sensory systems are specialized physiologically to detect changes in input and ignore constants. Our perceptual capacities themselves are not free of environmental influence; perception is not independent of cognitive interpretation and experiential context. The sensory input we apprehend as information is filtered through our expectations, which are themselves a function of prior experience and present context. So perception not only contributes to present learning but also is conditioned by prior learning (cf. Handel 1972, Neisser 1967, 1976, Fabrega 1977).

Perception demonstrates the importance of our capacity to store information (memory) and to integrate it, to compare it to previously stored information and to abstract from it generalizations (general lessons) that can be applied to the processing of future information or to the formulation of responses. Cognition we may define as those processes through which an individual acquires information, transforms it through integration and generalization, and uses it. Learning is a key component of cognitive process in that it represents the accumulation of information and the derivation of generalizations, but it is distinguishable from cognition in several respects. First, learning is cognition which results in a change in response to information input, whereas cognition includes those mental processes which do not result in such a change. Second, cognition involves also the apprehension of pattern and relationship among information inputs which underlie our capacity to generalize. Third, cognition includes the translation of stored information into behavior through decision making.

Knowledge is the body of information at an individual's disposal in the course of cognition.[4] Obviously, knowledge in this sense is constrained by memory, but it also is affected in important ways by the conditions under which it is tapped for retrieval. To explain this, we must consider the ways in which information is encoded and processed in the brain. Research on brain physiology indicates that we process information in at least two distinct ways, sequentially or analytically, and holistically or relationally. In most people[5] these two modes of processing are associated respectively with the left and right hemispheres of the brain. The two modes appear to be integrated in cognition by the connecting tissue bridge of the corpus callosum, which allows information to cross from one side to the other. In much of our cognitive process, we apparently alternate between those modes of processing, drawing on the complementary types of information each can provide. The analytic mode enables us to develop logical sequences of thought which compile information and allow us to derive logical conclusions from the sequence. The holistic mode enables us to apprehend pattern and relations, even when information is not complete. Since we usually are confronted with incomplete information, the latter mode is clearly essential for closing gaps in available information and developing working generalizations in the analytic mode. The two modes are interdependent, but each tends to be associated with particular types of encoding.

The analytic mode enables us to note discrete elements of information and it therefore is strongly associated with language. Verbal language is a system of labels for discrete items of information. In this sense it is an analytic code for encapsulating information for cognitive processing. Another example of an analytic code is the "language" of mathematics. Holistic or relational codes are applied to such phenomena as our apprehension of spatial or melodic patterns and that kind of knowledge we often label as "intuition" or "feeling." Although we utilize both in cognitive process, information encoded in one form may be difficult to retrieve in a different form. For instance, it is often easier to show someone how to perform an action such as knitting than to explain it verbally. Our knowledge of other people is often encoded as a kind of gestalt. If we are asked to retrieve such knowledge and encode it analytically, we may be hard pressed to specify the discrete components of that intuitive knowledge and indicate the basis of that knowledge in analytic form (cf. Deikman 1971, Ornstein 1973, Paredes and Hepburn 1976, ten Houten and others 1976, Fabrega 1977).

Stress also can affect the availability of stored knowledge for retrieval, as can the context in which it is sought (cf. Lazarus and others 1966 for a cross-cultural study of this phenomenon). The phenomenon of examination anxiety is a well-known example of the effect of stress and context on retrieval. The examinee's inability to remember information readily retrievable under less stressful circumstances indicates the difference between knowledge stored and knowledge at hand. A parent may have read carefully a manual of child rearing and know the "correct" procedures for handling his or her children, yet under stress react in terms of patterns learned at a much younger age. Even in the absence of stress, context can affect retrieval. A child may be able to calculate arithmetic problems perfectly in class, yet fail to apply that knowledge in situations outside of class. An individual may draw on stereotypes of groups such as women, blacks, Poles, or insurance salesmen in the context of one type of interaction, and yet use a less simplistic body of knowledge in another, in which the differences within those groups are of greater relevance than the supposed group characteristics. Because our integration of stored knowledge is generally incomplete, we can maintain even contradictory knowledge, as long as the contexts in which the knowledge is invoked do not force us to resolve the discrepancy.

Knowledge need not be "true." It need be neither linguistically encoded nor part of active awareness. It includes potentially all the information stored and the organization of that information into rules, plans, and theories, patterns and "intuition."[6] Much of cultural knowledge seems to be stored outside of conscious awareness. Because it is not put readily into words, it has been described as tacit (Polanyi 1966). Yet it is no less susceptible of transmission to novices and newcomers. As Spradley (1972) has commented, children and other novices typically learn both by instruction and by observation (through any of the senses) and inference.

Learning involves gradations of comprehension and commitment. Following Spiro (1966), Spradley distinguishes five levels of learning. These range from *learning about,* through *understanding, believing,* and *using* the belief to organize or account for behavior, to the ultimate level of "internalizing the belief so thoroughly that it is part of [one's] tacit knowledge and a violation would be unthinkable" (Spradley 1972b:22). Such a scheme for analyzing cultural learning is suggestive, but slightly misleading. We can learn about, understand, and use our understanding of given elements of cultural knowledge to organize or account for behavior without necessarily sharing the full commitment or belief otherwise associated with that knowledge. Anthropologists engaged in participant observation typically do this. It is also an alternative strategy for any individual participating in more than one cultural context.[7]

To the extent that elements of knowledge are assumed to be shared by group members, they are taken for granted as "natural facts of life." They become, as Garfinkel (1964, 1967) has documented, "routine grounds" of daily activity, "seen but unnoticed background expectancies." Such implicit understandings are made visible in their breach. Our assumptions about the meaning and use of time and of space, for instance, generally become apparent to us only when we are confronted with contrary or alternative perspectives. E. Hall (1959:15–30) describes the discomfort and confusion of U.S. and Latin American businessmen when they encounter one another's very different expectations regarding time. Misunderstandings often result as well from differing expectations and values concerning the use of physical space in interaction, as Hall (1966, 1974) has demonstrated in his research on proxemics. In light of our routine assumptions that the behavior of our fellows is meaningful, motivated, and guided by shared general standards, we treat their behavior as communicative. We decode and interpret it by reference to our stock of knowledge about types of people, types of actions, types of situations, and so forth. Generally, we become actively aware of this interpretive process only when the event we seek to "make sense of" resists ready interpretation in terms of conventional assumptions (Schutz 1944, Cicourel 1974). The influence of background expectancies on an individual's perception and interpretation of events must not be underestimated, as the cases discussed later indicate. At the same time, rendering such hidden assumptions visible allows us to reassess their validity and consider alternatives. The human capacity to learn, relearn, and learn throughout one's life enables us all to become multicultural in our perspectives.

Communication plays a crucial part in the transmission of cultural knowledge. While the part communication plays will be discussed in greater depth in the fourth chapter, three aspects should be noted. First, communication, like cognitive process, is comprised of many modes. These modes differ in the message complexes they can carry effectively. A picture may be worth a thousand words, but a sentence also can carry a message which pictures cannot convey. Second, most communication in daily life utilizes several modes simultaneously. This allows for redundancy in message-sending; essentially the same message may be transmitted in more than one mode, and the redundancy can reinforce the message. By the same token, contradictory messages also can be sent simultaneously. The importance of multimodal communication in every-day life reflects "our ability to attend simultaneously to multiple sources of information" which we process selectively (Cicourel 1974:164). Third, not all the messages conveyed in a communicative transaction are conveyed by a human sender. Context is an equally important message source. Because all human interactions take place in a setting, the setting itself and the ways in which it is defined by those interacting within it become significant sources of information, especially for the interpretation of the ongoing communication.

School classrooms are obvious examples of learning contexts. The class-room as an arrangement of objects and people in space, as a social situation, and as a system of rules and expectations, carries a mass of potential informa-tion which may amplify, complicate, or contradict information conveyed through formal instruction. Learning to learn-in-school involves learning a body of knowledge and skills that enables the student to "read" the context effectively and thereafter select particular types of information for concen-trated attention.

As a type of learning, learning to learn involves the acquisition of strate-gies for processing information (Bateson 1942, Harlow 1949). In systematic experiments designed to study learning capacities in other animals, the animals first must be taught the desired strategy for solving the problems chosen by the researcher. Then the capacity of the animal to cope with future problems presented can be tested effectively. Humans likewise are taught strategies for learning. The extensive capacity for generalization with which we are endowed genetically enables us to apply these strategies to diverse problems. Types of learning strategies favored differ cross-culturally and even across contexts within a given society, as we shall see later. This has important consequences for the process of knowledge transmission.

the study of primate learning

Learning is basic to human maturation but not only to humans. We share with other primates both a capacity and a disposition to learn, although these are more extensive in humans. All anthropoid primate species, including homo sapiens, exhibit the intertwining of biological and social factors in acquiring behavioral and cognitive competence. Because learning in nonhuman primate societies is less extensive, analyzing it is useful for pointing up certain general features of human learning.[8]

Most anthropoids live in groups composed of three to four to as many as seventy or eighty individuals. Even in the largest nonhuman primate group (usually known as a troop), every individual is known to every other. To varying degrees, all troop members are in continual face-to-face contact. Troop organization involves differentiation of members by relative rank, age, sex, and personal demeanor. To learn the particular patterns of organization character-istic of one's own troop, the individual must acquire observational skills and learn to control his or her own behavior according to the situation. For example, high ranking members expect deference on the part of lower ranking members and the young must learn to discern the relative rank of others and appropriate patterns of interaction with each of them. To adjust to the troop as an organized community, individuals must be able to evaluate complex social situations, to grasp the social field as a whole, and to coordinate their own behavior with that of others. The capacity for this kind of social awareness and self-control of behavior is similar between anthropoids and humans. The young primate also must acquire detailed knowledge of the physical environ-ment and its dangers in order to survive at all (Reynolds 1968, Jolly 1972, Kummer 1971).

Anthropoid childhood is quite long compared to that of most other animals. Infancy, the period of virtually complete dependence, lasts from one and a half to three years among most nonhuman anthropoids, compared to six years for humans. The prepubescent juvenile stage lasts until six or seven (compared to the human average of fourteen), with full growth requiring another year or two. With a potential life expectancy of nearly thirty or forty years, in addition to a large brain, an individual can acquire a considerable amount of experience. Learning is facilitated by troop organization. Sur-rounded by fellow troop members from birth, a child has a great many oppor-tunities to learn. As an infant develops locomotor skills, its network of social relationships widens. Through its exploratory activities, it is likely to come into interaction with all other troop members. Through their responses to its actions, they serve as socializing agents. Much of primate learning is observa-tional, especially visual. The primate penchant for imitating others and the reflex impulse to participate in whatever one observes others doing (social facilitation) both undergird the importance of observational learning. A good deal of learning takes place through interactions with peers and older troop members. In peer play and encounters with adults, the young primate rapidly learns the rules of acceptable social behavior and the consequences of violation of those rules. Some learning is achieved through direct instruction: a mother takes nonedible objects from her infant's mouth, an adult chases a child from a dangerous object, young females who handle others' infants clumsily or roughly are rebuked, physically or verbally, by the infant's mother; other behaviors may evoke a positive reaction. In all cases, learning appears to involve only the world–within–reach. Learning need not be vicarious, i.e., divorced from the context in which it is to be applied (Poirier 1973).

Curiosity, exploration, and play[9] all help amass in the young primate the knowledge and skills necessary to be a competent adult. Play, which begins as a nonsocial activity and develops into the predominant mode of interacting with juvenile peers, has a number of functions. Play provides practice in social adjustment and effective coordination with others under conditions of low risk. It seems to be associated with personality integration in the individual, probably in large measure through the practice it provides in role-taking and role-making. Social integration is also enhanced by the social bonds developed among peers through play. Through the heightened energy expenditure and exaggerated movements of play, participatory involvement of players seems to increase, and this appears to reinforce learning. Herzog (1974:14) among others has described the key function of play to be that it is

> perhaps the major channel through which juveniles acquire information about their physical environment, familiarize themselves with the social structure and conventions of their group, and test and improve their motor skills. . . . Ethologists and ethnographers agree that the young of all primate species are highly motivated to play, invest enormous amounts of energies in it, and grow up socially or physically retarded if deprived of opportunities to engage in it.

The troop in turn is helped by the activities of juveniles. The rambunctious curiosity of the young encourages them to explore their environment and test new things, while older troop members, more cautious and conservative, observe the results without endangering themselves and the knowledge they hold in trust for the troop.

In assessing the significance of play for primate learning, we must not restrict our concept of play to "rough–and–tumble and imitative activities" (Herzog 1974:14). In a more fundamental sense, primate dispositions to learn orient individuals to explore, examine, and test facets of their environment with no necessary instrumental goal. Curiosity itself is sufficient motive, learning sufficient reward. Play in this sense lies at the heart of all invention. Piaget (1952) points to play as the matrix of learning, linking it to development of the capacity for abstract thinking in the child. Imaginative thought, in his view, is internalized play. Play provides both for innovation in thought and for routinization of abstracted principles through self–generated practice.[10]

Accumulated knowledge is extremely important to a troop, for it enables members to adapt more flexibly to changing conditions than the trial and error experimentation of individuals alone permits. Because troop members learn from watching one another, discoveries by a single individual can eventually become shared by the whole troop. An example of this was observed in a Japanese macaque troop living on a tiny island. When sweet potatoes were introduced as a new food, juveniles were the first to try them. Before being eaten, the tubers were rolled and rubbed between the hands to remove adhering grit and sand. This macaques do with other foods; the only innovation thus far was in accepting the new food source. One young juvenile (named Imo by the observers) began taking her sweet potatoes to a brook and rinsing off the sand. Gradually other juveniles, watching, adopted the practice and were in turn watched by their mothers and siblings. Adult males ignored the newfangled notion of washing, though some eventually ate sweet potatoes. Because new generations of youngsters learned this behavior from their mothers, it eventually became an established tradition in the whole troop. Two and a half years later, when the researchers began to scatter wheat on the beach, Imo again tried something new; instead of picking the grains singly out of the sand, she took a handful of wheat and sand to the sea, dumped it in and, after the sand sank, picked the clean, floating wheat grains out of the water. Again the practice spread throughout the troop, and again adult males abstained (Kawai 1965).

The sociometric networks of learning in both cases consisted of those individuals in close daily contact watching and imitating one another. Dominant or high ranking individuals do not observe others in this way; on the contrary, they are the subject of observation by other troop members. If a dominant adult introduced a new behavior it quickly would spread throughout the troop, whereas it took several years for Imo's innovations to become common practice. Here again we see the balance between innovative and conservative behavior; both serve the troop. Under trying conditions, drought, for example, only the oldest member might remember water sources in similar circumstances in the past and be able to lead the troop there. The conservatism of older members is adaptive for the troop as a whole, since it protects the repositories of the greatest accumulated knowledge. The risk-taking innovativeness of expendable younger members helps to expand available knowledge.

Nevertheless, there is a limit on the knowledge that can be shared by the group as a whole in the absence of some form of symbolic communication. Anthropoid communication is complex and even subtle, but it appears not to involve the development of elaborate symbolic codes characteristic of human communication, especially language. This is not to say that nonhuman primates are incapable of symbolic thought, for laboratory research has indicated that this capacity is present in at least some anthropoid species. Even if an individual is capable of relatively complex logical operations and of grasping abstract conceptual principles which are at the root of symbolization, if he or she is unable to communicate that directly to another and thereby to develop *shared* symbolic knowledge, the limits this will set on the potential range of communication and on the accumulating stock of shared group knowledge are obvious.

human cognition and culture

Human knowledge is cultural knowledge. Because the content and style of human cognitive process are influenced by cultural milieu, ascertaining the universal characteristics of this process is not a simple task. Laboratory tests of nonhuman primates have yielded some suggestive evidence on primate cognition in general, but most psychological research on humans has been done in Europe and North America. The cross-cultural validity of these research results is not known. There is considerable evidence that the genetic endowment of all human groups is roughly similar, and efforts to document possible genetic bases for cross-cultural cognitive variation have been unsuccessful.[11] In recent years, systematic cross-cultural investigations of cognition have been undertaken which shed some light on the subject.

Most of the psychological research on cognition has been influenced heavily by the work of Jean Piaget. In his theory of cognitive development, Piaget contends that children develop logical structures in the course of interacting with their environment. These structures or "operations," as they are successively induced and mastered, regulate thinking processes and enable still more complex cognitive skills to be developed. According to Piaget, both the logical structures and their order of appearance in the individual are universal in the human species. Does their culture affect the rate at which individuals acquire logical skills, the order in which they acquire them, or the range of skills thus acquired?

One series of studies, carried out by psychologist Jerome Bruner and his associates (1966), was designed to test the effect of Western-type schooling on cognitive development. Hypothesizing that Western-type schooling structures learning experiences in such a way as to foster abstract modes of thought and formal propositional logic, Bruner and his associates compared test responses of (a) rural uneducated youngsters, (b) rural educated youngsters and (c) urban educated youngsters from other societies. Both sets of formally schooled individuals (rural and urban) performed much more similarly to U.S. children than to their rural cultural kin, but the conclusions drawn, that rural people unexposed to formal Western-style schooling are less capable of abstract thought than cocultural people of the same age *with* Western educational experience, were premature. Bruner and his associates failed to control for their subjects' familiarity with and understanding of the testing situation, and for their experience with the test content.

This problem has been tackled in a number of ways. The impact of test content on performance has been demonstrated in various studies, all of which show that unfamiliar content skews test results (e.g., Cole and others 1971, Price-Williams 1962, Okinji 1971, Deregowski and Serpell 1971 [cited in Cole and Scribner 1974], Irwin and others 1974). Deregowski and Serpell, for example, compared responses of Scottish and Zambian school children to a problem requiring that they classify objects represented in photographs and by toy models. The Scottish children classified both photographs and models in essentially the same ways; for them these two modes of representation were equivalent. Zambian children, on the other hand, classified the photographs with difficulty, but performed equally well with the models. Other studies indicate that the ability to "read" pictorial representations like photographs and drawings depends on learning conventions of perceptual organization (e.g., Miller 1973, Dawson 1967). Price-Williams (1962) investigated classification among educated and uneducated Nigerian children. When he used as his test objects plants and animals with which all children were equally familiar, he found no consistent differences in conceptual abilities between the two groups of children. Moreover, he found that while animals tended to be classified in terms of concrete attributes like color, size, or place where they might be found, plants were overwhelmingly classified in terms of the abstract attribute of edibility.

Other studies testing Piaget's theory of cognitive development suggest that neither the age at which specific logical skills are acquired nor the order in which they are acquired are constant cross-culturally.[12] While the factors which account for these differences are not yet clear, research directed to this question has focused on the specific life experiences of children tested[13] rather than on general characteristics such as exposure to Western-style schooling, urbanization, or "modernization." The relationship of the latter phenomena to cognitive ability is far from clear, although formal schooling at minimum may familiarize participants with "testing" as a situation.[14]

There are a great many sources of potential bias in cross-cultural cognitive testing in addition to familiarity with testing as a type of situation/event and with test content. For instance, nearly all the procedures used require that subjects verbalize their reasons for the choices they have made. While this may be the simplest way to determine the logical operation used by the subject in carrying out the test, how a subject explains her or his choices (or how an individual explains or justifies her or his action in everyday life) may not necessarily reflect the cognitive processes by which they actually arrived at that decision. Particularly, an apparently inappropriate verbal explanation does not indicate necessarily that the individual is incapable of the actual operations being tested. Nor does inept performance on a test indicate that the subject cannot make use of the tested skill in other situations, including practical applications. For example, Australian Aborigines tested by Piagetan tasks for mastery of the conservation of mass concept do poorly (Dasen 1972a, 1972b). Yet they live in semi-arid regions subject to recurrent water shortages and are practical masters at finding and storing scarce water. As Cole (1975:478) has phrased it, it is difficult "to believe that Aborigine adults will store water in tall thin cans in order to 'have more water' " or that "they think they will lose water when they pour it from a bucket into a barrel." It is likely that they would have died out long ago, had they not had practical mastery of the concept of conservation of mass. Heron (1971) found little correlation between performance on a Piagetan test and mathematical performance which presupposes the conceptual abilities which the Piagetan test theoretically taps. That is, students can do poorly on the first, yet well on the second.

Recent cross–cultural research indicates that certain logical operations are universal in the human species; at the same time it is clear that usage of these basic operations differs cross–culturally. In this sense there are many systems of logic (Cole and others 1971, Cole and Gay 1972, Cole and Scribner 1974, Scribner 1975, Scribner 1976, Luria 1977). For example, all normal humans are capable of conceiving relationship between events. But the way in which relationship is conceptualized, and the events (persons, objects) thereby related, varies. Consider the Trobrianders. Whereas Westerners are prone to see lineal relations—sequence through time or in space, one thing becoming another as an acorn becomes a tree, means relating to ends, causes to effects—Trobrianders prefer to see the pattern and noncomparative wholeness of each event. The yams in their garden do not become large and fat as a connected sequence of events. Rather, at each phase of growth (in our terms) the yam is a different entity. It does not become the following phase–entity; rather each phase–entity ceases to be when the next phase–entity appears. No temporal connection is made between these events; all the phase–entities of yam cultivation and the farming enterprise are part of a patterned, nontemporal whole. The satisfaction we take in lineal connection is taken by a Trobriander in this patterned unity.

Trobrianders are clearly capable of perceiving cause and effect as linked aspects of a single train of events, for in other situations they express an awareness of it. The events which they define in this way, however, are negatively valued. In their customs of gift-giving and gift-receiving, for instance, they view gift-giving as distinctly separate from gift-receiving, although the giver eventually will receive a gift from the original recipient. Gift-giving and gift-receiving are conceptualized simply as component parts of a patterned cluster of acts, unrelated to one another physically and temporally. If a person is thought to treat gift-giving and receiving as an exchange, as a sequence of acts linked by cause and effect, by giving a gift in the expectation of return, the person is considered despicable and the act of gift-giving loses its customary value (Lee 1949, 1950).

Experimental study of logical strategies has raised more questions than it has answered. Scribner (1976), in an evaluation of a number of these studies, points out that performance on the tasks (usually completion of syllogisms adapted to local cultural content) typically differs between schooled and unschooled subjects. The significance of this distinction is less obvious than it may at first appear. Schooled individuals had markedly higher overall scores than unschooled, "even 7-year-old second graders in a school system known for emphasizing rote learning rather than development of critical thinking" (Scribner 1976:489). This level of performance reflected a strategy, presumably learned in school, of restricting consideration to the evidence given in the test problem, rather than taking into account "extraneous" empirical factors. Most unschooled subjects used a mixed strategy, selecting situationally (in light of syllogism content) whether to approach it empirically or purely theoretically. When *only* the theoretical answers were analyzed, as instances in which solely logical considerations were at play, little or no logical error occurred on the part of the unschooled subjects. The error levels, in other words, were an artifact of the test and the *interpretation* of the task involved by those undertaking it.[15]

Rosin (1973) describes an arithmetic system of calculations devised by an unschooled (nonliterate) Indian peasant which incorporated "both culturally shared techniques and personal inventions" (Rosin 1973:7). He indicates that others in the village had also developed sets of computational strategies, each specific to the types of practical problems encountered in which such skills are needed. Play was involved as well:

> A person may memorize sums and multiples simply because he is fascinated by specific operations and number relationships and enjoys fooling around with them (Rosin 1973:8).

These logical strategies, then, may be instrumental and situation-specific (cf. note 15) but they may also be employed in nonpragmatic ways. Scribner and Cole (1973:557) have characterized the primary effect of schooling as "the tendency ... of school populations to generalize rules and operations across a number of problems," independent of the pragmatic relevance of the problem. At issue, then, are the conditions which promote the generalization of cognitive skills across situations and the application of such skills without reference to real-world contingencies or purposes.[16] Lave (1977) approached this topic by analyzing traditional tailors' apprenticeship training in Liberia, an alternative system of instruction to that of Western-style schooling. The two educational forms differ in several respects; Lave emphasizes in particular that schools favor deductive and context-free knowledge tranmission while apprenticeship utilizes inductive, context-related transmission. She found that both forms of instruction facilitated generalization of cognitive skills to unfamiliar arithmetic problems.

The study of cognitive skills and strategies is complicated by their situational application. Schooled subjects lend themselves to such research because of their familiarity with tests as situations and their orientation to generalized, theoretical applications of acquired skills to nonpragmatic problems. Nevertheless, determining which cognitive processes are actually in use during specific activities remains problematic. This difficulty is multiplied for researchers attempting to correlate cognitive processes, learning strategies, and behavioral styles. Differences in behavior (including language) do not necessarily reflect cognitive differences. Research on cognitive style has been hampered by the methodological difficulty of establishing these linkages, as well as by problematic theoretical assumptions.

Cognitive style refers to an individual's characteristic pattern or strategy for acquiring and processing information. As Kagan and others (1963:74) define it,

> cognitive style . . . refers to stable individual preferences in mode of perceptual organization and conceptual categorization of the external environment. One particular style dimension involves the tendency to analyze and to differentiate the stimulus environment in contrast to categorizations that are based on the stimulus as a whole.

Research indicates "that cognitive styles are independent of native ability and that they are definable without reference to specific substantive content" (Cohen 1969:829). There is considerable evidence that early cognitive training plays a critical part in establishing an individual's orientation in later learning, but the variables involved are not yet clear. Moreover, as Cazden (1966) has shown, the research conducted on this topic has not always controlled for variables that might seriously compromise the conclusions drawn.

Bernstein (1958, 1959, 1960, 1962a, 1962b) and Cohen (1968, 1969, 1971; also Cohen and others 1968), among others, report correlations between cognitive and linguistic style and socioeconomic class. Bernstein's experimental research focuses exclusively on language, although he links language use to a host of other social and psychological variables. Based on his sample of English working class and middle class boys (all about sixteen years of age), he asserts that the speech patterns of working class members differ characteristically from those of the middle class. Among the differences he found were more restricted vocabularies of working class subjects (as measured by standardized tests gauging academic achievement), more "restricted" or inflexible organization of grammatical elements in verbal utterances, and greater use of "sociocentric" phrases to express uncertainty, phrases that (he argues) call for affirmation rather than divergent response from fellow participants. In other words, working class speech patterns are hypothesized to be more predictable, composed of more routine and fewer elaborated structural units than is middle class speech. The latter is described as more open or "elaborated" in the manipulation of grammatical elements to convey meaning, favoring expressions that call for "individuated" or "egocentric" responses from other participants. Middle class speech patterns, Bernstein argues, allow for greater development of abstract concepts, generalization, and logical argument. From this interpretation of his data, Bernstein then extrapolates behavioral implications related to "restricted" speech styles, including low levels of conceptualization, lack of interest in process, preference for inclusive social relationships and group solidarity, and conservatism and acceptance of authority.

As Cazden (1966) and others (e.g., Leacock 1972, Labov 1969) have pointed out, Bernstein's research, although widely cited, is suspect in a number of ways. First of all, his empirical data must be evaluated in light of the conditions under which they were collected. Rather than observing speech patterns as they occurred in a range of daily life situations, Bernstein observed his subjects in the specialized context of a "tape-recorded, relatively undirected, discussion . . . on the [supplied] topic of the abolition of capital punishment" (Bernstein 1962a:38). To reduce his working class subjects' unfamiliarity with the test situation, he provided them with two preliminary practice sessions. Middle class subjects were provided with none. The way in which subjects interpret an experiment, its goals, their relationship to the experimenter, and the conditions in which it takes place all are critical to their response; but apart from the practice session provided, these variables were not considered in interpreting the results.

Because of the difference in the conditions themselves for the two groups of subjects, the results can not be assumed to be comparable. Another unexamined variable is the degree of prior acquaintance among the members of each conversational group. Of this Bernstein (1962a:38) says only that the working class "subgroups contained members with varying degrees of personal contact [while] the social and educational contact of the middle class group was not known." After the two practice sessions, we might reasonably infer that the members of the working class subgroups had a greater degree of mutual acquaintance than did their middle class counterparts. How significant might this difference be in accounting for the observed differences in speech? Bernstein argues in part that speech styles or "codes" are functionally related to particular forms of social relations.

> A restricted code is generated by a form of social relationship based upon a range of closely shared identifications self-consciously held by the members. An elaborated code is generated by a form of social relationship which does not necessarily presuppose such shared, self-consciously held identifications with the consequence that much less is taken for granted. . . .
> The community of like interests underlying a restricted code removes the need for intent to be verbally elaborated and made explicit. The effect of this on speech is to simplify the structural alternatives used to organize meaning and restrict the range of lexicon choice. A restricted code can arise at *any point* in society where its conditions may be fulfilled. . . . (Bernstein 1962b:233).

By incorporating in his test, conditions which increased the level of mutual familiarity among working class subjects, Bernstein also increased the likelihood that restricted patterns would be used. All this must be taken into account in assessing his claims of predictable or routinized speech habits among working class participants.

Another weakness in this research is that the data involve only observed speech patterns, while the analytic interpretation links those speech characteristics to specific cognitive processes and behavioral styles. For the latter and their relationship to speech styles, Bernstein provides meager evidence. Differences in speech styles, even when adequately documented, cannot be presumed to indicate disparate cognitive strategies; the relationship must be demonstrated. Likewise, delineation of social structural correlates of linguistic and cognitive strategies requires an examination of the range of contexts in which those strategies are applied.

In their experimental study of conceptualization, psychologists Kagan, Moss, and Sigel (1963) isolated three relatively distinct cognitive styles: analytic-descriptive, inferential-categorical, and relational.[17] They suggest that these represent preferred methods of organizing experience. Tests with U.S. children indicated that almost all were capable of easily providing alternative modes of conceptualization (Kagan and others 1963:83). Neither of the first two styles was related directly to language skill, although the third style, inferential-categorical, was. They also found each conceptual style associated with either of two orientations to test stimuli, egocentric and stimulus-centered. Egocentric orientation involves the tendency to classify concepts in terms of personal affective considerations; stimulus-centered orientation involves the tendency to classify concepts in terms of aspects of the stimulus itself. While these analytic concepts differ somewhat from those proposed by Bernstein in his egocentric-sociocentric distinction, their independence of conceptual style raises questions about the functional linkage hypothesized by Bernstein.

The analytic style differentiates the stimulus field, separating relevant from irrelevant parts. The relational style orients to the stimulus field as a whole, categorizing each part in terms of its relation to the whole. Users of the analytic style tend to resist the "distracting" influence of immediate perceptual experience apart from the focal stimulus. Users of the relational style, on the other hand, are less resistant to the influence of contextual experience.

R. Cohen argues that distinctive cognitive styles may be identified among U.S. children and asserts that these are functionally related to distinctive social environments which tend to be associated with low income and middle income status. Cohen and her associates (1968, 1969, 1971) have isolated four general types of cognitive style, two polar opposites and two combination types. Defining the polar types in about the same terms as Kagan and his associates,[18] she adds two components unsupported by their study. First, she specifically associates ego-centered orientation with relational style and stimulus-centered with analytic. Second, she contends that for school age children these polar styles are mutually incompatible rather than merely preferentially used. Each of the two combination styles, flexible and conflict-concrete, display some elements of both relational and analytic styles.[19] Unlike the other authors cited, Cohen emphasizes that all four cognitive styles allow for the acquisition of large bodies of information and the development of high levels of abstraction.[20] The styles differ primarily in the *mode* of abstraction used to process salient information from an event, and in the way in which this information is organized with respect to the individual and to the context as a whole. While many researchers treat the analytic style as superior to the relational, Cohen describes them as equally limiting. However, because most schools are organized so as to orient exclusively to the analytic cognitive style, students who use a predominantly relational style are at a severe disadvantage in the school context, in terms of both academic performance and other social and cognitive demands. Conventional tests of achievement and intelligence, including nonverbal tests often touted as "culture-free," are directed toward the analytic style favored in middle class education, handicapping performance, both in school and in experimental research, by those whose cognitive style differs. Polar relational type students are generally "poor achievers" and combination type students usually are "middle-range achievers" in academic subjects.

In some respects, analytic and relational cognitive styles reflect the differences between analytic and relational modes of information processing discussed earlier. The analytic cognitive style is characterized by strategies that emphasize the sequential, linear processing mode and treat parts or attributes of a given stimulus as meaningful in themselves, independent of the context in which they are embedded. Relational cognitive style, in contrast, involves strategies that emphasize the holistic, pattern-sensitive processing mode and treat stimuli only in terms of the contextual field in which they are embedded. Since analytic and relational modes of cognitive processing appear to be interdependent, although one may be dominant in a given individual's cognitive strategy, both polar cognitive styles presumably entail components of both modes of processing, though perhaps in different proportions.

We might also expect situational variation in individual cognitive strategy, with particular cognitive styles associated most strongly with particular types of situations. Cohen's relational style type resembles in many respects Scribner's (1976) description of "empirically-biased reasoning" discussed earlier. In light of Scribner's finding that use of this cognitive approach varied situationally, and that most subjects demonstrated an ability to use both theoretical and empirical reasoning, further examination of the hypothesized "incompatibility" of analytic and relational styles seems warranted. Cohen indicates that combination styles vary to some extent situationally, while polar styles are not situation-linked. It is not clear what range of situations was tapped to support this hypothesis, but most of the data appear to have been drawn from a battery of tests, supplemented by observations of participation styles in primary groups and of language use.

Cohen and her associates found cognitive style to be closely related to styles of family and friendship group organization and of individual partipation (and thereby to socioeconomic class), and infer causal factors in group organization that help develop a given style (Cohen 1971:46–48, 50–52). At the same time, she (1971:43) points out that differences in conceptual style have been observed among members of the same family. The relationship between social and cognitive variables is thus not determinate. Cognitive styles are also subject to modification: schooling, for example, can alter the dominant pattern of cognitive orientation. In no case is cognitive style an accurate index of learning *capacity*, although it is a factor in student *performance* on academic tasks and in the *evaluation* of students by school personnel.

Witkin (1967) and his associates, defining analytic ability somewhat more narrowly than the other researchers cited, found no correlation between socioeconomic class and analytic ability and verbally measured intelligence (Witkin and others 1966). Their research does indicate that socialization patterns which encourage the child's independence in various respects are correlated positively with the development of analytic ability (Dyk and Whitten 1965). This hypothesis has been supported tentatively by some cross-cultural research which links the mode of subsistence and other ecological factors with socialization practices, and these with analytic and relational cognitive styles (Dawson 1967, Berry 1966, 1971a; see also Witkin 1967, Witkin and Berry 1975).[21] Neither the components nor the correlates of cognitive style have been investigated adequately. Certainly the disparity in findings reported by various researchers suggests that we have a great deal more to learn in this area.

To determine the cognitive strategies which people use, the conditions in which they are developed, the situations in which they are applied, and their consequences for knowing and learning, we must investigate them within the sociocultural contexts in which they are embedded. The contexts, whether natural situations or contrived experiments, must be taken into account in our analysis. The stocks of knowledge which people bring to any event and their repertoire of cognitive strategies and interpretive frameworks are essential components of these contexts.

Analysis of learning must begin, therefore, with an examination of the social and cultural contexts of learning. In this chapter I have sketched briefly the basic elements of knowing and learning that infuse the diverse systems of transmission found in human societies. In the next chapter we will take up the concepts of knowledge transmission, education, and schooling as tools for the study of learning in sociocultural context.

notes

1. See, for example, Needham's discussion of the development of mathematics in China, Watanabe's (1974) observations on Oriental seismology and primatology, Mitroff's (1974) study of American geologists involved in lunar research, and Kuhn's (1970) classic treatise on scientific revolutions. Further discussion of the cultural conditioning of scientific knowledge is presented in the third chapter.

2. Wallace (1970) further argues that cognitive nonuniformity is necessary, in that the complexity of human social organization may depend on diversity among individuals and groups. Cognitive nonuniformity "permits a more complex system to develop than most, or any, of its participants can comprehend" from their individual vantage points. Also it liberates participants from over-saturation with information: it liberates them "from the heavy burden of actually learning and knowing" one another's motivations and cognitive maps (Wallace 1970:35).

3. The position I am developing here has been influenced strongly by the work of Alfred Schutz and Herbert Blumer. For introductions to their theoretical orientations, see Schutz (1970) and Blumer (1969). For studies of the "confirmation bias" in everyday thought, see Kuhn (1964), Wason (1968), Karmiloff-Smith and Inhelder (1974/5) and Mynatt and others (1977).

4. Knowledge, as I am using the term, does not include only "intellective" matters. The integral relationship of "affective" and "intellective" aspects of cognition is increasingly recognized (e.g., Kahneman 1973, Deikman 1971, E. Hall 1976, Kiefer 1977).

5. In left-handed people, lateralization tends to be less marked than in right-handed people. Hemispheric specialization also appears to be less entrenched in children.

6. E. Hall (1976:168–174) notes that some current research indicates that information is stored holographically. That is, memory is not in itself compartmentalized, although processing functions are. At the same time, he says, multiple programs (knowledge systems) can be learned without necessary conflict; presumably they are stored discretely.

7. The aspect of commitment (internalization, cathexis) in learning commonly is associated with the process of enculturation. The development of commitment at a deep personal level is then cited to account for individual resistance to cultural change. The degree to which cathexis of this sort is integral to the acquisition of cultural knowledge, or is variable among individuals or across cultural domains, needs to be taken as a topic for investigation. I do not mean to imply by this that affect is likely to be peripheral, for as indicated in note 4, affective and intellective aspects of cognition are intimately connected. What is at issue is the presumed power of culture: its nature and its source. E. Hall (1976) points out in this regard that the determinant power of culture is reduced when it is brought into conscious awareness, particularly through juxtaposition with alternative cultural systems.

8. See Herzog (1974) for a somewhat different treatment of this topic.

9. "Play" is notoriously difficult to define adequately, and analysis of it as a domain of activity is equally slippery. For two rather different approaches to the concept and the phenomenon, see Bateson (1955, 1956) and Reilly (1973). A fairly well-balanced selection of readings is available in Bruner and others (1976); this compendium includes articles on both human and nonhuman play.

10. Loizos (1967) argues that play properly should be distinguished from practice and exploration. She proposes that play be "described . . . as a positive approach towards, and non-rigidified interaction with any feature of the animal's environment, including conspecifics, involving stimulation through most available sensory modalities" (Loizos 1967:182). Play behavior uses motor patterns which appear in other contexts where they serve obvious biological functions (such as aggression and defense); but play behavior, contends Loizos, is qualitatively distinct from those nonplay patterns.

11. Substantiated evidence for a correlation between intellectual capacity and racial/ethnic stock is lacking. Some tentative evidence suggests that certain physiological factors such as eye pigmentation may affect perception, specifically color perception and susceptibility to certain types of visual illusions (Bornstein 1973, Pollack 1970, Berry 1971b, Jahoda 1971; however see also Bolton and others 1975, Stewart 1973).

12. See Dasen (1972b) for a review of cross-cultural research on Piaget's theory. Ember (1977) provides a useful overview of more recent studies and methodological problems in this research.

13. Price-Williams, Gordon and Ramirez (1969), for example, found that familiarity with pottery-making was a key variable in the performance of Mexican children on Piagetan conservation tests of mass and weight. Ember (1977:41) has questioned in this regard whether experience with pottery-making or simply with clay is the significant element. Dasen (1974) has argued that Australian Aborigines' experience in marking relative positions at waterholes in their territory facilitates their performance on conservation tasks related to length.

14. Familiarity with testing as a type of situation by no means insures that tester and tested share the same *definition* of that situation. Ogbu (1974:168–169) describes an excellent example of this when he contrasts the perspective of teachers and other testers with that of low income

minority children in a Stockton, California neighborhood school. While testers take for granted that the child is motivated to do her or his best, the child may not take testing seriously and thus fail to perform to capacity. See also Labov (1969:157–163) for a pointed discussion of the covert transaction which takes place in some testing situations.

15. Scribner (1976:494–500) proceeds to inspect performances on recall tasks (reported in Scribner 1975), in an attempt to determine the source of empirical bias on the part of unschooled subjects. Asking both schooled and unschooled subjects to repeat (recall and verbally replicate) syllogisms, she found that both groups made errors of similar types. However, schooled did *not* convert the syllogism from hypothetical to factual status, whereas unschooled commonly did. She argues that accounting for this requires us to consider into which "pre-existing schema . . . verbal logic problems can be assimilated" (p. 497) and terms this a "specialized language genre." This genre was absent in no group; however groups differed in the *situations* with which use of such a genre was associated: "the experimental or interview context may not have provided the appropriate cues to elicit the desired performance—the use of the logical genre (cf. Hymes 1974)" (Scribner 1976: 499).

16. Cole and others (1971:226–227) report that American school children tend to *overuse* certain logical operations, even when it violates the parameters of the specific problem set.

17. The definitions provided by Kagan, Sigel and Moss (1963:76) for these three styles are based on the conceptual organization of stimuli in relation to a perceptual field. Using an analytic mode, the subject "selects an element of objective similarity shared by two or more figures" in the field, differentiating it from the whole and labeling it by reference to that objective attribute. (E.g., "people holding something".) Using a relational mode, the subject focuses on

> a functional relationship between or among the stimuli grouped together. This functional relationship can involve temporal or spatial contiguity between objects or interobject relationships among the stimulus members. In this category no stimulus is an independent instance of the concept, and each stimulus depends for its membership on its relationship to other stimuli in the group.

(E.g., "people arguing with each other.") Using an inferential-categorical mode, the subject differentiates the field, as in the analytic approach, such that "any stimulus in the group is an independent instance of the conceptual label," but the concept derived involves not "a partial objective attribute" but "an inference about the stimuli grouped together." (E.g., "people who help others.") While Kagan, Sigel and Moss do not seem to agree, I would suggest that this last may represent a synthesis of the first two. Cohen's (1971:50) discussion of "flexible" cognitive style supports this suggestion.

It is also important to note that the apparent similarity of the analytic-relational distinction to Witkin's (1962) field independence-dependence notion is in fact not complete. Witkin (1963) himself, commenting on Kagan, Moss, and Sigel's study, contends that their respective uses of the label "analytic" are not synonomous.

> When we use the term analytic, we refer quite specifically to the ability to overcome an embedding context, that is to experience an item independently of an organized field of which it is part.. . . We should say that a person is being analytical when, in his cognitive operations, he is readily able to separate an item from its context.. . .

In assessing the literature on analytic modes of processing and cognitive styles, it is essential to bear in mind that the same labels often gloss different phenomena.

18. Cohen (1971:45–50) characterizes analytic cognitive style as a rule set that directs a person to be stimulus-centered, to be differentiating in perception, to seek/find nonobvious and generalizable attributes of a stimulus, and to define the meanings of these attributes in formal terms. Relationships drawn among objects tend to be "static and descriptive rather than functional or inferential," and tend not to involve process or motivation.

Relational style, in contrast, directs a person to be self-centered (to define concepts in terms of relevance to oneself), to be global rather than differentiating in perception, to find descriptive (unique, context-bound) attributes of a stimulus, and to formulate meaning in descriptive terms.

Relationships drawn among objects tend to be functional or inferential, and static rather than processual or motivational.

19. Flexible cognitive style combines analytic rules (to be stimulus centered, differentiating, and focused on formal attributes) with relational rules (to identify the unique as meaningful and to selectively embed percepts in context). Relationships in this case tend to be functional or inferential but also processual and motivational.

Conflict-concrete style combines analytic rules (to be stimulus centered and focused on formal attributes) with relational rules (to be global and descriptive). Relationships drawn are commonly static and descriptive or functional, rarely processual or inferential.

20. This is somewhat ambiguous, especially in Cohen 1971. In this article she develops more fully her model of the two combination types and, in the process, implies that abstraction is differentially developed in the four styles. Perhaps she means analytic-type abstraction in these cases.

21. For a critical discussion of this research, see Cole and Scribner (1974:80–90).

_TWO

EDUCATION AND THE TRANSMISSION OF KNOWLEDGE

To perpetuate organized relations among community members, new members must acquire behavioral skills and the knowledge necessary to decide when and where to use them. Yet cultural knowledge includes more than simply "recipe knowledge," i.e., what people must know to act competently (in accord with expected standards) in routine situations of everyday life. It also includes ideas about human nature and the place of humans in their physical and social environment, aesthetic preferences, values and affective patterns, beliefs about time and causality, and more. Knowledge of this kind may or may not directly affect the routine behavior of those who share it, but its transmission is important to maintain cultural continuity from one generation to the next.

In all societies, cultural knowledge is distributed differentially among members. Along with the effects of individual variability, structural factors in social organization play a crucial role. In all societies, stocks of knowledge differ to some degree between males and females, young and old. Insofar as power, wealth, influence, and prestige are unequally distributed, people differ in their access to and control over knowledge of various kinds. By virtue of their social positions, people also differ in the vantage points from which they view the social structure in which their lives are embedded. As a result, their ideas and values concerning it are likely to differ. We would expect, for instance, that a president, a legislator, a county sheriff, and a farmer would have rather different images of the working of the government bureaucracy, as well as variant attitudes toward that process. To the extent that members of a society specialize occupationally, each specialty will carry an esoteric corpus of technical and behavioral knowledge; usually access to this corpus will be controlled carefully by practitioners.

All societies are multicultural to a degree.[1] In societies in which more than one relatively *distinct* corpus of cultural knowledge is transmitted, one of the cultural groups is generally dominant in prestige and power or is in competition for this position with one or more of the others. This creates conflicts over cultural transmission which may affect educational process in a variety of ways. Since most societies today are socially stratified as well as multicultural and many incorporate multiple ethnic groups within their borders, such problems must be of focal concern in the study of education.

We must remember that the transmission of knowledge is subject both to conservative forces and to tendencies toward continual redefinition. On the one hand, any corpus of cultural knowledge active in a living group exhibits both resilience in the face of new events, which lends it the weight of tested learning and conserves it over generations, and a capacity for integrating new experience in such a way that it coheres more or less with established understandings. On the other hand, all cultural knowledge is subject to individual interpretation in the course of transmission, and to modification in the course of the individual's social experience. Since all social interaction (including that of cultural transmission) involves interpersonal communication, the processes of encoding and decoding the message complexes exchanged must include interpretation by the participants. This interpretation will be based both on each individual's repertoire of cultural knowledge and on the personal experience with which that knowledge is infused. The interpretive process itself, therefore, will affect the individual's apprehension of presumably shared meanings and understandings and preclude total consonance in the bodies of knowledge held by fellow participants. It also provides a crucial mechanism for the gradual modification of shared understandings in the course of social life, as people reinterpret their experiences in light of changing circumstances.

forms of knowledge transmission

In a broad sense, all knowledge transmission may be described as a form of *socialization* and *enculturation.* As processes these involve training in appropriate behavior with respect to other members of the group, including motor and social skills, and training in the body of knowledge which enables the individual to know what behavior is appropriate, to value it, and to seek to achieve it. Some scholars have found it useful to distinguish between socialization and enculturation in order to highlight particular facets of transmission. Herskovits (1947, 1964), for instance, reserves "socialization" to denote the processes by which an individual is integrated into a social group, while he applies "enculturation" to the processes by which an individual acquires competence in the prevailing "customs and knowledge" of the group (Herskovits 1964:325–329). This type of distinction implies gradations in learning comprehension and commitment similar to those discussed earlier and suggests their significance.

Social life requires certain basic modifications of individual drives and inclinations. Our anthropoid capacities for social awareness and self-control provide an essential foundation for achieving the adaptations necessary to function within a group. Infants, strangers, and other novice members must learn both to control their behavior (by selectively acting on and restraining their inclinations) and to take account of implicit and explicit features of the social environment in organizing their behavior. In order to behave "acceptably," in such a way as to evoke neither moral nor physical sanctions, an individual must acquire an appropriate set of motor and social skills. A child, for instance, learns to control elimination processes, to defer certain types of gratification, to control emotional expression, and to acknowledge rights of other people in specific domains. An adult novice may learn to use chopsticks or drive a dog sled, to display respectful deference before group members of high status, to question obliquely, to avoid direct eye gaze, or to touch only persons of the same sex. One can learn to behave in acceptable ways, however, without fully understanding the implicit *significance* of those behavior patterns and without acquiring the values and attitudes which accompany that behavior in other participants. In the same sense, one can come to understand the background knowledge associated with a particular behavioral skill (say, psychoanalytic theory) without mastering the skill itself (in this case, therapeutic application).

In its most inclusive meaning, enculturation entails acquisition of behavioral skills, knowledge of cultural standards and symbolic codes such as language and art, culturally sanctioned motivations and perceptual habits, ideologies and attitudes. To the degree that an individual acquires all of this, we might say that enculturation is "complete"; both comprehension and commitment presumably would be maximal. In fact the differential distribution of the total corpus of a community's (or society's) knowledge, the inherent variation of the versions of ostensibly shared knowledge, and the impact of specific life experiences and individual differences, all preclude complete enculturation.

Enculturation, then, is a matter of degree. It may take place at any age. Usually the transmission processes of childrearing result in relatively more thorough enculturation than do later exposures to a new culture, but this is not always the case. Enculturation may involve selected domains of a larger cultural corpus. A diplomat, for example, or a teacher may wish only to learn enough about particular cognitive/behavioral domains of a group to be able to communicate effectively with participants. An immigrant to a new land, on the other hand, may seek to acquire much broader comprehension and mastery in order to achieve acceptance as a member of the adopted community. Always, enculturation involves a particular group of people to whose ways and outlooks the individual is adjusting.

Potentially a person can acquire multiple stocks of cultural knowledge, achieving competence in divergent cultural repertoires. Often this creates little conflict for the individual; as with a second language versus one's native tongue, a second culture is used where appropriate as a guiding scheme for behavior and interpretation, but one's fundamental commitment to one's "own" (first) culture remains firm. For fully bicultural (or bilingual) individuals, commitment itself may be dual. So long as the situations in which such a person must apply one set of cultural skills do not overlap significantly with those in which the other set is appropriate, being a member of two (or more) divergent worlds may not be difficult. When the contexts are not distinct, however, the individual may find it difficult to juggle the multiple repertoires and even to maintain a coherent sense of personal identity.

For bicultural children (such as Americans with strong ethnic heritages distinct from the dominant culture of their community or region), school experience, which often provides their primary exposure to their second culture, can create just this sort of disjunction. Still in the process of becoming adept in the culture of their home, they then are confronted with a different set of expectations and taken–for–granted knowledge which may conflict with previous learning. Until they acquire facility in the implicit culture represented by the school, they are likely to be handicapped in their ability to use the school as a context for academic learning.

The processes of enculturation constitute the vehicles for transmission of all cultural knowledge. To analyze the variety of forms this transmission may take, two additional concepts are needed: education and schooling. As with enculturation and socialization, these terms have been defined in a number of ways. Often they are treated as synonomous in meaning. For our purposes, *education* will denote a subset of enculturation: a deliberate and systematic attempt to transmit skills and understandings, habits of thought and deportment required by the group of which the learner is a novice member. *Schooling* will denote institutionalized education in which learners learn vicariously, in roles and in environments defined as distinct from those in which the learning will eventually be applied.[2] Apprenticeship within a workshop would represent a type of education but not schooling, in contrast with study of the same subject in a vocational school.

While virtually all societies carry out some degree of systematic education, the extent to which knowledge transmission is systematized varies considerably. Schooling is instituted less widely, for it requires that a society be able to spare the active participation and contribution of students for the duration of their learning time. Thus formal schooling is found most commonly in relatively prosperous societies, although, as we shall see later, it by no means is found exclusively in industrial societies. Patterns of schooling vary along a number of dimensions such as typical duration, scope of curriculum, responsible agency, pedagogic strategies, and criteria of access. In some societies, schooling constitutes a minor part of systematic education, as in Puluwat; here aspiring navigators are taught largely through apprenticeship with schooling as a supplement. In many societies, schooling traditionally comprises several weeks or months of instruction in community lore, sexuality, and adult roles provided to adolescents in conjunction with coming-of-age ceremonies. In some societies, such as our own, schooling potentially extends for decades and constitutes a major part of the total educational system.

Because a school represents a kind of model environment for learning, divorced in a fundamental sense from the contexts in which that learning has its "real" application, it separates the students from their previous lives and roles, invests them with new obligations and responsibilities, and rewards them with new status upon completion of the educational process. Schooling is generally associated with formal rituals of status transition, but such rituals are not restricted to status changes effected by schooling. Other types of education too are often socially validated in formal ways, as when a person who has completed apprenticeship is initiated into the ranks of a craft.

All learning involves the learner's perception and processing of information. As every teacher knows, what we attempt to teach is not necessarily the same as what is learned. Instruction must be distinguished from learning. We should also bear in mind that not all instruction is deliberate or explicit. A mother may deliberately and systematically instruct her daughter in certain sectors of knowledge and skill such as cooking or farming or deportment. Other sectors of knowledge she may transmit implicitly, simply by serving as a model. The human propensities to imitation and social facilitation discussed in the first chapter contribute to the effectiveness of these less direct forms of knowledge transmission. Formal instruction always entails additional informal transmission, if only because of the communicative impact of context on the intended message exchange. For example, when a teacher in a typical American classroom is engaged in formal instruction on, let us say, mathematics, she or he is communicating a great many things not only about mathematics—a way of understanding relative quantities, a way of describing objects precisely, a way of thinking in logical steps—but also about the relationship of the student to peers, teacher, and self.

Although a great deal of research has been devoted to knowledge transmission, its forms and constituent processes, we do not have as yet a fully adequate theory to account for it. We do have several useful frameworks to guide our search for more complete understanding. Gearing and his associates, for example, are developing an analytic framework based on Wallace's concept of partial equivalence structures. Their focus is on face-to-face transactions and the controlled transfer of information as property within these transactions (Gearing 1973, Gearing and Tindall 1973, Gearing and others 1975, Tindall 1976). Hymes and others have emphasized intensive contextual analysis of communicative transactions and the development of communicative competence (e.g., Cazden and others 1972, Cicourel 1968a, 1972, 1974). At the other end of the spectrum, Siegel (1974), Dobbert (1975) and others have proposed systems analysis of educational transmission, while investigators like Carnoy (1974, 1975) and Shimahara and Scrupski (1975) have focused on the relationship between knowledge transmission as a process and the dynamics of the social structural system of which it is part. It is clear that we need the full spectrum of viewing angles, from microprocess to macrosystem, to comprehend knowledge transmission. No single perspective will suffice.

education and the distribution of knowledge

As a mechanism for the transmission of knowledge, education both reflects and affects social structure. As Kimball (1967:13) remarks, "when we examine the formal educational arrangements for each type of community . . . we can observe the broad congruency between education and the social and cultural aspects of a society." Education constitutes a kind of nexus between the corpus of cultural knowledge and the organization of social relationships, for it generally reflects the central priorities and values which orient behavior, the dominant modes of relationship, and the ways in which these are systematically inculcated in novice participants.

The institutional structure of any society is related to the distribution of knowledge, items of value (be they goods, skills, prerogatives, or prestige), and recognized means of access to both. To understand knowledge transmission we must explore these factors in some depth, but we remain handicapped because of the paucity of systematic research of adequate scope. To guide examination of existing studies, however, we should specify the questions such an inquiry would include.

1. What are the major bases of differentiation of knowledge repertoires among members of the society? These might include sex/gender, age, class, religion, race, or ethnic group, among others. In what ways and to what extent are certain kinds of knowledge denied to particular groups or individuals? In some societies, for example, males and females tend to have somewhat different knowledge repertoires, but a person of one sex is not excluded from acquiring knowledge characteristic of the other sex. In other societies, persons of one sex may be forbidden access to certain parts of the knowledge repertoire of the other sex, with enforcement ranging from a fine or social disapproval to death.

2. What are the main agencies of knowledge transmission? In the U.S., for example, the main agencies are family and peer group, the school system,

and mass media. What procedures does each use? What control does each have over the transmission process as a whole and over that segment in which each is most directly involved? What authority and responsibility has each agency over certification of the results of transmission? To what extent do such agencies cooperate or compete with one another and with what consequences?

3. What are the goals of the agencies of knowledge transmission? For instance, are their activites aimed at perpetuating the status quo or at effecting change, providing access to particular skills or knowledge or developing a general set of attitudes and allegiances? To what extent are these goals of selected groups in the society and to what extent are they generally shared goals?

4. To what extent are agencies of knowledge transmission controlled by particular cultural groups or social strata? This is especially pertinent in multicultural and stratified societies in which certain sectors of the population are politically or economically dominant. In more general terms, what is the relationship of these groups or strata which control transmission to dominant institutional orders[3] in the society?

5. In what ways is access to certain specialized bodies of knowledge controlled? Is access restricted, for instance, to kin of the specialists, to aspirants with requisite financial resources, or to those passing aptitude tests? What attributes and what procedures are necessary for achieving access? How is the use of restricted knowledge controlled after acquisition? For example, are specialists forbidden to reveal their knowledge to nonspecialists? Is the use of this knowledge dependent on the approval or certification of fellow specialists or some other agency? Are there sanctions against inappropriate or incompetent use?

These queries focus on the structural correlates of knowledge transmission in societies at a rather general level. If we narrow our focus to the organization of transmission within a community, additional factors must be considered. Because knowledge transmission is essential to the perpetuation of a "reasonable," "good," or "natural" way of living, the form of education is of interest to community members, even when it is for the offspring of others. While a child's earliest training may be carried out by a limited group of individuals, often kin (whom we may call primary socializers), others generally supplement this as soon as the child actively enters the larger community. Involvement may range from the tacit evaluation of the child's behavior (evaluations expected by the primary socializers); through participation in correcting, explaining, or modeling behavior; to engagement in systematic instruction. In the last instance primary socializers or the whole community allocates responsibility for systematic education to particular individuals. Examples include any specialization from a parent or hired tutor taking responsibility for systematic instruction, to a group class led by a professional instructor or a selected community representative. When the youth of a community (at least those of a single gender or class) are educated in some degree as a group, teachers are expected to be representatives of the community or class and of its standards and interests.

The organization of education in a community will depend on a number of variables. First, what types of knowledge are selected for systematic transmission and what methods are considered appropriate? The answer lies partly in the goals of the agency of transmission. Education may be designed to develop skills relevant to securing a livelihood or coping with social institutions, such as literacy and arithmetic. Or it may teach prevailing values and moral/religious ideology, as in catechism instruction. Community-wide education may be restricted to preparation for new roles, as in the initiation of adolescents into adulthood or premarital instruction.

Second, to what extent are all community members of a particular age subject to a common curriculum? This reflects the major bases of differentiation of knowledge repertoires. Are boys and girls taught different bodies of knowledge? Are children with varying social characteristics such as class, occupational group, or creed educated differently? How do these variations in knowledge transmission affect an individual's access to items of value, including prerogatives and prestige?

Third, to what extent is education defined as a community concern rather than as a concern solely of the household, kin group, or other primary socializers? If defined as a community concern, in what ways is education subsidized or supported by community members? The capacity of a community to subsidize may limit the scope of the system maintained. For example, in traditional Poro schools of Liberia, the scheduling of school sessions was dependent on the accumulation of a sufficient food surplus to feed the teachers and students for the duration of the session. Related to this is the degree to which the community itself is in control of its youths' education. When control is at least partly exercised by agencies outside the community, subsidy also may be provided by these agencies, and this may affect the degree to which community members support education in noneconomic ways.

Fourth, what is the community status of those being instructed and what are their expected responsibilities and privileges? Several issues are involved here. Is systematic instruction associated exclusively with certain life stages? For example, is education considered relevant and appropriate only for preadults or for children above a given age? If students are considered to be an economically productive group, community schools are likely to schedule instruction around seasons of heaviest labor demand. If students are considered economically nonproductive, or if their economic labor is valued less than their access to valued knowledge or status, the organization and timing of education will reflect this.

The status of students also is closely related to the status of instructors. In Jewish *shtetl* communities,[4] for instance, children were considered incomplete adults, of minimal interest to the community until they began their studies. At this point respect was accorded to them in proportion to their progress in learning. The first few years of schooling were devoted primarily to the mechanics of reading, under the tutelage of a minimally learned man. This instructor had very low social status, because of both his level of education and his means of livelihood, selling (rather than giving) learning and working with the lowest status members of the community. Subsequent instructors, who were Talmudic scholars in their own right and were supported in their studies by their families, were among the most respected members of the community. Their knowledge and the instruction they provided were highly valued (Zborowski 1955).

The status of those instructed is a function in part of the social differentiation among groups and classes in the society. In Jewish *shtetl* communities, schooling was a prerogative of male children, reflecting the unequal status of males and females in the community. Insofar as such differences affect access to valued items like power and privilege, educational curricula are likely to display analogous variation by group or class. Societies differ in the degree to which ascribed or achieved characteristics are bases for accession to responsibilities and prerogatives. In societies emphasizing achievement, curricula may vary less, although, as we shall see later, this lack of variance may not ensure equal access. In societies or sectors of a society emphasizing ascription, on the other hand, curricula for various groups may be designed to meet different goals.

In eighteenth-century Germany, according to Bruford (1935), the German aristocracy provided their sons with a kind of education distinctly different from that given to sons of the prosperous bourgeoisie. Only the latter attended the town grammar schools in which Latin, the language of scholarship, was taught. Sons of the nobility were instructed in "modern languages and the arts of dancing, fencing, and riding," skills "which made a young man welcome in good society" (Bruford 1935:66). These were primary, but secondary subjects included

> the study of the modern world, history . . . , geography, genealogy and perhaps some snippets of natural science, the 'curiosities' of botany, anatomy, physics and chemistry. Philosophy was considered pedantic, but time might be found for a little ethics. Law was important for future rulers and officials, and 'politics,' then, was of value to all. It meant the art of self-advancement by 'finesse' and civility . . . (Bruford 1935:68).

Finally, leisure activities of all kinds and "the 'science' of manners and deportment" (Bruford 1935:68) completed the curriculum, usually followed by the young man's grand tour of foreign courts at which final polish was acquired. In no sense were even the semiacademic studies intended as potential preparation for further learning. The goal of schooling was to acquire social skills necessary to succeed in the prime avenue of ambition—a career at court. As Bruford (1935:71) puts it, "the proper study of mankind was how to please the great."

The type of knowledge transmitted, the agency or agencies responsible for transmission, and the way in which access is controlled all carry important messages about the nature of the social system and the place of an individual aspirant in it. It is in part through such messages to learners that education contributes to the perpetuation of the status quo. Two examples will serve to illustrate this.

As in eighteenth-century Germany, preindustrial England was characterized by a rather rigid system of ascribed classes, each with a fairly distinct set of occupational roles confirmed by the prevailing patterns of education. For instance, the elite roles of churchmen, statesmen, and resident land owners were not considered to require specialized training in technical skills. Their education centered on classical languages, literature, history, and philosophy; proficiency in these subjects was the mark of a well-bred gentleman. The function of this classical education was to provide a body of shared symbols and values that imbued members of the upper class with a sense of their future role in the social and political elite. Since members of the upper class defined themselves as heirs and caretakers of a cultural heritage and social system which represented the flower of human progress, they sought to behave in accordance with these values. Elite education helped to develop a shared orientation and a commitment to the existing social order in most of its recipients.

In the West African societies characterized by the powerful secret organization of Poro (and Sande, the women's secret organization), social control was even more explicit, for every increment of specialized knowledge was bought with the coin of increased loyalty to the established power structure. Boys in Poro schools swore on their lives to keep their new knowledge secret. The consequences of this oath were made apparent during their schooling, when they witnessed the speedy and decisive punishments rendered by Poro officials on those who did not obey orders.

The schools were but one of the functions of Poro. Poro was the dominant force in regulating social, political and economic life. Although technically separate from the political system, in many areas it underwrote the power of political leaders. By grouping all adult men in a single organization, it crosscut the divisive ties of kinship and residence; this unity was particularly strong among those who had attended Poro school together. Within Poro, the highest ranks and accompanying knowledge were limited to certain families; achievement of all ranks required the payment of fees to Poro and tutor as well as instruction in the new knowledge. The power of Poro was rooted in the access of its elite to esoteric ritual knowledge and to the spirit world itself. This elite controlled both the daily life of all members and the rate at which upward mobility in the organization might be achieved (Little 1951, Gibbs 1955).

education and cultural values

The way in which knowledge transmission is organized in a society expresses its cultural values. The sectors of knowledge selected for systematic transmission, the status of learners and instructors, the goals and methods of instruction, and restrictions on access to bodies of knowledge all reflect fundamental beliefs and values of those who control and generally those who are served by educational institutions.

In the schools of Peyrane, a small French town, Wylie (1964) found knowledge treated as a closed system of principles, rules, and exemplary facts to be committed to memory and applied to one's own life. There are visible holes in this theory of knowledge, for portions of the state-controlled curriculum conflict with Peyranais reality. In spite of this conflict, school learning is respected greatly by the community.

Children begin school at four years of age and for two years learn the proper attitudes toward schooling:

> They learn to sit still for long periods. They learn to accept the discipline of the school. They even learn about learning—that is, they are impressed with the fact that to learn means to copy or repeat whatever the teacher tells them . . . they learn that their personality must be kept constantly under control (Wylie 1964:57).

Moreover, from the organization of the instruction, from the attitudes of teachers, parents, and texts, these children learn certain "basic assumptions about the nature of reality and their relationship to it" (Wylie 1964:73). Whatever the subject, the same method is used: a principle or rule is introduced for memorization, followed by concrete examples of the rule.

> The principle itself is not questioned and is hardly discussed . . . [Children] are given the impression that principles exist autonomously. They are always there: immutable and constant. One can only learn to recognize them and accept them. The same is true of concrete facts and circumstances . . . Nothing can be done to change them (Wylie 1964:73–74).

Similarly, children memorize general frameworks which then are filled out with related facts. Every fact is significant only in terms of the whole of which it is an integral part, in terms of the abstract principle which it exemplifies, and in terms of its relevance to human affairs, especially to daily life.

In the Jewish *shtetl,* lifelong study was a holy commandment, as was the sharing of learning. Knowledge in this community was first and foremost knowledge of the Torah and Talmud, the voluminous commentaries on the holy writ. Because these include extensive prescriptions for proper daily behavior as well as more esoteric knowledge, there was, in a strict sense, no secular knowledge to be transmitted.

The role of student was a highly respected one, associated as much with advanced age as with youth, with wisdom as with incomplete learning. Truth in any absolute sense was inaccessible to the human mind which can perceive only relative truth, subject always to interpretation.

> This relativistic and provisional approach fosters a tendency to analyze, to probe, to discuss every problem, every phenomenon; to see it not in one aspect but in multiple aspects. There is not the classic opposition between "yes" and "no." Everything contains both elements, negation and affirmation . . . (Zborowski 1955:138).

As noted earlier, the first years of schooling were distinguished sharply from later phases. Elementary instruction in the Hebrew language was conducted through rote repetition and memorization. Although children at this level were only three to five years of age, tutors were generally harsh and authoritarian. In subsequent phases of schooling, however, the relationship between instructor and learner changed radically, as did the definition of learning. Until a person had mastered the foundations of literacy he was unworthy of respect. When the boy (or very rarely a girl) finally began to study the Talmud, the core of Jewish scholarship, the teacher as authority was replaced by the teacher as guide, for true learning required individually paced study and creative synthesis. This relationship expressed not only the cultural respect for learning and the conception of learning as unending, but also the relativity of human truth and authority. "No scholar [is deemed] so wise that his words will not be weighed, examined and questioned" (Zborowski 1955:133).

We must remember that education and schooling are always embedded in a larger context of knowledge transmission. Lessons given through systematic instruction may be interpreted in light of lessons or messages derived from informal transmission. A Native American society, the Menomini of Wisconsin, exemplifies this (Spindler 1963a, Spindler and Spindler 1971). Although schooling was absent traditionally, a combination of systematic instruction and informal transmission taught children what they were expected to know as adult members of the community. Much of the traditional system of transmission is still active among present-day Menomini who hold to the old ways. Among them, children are respected as autonomous individuals throughout their growing years. Even before they are five years of age, they will have encountered people in many roles. Parents, elder siblings, grandparents, and other community members all treat children tolerantly and supportively. When hungry or fretful, children are nursed; they are weaned gradually and toilet-trained in a relaxed fashion. As Spindler (1963a:382) states, "encounters [with others] are nearly all favorable to the child." Punishment is very rare. It is assumed that reasonableness, respect, and verbal instruction are enough to produce good behavior. Traditional "Menomini believe strongly in the power of the spoken word" (Spindler 1963a:387). Young children are told stories which express cultural values, while from the age of eight to marriage, instruction is formalized in the "preaching" of elders, usually grandparents.

Cultural ideals transmitted include individual autonomy, emotional control, equanimity under duress, and quiet, expectant waiting. It is important to note that these are transmitted as much through the relationship itself between child and elder as by explicit daily training. The respect accorded children reflects the pervasive egalitarianism of the society. The use of modeling behavior and moral tales rather than direct verbal chastisement is typical as well of adult interaction. Verbal confrontation of individuals is absent, whether in supportive, decision making, or dissenting contexts. Just as elders wait for children to acquire mastery at their own pace, supporting each of their small successes but accepting lapses with equanimity, adults also await the outcome of their own fates without straining after particular results.

In the U.S., children generally are viewed quite differently. Autonomy is not considered an appropriate prerogative, nor is respect as full members of the community, characteristic among the Menomini, ordinarily accorded to the young. Some observers (e.g., Mead 1942) have argued that in the U.S. even parental love is commonly contingent upon the child's achievement. Social age is reckoned to a considerable degree by a person's participation in schooling. Adulthood as a stage of life is considered by many to begin with an individual's completion of formal schooling and entry into full-time remunerative work. Friedenberg (1963:90) describes the interface between U.S. adolescent experiences in high school and the adolescent's status in the society as the profound lesson of what it means to be a minor.

> First of all, they learn to assume that the state has the right to compel adolescents as well as younger children to spend six or seven hours a day, five days a week, thirty-six or so weeks a year, in a specific place, in charge of a particular group of persons in whose selection they have no voice, performing tasks about which they have no choice, without remuneration and subject to specialized regulations and sanctions that are applicable to no one else in the community . . . they do not participate fully in the freedoms guaranteed by the state, and . . . therefore, these freedoms do not really partake of the character of inalienable rights. [emphasis deleted]

They learn that the restraints and regulations are not limited to explicitly educational matters. Within the school the student is accorded little privacy and only trivial autonomy. Friedenberg (1963:93) states bluntly:

> The concepts of dignity and privacy, notably deficient in American adult folkways, are not permitted to develop here. The school's assumption of custodial control of students implies that power and authority are indistinguishable . . . In such a world, power counts more than legitimacy; if you don't have power, it is naive to think you have rights that must be respected.

Friedenberg is contending that the context in which academic lessons are taught is as significant a source of cultural transmission as the intended formal curriculum.

We may also question to what extent the community respects the formal studies of students in the first twelve grades. Beyond the basic skills of literacy and arithmetic, do students acquire knowledge highly valued by adults, as was the case in the Jewish *shtetl* and Peyrane? What kinds of knowledge are most valued? For instance, if we distinguish between scientific and humanistic knowledge, we would probably find that most people in the U.S. value the first more than the second. Scientific knowledge is generally considered more objective than humanistic knowledge, more concerned with "facts," and thus more suited to the solution of concrete problems. A source of national pride is "American know-how," our ability to devise technological solutions to problems. In advanced education especially, and in research aimed at accumulating new knowledge, the areas most respected tend to be those with visible results: applied sciences such as engineering, medicine, and dentistry, and service professions such as law.

It is also widely believed that objective truth may be discovered through the accumulation of scientific knowledge. Both school curricula and pedagogic methods used in instruction tend to emphasize the importance of facts and "right answers." Evidence supporting this is provided by ethnographic studies of actual U.S. classrooms. Henry (1955) describes the learned orientation of urban middle class elementary school students of "giving their teachers the answers expected of them." Henry argues that the essential theme is "giving the teacher what she or he wants" in order to secure approval and affection, although the answer sought is not always apparent. He found students engaged in frantic scanning for cues about the desired answer but little residual learning of a logical connection between questions and answers.[5] The importance of "right answers" and the conception of facts as discrete and unequivocal units of knowledge greatly influence the transmission process.

Knowledge transmission in any society is related to cultural values and social structure. Valued types of knowledge and cognitive strategies, the community status of teachers and learners, and educational goals and methods, are complemented by the allocation of instructional responsibility to particular members of the community or particular agencies, and by control over the acquisition and use of types of knowledge. We must look at knowledge transmission as part of a sociocultural system, if we are to understand it as both process and product. As product, it is a major force in cultural and social structural perpetuation, for it establishes the distribution of knowledge and skills on which the sociocultural system depends.

As process, knowledge transmission is subject to a variety of constraints which may reduce its potency in sociocultural conservation. Differences in individual ability and experience and in knowledge repertoires among constituent groups, and inconsistency or incompleteness in transmission all limit the effectiveness of systematic instruction as a conservative force. We will examine this dialectic relationship of conservation and change, structure and process in greater detail in succeeding chapters.

The analysis of knowledge transmission as a sociocultural phenomenon can be approached from a variety of vantage points. In the present chapter, I have indicated the types of variables which must be considered for a full analysis. In the next two chapters, we will consider types of theoretical perspectives and ways in which they influence our understanding.

notes

1. Goodenough (1971, 1976) argues cogently that multiculturalism is universal and that "the process of learning a society's culture . . . is one of learning a number of different or partially different micro-cultures and their sub-cultural variants, and how to discern the situations in which they are appropriate and the kinds of others to whom to attribute them" (Goodenough 1976:5). He further distinguishes individual personal outlook ("propriospect") from situationally appropriate "operating cultures," and these in turn from socially more-or-less shared "public culture" (Goodenough 1971:36–39). While this scheme is useful as a corrective to traditional treatments of culture as a homogeneous corpus, I have chosen not to incorporate it totally into the analytic framework presented for two reasons. First, on theoretical grounds, to describe each set of standards, expectations, values, and so forth which are situationally appropriate as a distinct (micro) culture risks obscuring the difference in degree of incongruity between what we might call allomorphic microcultures (all partaking of a common "macroculture") and between the disparate cultures typically associated with "multicultural classrooms" and other educational contexts in culturally plural societies. Second, in pragmatic terms, little of the available research allows documentary development of the detail of Goodenough's model.

2. Definitions of schooling vary markedly, in part as a function of the analytic goals of the definer. Two common types of usage emphasize, in the one case, the functional significance of schools for societal structure (e.g., Y. Cohen 1971) and, in the other, the cognitive significance of schools as environments for learning process (e.g., Bruner and others 1966). I have taken the latter approach. Herskovits (1947, 1964) provided an early anthropological perspective on education as a phenomenon not restricted to schooling. Arguing that education is universal in human societies while schools are not, he emphasized that education is commonly the province of the household. Schools, in his view, thus involve a shift of educational activity and responsibility to an agency other than the family. More recently Scribner and Cole (1973) have distinguished between noninstitutional formal education and institutional formal education (schooling). Formal education in general, in their view, entails deliberate organization for the purpose of knowledge transmission, special settings, and group responsibility. In schooling, they contend, there is greater discontinuity with daily experience outside the educational setting than is common in noninstitutional forms. Schooling involves instruction in techniques for processing information which then mediate later learning and in instrumental skills independent of the pragmatic contexts and ends to which they eventually will be applied. While my definition and theirs are similar, Cole and Scribner's analytic goal is to account for the cognitive effects of Western-style schooling. My analytic focus, in contrast, is the relationship between forms and contexts of knowledge transmission and transmission process as a sociocultural event.

3. An institutional order comprises all those institutions within a society which have similar consequences and intended ends. Western industrial societies display five institutional orders: political, economic, military, kinship, and religious orders (Gerth and Mills 1954:25). Institutional orders vary cross-culturally. Within a society, activities may contribute directly to more than one institutional order, or to none of them, although the orders may influence social action.

4. Descriptions of Eastern European *shtetl* communities are based on Zborowski's reconstruction, derived from historical sources and former *shtetl* residents' testimony. These communities no longer exist, although elements of the pattern described are still found in much Jewish rabbinical education. Other perspectives are available in many of Isaac Bashevis Singer's writings; more contemporary descriptions can be found in Chaim Potok's novels.

5. Goetz (1975) notes a similar phenomenon in a rural elementary classroom. However, the teacher described not only rewards right answers with approval but also seeks to encourage a degree of student autonomy. The teacher attempts to present questions to which the "right answer" can be derived by logical procedures rather than by second-guessing her hidden agenda.

THREE

THE STUDY OF EDUCATION

Analysis of the values and concepts which make up cultural definitions of knowledge has a dual significance. Not only is it necessary to ascertain the nature of knowledge in a particular society if we are to understand its transmission, but it is also important to recognize the cultural assumptions and values which form our own conceptions of knowledge as we attempt to extend it through scientific research. How we define science as an endeavor and how we define scientific knowledge affect our study of any phenomenon, including education. For this reason, clarifying the nature of scientific analysis is an appropriate prelude to our consideration of research approaches.

Among researchers in educational anthropology, concern with alternative methods of data collection and analysis has been growing steadily.[1] Interest has focused particularly on the respective strengths and limits of qualitative and quantitative approaches (e.g., Textor 1977, Hymes 1977, Wilson 1977). As Rist (1977) has underscored, evaluation of the relative merits of these approaches rests ultimately on the beliefs and values one holds about the nature of science and the nature of our subject matter. In this chapter we will take up the values and assumptions which shape our quest for scientific knowledge, relationships among alternative approaches to this quest, and implications for the study of education.

the nature of scientific analysis

Science is often thought of as a search for true facts. In this view science is conceived of as a set of objective procedures that assure the eventual emergence of "right answers" in much the sense described in the preceding chapter. Facts are assumed to be discrete and unequivocal, independent of cultural beliefs and values. Scientific method as an ideal is considered to involve a rigorous procedure of data collection and analysis through the use of quantified measurements and controlled experiments, deductive logic, and the scientist's neutrality with respect to any values which might influence observation or analysis. In this stereotype of science, the social sciences often are seen as "softer," that is, as less rigorous and less objective than the physical sciences.

In some ways this stereotype of science is accurate. Science involves the systematic investigation of phenomena in order to elucidate their nature, genesis, and consequences. It depends on the careful control of possible sources of bias or distortion both in the collection and in the analysis of data. In order for research results to be accepted as scientific, they must be supported adequately by evidence and explained logically. The misleading aspects of this stereotype, however, are equally important.

We can summarize the problem in terms of two ideals or goals: objectivity and truth. Both must be understood as goals which are at best approximated, but never attained. Even in physics, the epitome of rigorous science, it has been discovered that "pure observation," in which the observer has no influence on that which is being observed, is never completely possible. The tools one uses to observe necessarily affect the nature of the observation; in this sense, observation is an artifact of those tools. Moreover, atomic physicists have found that the act of observation itself influences the phenomena they seek to study.

Objectivity in all sciences is limited in three ways. First, perception itself always is filtered through conceptual processes. As Kaplan (1964:131) puts it, "observation is already cognition." We do not perceive simply raw sensory input but facts defined by our conceptual categories and expectations (cf. Hanson 1958, Kuhn 1970, and Kaplan 1964 for useful discussions of this process in science). Second, and related to this, is that our observations are conditioned by the questions we seek to answer. In other words, we focus on certain kinds of data and ignore other kinds in accordance with our research goals. The questions which guide research reflect the complex of assumptions and hypotheses which constitute the theoretical orientation of the researcher. Third, the act of observation, whether mediated through mechanical devices, as in many physical sciences, or through such tools as questionnaires, interviews, or simply the presence of an observer in social sciences, may affect the subjects of observation in ways that modify the nature of the data sought. This is significant especially in social science research.

These three limitations on objectivity have obvious consequences for the possibility of ascertaining unequivocally true facts. This is constrained further by translation, the verbal descriptions of our observations. Since language is itself a system of culturally defined categories for describing experience, the verbal translation necessary to make public our observations and analyses further removes data from the ideal status of "pure facts."

The implications of these factors are especially critical for social sciences because human behavior, unlike the behavior of molecules and machines, is motivated and intentional, constructed in light of acquired frames of meaning and relevance. Humans selectively perceive and unceasingly interpret the world of their experience. When they study other humans, the complexity of the reality multiplies geometrically. Social scientists may add both their own common-sense scheme of interpretation (which often differs from that of the people whose behavior they seek to explain) and the scheme they share with their discipline to the reality under study.

Interpretive schemes of social science disciplines (which are analogous to the cultural repertoires of other human groups) are composed of such elements as background assumptions, concepts, analytic frames and perspectives, propositions or hypotheses, and theories. As in other sciences, social science theories and analytic frames are idealized constructs designed not to replicate reality precisely but to isolate particular features and to articulate constituent processes. Reality itself is not subdivided into classes of objects and relations among classes except insofar as our means of perceiving reality causes us to categorize our perceptions. To analyze it, however, we must dissect the complex whole, breaking what is continuous into discrete elements and simplifying the complexity by focusing on particular facets. Analysis, therefore, is a kind of "intellectual shorthand" which makes systematic research manageable.

Concepts are the building blocks of analytic frameworks. A concept is an abstract idea that refers to specific empirical instances as members of a labeled class, and a bridge between theoretical analysis and the reality under study— the empirical world. Clarity of concepts is crucial to ensure identification of empirical instances and of the specific criteria by which they are identified. Without concepts, the empirical information to be discerned cannot be ordered and translated into analytically useful terms. Yet it has been argued by Blumer (1954) and others that the scientific utility of a concept may hinge on a certain slack in its definition.

Definitive concepts are precise in their reference, defining the objective attributes of empirical instances and thus prescribing how we perceive our field of observation. In social science, however, concepts cannot be rigidly defined and remain flexible enough to guide us in examining the empirical world. Specifying a concept's content precisely and using it to label given occurrences in social life do not establish the relevance or significance of that class of occurrences to the human reality we seek to understand. Rather, concepts are "fundamentally sensitizing instruments" (Blumer 1954:147) which enable us to discern commonality in an array of distinctive instances. As Blumer (1954:149) puts it,

> We recognize that what we are referring to by any given concept [e.g., "schooling"] shapes up in a different way in each empirical instance. We have to accept, develop and use the distinctive expression in order to detect and study the common.

Thus we formulate a concept such as "schooling" so that it can refer to a variety of particular instances. The formulation itself reflects the analyst's assumptions about the nature of the empirical phenomena to which the concept refers and the analytic ends to which the concept is to be put (see p.39 note two). Poro schools are quite different in appearance from French schools, but the concept helps us to discern the commonality. At the same time, careful study of the range of particular instances—for they are not the same—adds to our understanding of the *nature* of that commonality which leads us to label them both as schools.

All concepts sensitize perception and thus change the perceptual world through their guidance of thought in particular directions. Until Pasteur introduced the concept of the microbe, of an infinitely small form of life, many scientific problems could not be resolved. Similarly, the content of a concept may change as new features of empirical instances are noted and incorporated into the general concept. Scientific concepts share three characteristics. First, they constantly are related to one another and examined for mutual consistency and interdependence. It is this process which lends coherence to scientific knowledge and makes it systematic. Second, through successive applications, concepts are refined, the classes and relations they label are better understood, and the consequences of their use are clarified. Third, as abstract ideas, concepts make possible deductive reasoning which opens up new perspectives and raises new problems which transcend the immediate application. By extrapolating from a concept and considering possible logical implications, unanticipated directions for fruitful exploration can emerge (Blumer 1930).[2]

By means of concepts and propositions built upon them, theory organizes things known into a system. A theory is a way of making sense of experience by articulating interconnections or relations among types of events. Like concepts, theories are abstract and symbolic constructions. Neither, strictly speaking, *describes* the empirical world; concepts classify aspects of that world for the purpose of analytic description, while theories provide explanations or reasons for the aptness or "truth" of those descriptions. In other words, a theory is a systematic frame of reference that accounts for particular kinds of events.

Scientific theories, as explicit formulations of propositions which are subject to empirical test, may be derived by analytic induction (Glaser and Strauss 1967) or deductively from a set of premises. The test of any theory lies in its fit with empirical events, its capacity to explain, account for, or predict them. Theorizing as a cognitive process necessarily includes both deductive and inductive elements, for we theorize in light of our inductive knowledge of empirical events, reconstruct that knowledge into a deductive system of testable propositions, and test them through systematic examination of empirical evidence (cf. Johnson-Laird and Wason 1976:57–60).

All inquiry proceeds by means of theory although the theory may not be explicit. A theory is a way of looking at "the facts" as well as a way of organizing and representing them. Theory and its constituent concepts *define* facts by specifying what perceptual attributes are significant in an observational field. Facts and data are thus constructs of the observer, whether daily life or a set of questionnaire responses or a body of census information is the field of observation. Through the hypothesized relations among the classes of fact so assembled, a theory points us to additional angles from which to examine the field and thereby to new data. In this sense, theory shapes our very apprehension of data as well as the kinds of relations we are inclined to postulate among them. To the extent that the theoretical frame used is explicit, we are able to test its utility in explaining our observations or experience and to modify it if necessary to improve its fit and its consequent explanatory power. By making our theoretical frame explicit we also can, and are more inclined to, examine the assumptions or presuppositions on which the theory is built and their tenability. It also allows us to extrapolate further logical implications of the theory which then may guide further investigation.

Objectivity in analysis, like objectivity in observation, is inherently limited by selective perception, vantage point, purpose, and presuppositions. Scientific rigor does not depend on the use of methods detached from the empirical world under study such as standardized questionnaires, audio/video recording of behavior, or controlled experiment. The apparent rigor of methods that control for researcher effect by holding it constant is spurious and the "objectivity" achieved is fallacious (cf. Denzin 1970:8 on the fallacy of objectivism). Nor is rigor a function of quantitative findings or deductive analysis. Rigor and objectivity, dual values of the scientific enterprise, are represented by commitment to systematic consideration of negative as well as supporting evidence, reflexive examination of the researcher's perspective (including assumptions) as a source of bias, readiness to reexamine analytic procedures and results in the face of new information, and dialectic monitoring of the relationship between analytic constructs and the empirical world they are intended to represent. Objectivity and rigor, in other words, are styles in research work that are independent of particular types of methods or forms of analysis.[3]

Selecting the methods and types of analysis best suited to one's research goals is an important component of these styles. The next two sections will deal with the relationship between types of analysis and goals and with the limits and strengths of various methods as tools for research on education.

types of analysis

In surveying the types of analysis that are pertinent to the anthropological study of education we must consider three aspects: the level of analysis of particular cases, the goal of analysis, and the comparison of cases.

As indicated in figure 3.1, level of analysis refers to the degree of inclusiveness which characterizes the unit being studied. Theories focused on level 1 account for events in terms of states and processes within the individual, as when behavior is explained by biological or psychological factors. This is the domain of psychology and biology and generally enters into anthropological analysis only as it affects behavior at more inclusive levels. However, delineation of the cognitive categories and strategies of individuals has been attempted by some anthropologists as a prerequisite for documenting cultural sharing and cultural variation. Theories on level 2 emphasize interpersonal dynamics, including face-to-face communication. Sociopsychological analysis, including the study of communication process, is often most pertinent at this level. Levels 3, 4, and 5 all involve types of groups and group interrelations. Theories aimed at these levels emphasize the processes by which groups are maintained or modified over time and the dynamics of group competition and alliance. Although sociopsychological analysis is sometimes applied to aspects of these processes, functionalist and ecological types of analysis are utilized more often. Each of these analytic frameworks will be treated in depth in the next chapter.

In figure 3.2, the field of observation is divided into units of increasingly inclusive settings rather than into sets of human actors. In this case we can distinguish between theories (usually sociopsychological) which focus on the reciprocal relationship of the individual and group of which she or he is a member, theories (usually functionalist) which focus on the interrelationship of groups whatever their size or constitution, and theories (generally ecological) which focus on the interrelationship of a group or groups and the environment in which action takes place and to which it is adapted.

level 5 _____ inter-society

level 4 _____ { inter-society
                                      inter-community

level 3 _____ { inter-community
                                      inter-group

level 2 _____ { inter-group
                                      inter-individual (face-to-face)

level 1 _____ individual

FIGURE 3.1

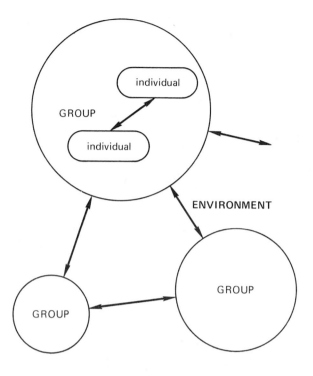

FIGURE 3.2

The levels in both schemes are quite similar, but they serve to clarify ways in which we delimit our units of analysis. These differences in level also reflect degrees of abstractness and generality in the explanations and in the goals of analysis. Imagine that we are looking at a society through a telescope. When we focus closely enough to make out the details of individual faces and demeanor, we lose some breadth of vision but we gain the opportunity to examine the actual dynamics of peoples' behavior as interpretive, goal–directed, and subject to complex types of influence and to chance in the course of their interaction. As we move further away we gain breadth and lose detail. With increasing distance certain large-scale patterns may become discernible that seem less subject to day–to–day contingency factors.

The goal of analysis in this sense depends on the type of explanation sought. Scientific explanation accounts for a phenomenon in terms of an intelligible system of which it is a part. Although some social scientists would argue that an adequate explanation also allows accurate prediction of future empirical instances, at best such prediction is likely to be only approximate, describing probabilities of phenomena occurring under rather specific sets of conditions. The scientific goal of specifying precisely the relationships between phenomena also is only approximated. Precision in explanations of human behavior is necessarily limited by the fact that observed conduct is the product of intentions and actions of variably motivated individuals, acting in variable contexts.

Returning to our levels of abstractness, we find that the meaning of "precise specification of relationships between phenomena" varies with the analytic level on which we choose to focus. For example, intensive ethnographic[4] study of a classroom may yield a body of detailed observations of classroom events and participants. Through analysis the researcher identifies types of events, participants, and situations, and types of relationships among them. Explanations then are developed to account for the patterns and relationships delineated. Smith and Geoffrey (1968), in their ethnographic study of an urban slum classroom, hypothesized that increased "personalized interaction" (interaction between a teacher and a single pupil) is directly related to increased pupil satisfaction and esteem for the teacher, and that these in turn correlate with increased classroom control. At this level of analysis, specification of relationships between component factors rests on the recorded detail of event-sequences and the researchers' knowledge of the dense context in which these processes are embedded.

Studstill (1976a, 1976b) focused on a level of analysis more abstracted from the daily lives of his subjects in his research on secondary school student failure rates in Zaire. All the secondary schools in a rural center (called Masomo in the study) were considered as parts of an inclusive state-controlled school system. Within this system, Studstill identified three networks of schools: Catholic, Protestant, and Zairian. Classroom observations and interviews with students, teachers, and administrators were used to supplement quantitative analysis of attrition rates in each network and correlated variables. The researcher accounted for the correlations in terms of systemic requirements, constraints implicit in popular expectations, and administrative policies of student admissions and the subsequent rationing of school output by failure. In this case, relationships among variables were specified numerically and supported further by qualitative systemic analysis. Documentation of the actual processes whereby high attrition rates are accomplished within schools requires qualitative study within the schools and the community.

The generality of explanation offered in the two cases clearly differs. Although comparison is involved in both, the comparative base of Studstill is greater by virtue of the question he posed and the methods he chose to investigate it. Smith and Geoffrey compared individuals and events within the classroom to determine variables in classroom process, including factors in student achievement. Studstill compared schools and networks of schools in order to determine system-level variables in student attrition rates. Smith and Geoffrey supplemented their classroom observations with less intensive consideration of the school–as–organization and the neighborhood it served. Stud-still supplemented his comparison of organizations with less intensive observations within them.

Inter-societal comparison involves even greater abstraction and general-ity. To compare education in Japan with that in Ghana, for instance, requires that we focus on patterns that are characteristic of a very large and quite varied population. In order to discern commonalities and significant differences be-tween the two societies, we set considerable detail aside as irrelevant to our analytic goals. In the most abstract form of comparison, the cross-cultural or cross-societal survey, the level of generality is such that it is almost beyond empirical test. The explanations generated by this form of comparison tend to be so general in their specification of relationships among variables, that it becomes difficult to apply them to the events in which actual individuals are involved and to ascertain their empirical validity. One reason for this is the problem of formulating concepts that can be applied broadly and yet retain specific meaning adequately reflecting the diverse cultural realities being com-pared. Nevertheless, generalization of this scope is useful for developing sug-gestive hypotheses which can be studied in detail in specific groups. Whiting and Child, for instance, utilized the Human Relations Area Files to secure information on socialization practices in seventy-five societies. From this data base, they developed a number of hypotheses about the relationship between such practices and adult personality. In order to determine the actual processes which might account for the correlations they found, they followed up their survey with intensive studies of six societies (Whiting and Child 1953, Whiting 1963; see also Harrington and Whiting 1972, Whiting 1977).

Another factor in setting goals for analysis is the relative importance accorded to structure and process. To study structural features of a social phenomenon is to study the patterned arrangement of relationships among individuals and groups. To study process is to focus on the ways in which these structural features are created, maintained, or modified over time, and on the processes of adaptation necessary to adjust to changing conditions. In the first case we look for relatively stable features of behavior and context at a particu-lar point in time. For comparison we select either multiple cases from one or several societies or multiple time periods in the same society, i.e., an historical approach. In the latter case we seek to isolate regularities in the processes involved; the scale of temporal concern varies with the level of analysis. Smith and Geoffrey were concerned with processes that took place from moment to moment or from day to day in a classroom while Studstill attempted to account for processes that were visible only in the course of students' school careers. Level of analysis, in other words, interacts with structural versus processual focus in establishing research goals. The more general the level of analysis, the more difficult it becomes to isolate the actual processes which result in ob-served structural regularities.

methods and evaluation of research

Methods are the procedural strategies for securing and analyzing data. Because the type of analysis achieved depends on the type of data collected and on the analytic procedures applied, methods play an important part in scientific research. They are particularly significant in evaluating research results, for they constitute the main basis on which judgments of validity and verification are made.

Anthropologists and other social scientists share many methods. Probably no procedures are used exclusively by a single discipline, though the frequency of use and the manner of application may vary. Often distinctions are drawn between qualitative and quantitative methods, between naturalistic and experimental methods, and between inductive and deductive analysis. Qualitative and naturalistic methods then are associated with inductive analysis and discovery, while quantitative and experimental methods are linked with deductive analysis and verification. This sort of classification oversimplifies the issues involved.

Qualitative research uses strategies that allow one "to obtain first-hand knowledge about the empirical social world in question" (Filstead 1970:6), usually through interaction with and observation of participants in the natural, on-going environments in which they live and work. Documents and other secondary sources may also be used in qualitative research in so far as they contribute to the development of empirically grounded analysis, that is, analysis closely tied to the world (events, processes) as experienced by its full participants. Qualitative research does not preclude quantification. Assessment of frequencies of types of behavior is basic to qualitative description; it is partly on this basis that judgments of typicality are made (cf. Wallace 1970:9–14). Where quantity appears to be significant in the sociocultural world being studied, qualitative researchers use quantification more extensively.

Quantitative research uses strategies that secure data, measurable by an analytic set of criteria, that can be rigorously tested for possible correlations by means of mathematical procedures. In this kind of research the criteria used to define and measure variables are generally independent of the sociocultural world(s) under study. Most quantitative researchers recognize that not all significant information can be measured or categorized readily by a detached (universal) set of analytic procedures, but they concentrate on data amenable to this procedure. The overlap between the two sets of strategies can be exemplified with interview responses. The responses themselves provide qualitative data about the opinions of interviewees (or at least about the answers the interviewees think the interviewer wants). When we abstract these responses from the whole interview as a sociocultural event, sort them in terms of a specific set of scales or analytic categories, and determine which are associated with interviewees of a particular sex, age, educational level, and occupation, we have quantitative data. Quantification can range from a simple count such as the Byers' (1972) report, of the number of times a child looks at the teacher and the number of times eye contact is made, to a computer-assisted calculation of possible mathematical interrelations among a host of variables derived from survey data on a large population.

Validity of research findings refers to the accuracy of fit between the researcher's analytic constructs and events in the sociocultural world experienced by participants. The analysis must account not simply for what we observe from our cultural-scientific frames of reference but also for what actors observe from their vantage points. Human action is always context-related. A person's purposes and motives, interpretations of "what is going on here" and "what does that mean for me," perceived options and constraints on action, and expectations of others all contribute to the behavior which visibly occurs. Social action multiplies these contextual factors by the number of participants involved. Thus the study of behavior–in–context as experienced by participants requires that we take into account the history of observed events, the way in which actors define the event and account for it, and the processes by which the event is accomplished by them. To achieve validity, a primary goal of the researcher must be to secure the most complete picture possible of actual social processes. This requires assembling information from the perspectives of a variety of participants and ascertaining contextual factors that affect those processes.

Reliability refers to the replicability of data offered as evidence. Could a second, independent researcher follow the procedures of the first and obtain the same data? This involves two elements. First, to what extent are the procedures used clear and repeatable? Second, to what extent are the concepts used to analyze the observed flow of events sufficiently definite that different observers could identify the same items as empirical instances of those concepts? Whereas validity measures the congruence between the empirical world and the observer's analytic constructs, reliability measures the congruence between the constructs of independent observers. Reliability is valued as an indicator of objectivity, on the assumption that observer agreement represents the elimination of biasing factors. Since two observers can share similar biases (including such perceptual filters as theoretical presuppositions and purposes), reliability is enhanced when observers who demonstrably diverge in orientation agree in their descriptions. Like objectivity, reliability is always a matter of degree. In actuality no two observers of human life ever observe exactly the same event; the passage of time, the particular personal–cultural vantage point of the observer, and the relationship of that person to the actors observed all render each observer's context distinctive. Secondary data like census information, test scores, and ethnographic depictions may garner more agreement among different analysts (and may not); but in these cases the prior processes of selection, organization, and formulation from which such data were constructed are usually obscured, and reliability at this sub–data level remains untested (cf. Garfinkel 1967, Cicourel 1968).

These difficulties in assessing reliability are troublesome, if only because of our scientific value for consensus as a cornerstone of credibility. The reliability of studies that follow accepted procedures and achieve results consistent with previous findings is less likely to be questioned than is that of studies diverging from the norm in either of these respects. The more detailed the presentation of data and procedures on which conclusions were based, the more credible a study will be considered. Since no study of human behavior, not even controlled experiments, can be replicated exactly, reliability must be assessed indirectly. Our choice of indicators of reliability is likely to reflect our assumptions about the nature of the observation process. And our evaluation itself influences the weight we assign to the body of data in question as evidence.

Related to reliability but distinct from it are testability and verification. These involve the scientific value for demonstrating the applicability or adequacy of an explanation/theory rather than simply asserting it to be "true." Demonstration aims at progressively inclusive limits of applicability. Does the explanation offered adequately fit the case at hand? That is, does it account for it plausibly and in a way which fits with other scientific knowledge? Does it fit better than alternative interpretations of the case in question? Does it account for other, similar cases? Does it account for cases of varying types not included in the original formulation?

The criteria by which we assess the adequacy of explanation[5] and the degree to which theories have been verified are not agreed upon fully. Most researchers agree that analytic propositions ought to be testable; at issue is what constitutes a test. Because it is logically impossible to confirm the empirical adequacy of a general proposition, we usually test it by seeking negative cases that might prove it false. Empirical cases that do not conform to our theoretical expectations stimulate closer inspection of both the case itself and the theoretical account. Often just such rethinking leads to significant advances in our understanding (cf. Glaser and Strauss 1967, Denzin 1970:30–58).

At the heart of scientific concern for verification is the central importance of evidence to substantiate scientific claims. What constitutes evidence and when is it sufficient to "prove" the claim? Qualitative and quantitative researchers often differ over the criteria to be used, as do scientists advocating different theoretical orientations. Quantitative researchers tend to emphasize reliability; careful method and technique in combination with rigorous definition of concepts, measurement of variables, and cleanly abstracted data, are expected to ensure the scientific adequacy of results. Qualitative researchers tend to emphasize validity of findings, in the sense of close fit between the theory developed and the empirical world it is intended to explain. Comparison of cases is more easily achieved at more abstract levels of analysis, for data at these levels are generally freed of much of the contextual significance of the sources from which they were constructed. If the contextual significance is to be preserved, the scope of feasible comparison is reduced. An alternative strategy for increasing empirical support for analytic claims is triangulation: the use of multiple sources of data, multiple techniques, and multiple theoretical frames in the collection and analysis of data (Denzin 1970:297–313).

In order to evaluate evidence adduced in support of any scientific claim, we must take into account the capabilities and limits of the methods used to produce it. Anthropologists typically have used a set of methods which emphasize naturalistic observation and qualitative analysis. Because they have tended to study lifeways of people significantly different in culture from themselves, they have most often chosen methods that would enable them to "get inside" the experienced world of others, to understand the cultural meanings in which human action is embedded, and to relate these to the social contexts in which action occurs. Such a composite set of methods is generally known as *ethnographic method* and the resulting descriptive analysis as *ethnography.* [6]

Prime among these methods is participant-observation. As its name implies, participant-observation involves the researcher more intimately in the social environment being studied than does nonparticipant-observation. As a research strategy, successful participant-observation requires both (a) the development of an acceptable "role" or "place" for the researcher in the sociocultural world under study, so that full participants can proceed with their ordinary concerns, and (b) the development of a degree of trust and rapport with full participants such that they become willing to share some of their thoughts and reactions with the researcher—to respond to her or him as a familiar person rather than as an intruder or stranger.[7] Participant-observation is most fruitful when the researcher also (c) speaks the language of the people studied, and (d) remains a participant-observer for sufficient time to sample a reasonably full range of situations and circumstances.[8]

The techniques used as part of participant-observation include observing with all one's senses and participating by talking with people, sharing in activities, and accepting responsibilities as a member of the group. Thus one is involved with those one studies, with the attendant advantages and disadvantages. Observation itself is always from a particular perspective, for no observer is without presuppositions and cultural frames that influence his or her perceptions. As a scientific method, participant-observation requires that the researcher (a) make as explicit as possible the frames of reference which may affect her or his perception,[9] (b) attempt to control possible sources of bias and distortion in recording observations, and (c) secure sufficiently rich and varied data that it becomes possible to falsify hypotheses or confirm them by triangulation.

Because observation is always from a particular perspective, "what is going on here" is never a straightforward set of "facts." Participants may offer a range of perspectives on this question, a range the researcher attempts to tap. The researcher's goal is partly to sort out those varied views, to discern the vantage points from which they emerge, the factors that affect them, and their effect on the actions of those holding these views and then to use them to construct a more complete picture of the event in question.[10] Participant observation, properly carried out, is a rigorous method of data collection, particularly useful for establishing the validity of analytic constructs. Its objectivity lies in the special training and set of relevances of the researcher. Unlike full participants for whom the events studied are "real life," the observer is detached from any immediate interest or stake in the outcome of the events except as data.[11] Reliability of results gathered by participant observation, however, can be difficult to establish. The procedures by which the gestalt of the lifeworld is dissected analytically may be partially obscure even to the researcher. The world encountered is also specific in many ways to the researcher in question—in time, in the roles enacted as participant and the relationships built, in the particular history shared by the parties involved. Successive studies and team studies provide some evidence of reliability, as does triangulation. Supplementing participant observation with interviews of varied types of participants (e.g., parents, teachers, children, administrators), study of documents (such as student papers, letters to newspapers, official records, personal journals, and recordings), nonparticipant-observation (such as noting arrangements of physical space in a classroom or school plant, monitoring rhythms of interaction, or observing children at play)—lends considerable credibility to findings supported by such diverse sources of evidence. Ethnographic method typically includes the use of multiple techniques in this way (e.g., cf. Becker and others 1961, Ogbu 1974, Wolcott 1967).

Nonparticipant-observation used alone restricts the observer's access to the perspectives of participants, to the cultural and personal meanings which motivate and inform action. Certain methods of this type (e.g., the use of documents) have the advantage of minimizing the effect of the observer on the events observed (see Webb and others 1966 and Denzin 1970:260–293 for discussion of such techniques). Most methods used in sociocultural research, however, necessarily become enmeshed in the flow of participants' lives.

Formal interviewing based on a standardized schedule of questions (as a technique distinct from the attentive listening and questioning engaged in by participant-observers as part of their routine interaction) is sometimes considered to be a more reliable data source than participant-observation, particularly when administered to an appropriate population sample. A key assumption here is that holding constant certain variables such as question form and sequence will reduce extraneous sources of bias. As Cicourel (1964:73–120) makes clear, the enhanced reliability achieved by this method is spurious. Interviewees may not interpret the questions in the way intended by the interviewer, yet this discrepancy may not be made evident within the interview. The interviewer, the interview situation, the negotiations between interviewer and interviewee, all influence the outcome in uncontrolled, and usually unmonitored, ways. If the form or content of questions reflect the researcher's interpretive framework rather than the interviewees', validity is also jeopardized. An alternative interview technique, developed to avoid presupposing relevant categories for talking about events, has been described by Spradley (1972a). This approach allows the interviewee greater freedom in setting the terms of the conversation and structuring its progress. Much anthropological interviewing is nondirective, and a good deal of that which is directed is deflected in its course as the interaction proceeds. Highly structured interviews conducted after relationships with interviewees have been firmly established and insight into the meaning and context of questions has been achieved, allows for maximal combination of reliability and validity.

Testing and contrived experiment engage experimenter and subject in a relationship similar to that of interviewer and interviewee. Often testing is carried out by researchers who have no relationship to their subjects other than that of "tester" or "interviewer." The significance to subjects of the test/interview and of the context in which it is carried out must be taken into account explicitly in the analysis of results. The hazards to reliability and validity of experimental research have been well documented (Campbell and Stanley 1963, Friedman 1967, Adair 1973, Bronfenbrenner 1976). Cross-cultural research based on this type of method raises additional problems such as the familiarity of subjects with the setting in which tests are conducted, with the form of test procedures and implicit rules of appropriate behavior, and with the content of the tests themselves. Since all societies are multicultural to a degree, these problems may be equally salient for studies within our society. (For a more detailed discussion of validity in cross-cultural testing, see Cole and others 1971, Cole and Scribner 1974.) To increase the validity and objectivity of experiment, Bronfenbrenner (1976) argues, we should make use of natural experiments, events occurring in a setting natural to the life-world of the participating subjects which allows us to examine the working of this ecological unit as a system.

Archival records and other documents, as noted earlier, do not entail the interpersonal dynamics of interviewing, testing, or participant-observation (once access to them is secured) but they require equal care in use as data sources. As in all other cases, the data they provide are dual constructs. First, these documents reflect the categories, intentions, and interests of those who originally compiled them. Second, the use of them as resources involves an additional set of decisions by the researcher that the information compiled may validly be "taken to mean" what she or he interprets it to mean, that is, as the basis for an analytic category or as an empirical example of a general concept. Thus both validity and reliability are problematic in this case as well.

Scientific use of all secondary sources, including questionnaire responses, ethnographic depictions, and organizational records entails interpretation and contingent decision making, as Garfinkel (1967) has documented. Quantitative data are not immune to this. Quantitative data, like qualitative, are constructs: selective abstractions and analytic reformulations of events in the empirical world. The translation of those events into numerical code logically requires either that there be some precise (demonstrable) correspondence between the empirical referent and the mathematical measure or that there be systematic rules of transformation by which equivalences are established between the two. In fact neither of these conditions seems to obtain in the social sciences.[12] Quantitative data, then, represent an essentially metaphorical rendering of sociocultural phenomena. In this sense they are neither more nor less objective than qualitative data.

Translation of data into mathematical code has certain advantages. Most notably, the logical manipulation of data by means of statistical procedures helps us to discern possible relationships among elements in the empirical world that might otherwise have gone unnoticed, and to gauge the probability that those relationships are significant. In so far as quantitative measures are associated arbitrarily with sociocultural phenomena, that is, in so far as the analyst presupposes the attributes of the phenomena to be measured, quantitative data have low validity. Thus quantitative measures are only as valid as the qualitative observations on which they are based. Reliability can also be problematic. Translation between qualitative data and numerical codes (coding) is not a determinate process; no matter how systematically rules for decision making are specified, judgment of cases is always a contingent accomplishment. Analysts not infrequently disagree as to what a given quantitative measure should be taken to represent empirically (e.g., Crain 1977 and Wentz 1977).

As an aspect of qualitative observation, quantified data can increase the credibility of research findings by providing *specification* of data adduced as evidence. A statement to the effect that "95 percent of the students in this school reported having a television in their home, and 25 percent reported having two or more" tells us more than the comment that "televisions are commonly found in students' homes." Systematic sampling of teacher-student interactions to monitor the ratio of supportive/neutral/denigrating behaviors provides essential evidence for the hypothesis that teachers respond differently to students of varying ethnic or socioeconomic backgrounds. Quantification, in other words, has a vital part to play in the process of triangulation. Triangulation, in turn, is a key method of verification of analysis, whether used by a single investigator or team or by independent investigators studying related problems.

Most research eclectically combines strategies and techniques in response to the requirements of the particular problem being investigated. Explanations offered are inspected by others and tested for adequacy by applying them to independently gathered data and by reexamining the original case in the light of alternative explanations. The most useful critiques (and the fuel of scientific growth) are those which seek to clarify the interrelationships observed by others and thereby refine analysis. Cazden (1966), for instance, has done this in her reexamination of test results reported by Bernstein on language differences between working class and middle class subjects, in order to identify unnoticed sources of possible bias in the research design. Less useful are critiques which demand that research conform to criteria for adequacy specific to the critic's theoretical orientation, without assessing the merit of other modes of analysis. The study of human behavior is served best by diversity of approach and flexibility of frame; while we seek simplicity behind the complexity of sociocultural events, we must remember that complexity underlies the simplifications of our theoretical constructs.

Because theories are frames of reference that account only for particular sets of events, no single theory is adequate to explain all phenomena. We also must bear in mind that competing theories may offer contradictory ways of explaining the same phenomena, and yet both be useful in developing understanding. The physicist Niels Bohr argued this about two competing theories of the nature of matter. Each accounted for some facts—those for which the rival theory could not account. Each failed where the other succeeded. Bohr contended that both theories should be accepted as valid and complementary, since both were necessary for a complete explanation, although they were mutually exclusive if applied simultaneously. Theories at best approximate the reality they are intended to explain. In the words of another physicist, "reality is too fluid and too rich to be contained in its entirety within the strict and abstract framework of our [scientific] ideas" (de Broglie 1939:281).

As we have seen, objectivity is a relative rather than an absolute characteristic of the scientific enterprise. The scientist's values influence the problems selected, the order in which they are tackled, the strategies and the theories used, and the evaluation of the answers produced. All scientific hypotheses and explanations are interpretive theories, comparable in most ways to the interpretive theories developed by thoughtful participants in the life-world under study. The critical difference, as I have said, is the detached framework of relevance and the mobile vantage point of the scientist compared with that of full participants.

Values are key in any study of human life because they influence observation and analysis in such basic and subtle ways. "Values," Kaplan (1964:384) reminds us, "enter into the determination of what constitutes a *fact*." They affect not only "our decisions where to look but . . . our conclusions as to what we have seen." The questions we formulate to guide our inquiry reflect our values and presuppositions and help to determine the answers we get. This is true both in daily life and in scientific work, but in the latter the ideal of objectivity prods us to clarify how our values affect our scientific decisions.

Objectivity as a value of scientists, then, entails a commitment to frank, public portrayal of procedures and evidence, including the sociocultural factors influencing interpretation, in order that results may be evaluated by colleagues and tested for merit.

In the next chapter we take up alternate analytic frameworks for the study of education. In each case the choice of analytic framework is linked to the nature of the questions posed; each framework orients the analyst toward certain kinds of data and rests on certain implicit assumptions. To compare the kinds of analytic results each generates, our focus will be on research applications to U.S. schooling.

notes

1. For evidence of this, note the recent establishment and rapid growth of the Council on Anthropology and Education Standing Committee on Ethnographic Approaches to Evaluation in Education; the frequent reference to methodological matters in the major journals of educational anthropology research; and the Special Issue of the *Anthropology and Education Quarterly* devoted to alternative research methodologies (May 1977).

2. To evaluate concepts as useful or illuminating, we must ask: Is the concept formulated clearly enough that other researchers can apply it with the same empirical results? To be scientifically useful a concept must "permit others to gain the same point of view and employ the same orientation" (Blumer 1930:160) as the originator. Does the concept refer to a class or relation that is significant in the field under study? A concept that has no empirical referent is empty. What implications does the concept have as formulated, either as tacit assumptions or as logical ramifications?

3. Rigor and objectivity represent scientific ideals but not always realities. Studies of scientific *practice* which are illuminating in this regard include Mitroff (1974), Kuhn (1964), and Mahoney (1976).

4. By "ethnographic" I mean *in situ* study of a sociocultural world (in this case a classroom). Briefly, ethnographic research involves deliberately inclusive focus such that contexts of action are delineated as carefully as behavior patterns themselves, and deliberate suspension of the ethnographer's habitual interpretive scheme such that the meanings of events for participants become a key component of the ethnographer's descriptive analysis. We will return to this topic later in this chapter.

5. See Kaplan (1964:327–369) for a discussion of varying criteria for explanatory adequacy.

6. Useful bibliographies in this area include Wolcott's (1975) annotated bibliography on ethnographic method as it relates to educational research, Burnett's (1974) bibliography on anthropology and education and Dwyer-Schick's bibliography (1976) on the study and teaching of anthropology.

7. This can create problems for the researcher as well, as Everhart (1977) documents. It also can take considerable time. Goetz (1975), for example, spent several weeks in the classroom she studied establishing her role as resident–adult–but–not–teacher vis-à-vis the students. Full trust was not established with the teacher until nearly two months after observations began.

8. A great deal may be observed in a single day in a school classroom, for instance, but one can discern from such limited observation neither the contextual significance of observed events nor the processual construction of events (both routine and irregular) by participants. In schools, observation for at least a semester, especially the fall semester (as in the studies of Smith and Geoffrey, Goetz, Everhart, and Cusick), is advisable, for this includes most of the long-term temporal cycle of the class as a social unit, from its initial establishment through the development of its routinized interaction patterns. Ethnographic community studies generally extend for at least a year so that the full annual/seasonal cycle may be tapped in observation.

9. Erickson (1973:4) suggests the following "test questions" for any ethnography. How did you arrive at your overall point of view? What details did you leave out and what did you leave in? What was your rationale for selection? From the universe of behavior available, how much did you monitor? Why did you monitor in some situations and not in others? See also Wilson (1977), especially pp. 261–262.

10. For a succinct summary of assumptions underlying participant observation as a method, see Wilson (1977). For more detailed discussion of the method itself, Bruyn (1966), Schatzman and Strauss (1974), Filstead (1970), and McCall and Simmons (1969) are useful sources.

11. Cf. Schutz (1953) on the perspective of the scientist compared to that of the full participant.

12. Cicourel (1964) critiques the epistemological presuppositions of sociological uses of measurement and mathematical representation. Both he and Garfinkel (1967) point out the indeterminacy of translation procedures in coding. Blumer's (1956) discussion of variable analysis is also relevant.

FOUR

ANALYTIC FRAMEWORKS FOR THE STUDY OF EDUCATION

All research depends on the use of specific analytic frameworks, and the type of analysis chosen reflects the researcher's goals. The utility of a given framework can be assessed only in terms of the questions we wish to answer. To point up the limits and strengths of the kinds of analysis most commonly used in the study of education, selected cases in which each has been applied will be discussed. To provide a firm basis for cross-cultural comparison, this chapter will concentrate on examples drawn from the U.S., giving particular attention to differences among analytic frameworks focused on the various levels discussed in the third chapter. Subsequent chapters will take up the relationships between structure and process, examined at different levels. We will look at education as a system in sociocultural context and as processes of interpersonal transaction, and then we will consider relationships between education and sociocultural change from both points of view.

Let us begin with the more general levels of analysis, examining first an analytic framework that focuses on structure. Because this framework has been highly influential in social science research, it constitutes a background factor even in studies oriented toward different goals.

structural-functional analysis

Structural-functionalism (also called functionalism) was formulated as a theoretical perspective for anthropology late in the nineteenth and early in the twentieth centuries. Its proponents emphasized the analytic importance of relations among social events and their organization into systems. This theory postulates that human societies are functional systems in that all parts of the social system contribute to the system as a whole. The function of each part is its role in maintaining the larger system as a working whole, and the system is assumed to be more or less self-contained, integrated, and in equilibrium.

Because the functionalist approach focuses on the integration of the system and its maintenance over time in a relatively unchanging (equilibrated) state, users of this analytic frame tend to concentrate on particular questions and forms of explanation. Talcott Parsons, in his analysis of a public elementary school class in Boston as a social system, asks how the structure of the class relates to its functions within the larger societal system, namely as an agency both of socialization and of role allocation. The level of analysis is detached from the detail of actual classrooms. He notes (1959:141), "In detail the relationship [between class structure and allocation function] is blurred," but at a distance formal relations among groups can be described by using statistical data on a sample of comparable classrooms. The questions he asks assume the existence of an integrated system maintained over time by the articulation of parts, each of which functions to equilibrate the social "machine" through its interrelation with the others. Thus he asks "how the school class functions to internalize in its pupils both commitments [to societal values and to performance of a specific type of role in society] and capacities [in the sense of both competence and responsibility] for successful performance of their future adult roles," and "how it functions to allocate these human resources within the role structure of the adult society." In both cases he is asking how the system works and how the requirements for its perpetuation are met. The type of explanation he offers is exemplified in the following passage, in which he discusses the peer group in relation to the school class:

> The importance of the peer group for socialization in our type of society should be clear. The motivational foundations of character are inevitably laid down through identification with parents ... and the generation difference is a type example of a hierarchical status difference. But an immense part of the individual's adult role performance will have to be in association with status–equals or near–equals. In this situation it is important to have a reorganization of the motivational structure so that the original dominance of the hierarchical axis is modified to strengthen the egalitarian components. The peer group plays a prominent part in this process (Parsons 1959:139–140).

Although he does not state that peer group relations are structured as they are in order that the system may be maintained, he implies that the system's maintenance requires the "reorganization of the motivational structure" and that the significance of the peer group is first and foremost that it fulfills this systemic need. If we translate the argument into a list of premises and propositions, this becomes apparent. Tacit premises on which the argument is based include: (a) the society is a working system; (b) working systems require that component institutions contribute to the maintenance of the system; and (c) working social systems require that participants be motivated and trained to facilitate system functioning. With this as a foundation, Parsons postulates first that children's early socialization is characterized primarily by hierarchical status relationships which create a particular kind of motivational structure. Second, he postulates that adult life involves an individual in a high number of roughly equal status relationships which, by implication, require a different kind of motivational structure. Third, he postulates that children's peer group relationships provide models for adult equal-status relationships and bring about a change in motivational structure (largely by reducing dependency on the family). On these bases he concludes that the peer group as an institution contributes to the stable working of the larger social system, that its function is to maintain the social order by preparing the child for adult roles. Since the conclusion derived is almost identical to the premises, the argument is circular. More importantly, neither the passage cited nor the essay as a whole go behind the idea of "system" to examine the applicability of the concept to the problem being analyzed.

While functionalism as an analytic frame has been much criticized for its assumptions and the type of explanation commonly resulting from its use, its utility as a set of sensitizing concepts remains noteworthy. When it is applied carefully to sets of role-relationships and institutions that do in fact form more or less bounded systems, it can be quite illuminating. Burnett (1969) has analyzed ceremonial events in a small high school as rituals that help to maintain and restore equilibrium in the school social system. These rituals pace both the annual cycle of seasons and the four year cycle of student status transition. Spindler (1963b) and Wolcott (1973) describe the role of school principals in the organization of the school system. As a formal organization, a school system is a functionally integrated whole, with "certain conditions of existence that must be secured and maintained if the organization is to function and fulfill its obligations within the framework of the larger society" (Spindler 1963b:235). The principal's role, writes Spindler (1963b:238), is a balancing role.

> His job is in large part that of maintaining a working equilibrium of at best antagonistically cooperative forces. This is one of the reasons why school administrators are rarely outspoken protagonists of a consistent and vigorously profiled

point of view. Given the nature of our culture and social system, and the close connection between the public and the schools he cannot alienate significant segments of that public and stay in business.

As a mediator-administrator in the larger bureaucratic organization, the principal is generally more aware than the teachers supervised or the families they serve of the processes that contribute to the school system's stability and the forces that threaten its equilibrium.

It is this attention to the tenuousness of the equilibrium, to the need for constant negotiation among competing groups, and to the constant interplay between the particular setting of a school and the actual behavior of its participants that marks Spindler's treatment as a radical departure from the traditional brand of functionalism represented by Parsons. In contrast, Spindler's and Wolcott's approach in the studies cited may be classed as "ecological" as well as "functional."

ecological analysis

Like functionalism, ecological theory presumes systemic relations and the interdependence of component parts. However, while functionalist analysis tends to focus on stable structural features and on the maintenance of stability over time, ecological analysis also considers the processes that generate, maintain and change the prevailing network of interrelations. It can do so because it includes in analysis the physical and social environments in which social systems are enmeshed. Ecological analysis thus has a potentially wider scope than functionalism and is applicable to the most inclusive level of analysis. Although ecological approaches are applied most often to the more general levels analyzed also by functionalist frameworks, they are also useful in the analysis of less inclusive units of study. The ethologist Nikolaas Tinbergen (1974), for example, has examined the relationship between the environment and the education of autistic children, noting the significance of environmental stress in inducing and exacerbating autistic responses.

Ecology, in a general sense, "deals with organisms in an environment and with the processes that link organism and place" (Shepard 1969:1). Anthropological ecology has been described by Bennett (1969:10–11) as "the study of how human utilization of nature influences and is influenced by social organization and cultural values." As a framework for the study of educational systems and processes, ecology might best be thought of as the study of the reciprocal influences of sociocultural organization and the environment, both physical and sociocultural. Its strength relative to functionalist approaches is that it adds to a functionalist description of how a system works, an analysis of the relationships between system and context. This enables a more effective investigation of why the system works as it does.

Explanation from an ecological perspective requires first that the researcher identify the environmental factors most important in constraining or encouraging behavior by participants in the social unit. Assuming that sociocultural organization is the product of adaptive processes, whether they are responses to past or present conditions, the ecological analyst seeks to isolate the physical, social, and cultural variables influencing the outcome of these processes. Bennett (1976) has suggested that the basis of human ecology is the human capacity for self-objectification, learning, and anticipation. Humans conceptualize themselves as able to act upon their environment. We symbolically construct our environment (and ourselves) through the processes of selective perception, organization, and interpretation discussed in the first chapter. The human capacity for learning enables us to store experience as precedents, which also promotes the preservation of outmoded (maladaptive) problem solutions. At the same time, our capacity for foresight and intentionality (anticipation) enables us to respond in novel ways. This type of ecological perspective directs our attention to the openness of the system we examine, in contrast to the implicit closure of functionally interpreted systems,[1] and to interpreting actors who are guided by precedents and values, purposes and interests, and who cope with their environments in interactive ways.

Following Bennett (1969), we may distinguish several key concepts for ecological analysis. Adaptation as a general concept refers to the process of adjustment to existing and changing conditions. Within this, adaptive *behavior* denotes the actual ways people devise to cope with their fellows and available resources to attain goals and solve problems. Adaptive behavior is part of the choice making which weighs the costs and benefits of alternative lines of action. Adaptive *strategies* are the larger patterns formed by the many separate adjustments people devise. A principal faced with an irate parent will respond to the immediate problem by evaluating the possible alternatives and their probable consequences, and attempt to place that problem into a larger strategy designed to balance the conflicting interests of the many groups to whom he is responsible. Adaptive *processes* are the changes introduced over relatively long periods of time by the repeated use of such strategies or adjustments, as in the evolution of the principal's role from that of a supervisor of teachers to that of a major participant in a public relations enterprise. While most often applied to the more inclusive macro-levels of sociocultural analysis, such as the relationship between community social structure and its physical-social environment, ecological perspectives are equally useful at less general analytic levels. In many ways, such a framework can bridge these levels by providing a common set of concepts and principles for understanding both individual action and the conduct of collectivities as inclusive as societies. Thus we can consider both the micro-environments of educational processes and the macro-environments of educational systems from an ecological standpoint.

Consider, for instance, the relationship between education and physical environment. To assess this we need to determine how participants perceive the physical settings in which education occurs or is attempted and how these perceptions vary with factors like age, role, and cultural background. We need also to determine how certain kinds of behavior are constrained or facilitated by these settings, and to what extent participants seek actively to modify them.

Jackson (1968) points out that by the time an American child is ready for junior high school, he or she already will have spent some seven thousand hours in school. "Apart from the bedroom (where he has his eyes closed most of the time) there is no single enclosure in which [a child] spends a longer time than he does in the classroom" (Jackson, 1968:5). Moreover the classroom is a relatively unchanging environment:

> School bulletin boards may be changed but they are never discarded, the seats may be rearranged but thirty of them are there to stay, the teacher's desk may have a new plant on it but there it sits, as ubiquitous as the roll-down maps, the olive-drab wastebasket, and the pencil sharpener on the window ledge (Jackson 1968:6–7).

Patterns in the use of space in American schools are deeply rooted and significant features of the learning environment. Robert Sommer (1969) points out how rigidly student movement is controlled in school buildings and classrooms. "Everywhere one looks there are 'lines' " to be waited in, straight rows to be sat in which "tell the student to look ahead and ignore everyone except the teacher" (Sommer 1969:99). Friedenberg (1963) reminds us that there are not only lines but also total adult control over sanctioned movement on the part of students and a complete absence of any private space to which a youngster may retreat.

The options for alternative use perceived in a given physical setting depend largely on one's cultural repertoire and background experience. Even in instructional spaces designed for maximum flexibility, teachers accustomed to definite routines of space-use may ignore or fail to perceive available alternatives. In a midwestern U.S. elementary school designed around the "open classroom" concept, Goetz (1975) found that teachers uniformly disregarded the potential for cooperative use of classroom space. Each classroom was divided into independent single-teacher units by movable partitions, treated in practice as fixed features of physical setting. Smith and Keith (1967, 1971), in a case study of school innovation, discuss the impact of radical changes in physical plant design on school organization and educational process. In this case, school personnel supported the theoretical potentials for pedagogic change built into the design of the new school plant and participated in the development of requisite organizational and curricular schemes. In practice, many adaptive strategies developed by teachers and students in the old building were carried over to the new. In some respects, however, the new facility

> made it very difficult for the teachers to utilize the more traditional procedures.
> It forced them, . . . as intended, to more individualized, differentiated activities
> (Smith and Keith 1967:129).

Smith and Keith's observations extended over the period of transition. Their analysis thus focuses on organizational problems rather than on their long term solution. As an ecological study, their research documents the interconnection of responses to physical environment with the participants' goals, skills, and values, the organization of school personnel and decision making processes, curricular development, and community response (cf. also Gump 1976).

The options available to the typical U.S. school teacher are restricted by more than the design and fixtures of the classroom. For instance, because classrooms are rarely soundproof, classroom noise must be kept below certain defined limits to avoid interfering with other groups. Noise also must be minimized in many schools because it is interpreted as disorder and nonlearning. The distance between a classroom and other classrooms or facilities such as the cafeteria, lavatories, and recreation areas may require that students travel through the building several times a day and that norms of conduct be established for these periods of traffic. If cultural values emphasize order and conformity to regulations, students may be required to walk silently and in single file through hallways, subject to official challenge. Far more than the physical plant itself, then, cultural values and expectations and social structure influence how physical settings are used and how the educative process is organized. We may say that features of physical settings encourage and constrain educative encounters through their interpretations by participants, and that settings are "set" largely in response to cultural and social factors.

To analyze the sociocultural environment of American schooling, we need first to look at the groups involved directly or indirectly in the schooling process. Using the classroom as our vantage point, we see that the class itself —students and teacher—represent segments of the community, possibly distinct or even conflicting segments as when they are members of different ethnic groups or socioeconomic classes. Within the formal organization of the school system, the teacher is subject to evaluation and control by the administrative hierarchy, symbolized by the principal. Other teachers, as peers and professional colleagues, also form an important part of our teacher's social environment. The nonacademic staff provides regular supporting services which may affect the teacher's instructional choices; procedures that impose extra work on the maintenance staff, for instance, may be frowned upon. Evaluated by the achievements of their former and current students, teachers may feel constrained to stress certain skills which others will expect the students to have acquired, even when they themselves question the importance of these skills.

Through their students they are linked with the families and neighborhoods of the school. These families may or may not participate actively in formal auxiliary organizations such as the PTA, but their perceptions and interpretations of the school and the school-related experiences of their children do affect the children's interpretation and response to school. When parents become more vociferously involved, they may become lobbies for particular choices in curriculum or classroom organization, exerting both direct pressure on the teacher and indirect pressure through the administrative staff. Obviously teachers, like principals, often are subject to many irreconcilable demands and expectations. Besides the direct service relationship between the teacher and her or his students' families, the school and its personnel also have a transactional relationship with the community. Public schools depend on taxpayers for goodwill and fiscal support to maintain and improve their facilities and programs. Because school systems are considered community institutions, they generally are overseen by a board of education typically composed in part (if not wholly) of citizens who are not professional educators. Election or appointment of board members ties the school system directly into the political sphere of the community, and as the political sphere is intimately linked with the economic, into the latter as well.

Ogbu's (1974) study of schooling in a low income, ethnically heterogeneous neighborhood depicts the interconnections among these groups: students, parents, school personnel, and "taxpayers"—those prosperous community members who lived outside the neighborhood and effectively controlled community-level decision making with respect to schools. The divergent viewpoints, interests, and strategies of each of these factions, coupled with their differential access to economic and political resources, help perpetuate a high rate of school failure. School performance of low income minority students, Ogbu argues, is an outcome of the adaptive strategies they adopt to cope with conflicting pressures of teachers, peers, and parents in the face of limited occupational opportunities. The result of the combined strategies of students, parents, school personnel, and taxpayers is an adaptive process which effectively maintains the community status quo.

Horton (1971), in his analysis of a suburban school system, points out the importance of an additional agency, the "educational world," i.e., the complex of professional associations, teacher training and educational research institutions, "publishing enterprises, accrediting and regulatory agencies, and governmental advisory bodies and commissions; all of which are in turn linked with the universities and other institutions of the intellectual establishment" (Horton 1971:185). The impact of this sector on schools and schooling is channelled most directly through the participation of school personnel in training institutions and professional organizations; but the indirectness of other influences from this arena does not lessen their force. The same may be said of each of the constituent sectors of education-as-an-ecological-system. Smith and Keith (1967) note the impact of inadequate support from the university sector in providing resources to school personnel when they must implement innovations born of researchers' educational theories.

The "educational world" constitutes one of several extralocal forces impinging on a community's school system. Funding sources (often federal) and their prerequisites for eligibility, and regional or national pressure for curriculum modification, as in the revamping which followed in the wake of Sputnik, are others. From another angle, the school system may be seen as a competitor in education with mass media of various kinds, particularly those extralocal in origin. Certainly media content and form are a source of pressure for curriculum reform and an alternate agency of cultural transmission which classroom teachers must take into account in their instruction. School systems are directly affected also by competing interests of school personnel, whose investment in status mobility within professional reference groups may conflict with other organizational goals and strategies of the schools.

When we expand our scope to this breadth, it becomes extremely difficult to specify the complex interrelationships which affect the classroom microworld from which we began. Ecological analysis, like any other systematic research, requires that we select an area on which we concentrate—for example, the interface between the school as a community institution and the various community interest groups competing for influence. Other facets of the total ecological relationship then can be traced out in less detail or as they emerge as important to the problem at hand (cf., for example, Kelley 1977).

Barker and his associates (Barker and Wright 1955; Barker and Barker 1961; Barker and Gump 1964) have developed a distinctive ecological approach with considerable promise for the study of educational processes. Concerned with the relationship between individual behavior and its ecological environment, they formulated the concept of "behavioral settings" as the structural units comprising environments. Behavioral settings are locales bounded in time and space in which varied but stable patterns of conduct occur. Any context which is defined by participants as a place-time in which certain activities are appropriate and others inappropriate, and which is understood to exist independent of an individual's participation, is a specific behavioral setting. A classroom is but one behavioral setting in a high school; others include the class play, the senior prom, the basketball game, the junior class carwash, the chess club, the library, the student council meeting, the contest for track queen, and career day. Behavior settings are "homeostatic systems" which tend toward functional equilibrium or stability through the many forces that play upon them. In a school class these forces include internal elements such as the time schedule, the arrangement of furnishings, and rules of behavior; elements which link the class setting and external conditions, such as the school's master time schedule and regulations; and elements which link the setting with its components, such as student maturity and textbooks.

In a comparative study of high schools with large and small enrollments,

Barker and Gump (1964) found that size alone affected the relationship between students and school settings. In the small high school, for example, students participated in more of the available settings, a much larger proportion of the students held positions of importance and responsibility in the behavior settings they entered (with commensurate differences between small and large school in the kinds of satisfactions reported by students), and students felt more external pressure and obligation to participate actively in the various settings of their school. This research is important especially for its emphasis on the environment as experienced by the participants. As the authors point out,

> it is possible to study schools in terms of such variables as the social class of students, the training of teachers, and the extent of curricular offerings; but students do not respond directly to these variables. Students respond to the sectors of the social environment in which they live (Barker and Gump 1964:199).

The importance of cultural assumptions and values as aspects of settings must not be underestimated, for they often underlie practical actions and choices of the participants. It is practical, for instance, to seat children in rows facing the teacher, for it directs their attention to the instructor. It is also an expression of a cultural pattern that defines "child" and "teacher," "status," and "knowledge," and their interrelationships. History too is often a critical contextual factor, as Fox (1972) shows. Not only does it underlie present conditions, but also it influences how community members define them and how they respond to perceived options and constraints. The history of an event or community or nation as a body of ideas and beliefs is part of the cultural knowledge which we must consider in our analysis.

Ecological analysis is pertinent both to the study of systemic processes, the processes which constitute the adaptational dynamic of social structures, and to the study of intragroup and individual–environment transactions. Its utility in the study of education depends, however, on another type of analysis which we will label "sociopsychological."

sociopsychological analysis

Sociopsychological analysis is crucial to ecological analysis, because it delineates the relation of ideas and values, attitudes and inclinations, perception and interpretation, to the adaptive processes on which ecological research focuses. We could designate the sociopsychological approach as primarily cultural, since the cognitive-affective elements of human behavior are influenced heavily by cultural milieu. But we must also bear in mind the relationship between cultural knowledge and the social matrix in which it is acquired and used, as well as the relationship between socially shared cultural expressions and the individuals who use them.

Three avenues of investigation are particularly important to the study of education. One is the definition of participants by themselves and others, the second includes the conceptual content of cognition and cognitive strategies, and the third, communication, relates the first two.

IDENTITIES AND ROLES

The characteristics attributed to participants in any interaction are the product of social processes. Such definitions are mediated by cultural values and expectations. To some extent these definitions are also negotiated in the course of social interaction. Their importance lies in their contribution to the interpretive accounting in which people engage in daily life. They become, as Robbins (1973) has pointed out, part of the theory of motivation which we use to explain and predict the behavior of others.

Personality represents one type of definition. Although the way in which desires, needs, learned patterns of conduct, and evolved coping strategies are organized in a given individual is partly a function of her or his biopsychological uniqueness, they also reflect the interplay between individuals and the sociocultural milieu. Shared practices of socialization and enculturation in combination with the routines of daily life tend to elicit certain types of adaptive response in each individual. The labels used to differentiate among personality types are themselves cultural, reflecting shared concepts of types of persons and types of behavior. Generally, the more closely the templates of personality and the resulting behavioral style approximate the norm favored by their society, the more successfully individuals gain esteem and acceptance as "good," "decent," "upstanding" members of the community. The fundamentals of personality everywhere seem to be established early; although learning is a lifelong process, personalities once crystallized resist major modification.

Identity, another type of definition, refers to two potentially divergent but interrelated phenomena: both the categories used by others to define the individual within the group (social identity) and the categories, images, and ideals used by the individual to define herself or himself (personal identity).[2] Personal and social identities interpenetrate, for we develop our concepts of self in the course of interaction with others and in light of the responses we evoke from them. While identities, like personality, are a product of interaction, they also are situational and highly subject to change.

The categories used to define social identities depend on context. To his classroom teacher, Joe's social identity may include the attributes of a third grade boy, slow in reading but quick at math, hot-tempered and prone to get into fights. At home Joe's social identity may include such attributes as the oldest son, good at fixing things, and a helper with chores. In his peer group, Joe's social identity may be built up of attributes such as a pal and occasional leader, the owner of a green bike, and a good ball player. His personal identity (which also varies situationally) will reflect the perceptions of others, for it is formulated and synthesized in the course of his interactions in every context. The bases of identity attribution range from obvious to subtle. A person's appearance, manner of movement, and other visible features are readily available indicators as are language and communicative style. Place of residence, occupation, kin and friend affiliations, relative affluence, religious or political orientation, temperament, skills, and "reputation" (as a cumulative designation of social standing relative to a given set of values) may also be relevant. As such indicators suggest, social identities tend to be based on attributes of "types of people" rather than on unique characteristics of individuals. Some attributes are fixed, while others can be modified or manipulated by the individual. While identities are perhaps most tenuous in the young, who have not yet firmly established their repertoire of roles and types of relationships, identities are subject to change at any age if there is a serious discrepancy between an individual's self-image and the identities recognized by others.

Personality and identities are closely intertwined. An individual's personality influences the modes of expression and action she or he characteristically employs and these, in turn, affect the identities others accord to her or him as well as the personal image formed. When the personality configuration characteristic of an individual resembles one of the types most valued or expected as normal by members of the group with whom she or he is interacting, the individual is less likely to be accorded negative or low esteem identities by them. However, because such expectations and values differ culturally, personality configurations and patterns of behavior appreciated by one group, such as that in which an individual is first socialized, may be defined as deviant by members of a different group with a different set of cultural standards. In these cases, negative identities are likely to be attached to the inadvertent deviants by members of the second group. Human propensities to categorize experiences lead also to stereotyping of people. Individual members of a group often are assumed to have the characteristics associated with the group as a whole.

In many U.S. classrooms, young people are confronted with social identities quite unlike those acquired at home and with friends. When the student and teacher are cocultural in that they share a middle class Anglo background or orientation, disjunction in identities is less likely. Nor is disjunction necessarily the result when teacher and student are of different ethnic backgrounds, if the two orientations are congruent in situationally relevant respects. DeVos (1975b:36) comments that immigrant Japanese parents and the Japanese-

American community emphasized values of conformity, respect for authority, and the importance of academic education that converged with the values and expectations of U.S. school personnel. This facilitated the academic success of Japanese-American students and influenced teachers to attribute positive social identities to them. On the other hand, parental pressure to learn the Japanese language was countered by peer and school pressures toward student identity as Americans. When student and teacher are neither situationally nor generally cocultural, the disjunction that results can have serious effects. Teachers who lack training in cultural differences often evaluate each student's manner and behavior by middle class Anglo standards. The resulting classroom identities define the limited and largely negative expectations teachers (and by extension the sociocultural world which teachers represent) have of minority students.

The alternative responses open to these students are limited; they can withdraw commitment and vulnerability, presenting impassive and impenetrable facades that defeat instructional efforts, they can rebel (and acquire the label of "troublemaker"), or they can internalize the negative identities and become exactly what they are expected to become. Were these identities just idiosyncratic constructs accorded by individual teachers, students might overcome their effects in other educational contexts. Because such evaluations become permanent information in school records, however, and because they result from cultural disjunction as much as from the personal insensitivity of a particular teacher, they can become self-perpetuating social identities in the course of the student's school career.

In a comparative study of four city schools, serving respectively lower and middle income black and lower and middle income white neighborhoods, Leacock (1969) reports significant differences in the identities allotted students by teachers and in the styles of interaction conveying these messages. Combining data collected from second and fifth grade classroom observations, interviews with teachers, and interviews with children, Leacock documents "the way a pervasive atmosphere, stemming from the very structure of our society, expressed in the organization of the school system and embodied in the teacher's assumptions about different groups of children, adversely affects the teacher-student relationship and the teaching function." She discusses three types of teacher behavior toward low income students of both races "(1) derogation of children through negative evaluation of their work; (2) negation of children through failure to respect contributions offered from their own experience; and (3) relating to the children in ways that prepare them for subordinate social roles in which they are not expected to show initiative or take responsibility" (Leacock 1969:169). Importantly, Leacock notes that this phenomenon is not simply a function of the quality of instruction, for the research indicated that teachers were not uniformly better in middle income schools. At the same time, "a poorer teacher in a 'good' school was more successful in her classroom than one in a 'poor' school," for students responded "to the higher standards and higher expectations" (Leacock 1969:168–169). In the lower income schools, what was observed was not an attempt to impose middle class goals on the students,

> but rather a tacit assumption that these goals were not open to at least the vast majority of them. The "middle-class values" being imposed on the low-income Negro children defined them as inadequate and their proper role as one of deference (Leacock 1969:169).

Ogbu (1974) describes identity attribution both within a school and in the wider community. "Taxpayers" (see above p. 67), including many teachers, type low income minority parents as uneducated, uncommitted to the value of schooling, and unconcerned with their children's academic success—an identity which, Ogbu shows, is based on inaccurate assumptions. These assumptions nevertheless affect the ways in which teachers and other school personnel label the children as students and interpret their behavior. In the eyes of many parents, teachers are more committed to the quality of schools in their own residential neighborhoods than to that of their workplace, unconcerned about or inept at teaching, convinced that the low income minority students they teach are incapable of learning as fast as other children, and uninterested in cooperating with parents to ameliorate student learning problems. Identity attributions of these sorts serve as bases for theories of motivation which participants use to account for perceived behavior and guide their own responses. Thus they are key variables in the formulation of adaptive strategies. Teachers, convinced that students are slow learners and that this is a function of their "culturally disadvantaged" home environments, adopt teaching strategies that do not challenge students, grade them on bases other than the actual work they do in class, and assume a patronizing role with parents. Parents, aware of their negative social identities in the eyes of school personnel and of their relative powerlessness, tend to adopt strategies of accommodation in their infrequent interactions with teachers, avoiding confronting teachers with their dissatisfaction and disagreement. Obgu indicates that this sort of strategy in combination with visible "involvement" (contacting the teacher about one's child's performance, working in the PTA) is interpreted by teachers as an indication of "interest" and the "right attitude." This in turn affects the teacher's perception of the child, modifying the identity accorded.

The attribution of negative or restricting identities to minority groups low in social prestige and its impact on performance evaluation has been explored in a number of studies. Wax and others (1964), Hobart (1970a), and others have described an initial display of student involvement and enthusiasm in early grades which dissipates thereafter. Coombs and others (1958) and Wax and others (1964) also report normal test scores on IQ tests in early grades which fall off in each successive grade. Students as individuals become increasingly indistinguishable from their acquired classroom identities. One factor in this process may be what has been dubbed the "Pygmalion effect": the effect of teacher expectations on student performance. In their widely cited study of the effects of positive teacher expectations on children's performance, Rosenthal and Jacobson (1968a) found that the gains made by children marked by teachers as promising (though actually randomly chosen by the investigators) were particularly evident in the first and second grades. Thereafter the gains decreased and in the fifth grade had no significant effect until the second year of study. They found an unfavorable response to children who made intellectual gains when they were not expected to, particularly in classes labeled as "slow" or "low track" in a school serving mostly low income families.

> The more they gained the more unfavorably they were rated. Even when the slow-track children were in the experimental group, where greater intellectual gains were expected of them, they were not rated as favorably with respect to their control–group peers as were the children of the high track and the medium track. Evidently it is likely to be difficult for a slow-track child, even if his IQ is rising, to be seen by his teacher as well adjusted and as a potentially successful student (Rosenthal and Jacobson, 1968b:22).

The dramatic findings of this study have not been replicated fully in subsequent research. It has been fairly well established that, early in their classroom careers, children are typically identified by their teacher with their probable level of achievement (cf. Dusek 1975). Rist (1970) found this true even at the kindergarten level at which neither academic record nor demonstrated skills existed as information sources. In the kindergarten class he studied, composed of black children and a black teacher, children very early were sorted into ability groups; the only information available to the teacher at this time, according to Rist, was the socioeconomic background of each child. There was no shifting of individual children from one ability group to another during the year, and children performed at the level of the group to which they had been assigned. Brophy and Good (1970), based on controlled observation in four first grade classrooms, report that teachers treated children of whom they had high expectations differently from children of whom they had low expectations. They noted:

> Despite the fact that the highs gave more correct answers and fewer incorrect answers than did the lows, they were more frequently praised when correct and less frequently criticized when incorrect or unable to respond. . . . When the highs responded incorrectly or were unable to respond, the teachers were more likely to provide a second response opportunity by repeating or rephrasing the question or giving a clue than they were in similar situations with the low. Conversely, they were more likely to supply the answer or call on another child when reacting to the lows than the highs (Brophy and Good 1970:372).

Thus the same item of behavior is interpreted and responded to differently, depending on the previously attributed identity of the child. Varying expectations by the teacher have been shown to correlate with the students' level of academic achievement (Brophy and Good 1970, Dusek and O'Connell 1973, O'Connell and others 1974). Still undetermined are the way in which teachers form expectations of students, and the precise nature of the relationship between such expectations and attributed identities and student academic success.[3] Teachers use many sources to formulate their assessments of individual students. It also is apparent that student-formulated identities are influenced directly and indirectly by those assessments.

Classrooms are complex social groups. Teachers are not the only allocators of identity within this context; indeed, the identities allocated by peers are often more personally relevant to students. When the criteria for attribution of valued identities by teacher and peers conflict, students may opt for the standards of their peer group. Students participate in the construction of their classroom identities, as McDermott (1974) has argued, although that participation may not be completely deliberate. Identities can be strategically manipulated by controlled behavioral display or presentation (Goffman 1959; cf. also King 1967). The identity aspirations of participants are relevant, therefore, to the negotiation of identities as a social process. McDermott describes the negotiation of identity as an essentially political process, arguing that academic failure and its associated identity is a strategic accomplishment for many black children, allying them with their classroom peers and their local community. Equally, it can be argued that the teacher's gatekeeping role, as evaluator of academic ability and achievement and as transmitter of knowledge prerequisite to valued status in an Anglo-dominated society, is a highly political one. In many classrooms, student-teacher transactions can be understood as processes of political conflict in which students win the battle and lose the war. In any case, when negative identities have been attributed by teachers early in school, students seem to become increasingly impervious to changes in teacher attitudes that might signal available identity shifts. Perhaps they simply become unwilling to take the risks necessary to test it. Once formulated and ratified in the course of subsequent interaction, identities can acquire a determinative power for all users that affects interpretation of further interaction and events.

Teacher identities are also important in classroom interactions. Attributes such as strictness/permissiveness, fairness, effectiveness, and personal distance are common elements of U.S. classroom teacher identities. To some degree, a teacher's personal identity is less subject to the influence of student-attributed social identities than are student personal identities to those of teachers. This is partly because the teacher role normatively includes evaluation of participants, whereas the student role does not, and partly because of the status differential between teacher and student. One very widespread teacher identity might be labeled semi-parental in that attitudes expressed toward students and sanctions applied to their behavior, center on love, approval, acceptance, and the threat of their loss. Both Henry (1959, 1963) and Leacock (1969) describe the heavy use of terms of endearment, tactile displays, and other parentlike expressions among middle class oriented teachers (that is, by teachers with middle class values and patterns, whatever their own class background). Talbert (1970b) suggests that styles of certain types of black teachers, while seeming to express a lack of respect for students and a harsh, nearly authoritarian stance, may in fact reflect distinctive child rearing practices of black mothers.

Identity is thus closely related to role, though the two are not synonomous. Role refers to recurrent patterns of conduct associated with particular types of interpersonal relationships. As aspects of types of relationships, roles entail certain mutual behavioral expectations, regardless of the particular persons involved. Knowledge of appropriate patterns of conduct and the circumstances to which they apply is part of cultural knowledge. Most members of the group sharing this knowledge are likely to have similar definitions of adequate role performance or transgression. An individual's role performances thus will influence the social identity attributed by those with whom the person interacts. How well a student's behavior conforms to the normative expectations of a given teacher generally will influence the social identity attributed to the student by that teacher. How an individual performs the student role will reflect both his or her conception of that role and the particular style associated with his or her personality and sense of personal identity.

Teachers are also subject to the pressure of role expectations, those which they hold, those which their professional superiors and colleagues hold, and those which their clients (students and their parents) hold. In a Kwakiutl Indian village on the Northwest Coast, Wolcott (1967) found these sets of expectations were not fully congruent. Villagers generally defined the teacher role to include the attributes of transient white outsider, disciplinarian, repository of facts and model of moral infallibility, and effective manager of school activity. Teachers were expected to consider themselves superior to Indians, to be insufficiently "qualified to do more than 'teach Indians'," and "to have a hard time managing the classroom" (Wolcott 1967:82, 83). A given teacher's role performance was evaluated by this set of role norms, and the resulting judgment contributed to the teacher's social identity in the village. For instance, running the school "the right way" was

> measured primarily by three criteria: opening school everyday, starting it on time, and keeping pupils busy. When villagers judge that the teacher is running a good school, based on these criteria, they refer to him as a "good teacher" (Wolcott 1967:81).

These normative expectations were specific to the teacher role; villagers themselves did not engage in overt disciplinary action with respect to their children, nor were punctuality, the display of knowledge, sobriety, and other such values notably emphasized in nonschool village life.

The interrelation between role and identity illustrates the interconnection of structure and process. Roles represent relatively stable sets of norms of conduct at a given point in time. Role, as the term is used here, refers to typified expectations for types of transactions in associated types of settings. These expectations influence the interpretations others make of the person presumably responsible for "enacting" the role, and often influence directly the behavior of that role-enacter. In practice, a role represents only a set of guidelines for the actor's behavioral strategies and/or other participants' interpretations and evaluations of the behavior displayed. In this sense, role behavior is a mutual accomplishment of all participants. Role expectations are themselves products of social negotiation, as we can see in the changing definitions of appropriate parent-child, husband-wife, and teacher-student roles. Identity is also a social accomplishment, derived in part from the expectations and typifications of fellow participants. Whereas a role is a set of expectations associated with a type of actor/activity in specified contexts, independent of the particular individual who enacts the role, an identity involves the attribution to an individual of a set of socially meaningful type-characteristics. The way in which one's role-linked behavior is evaluated may contribute to one's personal and social identity. ("Kwakiutl children do not perform well on academic achievement tests [test–taking being one component of the student role in Western–style schools]; Kwakiutl children are stupid/culturally disadvantaged/unmotivated.") Similarly, one's identity may influence evaluation of one's role-linked behavior. ("For a man, Joe teaches kindergarten quite well.")

COGNITIVE MAPS AND STRATEGIES

Both roles and identities rest on cultural conceptions, and their realization in particular forms depends on the behavioral strategies used by individuals in coping with specific situations. The cognitive frameworks and strategies involved are thus important in analyzing the part roles and identities play in the educational process.

Cultures differ in their assumptions about human nature, motivation, and the function of tutelage. Cultures which emphasize the malleability of children are likely to emphasize very careful, deliberate instruction of the young so that they will grow up to be respectable group members. Teaching procedures in such cultures will differ radically from those which view children as distinct personalities at birth, receptive to training in skills and knowledge but not to the shaping of personality. Conceptions of the function of instruction reflect those of the status of learners, their nature, and the types of behavioral and cognitive competence sought. We may compare the Lockean conception of the child as a blank slate to be inscribed by tutelage to the nineteenth-century U.S.

conception of the child as a bundle of animal impulses to be controlled and reformulated through discipline (Sunley 1955). The encouragement of rapid learning as a source of admiration, as among the Tallensi (Fortes 1938) and Eastern European Jews (Zborowski 1955), contrasts with the discouragement of individual display of exceptional capability, as among Samoans (Mead 1939) and Hopi (Eggan 1956). Teachers may be conceived of as authorities not subject to question, as in Burma (Nash 1970), or as guides in a self-directed or self-paced course of learning as in Jewish *shtetl* schools, as semi-parents in the sense described earlier in many U.S. schools or as representatives of an alien system as in many Native American schools. The specific conceptions held by teachers and learners of their mutual roles significantly affect instructional process.

Since children learn to interpret and evaluate their own experience through the frames of reference used by those around them, they quickly acquire the prevailing attitudes toward learning, learners, and teachers. But when they are confronted with disparate frames of reference in their homes and in school, severe disjunction between the two may hamper their attempts to adapt successfully in the school context. In the U.S. this is a problem for many children of non-Anglo and non-middle class backgrounds. Even within the sector of the population sharing a general Anglo cultural heritage, different conceptions of appropriate teacher-student roles and instructional procedures are apparent. This has been expressed in the recent growth of parental demand for alternative types of schooling, from instruction emphasizing basic skills in reading, writing, and math, with teachers cast in more authoritarian and disciplinary roles, to instruction allowing more student input and self-pacing, with teachers cast as guides and facilitators of individual student development. This diversity underscores the importance of ascertaining in each society, the range of variation as well as the shared conceptions of teachers, learners, and learning.

Other types of concepts also affect educational process. The importance of concepts of knowledge itself, as illustrated in the widespread U.S. value for "right answers," and of the status of learners and teachers in the community was discussed earlier. Different types and phases of education often are associated with variant conceptualizations of knowledge, relative status, teacher-learner roles, and the function of instruction. The distinction made in *shtetl* communities between preliterate and literate children and their respective tutors is a vivid example. It would be useful to investigate in the U.S. how such differences affect educational process at each level of schooling from the primary grades through college and advanced education, in academic and vocational curricula, and in public and private or alternative school systems. At what level do people conceive both systematic, deliberate instruction and schooling to begin? Are organized activities for preschoolers guided by selected adults considered a form of schooling? Do parents see their role as including systematic and deliberate transmission, and what relationship do they perceive or expect between this activity and that available through other organized sets of role-relationships, such as those of peer groups, schools, and mass media?

Concepts such as these and their associated values are important components of participants' attitudes toward educational process. Attitudes are dispositions to interpret events in particular ways. The analysis of attitudes must take into account the complexity of their genesis in previous and current experience, the consistency of their influence on interpretations of events, and the degree to which participants are aware of their own attitudes.

The attitudes with which teachers begin instructional careers may be reinforced or modified in the course of interaction within the classroom, in the school system, and with the community as a whole. In a study of neophyte teachers in New York City ghetto schools, Fuchs (1969) found that much of their outlook resulted from their ignorance of the larger system in which they were operating. Much of their first year experience in that system was designed to develop attitudes favored by more experienced colleagues. Impassioned narratives like those of Herndon (1968), Kozol (1967) and Kohl (1967) describe the trials of teachers who do not choose to adopt the attitudes prescribed. Sarason (1971) points out how faculty and administrator receptivity to change in schooling procedures is diminished by interaction with outside consultants who do not appear to comprehend the school's complex problems.

Teachers' professed attitudes are not necessarily congruent with their actions. Henry (1959) and Leacock (1969) report that some teachers described their teaching methods as far more stringent and control-centered than their actual classroom style proved to be. Attitudes are complex and only partially verbalized ways of interpreting that are influenced by many situational factors. If we wish to know which teacher attitudes are relevant in classroom settings and how they affect the educative process, we must realize that teachers themselves will be able to verbalize only some of their attitudes, that there may be a discrepancy between those they profess and those they display in interaction with students, and that some may be the result of careful deliberation while others are taken for granted background expectancies.

The same holds true for other participants in the educational process. Goetz (1975) found that both the students and the teacher she studied were well aware of the value for right answers and of its potential conflict with values like "finishing work"; but neither students nor teacher seemed aware of the full range of contexts in which these attitudes were implicit.

The interpretive schemes which participants bring to bear on their experiences in educational and other transactions, once again, are partly cultural products and partly products of varied individual experience. The relative influence of the two sources is not always apparent, although we generally assume that those interpretive strategies which are widespread within a group indicate cultural sharing. The complexity is illustrated by research on cognitive style. The studies discussed in the first chapter indicate that cognitive styles are influenced by early experiences, including patterns of socialization, and that they tend to correlate with styles of interaction and group organization. On the other hand, it appears that *use* of a given cognitive style does not necessarily denote an inability to use others. Personal preference, situation, and other variables as yet undetermined may affect their application. The choices made have important consequences, not only for the mode of learning they facilitate but also for others' interpretations of the person's behavior.

Witkin and others (1966) and Cohen (1968, 1969), for example, agree that cognitive styles directly affect school performance and that the "deviant" cognitive styles have a definite impact on individual educational careers, although they differ in some details of their findings. Witkin and others (1966:313) suggest that students with deficits (or differences) in verbal skills are more likely to be labeled as "retarded" or "slow" than students with other kinds of deficits.

> For example, the child with particular impairment in the analytical area, but with relatively better verbal-comprehension competence, not only may escape the selection filter which leads to classification as retarded but may even be considered "a good child" by his teachers. We know from our studies that field-dependent children, low in analytic ability, are often conforming to adult authority. This characteristic, together with their ability to "talk nicely," is apt to be particularly pleasing to teachers. Even if such children should be referred for testing, their analytic deficit is not as likely to make for a low IQ (especially if a Binet-type test is used), and so they may avoid the "retarded" label (Witkin and other 1966:313).

When cognitive styles which are less valued by those influential in labeling learners are correlated with other cultural differences, the learning situation can become even more problematic for all participants. That many researchers in this area impute differential value to alternative cognitive styles further enhances the likelihood that negative or inferior identities will be accorded to "deviant" individuals in schools. Bernstein, for example, treats the working class speech habits he observed as diagnostic of communicative and conceptual deficiency in the working class group relative to the middle class. Kagan, Sigel, and Moss, and Witkin and his associates have implied in their research that analytic style and field-independence in conceptual organization are superior developmentally to field-sensitive, relational cognitive style. In this the investigators have taken a cultural value and raised it to the level of a scientific premise.

Ramirez and Castaneda (1974) argue that both sources of identity attribution, those implicit in much cognitive research and those institutionalized in U.S. schools, have had important consequences for the Chicano children they studied. These children, they found, are typically field-sensitive and relational in cognitive style. In concert with other role expectations, behavioral strategies, and values, this style contributes to learning difficulties in school and to the development of negative personal identities, due to the cultural disjunction they create in Anglo-oriented schools. In order to succeed in this learning situation, Chicano children must renounce many of the values central in their homes and ethnic community. Because researchers have tended to assume the relative superiority of analytic modes, the adaptive and maladaptive features of each style have remained largely unexamined. For the same reason, fundamental relationships between the analytic and relational modes, and situational factors in their use have been little explored.

Preferred cognitive style is pertinent to learning strategies and their congruence or disjunction with instructional strategies. Based on their research among the Kpelle of Liberia and subsequent comparative study of U.S. school children, Cole and his associates (1971:233) concluded "that cultural differences in cognition reside more in the situations to which particular cognitive processes are applied than in the existence of a process in one cultural group and its absence in another." This may be equally true of cognitive style. Comparing test responses of Kpelle with varying amounts of Western-style schooling and of unschooled Kpelle, they found that schooled Kpelle tended to use particular procedures of organizing information more consistently across a variety of situations than did the nonschooled, but that no cognitive procedures seemed to be totally absent from the repertoires of the non-schooled. Western-style schooling, it seems, trains students to favor the use of particular procedures and to use them in a wide range of circumstances. U.S. schoolchildren, the researchers contend, learn to use taxonomic categories so thoroughly that they attempt to use them even in problems to which they do not apply.

> The use of [taxonomic] categories is ordinarily considered by Western psychologists to represent a higher level of cognitive development than the use of functional categories. Yet so strong was this tendency [to use them] that where the conditions of the problem made taxonomic classification difficult, or even impossible (as, for instance, when the child had to choose an item to place between a file and an orange), the American children would violate the instructions in order to maintain taxonomic classification. Instead of choosing an item that went with both of the constraint items, they would choose an item that was part of the same taxonomic class as *one* of the constraint items and ignore the other. The Kpelle subjects, even the high school subjects who used taxonomic classification widely, would not violate the conditions of the problem in this manner. Their performance indicated that they were capable of taxonomic classification, but they used the taxonomic mode under a narrower range of circumstances (Cole and others 1971:226–227).

Learning strategies also reflect varying emphases on channels of learning and instruction. Although this will be explored in greater detail later, an example will clarify its significance. In a discussion of learning styles among Native American children, Cazden and John (1971) summarize evidence that learning in these cultures is more visual than verbal, more by independent observation than by verbal instruction. Within many Indian communities, visual acuity and discrimination traditionally have been emphasized, and interpersonal communication involves the use of very subtle visual cues. The cultural expectation of a learner's autonomy as opposed to dependence on step–by–step guidance to mastery, combined with the emphasis on visual learning, creates a particular type of learning strategy. Werner states the basic principle of this strategy among the Navajo, suggesting a contrast between contemplation in Navajo and empiricism in Anglo learning strategies.

> The Navajo approach . . . stresses the acquisition of competence as a prerequisite for performance. Navajos seem to be unprepared or ill at ease if pushed into early performance without sufficient thought or the acquisition of mental competence preceding the actual physical activity. . . . This philosophy of learning can be summed up in the following 'artificial' proverb: "If at first you don't think, and think again, don't bother trying."
> The Anglo approach stresses performance as a prerequisite for the acquisition of competence. . . . The comprehension of the principles is perceived as a corollary and automatic by-product of the ability to perform. This philosophy of learning can be summed up in the well-known proverb: "If at first you don't succeed, try, try again" (Werner 1968:1–2, cited in Cazden and John 1971:262).

In Anglo schools, Indian children encounter inevitable cultural disjunction. Rohner (1965:334–335) describes this for Kwakiutl who "typically learn by observation, manipulation and experimentation in their native setting, but. . . . must learn by verbal instruction, reading and writing in the classroom."

We must not discount knowledge which is conveyed through nonvisual channels, even though many skills are learned through careful observation with little verbal instruction. Among the Menomini, for example, young people are instructed in cultural values, beliefs, and morals directly through "preaching" by their elders and indirectly through stories, as well as through prevailing patterns of conduct. Clearly the emphasis on visual learning strategies for acquiring fairly discrete types of knowledge and skill, as suggested by Cole and others, is situational.

Learning and instructional strategies are not the only strategies which affect educational process, for learning is not the only goal of participants in educational transactions. Learning situations are complex interpersonal transactions which involve multi-faceted relationships among participants. This is apparent in Goetz's comparison of strategies used by a third grade teacher and those used by her students. While the two sets of strategies were partly complementary, they also were partly divergent. One of the prime goals of this teacher was to increase student autonomy. She sought to induce children to relinquish their definitions of school-related activities as "have–to" behaviors, required by external authority, in favor of the definition of those behaviors as personal "need–to" or "want–to" behaviors.

> For example, if she assumed that most of the students would not "want to" memorize multiplication tables, or even feel the "need to" do so, she might devise learning games which incorporated this behavior, or she might instruct the child to practice multiplication tables with flash cards in pairs of their choice. She would be using strategies which she found most children would voluntarily respond to (since they incorporated at least two of the children's own values) in order to engage them in behaviors with which she expected they might ordinarily merely comply (Goetz 1975:231–232).

Among the students' prime values were mastery (knowing what to do and how to do it), expansion of responsibility, opportunities for interaction (especially with peers), play work (as opposed to "hard work"), approval of others, self-expression, and maximizing novelty. One of their strategies was to attempt "to maximize those behaviors which they perceive[d] as autonomously directed and to minimize those behaviors which they [saw] as externally dictated" (Goetz 1975:227).

Differences in strategy derived from such factors as the disparity of status between teacher and students. While there was some sharing of control, most remained in the teacher's hands; when opportunities for choice were sanctioned, it was always from a range specified by the teacher. The teacher also was understood to be the leader and the children followers. Initiation of activities was predominantly the teacher's role, and she engaged in a far greater proportion of planned and anticipated actions than did the children. They, in turn, more often engaged in response behaviors in the face of initiating behaviors by the teacher.

This disparity of status and in the degree of control over events underscores the difference in potential relevance of cultural repertoires of student and teacher participants. While students interpret and respond to school events in light of their own goals and values, they are confronted with a world structured in ways consonant with the culture represented by the school and generally also by the teachers. To the extent that students and teachers share a cultural heritage, a mutual meshing of interpretive schemes is likely to develop within the limits set by differences in role and goals. Yet in the final analysis, all educational encounters are intercultural, if only because the world of children and other novices is not isomorphic with the world of adults and other "experts." For this reason, examination of the frames of reference of various participants is essential, particularly the processes which mobilize these frames as active components of the interpersonal transactions. Research of this type brings into focus the dynamics of intercultural and interpersonal communication.

COMMUNICATION

When we think of interpersonal communication, we think first of verbal exchange, for so much of what we intend to convey is encoded in words. There are, of course, a great many other ways in which we communicate with one another as well: gestures, facial expressions, and postures; paralinguistic sounds like intonation, voice loudness, and meaningful (but nonlinguistic) sighs, grunts, laughter, cries and so forth; the distances we maintain from others and the tactics we use to bridge or sustain the distance; clothing, and accoutrements we carry with us; deodorants and scents with which we modify our body odors. Still less do we think of the information implicit in the physical features of settings, the choice and placement of objects in space, and the manner in which we interact with the setting, and action itself.

Many theorists view human communication as a loop similar to that in figure 4.1. Each communicative act is considered one in which a *sender* transmits a *message* to a *receiver*. The sender (which may be an individual or a group) translates information into *symbols* which she or he expects to be understood by the receiver; the symbolically encoded information (or message) upon receipt is decoded, information is extracted from the symbolic code, and the receiver may then respond, thereby becoming the sender of message 2.

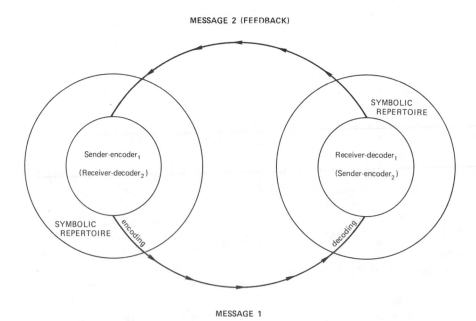

FIGURE 4.1

Notice that for the communicative act to be completed, the message must be received and decoded, and that this must be through the receiver's symbolic repertoire, which may not be identical to that of the sender. The only way for the sender to determine whether the information intended (and encoded) by him or her is the same as that actually decoded by the receiver, is by evaluating any perceived response. No response may mean that the information transmitted was not so received, but it may not. Thus a sender uncertain about the fate of message 1 may transmit a second message intended to elicit some discernible evidence of receipt. Let us say, instead, that the receiver–decoder of message 1 responds perceptibly by encoding and transmitting message 2. In this case, upon decoding message 2, sender 1 may have indirect evidence of the information decoded by sender 2 from message 1, as well as additional information decoded from message 2.

When both sender-receivers speak a common language, they are likely to take for granted that they also share substantial portions of their respective symbolic repertoires. However, because cultural knowledge is neither homogeneous nor consistently distributed among members of a group (much less among all speakers of a given language), the assumption of symbolic sharing may or may not be a valid one. If I take for granted that the intended meanings of my messages are obvious and therefore the same as the meanings decoded by those with whom I interact, I may not become aware of a serious discrepancy between the two sets of information until I receive a message that does not make sense, a message not only unexpected but unexpectable in view of what I had understood to be going on between myself and my fellow communicator. As long as I can decode and interpret messages received as "sensible" in relation to my understanding of the situation, I need not consider as problematic my fellow communicator's decoding of my intended meaning. This is the nature of routine communication.

In the absence of some shared symbols and meanings, communication obviously would be minimal. Yet even when symbolic repertoires are largely shared, intended transmission of information may not be realized fully. The interpretation of any message received and decoded also is subject to a great many contingencies beyond the message content itself, contingencies such as the receiver's definition of the situation, previous experience, and interpretation of the communicative context. The probability of the correct inference of intended meaning is directly related to the redundancy of contextual information. The more information that constrains possible interpretations, the more redundancy is present in transmission.

Redundancy in any communication is increased when multiple channels are used, for information conveyed in one channel can be amplified or qualified by that conveyed in another (figure 4.2). From the receiver's standpoint we may think of channels as correlates of perceptual capacities; we receive information through aural, visual, tactile, kinaesthetic, olfactory, and gustatory

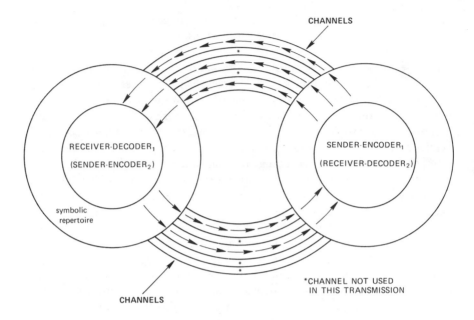

FIGURE 4.2

senses. In most face-to-face communication, at least two channels are in simultaneous use (aural and visual), often more. Thus in interacting with me you receive my words and paralanguage aurally; at the same time you visually perceive my facial expressions and body movements, you notice whether my eyes are focused on yours or are directed elsewhere, and you compare the information load, the meanings you infer from these various percepts as part of your interpretation of my message. Equally, the setting, social context, and definition of the situation contribute to the information which enters into that interpretation.[4]

Two nonverbal systems of communication that have been studied systematically are kinesics and proxemics. Kinesic communication, or body movement as an expressive system, conveys messages received visually, especially facial expressions, gestures, and postures. Some elements of kinesic behavior appear to be grounded in the autonomic nervous system and are common to all humans. Smiling is an obvious example; pupil dilation and contraction when an individual is experiencing strong emotion of some kind, is a more subtle one. Kinesic patterns also show considerable cross–cultural variation. Not only do particular facial movements, gestures, and so forth carry culturally-defined messages but they also are associated with specific situations in which those messages are appropriate. A Japanese typically will smile when conveying tragic news, while Anglo-Americans will avoid smiling under the same circumstances. Accurate decoding of the facial messages in each case depends on mastery of the kinesic code involved (Birdwhistell 1970, 1971, Ekman and others 1972).

Proxemic communication, or culturally patterned use of space, employs a variety of perceptual channels. The amount and kinds of touching appropriate in various situations, the amount and kind of eye contact, loudness of voices, the orientation in space of people's bodies to one another, as well as the distances appropriate to maintain, all are aspects of spacing that carry meaning. Edward Hall (1966), the pioneer and chief researcher in this field, has shown that proxemic patterns pervade cultural systems so thoroughly that architecture, design and placement of furnishings, attitudes toward nature, and even styles of art also are affected by them.

For example, each of us defines our personal space, the distance we prefer to maintain from nonintimates during interaction. When these territorial zones are invaded, we are likely to respond with anxiety, anger, or withdrawal. In large measure, personal space is culturally patterned. For northern Europeans and North Americans of similiar cultures ("Anglos"), a comfortable distance for nonintimate, face-to-face interaction is about three feet or just out of arm's reach. In Mediterranean and Jewish cultures, closer interpersonal distance is more comfortable, close enough that participants can touch one another in the course of interaction. Arabs prefer to be close enough that they can feel the warmth of the other participant's breath. Few of us are consciously aware of such features of our cultural orientation. We know what feels "right" and "comfortable" and we respond to others coming too close or moving too far from our "comfort zone" by attempting to control the distance ourselves or by interpreting the other person's behavior. If we interact with someone who prefers a greater distance, we may find that person cold, aloof, or arrogant; a person who infringes on our personal space we may think of as pushy, aggressive, or lecherous (cf. also Hall 1975, Scheflen 1972).

In analyzing the communication processes involved in knowledge transmission, we must consider the many types of messages exchanged. We also must investigate (1) the definition of the situation ("setting" in Gearing's [1975] terminology) each participant brings or evolves in the course of interaction, for this constitutes the frame within which he or she will interpret the communicative import of events; closely related to this is each participant's agenda, which Gearing (1973:2) has defined as "an expectation as to how the encounter promises or threatens to unfold"; (2) the cultural significance associated with channels and senses used in communicative events; (3) the interplay among channels of transmission; and (4) the complex message transmissions themselves.

In every communicative situation both sender-encoders and receiver-decoders are concerned not simply with the abstract transfer of information but also with signals that may clarify how the message is to be interpreted. Effectiveness of communication may well depend on each participant's ability to decode accurately such messages-about-messages (meta-messages). The meta-messages intended by the sender may not be those decoded by the receiver. Despite my best efforts to send signals attesting to the sincerity of my message, you may infer that the message is in fact a lie; the behaviors you intend to convey your confidence I may read as pomposity. This type of disjunction occurs with some frequency among people sharing substantial parts of their symbolic repertoires. Needless to say, it happens still more often and far more acutely between people of different cultures whose symbolic repertoires overlap minimally, if at all.

Communicative competence, as Hymes (1972) has pointed out, requires the ability not only to convey information in one or more available channels, but to match channel form, content, and style to specific contexts and situations—to use communicative skills appropriately. Within a person's communicative repertoire may be multiple codes, each constituting an alternate system for message transmission. Socialization entails in part the acquisition of these codes; mastery of the code(s) valued by a given group generally is prerequisite (though not necessarily sufficient) to the attribution of the social identity of member. Aspects of communicative performance also are commonly used in attributing social identities and even as inferential evidence of cognitive capability (cf. Shuy 1970, Williams 1970, Seligman and others 1972). To analyze communicative events and the relationship between communicative strategies and knowledge transmission, we must take into account the communicative-interpretive repertoires of participants, their respective definitions of the situation and context, and their respective interests and purposes (cf. Cazden 1972).

Consider once again a U.S. elementary school classroom: with what definitions of the situation do participants begin and how do these evolve over time? As noted earlier, neophyte teachers are expected to learn how the school works as an organization; their first years also are spent learning the prevailing values, categories, and behavioral norms associated with their roles as teacher and colleague. As we might expect, new teachers also often have a rather different conception of the classroom as a sociocultural situation than do more experienced teachers. Teachers of low income students may make different assumptions about the classroom than teachers of middle income students. At the secondary level, teachers of remedial or vocational classes are likely to define the situation differently than teachers of accelerated or college preparatory classes. In other words, the prior cultural heritage or class orientation of the teacher is only one factor in her or his definition of the situation. Equally important is the teacher's ongoing experience in the classroom and in the school. The evolving definition is constructed from assumptions about the students as types of people, about one's own goals and available means to implement them, about probable expectations of other participants, about the school as a context in which to work, and about ecological constraints on what happens in the classroom.

Wolcott (1967) reports that even teachers who began their sojourn in the Kwakiutl village school of his study with positive and hopeful attitudes toward the students, were rapidly worn down by the difficulties encountered. Their initial definitions of the situation, based on previous experience in quite different school contexts, changed markedly in the course of their (often brief) tenure, as did the goals which they sought to implement and the strategies they used to achieve them.

For teachers, this definition of situation may be more or less explicit, for their role entails thinking about organization and long-term objectives. Students, particularly at the elementary level, may use less systematic frames of reference, but they too define the situation from their own vantage point. They arrive in the classroom with a range of applicable and inapplicable images, from home and peers, from previous schooling experience, and from media to which they have been exposed. One of the first lessons they are expected to learn, however, is the "official" situation definition. Classrooms are places in which certain types of events have priority over others. There are particular kinds of limits, varying with the classroom, on the alternative courses of action open to students. In time students learn that there are types of students (like "dumb kids," "smart kids," "good kids," "bad kids"), and types of teachers, types of activities and types of sanctions. All of these enter into their evolving definitions. Kindergarten and primary grades are often tacitly or explicitly understood by educators to provide for enculturation in the official situation definition and in the skills necessary to achieve it, such as "paying attention," "following instructions," "sitting still," "waiting for a turn," and so forth.

The direction in which the situation definitions of all participants change in the course of their interaction with one another, depends heavily on the communicative events in which they share. As Gearing (1973:3) points out, their definitions may converge or diverge. These frames of reference both influence the interpretation of ongoing communication and evolve under the impact of this communication. To exemplify this we will consider messages typically sent in conjunction with formal instruction through the five channels listed above.

Audial Channels. Verbal transactions in the classroom, while in part student-initiated, are largely initiated, controlled, and personally dominated by the teacher. For the teacher, verbal messages from students are to a considerable degree "data," that is, bases for evaluation of the speakers. Student messages are subject to scanning not only for the "correctness" of the information conveyed but also for acceptability of topic, form (Standard American English, or SAE), and manner of presentation.[5] Teacher responses to student verbalizations in early grades not only provide feedback on the particular transmission attempted but also inform the student that future verbal messages will be treated in the same way. As a defining characteristic of teacher-student interaction, this function of student verbalization is reinforced by other messages which emphasize performance evaluation and competitive achievement (cf. Philips 1972).

Student-teacher verbal interaction may be limited and paced by concurrent message transmissions of this sort. This becomes apparent when we look at student-student verbal interaction. Students who appear withdrawn, taciturn, or verbally inept in the classroom often are observed to be quite effective and active verbal conversationalists with peers, inside or outside the classroom context. Opportunities for student-student verbal interaction within the classroom usually are controlled carefully, limited to the times and types of events specified by the teacher.

Student verbal behavior in the classroom cannot be understood apart from student definitions of the situation. These involve a definition of the classroom as a type of setting of types of events, expectations concerning teachers as types of persons (e.g., adults, whites, middle class), learned patterns of interaction valued outside the classroom, and evaluation of the relationship of the classroom or school to the student's interests and personal goals (agenda). Ward (1971) found that children and adults in a rural black community near New Orleans did not converse. Adults gave directives to children, but the bulk of the children's verbal activity was with the community of children—peers, caretakers, and charges.[6] These children tended to be verbally unresponsive in classrooms as well. Boggs (1972) found that Hawaiian children would not respond individually to direct questions from an adult, nor would they ask questions of an adult when interacting dyadically. They were quite verbal, however, in communicative exchange with peers, in collective interaction with adults, and in spontaneous (self-initiated) remarks directed to the teacher. These patterns of communicative transaction apparently reflected strategies developed out of school. While Anglo teachers attempted unsuccessfully to impose their own structures of participation, Hawaiian and Hawaiian-oriented teachers were able to coordinate their instructional strategies with the student patterns, largely by avoiding direct questioning of individuals and allowing them to relate to adults as a group (see also Howard 1972).

Sharing a verbal code does not necessarily indicate that "participant structures" (Philips 1972) are shared. In a comparative study of first grade classrooms, Mishler (1972) found that teachers differed markedly in their use of language as a resource for guiding student learning, focusing attention, and maintaining control. Each strategy called for different patterns of student verbal response, with some variation in the participant structures within which these responses were "properly" to be lodged. Clearer examples are provided by the studies of Dumont (1972) and Philips (1972). As they emphasize, when teacher strategies conflict with those of students, productive communication is likely to be thwarted.

Noting the consistent complaint by classroom teachers of many cultural varieties of Native Americans, that students are shy, withdrawn, unwilling to compete, and unresponsive to questions, Dumont (1972:345) points out that "these same children were amazingly different outside the classroom: they were noisy, bold, daring, and insatiably curious." Dumont (1972:349) discerned that the students' silence in the classroom was quite deliberate, a strategy "in a network of student defense needed to deal with the conflict resulting from cultural differences." Observing two Cherokee classrooms in session, one typically at a stalemate and one atypically successful and lively, the researcher was able to show by contrast the cultural bases of classroom conflict. In the first classroom, the teacher, ignorant of Cherokee values and goals, repeatedly insulted the students by his preaching, condescension, and rudeness. The individual autonomy which Cherokee value was totally denied to these young people. Students have a degree of power in this situation, but it is empty in its consequences, for neither side wins.

> It . . . became clear that the many modes of student silence were highly refined means of selective interaction, subtly ensnaring the teacher in order to teach him those forms of teaching and learning with which they were comfortable and with which they could work. In doing this they religiously maintained one fast and democratic rule: we don't change unless you do (Dumont 1972:357–358).

In the second classroom, the teacher was subdued, calm, and consistently respectful of the personal identities of his students. His teaching strategy involved an openness to alternatives chosen by the students and a supportive atmosphere in which experimentation could take place, in which students could teach themselves and one another, using him as a resource or ignoring him in their own pursuits. In this way he acknowledged the autonomy of the students and allowed dialogue to emerge among equal participants. In Cherokee terms he was a good teacher, one worthy of respect and response, because he did not attempt to violate their autonomy and integrity by the imposition of authority; he was a good teacher because he offered assistance in ordering knowledge and clarification of the unknown within a framework of harmony and good feeling.

Based on observation in Warm Springs Indian, mixed Anglo-Indian and Anglo classrooms, Philips (1972) describes similar cultural conflicts in typical classroom strategies. Anglo teachers attempted to implement four general types of participant structure, depending on the learning task at hand. All of these presupposed the teacher's role as the controlling authority and the central node in a system of dyadic/collective relationships. In two of these formats, the teacher directly controlled verbal exchange (the dominant mode of activity), addressing or soliciting response from the group as a whole, a sub-group, or an individual in the presence of the group. In these situations,

Indian students were almost uniformly silent. In the other two formats, teacher control was relatively indirect and transactions did not entail individual public display. When students worked independently at their desks with the option of initiating communication with the teacher, Indian students did so as often or more frequently than Anglo students. Participation of Indian students was greatest when students worked on projects in small groups. They became most fully involved in the learning tasks under these conditions, talking a great deal to fellow group members and competing with other groups. Anglo students, in contrast, seemed to have more difficulty just organizing the group effort; they relied "more heavily on appointed chairmen for arbitration and decision-making" and gave less evidence of competing directly with other groups in the class (Philips 1972:379).

The interplay of strategies here is revealing, for Anglo and Indian students tended to respond differently to the structures provided by the Anglo teacher. Those which conflicted with structures prevailing in their home community evoked tacit resistance from Indian students. Those structures which could be adapted to their own interactional strategies were implemented most fully for their own learning purposes. Anglo students' difficulty in handling group tasks may have reflected the absence of appropriate patterns in their previous experience. As important may have been their acceptance of the teacher's self-definition as pivot of all classroom interaction. For these students, competitive display in teacher-controlled events apparently was consonant with their own definition of appropriate interactional strategies. Indian patterns of learning, on the other hand, involve extensive observation, followed by performance only when the learner feels the necessary competence has been achieved. This trial is not public; the individual does not invite a witness until she or he has achieved success. In combination with the value for individual autonomy and an emphasis on nonverbal channels of instruction, this private pacing of competence demonstration ensures a lack of verbal response to standard Anglo instructional strategies.

In analyzing verbal transactions, we must look at messages sent and received in both their immediate and cumulative aspects, for each is awash in a stream of simultaneous communication and embedded in the cumulative sedimentation of previous transactions. For teachers and students who share verbal codes and norms of verbal conduct, as when all come from a similar cultural milieu, these transactions may be relatively unproblematic. When teacher and students do not share these, as when middle class Anglo teachers instruct Appalachian or Chicano or black or Native American students, verbal transactions may become a major source of misunderstanding and anxiety (cf. Lein 1975). Because the classroom itself is part of a larger context, conflict in communicative strategies also carries meaning beyond the immediate events in which it is manifested.

Students who do not use the teacher's linguistic code with facility, Gumperz and Hernandez-Chavez (1972) found, elicit different code usage from the teacher than do students who share the code. With a slow reading group, one teacher observed concentrated on details of language form such as spelling, pronunciation, and basic syntax. She addressed the students in "pedagogical style," with deliberate enunciation and artificial rhythm, and insisted on formal responses in similar style from the children. With an advanced reading group taught in the same room, she spoke in a more natural style, ignored minor deviations in form, and treated words in context as part of a larger communicative event. That the two groups of students did not share a common situation with respect to language transactions, was evident. Advanced readers received greater acceptance of their communicative efforts than slow readers, more positive response and less emphasis on ideal verbal form, and, by implication, more positive valuation as persons. Given the fact that most students in advanced reading groups were white or Oriental, while most students in slow reading groups were black or Chicano, student inferences about their classroom identities probably reinforced their experiences and the expectations they developed outside school. Because instructional strategies which focus on form to the exclusion of social meaning inhibit the learner's development of verbal expression,[7] students in the slow groups were further retarded in acquiring the code being taught.

The choice of a code entails the choice of the associated identity. Respect for the code(s) a child brings to the classroom communicates respect for those identities and the social worlds in which they are appropriate. Recognizing the social meaning of code selection or code switching seems to be essential to effective instructional strategies. Communicative codes are in themselves adaptive strategies, adapted to their social contexts. Labov (1969) has pointed out that the verbal strategy of responding to questions with monosyllabic answers is adaptive in the streets of a black slum, where questioners may be anyone from welfare workers to police. Children whose linguistic codes are treated as negative identity attributes may find minimal verbal response in classrooms equally adaptive. Bilingual students, such as those with competence in both black English and Standard American English (SAE) or Spanish and SAE, may shift to the deviant code in the classroom for particular communicative purposes. That switch is a verbal message that may be decoded as a sign of ineptness in the standard code or as a symbolic statement. When the teacher is unaware of the symbolic import of such a switch or is uninterested in it, student use of such code switching becomes a semiprivate communicative transaction with fellow code users; as such it can serve as a political strategy for reaffirming positive aspects of identity and lines of student alliance (cf. Mitchell-Kernan 1972).

Communication in classrooms, indeed in all educative encounters, has an intrinsic political dimension. As Gearing and others (1975) point out, all educative transactions involve the controlled transfer of information, and thereby control access to status transformation from novice to "old hand." Differential control over information implies hierarchy, although in practice this may be emphasized or muted. In U.S. classrooms, the manner in which teachers address students, and the content and form of teacher-initiated messages are often distinctly different from the range of manner, form, and content acceptable in student-initiated transmissions. The timing of verbal message-sending is controlled largely by the teacher and the proportional quantity of verbal transmission typically is far greater for teachers than for students. This asymmetry, which reflects cultural values concerning the relative superiority of adults versus children and teachers versus students also can be seen as a cultural lesson in hierarchy and dominance/submission to be mastered as a social skill. The dominant position of SAE in multicultural classrooms also contributes to this lesson in hierarchy, for when other dialects are tacitly or explicitly dismissed as "incorrect English" or "non-English," the speakers of these languages are effectively denigrated. It is likely that this exclusive approach to language in combination with the evaluation of all verbalization (as well as of other message transmissions) contributes heavily to the withdrawal from the schooling process noted by many observers of minority and lower income students.

Students are not without power of a sort in the classroom situation. Withdrawal itself, as the Cherokee demonstrate, can be a manipulative as well as a defensive strategy, as can selective nonresponse such as Hawaiian students display. Verbal codes are closely linked with behavioral patterns that together structure communicative transactions in distinctive ways. Philips' (1972) delineation of these contrasting participant structures in a mixed Anglo-Indian classroom shows clearly that language is but one element in the communicative strategies implemented by students and teachers.

Visual Channels. The arrangement of objects and people in space is one of the first sets of messages to confront students as they enter the classroom, and one of the first decisions to confront teachers (cf. Kohl, 1970:34–47). If we examine the ways in which space is utilized in American elementary classrooms, we find considerable consistency. Basic furnishings typically include desk space for students, distinctively different and greater desk space for the teacher, storage spaces, chalkboards and bulletin boards, a wastebasket, and possibly additional work surfaces. Student desks usually occupy the center of the room for routine work and form an orderly arrangement of parallel rows. Usually the teacher's desk is at the front of the room, often in the center and even when it is not, its size and separate placement signal the dominant status of its user.

The characteristic features of classroom proxemics begin here, for each classroom member has a definite object-in-space (desk) which is associated with the individual as a group member and constitutes part of her or his classroom identity. On the one hand, it is a space where the individual can leave personal belongings and to which she or he can return with a proprietary sense of territory. On the other hand, it is a space from which the student can be excluded or to which she or he can be confined at the will of the teacher, as when the teacher banishes a student to the corner, or requests that someone return to his or her own desk, or cautions students not to look at others' desks during an examination.

The territory of the classroom is divided into zones with specialized definitions and associated rules of conduct. In the classroom Goetz (1975) describes, zones on the room's perimeter were designated as specialized activity centers and access was controlled by factors such as a student's progress on other work assigned and group involvement in a particular task. In many classrooms movement by students outside the immediate zone of their desks is strictly regulated; in others, movement in the room is relatively free much of the time, as long as off–limit areas are respected and proper decorum observed.

The arrangement of students in space orders both student-student and student-teacher interaction. Particularly when students are expected to remain at their desks most of the time, interactions with peers are encouraged and constrained by sheer proximity. Teachers, in turn, are able to utilize these built-in limits by separating "talkers" or "troublemakers" from one another or from other students. Students routinely face in a single direction, usually countered by the teacher facing them or oriented toward them while instructing. By arranging students in rows facing forward the teacher is able to maximize his or her own visual access to kinesic information from students and opportunities for eye contact. Although studies have shown that student-teacher eye contact is not a reliable indicator of actual student attentiveness, middle class Anglo teachers often seek it intuitively because it is part of their cultural pattern.

Eye contact does not carry the same meaning in all cultures. In black and Puerto Rican cultures, for instance, sustained eye contact is considered rude and disrespectful; children are taught to direct their gaze away from others' eyes. If their teacher is unfamiliar with this pattern, she or he may interpret such students' eye movements as evasion, defiance or shame. The children at the same time interpret the teacher's sustained direct gaze and insistent "Look at me when I'm talking to you!" as demeaning and threatening.

Rhythms in the sequencing of eye contact also are relevant. Byers and Byers (1972) analyzed filmed transactions among two black girls, two white girls, and white teacher in a nursery school setting. They found that the more active black child looked or glanced at the teacher more than twice as often as the more active white child, yet successfully caught her eye or exchanged facial expressions only half as often. Careful study of the film indicates that the white child timed her glances at the teacher to catch pauses of general "searching the scene" behavior of the teacher, whereas the black child's attempts were not so timed. The teacher, though sensitive, was unable to coordinate with the black child's cues. The ability to interpret correctly and respond appropriately to kinesic clues requires shared protocols.

Visual communication by participants occurs also through wall displays and chalkboard inscriptions, clothing choices and dress codes, and demeanor. Teachers frequently use these as tools in systematic instruction, but they also are significant in informal communication. The display of completed student work, the use of chalkboards in publicly testing student performance competence, responses to student costume and demeanor, all contribute to the formulation of a student's classroom identity. Students who chafe against the restrictions of school regulations and norms often seek a covertly defiant outlet. These may take fairly dramatic visual form as postural or gestural displays, graffiti, or costume. When students and teacher do not fully share communication codes, they may take forms that are not recognized by the teacher, though recognizable to peers, as in the use of subtle kinesic shifts.

Olfactory and Gustatory Channels. These are of relatively minor importance in U.S. classroom communication. Yet as Jackson (1968:7) notes, even the smells of American classrooms seem to be fairly standardized. There is

> a sort of universal smell [of wax and cleaning fluid] which creates an aromatic background that permeates the entire building. Added to this, in each classroom, is the slightly acrid scent of chalk dust and the faint hint of fresh wood from the pencil shavings. In some rooms, especially at lunch time, there is the familiar odor of orange peels and peanut butter sandwiches, a blend that mingles in the late afternoon (following recess) with the delicate pungency of children's perspiration.

These odors, Jackson concludes, though so familiar that teachers and students cease to be actively aware of them, are unmistakable markers of the identity of the setting.

In elementary and secondary school classrooms, personal scents and odors often serve as markers of identity. The use of added scents, especially at the elementary level, tends to be limited to the teacher and thereby marks his or her adult status vis-à-vis students. However, teachers and students alike use the unintended messages of personal body odor as a basis for evaluation of individuals. In this way olfactory information can contribute to the development of social identities. Students who do not present the culturally favored "neutral" or mildly soapy odors of recently washed skin and fabric, students who smell of cigarette smoke or unexpected odors are likely to be perceived negatively by Anglo-oriented teachers and by students who share these values. Students also may negatively perceive teachers whose odors fall outside certain accepted categories (see also Largey and Watson 1972).

Gustatory communication between teacher and student tends to be confined to ceremonial occasions at which refreshments may be shared. Since meals usually are consumed in the company of peers, they serve as an implicit reminder of the differing status of faculty and students. Discussion of food and nutrition, however, can present further bases for identity attribution. The identification of "good" food habits with the meal patterns of middle class Anglo cuisine, for instance, implicitly devalues alternative cuisines chosen for cultural or economic reasons. The implications of this message can further crystallize the personal and social identities children acquire in school.

Tactile Channels. Although secondary in teacher-student communication, tactile messages are not uncommon in U.S. elementary classrooms. Henry (1955, 1957, 1959) found considerable tactile communication in middle class suburban schools, often associated with verbal terms of endearment. Teachers in such classrooms, Henry (1959) argues, are under pressure to implement two conflicting goals: maintenance of order and academic standards, and encouragement of initiative and spontaneity. He observed two types of coping strategy, both styled after "permissive" middle class patterns of parenting. In the first strategy, the teacher elicited the affections of students by means of tactile and verbal messages of endearment and used the corollary fear of loss of (the teacher's) affection to control student behavior. In the second strategy, the teacher formally abandoned a role of authority, leveling the distance between teacher and children, and then exercised control through covert manipulation of peer interaction.

Tactile messages are not always positive in affect; they may have negative or mixed valences. Corporal punishment is used in many schools, although it is usually rather strictly regulated. Tactile contact that is not directly punitive is common, as when a teacher pulls fighting students apart or turns a student by the shoulder. In either case, positive or negative, we need to ask who does what to whom under what circumstances. Further, how does the intended tactile message compare with the message received? And what significance is accorded it by participants in view of other messages previously or simultaneously conveyed?

In their analysis of filmed nursery school transactions, the Byerses (1972) found that tactile communication, like eye contact, was characterized by culture–specific patterns of rhythmic organization. Thus, attempts at tactile contact by the white teacher and black child were mostly unsuccessful because they were not appropriately synchronized.

Like other message systems in the classroom, tactile patterns are characterized by asymmetry. To some extent in the primary grades, and clearly thereafter, teachers dominate the initiation of tactile contact and control its course and duration. In Anglo culture, tactile prerogatives of this kind are associated with status; the boss can put a friendly hand on his employee's shoulder, but the right is not reciprocal. Throughout the contexts in which they live, children in the U.S. are subject to tactile invasion of their personal space.[8] While the parentalization of teachers may make this tactile exchange acceptable and meaningful as a gesture of parentlike affection and control, we do not know if this is the case, particularly for children unaccustomed to the parent-type modeled and in light of the full spectrum of messages being received.

We still know very little about the interplay of communication modes in classroom settings and in educational process in general. Because individual interpretation plays such a crucial part in all communicative transactions, systematic analysis of the processes involved would lead us to comparison of that knowledge intentionally transmitted in educational encounters with that knowledge actually decoded by receivers. On this basis we could resolve more adequately the question of why the two are often not the same. Because individual interpretation is always influenced by culture, analysis of communication process allows us also to investigate the foundations of cultural sharing, variation, and change.

The three aspects of sociopsychological analysis discussed are interdependent. Each represents an analytic angle from which the study of educational process can be approached. Together they also provide a framework through which the relationship between structural and processual aspects of knowledge transmission can be integrated. Basic to such an endeavor are the concepts of "context" and "adaptation."

At the micro-level of individual cognition and interpersonal transaction, context involves the physical and social circumstances, as they are defined by participants, in which events take place. Because the process of definition and interpretation is conditioned largely by cultural orientation, contexts are a focal concern in anthropological analysis. At the macro-level of group organization and social system, context includes the social structural and environmental features which constrain and facilitate system operation. While context reflects the ongoing processes of participant interpretation, it also represents structural features which participants encounter and which may affect them even when not consciously perceived. The sociocultural world in which we live is not merely a product of our own independent interpretations and patterns of behavior, but also of the complex interplay of the interpretations, strategies, and actions of the many participants with whom we share that world. Much of each individual's apprehension of the world is predicated on the cultural definitions and networks of social relationships which precede his or her entry into that world. The established systems of the sociocultural world are resilient, for the patterns and contexts of action they support set limits on the alternatives available to any individual. In this sense, social structure is an obdurate fact to which participants must adapt. At the same time, the conditions to which societies must adapt do not remain constant over time. This source of change, combined with changes in the modes of interpretation prevailing among participants, contribute to sociocultural change as an inherent feature of human group life. This is the crux of the relationship between structure and process.

Adaptation has been defined as the process of adjustment to existing and changing conditions. Thus adaptation involves the interpretation of contextual features and response to them, in light of an individual's or group's goals. On the micro-level, adaptive behavior and strategies reflect the sociopsychological processes discussed above. Insofar as adaptive behavior is patterned and recurrent over time, it affects macro-level system organization. In this sense, we can speak of the adaptive processes through which an educational system responds to changing societal structure, as with the advent of universal compulsory schooling in the U.S. Behind any adaptive process lies a multitude of individual choices and actions, yet for particular analytic purposes we may choose to focus on a level which precludes consideration of such detail. In this way, it becomes possible to delineate processes of broader scope. We may analyze the relationship between the development of the U.S. economy and the emergence of a system of compulsory education, noting the effects on the labor force of restricting adolescents' participation and of socializing them through schooling for work in industries and other bureaucratic organizations (cf. Bowles and Gintis 1976, Katz 1971).

The utility of the various levels and types of analysis discussed resides in the light each can shed on particular types of questions. None is sufficient for total analysis; each neglects certain aspects of the problem of knowledge transmission while focusing on others. As long as we bear in mind the ways in which the analytic frames which we apply selectively filter the knowledge we construct, we can use them effectively to extend our understanding. In combination, these analytic perspectives allow us to articulate diverse research findings into a coherent and relatively comprehensive system for understanding knowledge transmission in human societies.

In the following two chapters we will examine comparatively the way in which educational systems work from a macro-level point of view, and then educational process from a micro-level point of view. We then will consider the problem of change from a combined perspective.

notes

1. Von Bertalanffy (1968) distinguishes between closed (mechanical) and open (living) systems (though not specifically with reference to social systems). In part, his definition of open system rests on the exchange of components between system and environment and on the regulatory processes which maintain open systems in a steady state (dynamic equilibrium). This definition is useful for many ecological theories, but is somewhat more restricted than is apt here. One important issue is the degree to which "systemness" itself may be presumed; while it is a useful analytic assumption, it also risks misrepresenting what we seek to analyze. By openness, therefore, I am referring to the contingent character of order and integration in any sociocultural organization. As Khleif (1971:144–145) has remarked, "equilibrium in a social system . . . is but a case

of constant change;" and society is a "negotiated order" (Strauss and others 1964:146–153, 373–377).

2. The concept of identity has been discussed at length by several authors, among them Goodenough (1963:176–251) and Robbins (1973). As an analytic concept, identity has been defined and subdivided in a variety of ways (see e.g. Goodenough 1963, Wallace and Fogelson 1965, Miller 1963, Goffman 1956). Miller and Goffman suggest a threefold classification in which personal identity or self-concept is distinguished from *subjective* social identity (how a person *thinks* others view or label her/him) and *actual* social identity (how others *actually* view her/him). My usage here is thus less finely drawn. Of key importance, whatever analytic scheme is used, is the dialectic and interpenetrating relationship of identities.

3. Dusek (1975), in a critique of experimental research on the Pygmalion effect reported by Rosenthal and Jacobson (1968), asserts that "the evidence supportive of the notion that teachers bias children's education in elementary school classrooms is not compelling" (Dusek 1975:679). However, the definition of bias used is an artifact of the method of controlled experiment. Researchers cited by Dusek used an interventionist design in which teachers were supplied new information about randomly selected pupils, supposedly based on performance scores on special tests. In fact, the pupils involved were evaluated by the researchers as "objectively similar" in aptitudes, although the teacher was told that their respective test scores were markedly different. That no significant difference in classroom behavior or assessment was noted among the teachers studied establishes only that no single item of information is likely to overturn the collected body of information upon which most teachers draw to determine a student's classroom identity. Such research results may also reflect a conditioned distrust of university researchers by elementary and secondary level teachers, partly because of widely publicized deceptions such as the Rosenthal and Jacobson study. (Cf. also the discussion of change in U.S. schools in the seventh chapter.) Resolution of the controversy over the "reality" of a Pygmalion effect in classrooms requires long term naturalistic observation in the classroom, and inclusion of the larger context in which that classroom is embedded as a subject of research. Cf. Cicourel and Kitsuse (1963) for a study of the school as a system for allocating student identities and manipulating student achievement levels.

4. Henry (1963:289–290) has argued that noise, a component of many communication models, is highly relevant to educational transactions. Noise, defined as the uncontrolled, random elements in the communicative exchange, becomes part of the unintended transmission. I have included this component but not the label, because the label implies that we can make a clear empirical distinction between noise and not-noise. Even "the shuffling of children's feet" which Henry cites as noise is a positive message rather than an incidental event, although it may be *interpreted* as "noise" by a participant. Noise as a concept is most useful, I would argue, in analysis of participants' interpretive categories.

5. It is important to note that extrinsic factors like demeanor and appearance commonly contribute to evaluations of "verbal" skills (cf. Seligman and others 1972).

6. Horner and Gussow (1972) studied children's linguistic environments in a black urban ghetto in upstate New York. By "bugging" the clothing of two three-year old children, they were able to monitor verbal transactions in the two respective households. By far the greatest proportion of each child's verbal interaction was with its mother, secondarily with playmates up to about eight years of age, although there were definite differences between the two children in the total interaction pattern. Consonant with Ward's findings, two-thirds of all verbal behavior directed to the children by their mother involved directives.

7. There is no evidence that linguistic form itself is a salient factor in a child's ability to learn in the classroom (cf. Labov 1969).

8. I do not mean to imply that children do not enjoy tactile relations; clearly many do. However children are rarely consulted before adults, whether strangers or kin, initiate contacts, and they often express annoyance or aversion, to their parents' embarrassment. The expanding cultural awareness of U.S. youngsters may account, at least in part, for the strongly negative response young boys develop to preferred tactile exchange. It is "sissy stuff" because it is the role of an inferior to be touched, of mama's boys (eternal children) and females. Girls, trained to acquiesce to affection and condescension, typically do not reject overtures so explicitly.

FIVE

EDUCATION AS
A SOCIOCULTURAL
SYSTEM

All knowledge transmission in a society or group comprises a system, in that each transmission event is conditioned, potentially or in fact, by every other. In practice, some events are more closely connected than others. The life paths of a factory worker or farmer may never cross that of a scion of a wealthy family, and these in turn may differ significantly from that of an imprisoned criminal. The educative encounters in which each engages may be distinctive in various respects. Yet indirectly these events are linked, since each constitutes part of the sociocultural context of the others. Much of the knowledge transmitted in any group is implicit in the structure of existing relationships, the known history and prospects of those relationships, and the perceived options and constraints with which they confront an individual. In the largest sense, education as deliberate, systematic knowledge transmission cannot be understood apart from the total transmissions of socialization/enculturation.

To focus on education is to focus on those events which entail, at least in part, deliberate attempts to transfer knowledge from one person/group to another. This is a complex matter in any society, for multiple agencies, multiple communication modes, multiple purposes, and multiple modes of organization of educative transactions are involved. Analyzing education as a sociocultural system requires mapping the social distribution of knowledge and associated values, as sketched in the second chapter. It also requires identifying the full array of types of educative transactions and contexts which occur in the society, to ascertain their interrelations.

Such an ambitious task with respect to a society has yet to be systematically undertaken.[1] Both sheer scope and the unevenness of available data would hamper the efforts of a researcher attempting this kind of analysis.

Most analyses of systemic aspects of education have focused on schools and school systems. The boundaries of the system in this case are relatively easy to establish. With adequate historical data we can document its development as a system as well as the dynamics of its operation as an institution in a larger sociocultural framework. In this chapter our focus will be on schools as systems. But it is essential to remember that schools are always part of a more inclusive educational system, and that societies which do not have schools nevertheless have educational systems.

analyzing educational systems

While education is universal in human societies, formalization of educational processes and the development of schooling are not. Mead (1943) has suggested that formal instruction outside the family is likely to be sought when the social structure becomes sufficiently differentiated that a child may take on adult roles different from those of his or her parents. Moreover, if essential or desired skills are too complex to be taught easily (or if parents are not themselves sufficiently proficient to teach them), they are likely to be taught by someone less closely related to the child (Hagstrom 1968).[2] The development of schooling, as noted earlier, is also contingent upon such factors as community ability to subsidize instruction and to spare students from other more immediately productive tasks, and the interest of particular groups in controlling access to a corpus of knowledge and in recruiting members to ensure the perpetuation of the group and its knowledge.[3]

Within these limits, schooling is found in a wide range of types of societies, including small-scale societies with subsistence economies and unwritten languages (often labeled as "primitive"). The Poro schools of several West African societies are an interesting example, not only because their systemic characteristics are fairly clear, but also because their nature and origin have been the subject of controversy. Jules Henry (1960:277) has argued that these schools, similar in many ways to those of the "literate" world, must be "a combination of native initiation rituals and the white man's idea of a school." Henry's argument, and that of others with similar interpretations of Poro schooling, presumes that societies of this type (i.e., small-scale, nonliterate, subsistence societies) are qualitatively different from "literate" societies. The differences postulated include those listed below.

Nonliterate Societies	*Literate Societies*
Limited and relatively unchanging corpus of knowledge	Extensive and expanding corpus of knowledge
Learning predominantly informal, unsystematic	Learning predominantly formal, systematic
Training predominantly in morality, ethics, religion	Training predominantly in "objective knowledge" like mathematics, science, history, literature
Knowledge transmitted predominantly concrete, pragmatic, and relevant to child's life	Knowledge transmitted largely abstract, peripheral to child's life
Teaching as single aspect of adult's or craft specialist's role	Teaching itself as specialized occupational role
Absence of formal schools	Presence of formal schools

This typology illustrates one of the ways in which assumptions influence scientific inquiry. With such assumptions, based on a survey of a select sample of societies, researchers are prone to interpret further cases as if the assumptions were proven facts, rather than tentative schemes for organizing complex data. Mead (1943:634) falls prey to this when she writes, "There are several striking differences between our concept of education today and that of *any* contemporary primitive society" (emphasis added), adding in a footnote that her "discussion, unless otherwise indicated, is based upon South Sea people only." The assumption that cultural knowledge is limited, tradition-bound, and relatively nonabstract in any human society is questionable. The derived postulate that schooling therefore is unnecessary to sociocultural perpetuation in "nonliterate" societies thus is dependent on a very weak initial premise. Whatever initial assumptions underlie our analyses, we must be prepared to test and modify them in the face of empirical evidence.

Let us consider the case of Poro schools. Although we lack specific historical documentation of their development, available ethnographic evidence does not support the contention that they were styled after Western institutions. Whatever their inspiration, they became integral features of the societies in which they developed, adapted to indigenous cultural goals. Among the Mende, Kpelle, Vai, Mano, and related societies of West Africa, social, economic, and political life were largely controlled by the Poro men's secret society. As noted in the second chapter, Poro also controlled access to knowledge of various kinds, partly through the schools which it organized and ran. Although today these schools have changed greatly because of the social, political and economic transformations of West African societies, formerly they were crucial life experiences for all members of the community. Under the jurisdiction of Poro and Sande (a similar women's secret society), separate schools for boys and girls were held in special sections of the forest outside the towns. Upon initiation into the school, which required payment of a fee by the child's parents, boys were considered socially "dead." Such separation was less radical for girls. Depending on the district, schooling lasted from several months to eight years,[4] with the boys' schooling generally longer than the girls'. In the boys' school (which has been described more fully than the girls'), novices were instructed both in general cultural knowledge and skills and in specialties such as weaving, leatherwork, medicine, folklore, dancing, bridge-building and so forth, according to individual aptitudes. In many districts boys constructed small towns in which they lived for the duration, learning to hunt and farm, to gather and use herbs, and to defend their towns from staged "enemy" attacks. In all these activities they were evaluated carefully and reinstructed so that they might develop proficiency and precision in all their endeavors, as well as discipline, endurance, and the ability to follow orders. When their schooling was completed, successful graduates were "reborn" and returned to their communities as publicly recognized adults. Those who were unable to endure the hardships of the school curriculum did not survive and were not to be mourned, for they had died socially upon initiation.

While males had greater access to highly specialized and valued knowledge and to power and rank, where Sande organizations were strong, some girls also had access to the upper echelons of knowledge and power. In traditional Kpelle society, for instance, Poro was ritually supreme for the four years of boys' schooling, ceding ritual supremacy to Sande for the following three years, during which the girls' school was held (Gibbs 1965). According to Harley (1941, 1950), some girls were traditionally consecrated, socially, as men, and initiated into Poro rather than Sande. From this cadre the ritual consort of the highest local official of Poro was chosen, and her power was very nearly equivalent to his.

Although fees were charged for initiation of each child, these schools were open to all community members and were virtually compulsory. Students were evaluated upon entrance for aptitudes, interests, and ambitions. Part of the curriculum was common to all, and part involved specialized training according to these evaluations. Teachers were community members of good moral reputation and specialists in the topics covered. They and the school were administered by a headmaster endowed with exceptional wisdom, knowledge, and the culturally emphasized virtues of courage, respect for law, courtesy, and public spirit. For the duration of the school session, these adults were full-time specialists in schooling, often staying with the students in the bush and returning to the towns for further supplies. Instruction was carried out exclusively by individuals who were in no way related as kin to the students, for it was felt that kin might be inclined to treat them too leniently. Indeed the total separation from family was designed to prevent the favor and sympathy which students might hope to receive from kin. More importantly, it served to reorient the students, especially boys, from their initial narrow kinship commitments to responsibility to the community in general and to their peers in particular.

The pervasive power of Poro and Sande in daily community life tied schooling into the sociocultural system in many ways. By teaching loyalty and obedience to those in authority, as well as in particular kinds of knowledge, Poro schools underwrote the power of the reigning elite. Bonds created by attendance at the same school helped to crosscut potentially divisive loyalties based on kinship and residence. Loyalty to fellow Poro members took precedence over loyalties even to close kin. At the same time, access to the highest ranks and the associated specialized knowledge was restricted to certain families, so that the loyalties of the elite—those with access to the most highly valued cultural knowledge—were doubly reinforced by both Poro membership and kinship.

The whole community was involved in Poro activities, whatever the rank of individual members, through the power of Poro to rule all in the regulation of political, economic, social and religious affairs. Schooling required contributions by all families in the form of food subsidy. During school sessions community members, especially women, had to extend themselves beyond their ordinary productivity to supply adequate food. No request by a representative of Poro could be refused (Harley 1941, 1950; Watkins 1943; Little 1951; Gibbs 1965).

With the massive transformations of the social order brought about by colonial domination and the establishment of multicultural societies, Poro schools changed. With the advent of alternative routes of achievement and a different set of options and constraints, Poro schools became much reduced in duration and curriculum. Little (1951) observed in Sierra Leone during the mid-1940s that full Poro sessions lasted only seven months and new initiates might remain only a few weeks. The amount of technical knowledge imparted was reduced with this change, as was the traditional requirement of total isolation from the community. Contrary to their traditional alternation, Poro and Sande schools convened at about the same time, for the economic drain on the community was no longer as great. Interestingly, the Sande curriculum, while similarly reduced in terms of traditional content, was adapted more readily to changing conditions than that of Poro, for the Sande society incorporated such revisions as the introduction of government-trained young women to teach "modern methods of mothercraft and hygiene" (Little 1951:130).

In some areas such as Liberia, Poro activity was completely suppressed and its only remaining functions were drastically modified. In combination with the secret nature of Poro business, this severely hampered researchers' access to information about schooling and other Poro activities. Most of the available ethnographic information was collected during the period when Poro power was breaking down (cf. Harley 1950:v–vii). Where this was due to official suppression, only very sympathetic and skillful researchers were able to secure information. Lancy (1975:380n), found in Liberia that his "attempts to elucidate the nature of the bush [Poro] school were continually discouraged."

The above sketch of Poro schooling and its treatment by a variety of researchers serves as an illustration of three points. First, the way in which available data are analyzed reflects a number of choices by the analyst. Assumptions about the nature of the phenomenon being studied can have far-reaching consequences for subsequent interpretation, just as analytic frameworks can. Second, the impact of colonial expansion, industrialization, and increased intercultural contact has complicated the study of traditional educational systems in non-Western societies, particularly those without written historical records. To derive a general theory which would account for cross-cultural differences in the development of schooling, we would draw ideally on data from societies with various types of social structure from different areas of the world. In fact, we lack the data to do so. This is partly because many early ethnographers had a narrow conception of education and schooling that did not encompass the full range of phenomena that constitute education in a community. As a result, they failed to note many events important to system analysis. When knowledge transmission was closely tied to access to power, whether spiritual or mundane, many observers were unable to secure sufficient data to provide adequate descriptions of the structure of education. For systems that have changed markedly in the last two centuries, historical data are essential. Yet for most of the world's societies we have only fairly recent historical documentation specific and accurate enough to determine the actual sequence of events leading to the educational forms observed. The decline of Poro schools from a vigorous formal system of education to less elaborated rituals of transition from child to adult status, illustrates the importance of an historical perspective for documenting even the existence, much less the genesis, of a particular type of educational system.

The third point to be underscored here is that the unevenness of available data increases the significance of analytic orientations. To sort out the key variables in the development of particular types of educational systems requires either detailed historical evidence or a theory which enables us to fill in gaps in data by reference to an expected pattern. In the latter case we must take special care to ensure that our assumptions and analytic speculations are supportable.

Analysis of education as a system in sociocultural context calls for macro-level analytic frameworks. As we noted earlier, such frameworks often sacrifice detailed consideration of micro-level process and variation in order to focus on general patterns of structure and development. Use of such frameworks is therefore especially susceptible to the hazards just discussed. Structural patterns may be explained theoretically by asserting that these patterns are the result of certain developmental processes; the danger lies in neglecting to support empirically the premises on which the theoretical account is predicated. If analysis is conducted exclusively at the macro-level, detailed evidence which might call those premises into question may be neglected.

As an example we will consider the problem of the relationship between school systems and industrialization. Functionalist explanations of the development of educational institutions interpret the growth and specialization of schools as adaptations to changing social needs. Some proponents assume further that the relationship between education and social structure is relatively simple in nonindustrial societies, that the transition from "simplicity" to "complexity" is due to some aspect of the industrialization process itself, and that the particular form which schooling takes under conditions of industrialization is functionally related to the needs of this process. Thus the characteristics of school systems in industrial societies are postulated to include specialized training for a highly differentiated division of labor, formal educational qualifications for entry into occupations, social mobility through school achievement, a rationalistic educational philosophy, and the incorporation of changing scientific knowledge in the curricula (cf. Shipman 1968).

This kind of explanation does not really account for the development of particular educational systems in particular societies, as Vaughan and Archer (1971) have shown. Comparing the evolution of school systems in England and France during the late eighteenth and early nineteenth centuries, they point out that distinctive structural and cultural factors in each case set the pace and direction of educational change.

In many respects schooling in preindustrial France and England was similar. In both countries, formal education was voluntary rather than compulsory, locally administered, privately financed, and mainly an institutional arm of the Church. The goal of instruction was primarily religious. Although not formally standardized in either case, the curriculum was devoted mostly to catechism in elementary schooling and to classical studies in secondary and higher schooling. In neither case did influences external to the sociocultural system noticeably affect the course of educational change, beyond some delay or acceleration of pace.

When we turn to the period of change itself, however, we find that England far surpassed France in the rate of industrialization. The societal needs engendered by industrialism remained largely unfulfilled by the school system, which did not change much from its preindustrial form until late in the nineteenth century. A unified state school system was not achieved until 1945. France, in contrast, led dramatically in the development of the type of school system characteristically attributed to industrial society. Its educational changes "pre-adapted" it to a course of industrialization not yet developed fully.

Vaughan and Archer attribute the reasons for this divergence largely to differences in the orientation, resources, and strategies of interest groups most active in seeking educational reform in each country. In France this was the revolutionary bourgeoisie and in England, the entrepreneurial middle class. There were many similarities between the two. The nature and interests of both groups led them to attack the domination of formal education by the established churches; both sought to reorganize schooling to fit the new tripartite class structure rather than the feudal class model reinforced by religious education. Both sought a state-organized, administered, and financed system, and both sought to incorporate vocationally-oriented instruction within this state school establishment. The differences between the two groups, however, were pronounced.

Their resources and strategies were different. The bargaining power of the French bourgeoisie came from their legislative control in the Revolutionary Assemblies and their subsequent control of key administrative posts. Their resources were by and large political, and their strategies used legislative power to break the Church's scholastic monopoly. This they accomplished by confiscating Church school buildings and prohibiting clerical teaching orders. Only by mobilizing state funds to support the new school system, did the bourgeois reformers gain access to financial resources. The opposite was true of the English entrepreneurial middle class. With virtually no access to political power, their resources were largely financial. Their bargaining power depended on their capacity to organize voluntary subscription for all levels of instruction in order to establish competitive alternatives to existing school institutions. In this way they sought to restrict the Church monopoly but not necessarily to drive out the clerical educators.

In both cases the strategies chosen were determined largely by the resources available, but they also reflected the groups' divergent interests and orientations. The French bourgeoisie sought educational change oriented to professional and bureaucratic administrative roles. They stressed secular nationalism, rationalism, and administrative efficiency. Equality of formal educational opportunity was considered necessary to achieve maximal competence at all levels. It was to be ensured through creation of an integrated academic ladder to be climbed on the basis of merit alone, with the provision of state aid for the secondary schooling of the most able students. The reformers promoted broad, uniform curricula throughout France in the interest both of equality and of nationalism. Specialization was postponed until advanced levels in their belief that knowledge led to moral virtue. Prompted by the desire to divest clergy of their influence as teachers, the reformers established specific levels of competence to be met by teachers at each scholastic level. Teachers were organized into a civil hierarchy bound by a deliberately fostered esprit de corps, in a policy designed to create a pedagogic cadre as faithful to the state as the clerical orders had been to the Church.

The English entrepreneurial middle class reformers sought educational change oriented to economic roles and in line with the ideological precepts of

classical laissez-faire economics and utilitarianism. Unlike their French counterparts, they did not challenge the traditional social criteria of academic
advancement. They did not seek the hierarchical integration of schooling
institutions to facilitate social mobility. They did not advocate standardization
of curricula nor did they seek as radical an exclusion of religious content.
Rather, they envisioned curricula adapted to the industrial specializations of
geographic regions and of social strata, changes which would adapt the potential labor force to new economic roles. They advocated both differentiated
schooling for various social classes and early vocational specialization where
appropriate. Though interested in improving the quality of teaching, there was
no suggestion of ensuring uniform training or developing a teaching corps as
in France.

The French reformers successfully challenged the Catholic domination of
schooling, gradually replacing that system with one totally under state control.
The English succeeded only in winning some concessions from the dominant
interest groups. Even if the English reformers had been as successful as the
French at that time, however, the resulting school systems still would have
been substantially different, for the cultural orientations of the two groups
diverged. Commenting on the importance of cultural frames in the social
processes leading to educational change, Vaughan and Archer (1971:220)
observe that

> decisions of this kind, about the particular arrangements best able to meet a
> given end, always depend upon 'judgments of appropriateness' derived from the
> ideology. It is this interaction between interests and ideology which accounts for
> educational differences in two societies, with similar types of groups dominating
> [schooling] and where similar structural relations prevail.

Vaughan and Archer's analysis represents a multilevel approach to the
study of school systems. By combining consideration of general structural
patterns with an analysis of the actions of particular interest groups, they were
able to delineate the actual social processes which underlay structural change.
By distinguishing social processes from the cultural knowledge drawn upon by
actors in these processes, they were able to advance a convincing explanation
for the differences in the strategic decisions made by the participants and in
the impact of those decisions on prevailing institutions. In many respects their
approach resembles the ecological approach described in the fourth chapter,
for they focused on adaptive strategies and resulting adaptive processes within
specific sociocultural environments.

In the next three sections we will examine in some detail two school
systems. Although both systems were influenced both by Western political and
economic expansion and by Western academic models, they represent distinctive sociocultural adaptations to changing conditions. By analyzing their de-

velopment, structural dynamics, and relationships to sociocultural context from a multilevel point of view, we will be able to see the relationship between structure and process in the operation of educational systems.

evolution of school systems

Because it is characterized by a distinctively non-Western culture, Japan provides illuminating contrasts to the cases of England and France. The circumstances surrounding the development of industrialization and the contemporary school system also were markedly different. Japan's course of industrialization and academic reform was planned and effected by the ruling elite in response to external threats by the West in the last half of the nineteenth century. They chose to model the pre-university portion of the new school system on that of France. Like France, Japan emphasized the needs of the state and the development of civic pride and loyalty. Curricula were uniform and under the aegis of the state Ministry of Education, academic levels were integrated hierarchically into a ladder of potential mobility, and student progress through the system was based theoretically only on merit. The processes of education within this administrative structure were strongly influenced first by U.S. models and, near the turn of the century, by Prussian models. The actual development and operation of the Japanese system, however, reflects distinctive features in its sociocultural milieu.

The decision to "modernize" was made by an oligarchic elite which seized power in 1867, toppling the Tokugawa regime and returning the emperor to a revered status as symbolic father of the state. By identifying the nation under imperial leadership with the extended family central to the lives of most Japanese, they facilitated the extension of strong local loyalties to the larger "family" and its supreme head. By establishing a national system of schooling aimed at systematically teaching Confucian values of loyalty, filial piety, thrift, and diligence, as well as literacy and tools of scholarship, they ensured popular commitment to the changes introduced.

"The Japanese family system," as Dore (1958) points out, is a key concept in the symbolic code of Japanese identity as a people. The family (*ie*) had been traditionally the major unit of social organization, far more important than the individual, and "represented externally by a family head who exercises wide powers of control over family members" (Dore 1958:94).

> In Japan the habit of modelling the structure of social groups outside the family—occupational, educational, recreational, political, artistic, criminal—on the pattern of the family, has been developed with a consistency rare in other societies ... the duty of obedience in these non-kinship structures (*chuu*—loyalty) is equated with filial piety; and the love, the favours, shown by the superior to the inferior are designed [sic] by the same term—*on*—whether it is parent, teacher, master or feudal lord (Dore 1958:94).

Traditionally, family members were expected to be concerned first and foremost with the honor or interests of the *ie*. A person's every action reflected on his or her own honor and also on the honor of the *ie*.

The radical expansion of opportunities for social mobility introduced by the new school system was limited in part by the ability of the student's family to pay the costs incurred. But the new emphasis given to individual achievement as a means of national improvement legitimated personal ambition by traditional moral sanction: giving one's best to the State and bringing honor and wealth to one's family. As in other societies that attempt to incorporate a meritocratic academic system into a highly stratified social structure topped by an entrenched elite, Japan's elite was (and is) disproportionately represented among those who achieved greatest scholastic success. Financial advantage permitted the hiring of private tutors to supplement school instruction, tuition at private schools with excellent records of student success in passing university entrance examinations, and support of students throughout a lengthy academic career. Personal connections were not relevant to the passing of examinations, for these were strictly impartial, but with high examination scores, personal (family) ties could ensure success in securing a suitable occupational position. In any event, the reform demonstrated to most middle class Japanese that ability, not attributes of birth, was the most important factor in socioeconomic mobility. At the same time, ability required nurturing, and academic success was secured as a family enterprise and a family achievement (Dore 1958; Vogel 1968).

Whereas Japan instituted its current school system in a deliberate strategy to offset the possibility of domination by another power, many other societies have developed formal educational systems as a consequence of domination. Ghana's school system is a case in point.

Formerly known as the Gold Coast, this region became part of Great Britain's expanding empire in the nineteenth century. For two centuries before, the coastal societies, whose descendants are members of the present-day nation of Ghana, had been engaged in lucrative trade relations with various European trading companies. The Africans had the military strength, the political know-how, and the trading skills to keep their sovereignty intact. During this time, however, the expansion of trade into a major economic institution[5] and the development of mercantile towns on the coast helped to bring about major changes, both in the social structures of the societies directly involved and in the balances of power with societies further inland. In the towns the trading companies provided some formal education (in English, arithmetic, and Christian catechism) for children of the traders, both African and Euroafrican; these were the earliest Western-style schools.

Partly in an effort to protect the interests of British merchants, Great Britain gradually acquired political control over much of the coastal area, eventually extending hegemony inland to include most of present-day Ghana. The growth of British control was paralleled by the gradual expansion of facilities for formal education, largely under the aegis of missionaries, during the latter half of the nineteenth century.[6] As in England at that time, government support of schooling was quite limited. Instruction was provided by voluntary organizations, mostly missionary societies, with minimal government control and modest financial assistance. The distribution of schools thus was quite uneven, for not all peoples in the territory were equally receptive to missionary activity or schooling. Foster (1965b:86) remarks that "the pattern of distribution of schools closely followed the pattern of differential demand."

These differences in demand Foster attributes largely to the degree of involvement of a given society or community in the economic and political transformations occurring in the country.[7] In areas where the developing exchange economy (and its occupational structure) offered economic opportunities more promising than subsistence farming, interest was likely to be greatest, for the key to most of the new occupations was European-style schooling. Missionary evangelism usually was of little intrinsic interest; it won a hearing through the missions' provision of the desired instruction.

Two themes emerge as central in the evolution of Ghana's school system. First, European-style schooling attracted a growing African clientele because of its relationship to the new European-dominated economic and political structure. Second, the content and orientation of that schooling as it developed over time reflected a series of cultural misunderstandings.

By 1900, British dominion over the Gold Coast was complete. Represented by an administrative bureaucracy, the colonial government itself absorbed a goodly number of schooled Africans into the lower ranks. Particularly in the coastal areas (also the site of the administration), European commercial enterprises dominated the economy and provided additional occupational opportunities. Through the development of cocoa as a cash crop, an increasing number of inland farmers also entered the commercial exchange system. These transformations of the economic and political spheres were ultimately under the control of the British; this was apparent to all participants. It also was clear that access to desirable opportunities was dependent on literacy in English and a formal education. As early as the beginning of the eighteenth century, some Gold Coast Africans had acquired a university education and many more were receiving primary and secondary English-style schooling. The inescapable reality, however, was that Africans were not permitted to rise into occupational posts of the highest ranks; these were the exclusive prerogative of the Europeans. Moreover, as in Japan, the numbers being schooled outpaced the growth of occupational opportunities. This, along with the restrictions imposed by the European monopoly over the most desirable positions, encouraged the emergence of nationalist sentiments for independence from colonial rule.[8]

The second theme, closely related to the first, involves British attitudes toward the colony and its inhabitants, their perceptions of African goals and motivations, and African attitudes and their perceptions of British motivations. Throughout the century and a half in which Western-style schooling was being introduced systematically by the Europeans, there was a fairly constant concern for "adapting" the curriculum to the African context. Certain basics, such as Christian catechism, were universally considered by the Europeans to be indispensable. There nevertheless was widespread sentiment for vocational and technical training rather than "academic" instruction.[9] That this agreed with English school reform at home is seen in their attitude toward the colony. We noted earlier that the English reformers were not seeking to extend academic instruction to the working class. Rather, they advocated differentiation of school curricula for particular social/occupational strata and for particular regions, with early vocational specialization for the stratum constituting the basic work force. The recommendations made for schooling appropriately adapted to the colony focused on farming and animal husbandry (housekeeping for women) and artisan skills. The colony was envisioned as a distant peasantry which, with England's guidance, could become as happy and productive as the working class at home, contributing to the prosperity of the larger society (or empire). When Africans persisted in demanding academic instruction on a par with that given in England, and sought white collar jobs in preference to manual labor, there was much worry that schooled Africans thought themselves above working with their hands and that the dignity of all types of labor had not been emphasized enough. With some exceptions, there was little understanding of the African perspective. It is perhaps not too strong a statement to suggest that the Africans were seen as "uppity" inferiors, imitating their betters and attracted by the glitter of white collar work, with no pragmatic basis for their actions.

As Wallerstein (1964) and Foster (1965b) make abundantly clear, African goals and strategies were pragmatic to the core. The British themselves lavished no great respect on those occupations they were exhorting the Africans to take up; the prestige rankings used by the Europeans were apparent to the Africans. More to the point was the fact that prestige was directly related to the salary and security perquisites of any occupational position. African aspirations were not for prestige per se but for access to the greatest returns on their schooling investment in the form of salary, security of tenure, and influence. What they aspired to was not necessarily what they realistically expected to attain; they were aware of the limits on their alternatives. They viewed European advocacy of vocationalism and "adapted" curricula as attempts to keep Africans in inferior positions and to buttress the European monopoly of power. European-style schooling was in an important sense a symbol of that power, and obstacles to full-fledged European schooling constituted obstacles to achieving power and autonomy.

In Japan, the introduction of the new school system resulted from actions taken by a dominant elite, but their goals included unification of the society as a whole into a strong and independent nation. They adapted the borrowed model to cultural values while providing new options to many, including access to new sources of knowledge and prestige. Theoretically, at least, no ceilings were placed on the ambitions of the able. In Ghana, the new school system was introduced by a dominant elite. In this case, however, the elite itself was fragmented in that it included government administrators, mission groups often in competition with one another, and entrepreneurs seeking particular occupational skills. Nevertheless, to a considerable degree the goals of this elite were shared. They sought modification of cultural values through the introduction of Christianity and Western (especially capitalist) ideology, training which would serve the interests of their home societies through the creation of a skilled labor force, and a continued monopoly of power by the expatriate elite. The actual course of development of the Ghanaian school system therefore mainly resulted from the conflict between the European administrators of the emerging system and their African clientele. Unlike their English and French counterparts, African interest groups had little economic or political power before mobilization of the nationalist movement. While they were in many respects a voluntary clientele, the transformations of the economic, political, and social order brought about by colonial domination created new constraints as well as new options to which they had to adapt.

Now let us consider the way in which these systems operated. We shall see that in neither case did the system which actually developed resemble exactly the vision of its originators. Rather, both were adapted over time to unanticipated, changing conditions.

dynamics of school systems

The Japanese visionaries who set the country on its modern course showed remarkable insight in their academic program, for it melded borrowed structures with traditional values and reinterpreted traditional values in the service of national goals. By imposing compulsory elementary schooling and uniform curricula throughout the country, they sought, as the French reformers had, to develop a national culture. They emphasized "moral education" in the lower grade levels, which was designed to engender a strong sense of national identity and loyalty. Specialized training followed.

The Japanese academic system as an avenue of individual mobility is a highly structured selection mechanism for allocating social roles. Before World War II, six years of compulsory schooling (separate for boys and girls) were followed by an array of schooling options, most of them exclusively for males. A student might terminate his or her education at that point or seek to enter a school that provided terminal general or vocational training. If a student aimed at advanced schooling, however, he faced five years in middle school and three years in high school as preparation for the university. Because each route to further schooling depended on the results of an entrance examination, a child's future chances were established to a considerable degree in the first six years. The most radical constriction of available options took place in the transition from middle school to university preparatory school. Not only was a university degree essential for high status positions in business or government, but universities themselves—as well as all schools leading up to them —were ranked in terms of quality and prestige. Thus certain options were open only to those with degrees from Tokyo University (the top ranked Imperial University) and entry to Tokyo University required first-rate preparation and examination scores. Students at top-ranked high schools had the highest chance of acceptance by Tokyo University, because of their superior training.

The relatively slow development of other universities fixed quite early the characteristic features of academic mobility.[10] Because there were so few available university places for high school graduates, a rigorous examination system was used to select entrants. This, in turn, fostered extreme competitiveness and elitism. Once university education came into full operation, the graduates eventually filled all available niches in the state bureaucracy and in the upper reaches of the private sector. One's career no longer could be guaranteed simply by a university degree. National mobilization for war took many of these graduates. Following the war, however, the inflationary spiral continued, for reforms demanded by American Occupation officials included three additional years of compulsory schooling (all coeducational) and the "democratization" of curriculum and structure. With the increasing availability of higher schooling to meet the mounting numbers of aspirants, universities and other schools of advanced training continued to be both ranked by prestige and quality and distinctly associated with the occupations in which their graduates tended to find positions. But a university degree now became necessary for entry into an increasingly wide range of white collar jobs. In spite of government efforts to equalize the quality of schooling throughout the country, Tokyo University remains the first-ranked, government-supported national university; national universities as a whole out-rank private institutions, and older institutions out-rank newer ones (Passin 1965).

Today in Japan, academic education is by far the most important avenue of social mobility. In its concern for national integrity, until very recently the government has been systematically raising academic standards, thus increasing the competitiveness of the system. Despite government subsidies and grants, much of the financial support of schooling institutions must be borne locally. While fees assessed on parents of school children may be waived in cases of hardship during the first nine years, expenses for books and maintenance can be difficult for the poor to manage. Unless their children show exceptional ability, they may necessarily leave the academic ladder early. In some ways, the burdens on families may be greatest when aspirations for children are highest.

Because admission to secondary schools and universities is determined almost exclusively by state entrance examinations,[11] all efforts must be directed toward maximizing examination scores. Entrance into the best schools at the lowest levels (kindergarten and first grade) helps to assure academic success at succeeding levels; examinations for admission to the elite schools are common even at the beginning level. The next nine to sixteen years involve major investment of family resources, personal and financial.

From the first day in elementary school, children are assigned homework. This is as much a parental demand as a pedagogical choice of teachers. Because the first nine years are preparation for the first major selection phase, children are under ever-increasing pressure to study hard. Teachers regularly recommend to parents that students spend more time studying, to which ambitious parents agree with alacrity (Singleton 1967). Mothers, particularly, become directly involved at this stage, assisting with homework, consulting regularly with the child's teacher, and providing inducements to the child to study diligently. Vogel (1968:54–55) describes the extent of such involvement in a middle class suburb of Tokyo:

> Even if a tutor is hired for brief periods, the ultimate responsibility for helping with (or, from the child's view, hounding about) the homework is the mother's. The work is usually sufficiently difficult so that the child cannot do it without his mother's assistance, and the typical mother [who studied a prewar curriculum] cannot do the work without some preparation . . . Many mothers read their children's books and study other books while the children are in school, and others consult with tutors or school teachers to keep up with their children's work.

Examination performance at middle school and high school admission levels are the key to future choices, for the better the school qualified for on examination at each level, the better training the student can expect for the next examination. In the preceding year, the mother gathers as much information as she can about costs, entrance requirements, and various schools' reputations for placement of their graduates. This is a popular topic of speculation and comparison among all members of the community. Newspapers and other mass media devote considerable space to it, and parents interviewed in three separate field studies were exceptionally voluble (and knowledgeable) about the topic (Dore 1958; Singleton 1967; Vogel 1968). As Rohlen (1977:53) comments, depending solely on the public school to prepare a student for future academic success is "almost unheard of." Tutors, cram schools, a variety of written study guides, practice tests, other information resources, and a heavy dose of parental supervision are all used to supplement. The quality and quantity of private supplementation reflects the financial burden a family can afford, but tutoring is now common in lower income families. A 1975 survey in the city of Kobe indicated that more than half of all sixth-graders received supplementary academic assistance of this sort (Rohlen 1977:53).

Teachers themselves inevitably are servants of this system of intense exam-oriented competition. They train students in test-taking as well as subject matter, and counsel students and parents about the aspirant's chances of success on the examination. In those locales where an individual must specify to which school she or he seeks entrance before taking the exam, accurate assessment of expected performance is critical. This is a judgment for which the teacher is held primarily responsible. If the student chooses too high-ranking a school and fails to perform adequately on the exam, she or he cannot enroll the following year. If the student scales down aspirations and out-performs the entrance requirements of his or her chosen school, the chance for greater eventual success has been lost (Singleton 1967).

In Kobe, according to Rohlen (1977), there is relatively little competition for the better public high schools, because teachers adjust the number of students they direct toward each, according to the number of available spaces. Nevertheless, only half the aspirants to public academic high schools are actually admitted. At the lower-ranking public vocational high schools, competition for admission is particularly fierce, for it constitutes the last available avenue to a public high school diploma. Failing this option, recourse can be had to private (and thus more costly) high schools, night school, or supplementary training to prepare for retaking admissions examinations for more desirable school places.

A great many students do fail examinations. Given sufficient commitment and financial backing, they may resume studies independently, retaking an examination until they achieve their original or a more modest academic objective. (Indeed a Japanese commentator has described the academic ladder as a "6-3-X-3-X-4" system, to represent the years of independent exam study as part of the institution.) To exemplify the institutionalization of the interim years of study for retaking examinations, consider the following figures provided by Dore (1967:139). In 1957, only 28 percent of the successful applicants to top-ranking Tokyo University were taking the exam for the first time; 46 percent were on their second attempt, 18 percent on their third, and 8 percent on their fourth or more. In all state universities in the same year, only 52 percent of the successful entrants were coming straight from high school. In 1975, according to Rohlen, 45 percent of the freshmen enrolled in Tokyo University had retaken admission examinations at least once. This reduction reflects partly the expansion of university enrollments as a whole;[12] in addition it reflects the expansion of cram schools and other private supplements to academic preparation (Rohlen 1977:38n, 54–55).

The Japanese school system can be analyzed as a functional system for allocating social rank, distributing opportunity for upward mobility, and en-culturating young people in the workings of bureaucratic organization. At each successive level of the system, future opportunities for individual students are further defined, often constricted, sometimes expanded. Parental support and investment in student school careers represents an attempt to fend off, minimize, or counter constriction and to maximize the level and rank of academic education their children will achieve. In some respects, the families who are the clients of the school system and the administrators of the system are at odds. While the official goal of the meritocratic system is to equalize opportunity for academic education through national examinations and a network of low cost, high quality public schools at all levels, families are directly concerned with academic outcomes in a highly stratified society where adult social rank correlates closely with academic careers. Thus it is in each family's interest to devote all the resources it can muster to maximization of its children's academic success, a burden which inevitably unequalizes real opportunity for lower income families. This contributes to the perpetuation of the system, even in the face of official attempts at reform. For example, Rohlen cites official reforms in the system of admission to Tokyo public academic high schools, reforms intended to distribute academic opportunity more equitably. The hierarchical ranking of high schools was officially abolished, and with it, application for admission to a specific school on the basis of examination scores. Instead, students were randomly assigned to a high school by computer. If ranking among these schools were eliminated, officials reasoned, students whose families could not afford massive private supplementation might still have an even chance at high quality, low cost preparation for university entrance examinations. Many difficulties beset this reform attempt. Most debilitating was parental response. Even many lower income families interpreted it as a liability in their quest for maximizing their children's academic futures. The result was an upsurge of investment in the private sector. The top-ranked private high schools have always had exceptionally high rates of public university admission; now the better private high schools are also outstripping the public academic high schools in rates of admission. As a result, the economic crunch on lower income families trying to facilitate their children's academic mobility is worse than before (Rohlen 1977:53–70).[13]

The adaptive strategies of families with children enrolled in the Japanese school system can be understood only in light of the larger sociocultural system of which it is a part. We will explore this more fully shortly. Two factors, however, are of particular importance here. First, we must note the centrality of the school system and student careers in the lives of Japanese of all social strata. The school system itself constitutes a highly articulated mechanism for social differentiation. To a far greater degree than in the U.S., discrete career channels and allocation processes are built into the school hierarchy. At each level future options are further restricted. Not only the *level* of education attained but also the relative *rank* of the school(s) in which that level is attained becomes an inextricable part of the individual's social identity, both delimiting access to particular occupations and defining one's rank within them. This is reinforced by the pervasive *belief* in equal academic opportunity in all classes, a belief which persists in spite of the actual economic

advantage of higher income families in providing the necessary private supplementation to public schooling. This belief is associated with the identification of academic achievement with "character, ability, and modern virtue." As
Rohlen (1977:37) puts it,

> The formula ability + hard work = educational achievement = elite status is
> a powerful one in Japan and its power hinges on the assumption that public
> education provides a very high degree of equal opportunity.

Because individual social identities are closely linked to family identities,
family stakes in individual success are very high. For all these reasons, pressure
on individual students is acute. For some the accumulated tension and anxiety
about failure prove too much.

> For those who aspire to the new middle class, the opportunities for mobility
> are highly compressed into one period of life, late adolescence. The intense
> concentration of pressure for finding one's position in life during this brief time
> is undoubtedly related to the fact that Japan is the one country in the world
> where the suicide rate is high in the late teens and early twenties and declines
> during middle age (Vogel 1968:44–45).

In Ghana, as we have noted, schooling was neither state-controlled nor
compulsory at its inception. The school policy of the colonial government
resembled that of Great Britain. Wallerstein has pointed out some of the
ramifications of this policy in a comparison of the British Gold Coast with its
neighbor, the French colony of Ivory Coast. In the latter, schooling was
largely, though not exclusively, in the hands of the state. Because Gold Coast
school facilities were largely in the hands of the missionaries who had their
own interests to further, they had more motivation to meet and to seek to
create demand. This had the positive effect of forcing them, in many cases, to
respond to the African push for solid academic instruction with appropriate
revisions of curriculum. That this was not complemented effectively by the
development of opportunities to use this instruction, reflected the laissez-faire
policy of the British in contrast with the rationalistic policy of the French. As
Wallerstein (1964:39–40) summarizes,

> . . . The British educational policy was haphazard and neglected placement [of
> graduates and other school leavers] . . . whereas the French educational policy
> . . . was more systematic. The French trained only those for whom they were
> willing to find a position in the colonial structure. But the British trained without
> regard for this, and they did not expand the positions available for African
> placement to meet the expanded supply.

As primary schooling became more widespread, provision of secondary
schools became an important goal, especially on the part of schooled Africans

and early nationalists. By the end of the 1800s, four schools gave postprimary instruction; all were completely staffed and supported by Africans (Foster 1965b:102). Within another few decades a model secondary school (Achimota) had been instituted by the colonial government with the goal of developing an indigenous university. In 1948 the first university was established, unmistakably in the British mold. As Ashby (1966:234) observes,

> Clearly the pioneers had no choice but to adopt the pattern of an English university. Equally clearly this was the pattern the Africans themselves wanted. The African intellectual, educated in London or Cambridge or Manchester, would have been indignant at any softening of standards, and substitution of easier options, any cheapened version of higher education.

The insistence on high standards was vindicated, for a decade later, students in East and West Africa took the degree examination of the University of London itself and passed at the same rates (about eighty percent) as the internal candidates of the university.

In 1951 Ghana was granted self-governing status, in 1957, independence. Its legacy from the colonial era, however, included an economy growing far too slowly to absorb the rapidly expanding number of school-educated people. In the early 1960s, the structure of the academic system provided six years of primary school, two to four years of middle school, five to seven years of secondary school, and three years of university. Schools themselves still were not distributed evenly throughout the country, with the predictable consequences of lower access to advanced schooling for some groups. However, financial assistance was increased. The abolition of fees for primary schooling, more government aid to secondary schools, and an increased number of secondary schools of various types have created a ranked system similar in some ways to that of Japan. Although, theoretically, all schools subsidized to some extent by the government are equal in status, since their students follow the same curriculum and prepare for the same public examination, in fact they are generally acknowledged to be of differential merit. Selection for secondary school is based on fierce national competition. While it is ostensibly possible for any middle school student to choose any secondary school in Ghana in listing his or her preferences (in conjunction with the examination), the highest ranked schools may select freely from the best candidates and the remaining schools must divide the remainder. At the same time, more capable students increasingly are taking the secondary qualifying examination earlier in their middle school phase, leaving the latter years of middle school to terminal students.

With the increased level of general academic education, academic qualifications for certain occupations also have risen. Because the available jobs are not expanding at a rate equal to the number of school leavers, even at the secondary level, how students perceive their actual options is of interest. How closely do they reflect the realities of their situation? From interviews and autobiographical essays collected from middle school and teacher training college students in northern Ghana, Grindal (1974) concluded that these students assumed a direct correlation between academic achievement and future success, tempered only by fate. Their expectations, he says, were unrealistically high; in contrast, southern students were much more aware of the limited possibilities for educational and occupational advancement. In opinion surveys of southern Ghanaian students, Foster (1965b) found that the young people clearly distinguished between the kinds of jobs they would like to have and those they expected to get when they left school. He reports that middle school students indicated "an overwhelming interest in skilled trades involving distinct manual activity", and that "a substantial minority . . . express[ed] a preference for entering farming or fishing" (Foster 1965b:207). Despite the modesty of those ambitions, he observes, in all likelihood "a high proportion of these pupils will be unable to find any sort of paid employment however humble it may be" (Foster 1965b:208).

Secondary school students (a far more selected group than middle school students) had more ambitious aspirations, with slight differences apparently due to socioeconomic background and gender. Among boys the largest single block of preferences was for the medical, scientific, and technical professions —45.9 percent, compared to 32.5 percent for girls. Secondary school teaching was aspired to by 14.8 percent of the boys, 22.9 percent of the girls, and higher administrative and commercial posts by 14 percent and 8 percent of boys and girls respectively. Students of more favored socioeconomic backgrounds expressed greater preference for medicine, while their less favored colleagues leaned toward teaching. Asked about their expectations if they were unable to proceed beyond the fifth year of secondary school in which they were then enrolled, their responses changed significantly. Virtually none believed they would be able to obtain professional or semiprofessional employment. This belief was largely independent of socioeconomic background, rural or urban origin, and gender. "There can be little doubt", according to Foster (1965b:282), "that each student perceives his own level of [scholastic] achievement as being the overwhelming factor determining his occupational future."

The relationship between schooling and occupation, then, is seen as fairly direct by Ghanaians, and the school system is a crucial avenue for individual mobility. Students from favored backgrounds have a greater likelihood of being able to achieve maximal schooling:

> Although professional, technical and clerical workers constitute only 7 percent of the Ghana adult male labour force, they supply 34 per cent of our male students and no less than 66 per cent of the female students. Whereas farmers and fishermen, who account for over 62 per cent of the employed adult male population, provide only 37 and 12 per cent of these respective samples (Foster 1965:242).

These figures are reinforced by indications that level of paternal schooling and urban background also increase an individual's academic chances. At the same time, the chances of less favored individuals are by no means slim. Even in the two most highly ranked secondary schools in Ghana, just under one-fifth of the male students had totally unschooled rural parents, although these schools have comparatively high ratios of students from favored backgrounds. Ethnic background, too, is differentially represented in higher schools, primarily because of the uneven distribution of lower schools, historically and today. Yet in this case as well, ethnic groups seem to be moving toward parity, as access to schooling is increased in all parts of the country. It is noteworthy that the most highly ranked schools show the greatest ethnic spread among the students.

This discussion of the dynamics of the school systems of Ghana and Japan reflects in part differences in the types of studies conducted. For example, for Ghana we lack information on the strategies which students and their parents use to cope with the system, since available research has been concerned mostly with system development and operation. For Japan, this type of research is complemented by intensive studies of particular schools and families, allowing us to delineate more specifically the interaction between individuals and the system. The case of Ghana also differs significantly from that of Japan, however, in that Ghana is far more heterogeneous culturally. Composed of a great many distinct ethnic groups, Ghana has been faced with the necessity of developing a nationwide culture and unified society to a degree that Japan has not. Those groups whose cultures rendered them most receptive to European values and those who most successfully adapted themselves to the new economic and political conditions tended to have a distinct edge in access to schooling and to the rewards that schooling potentially bestowed. In the wake of independence these inequalities became volatile political issues, complicated by the economic weakness of the new nation. The financial resources available to Japan through its simultaneous industrialization have not been available to Ghana.

Further differences between the two school systems appear when we consider their relationships to other sectors of society, although again our comparison is limited by the types of research which have been conducted in each country.

school systems in sociocultural context

In Japan, as in Ghana, rising enrollments have reduced the market value of schooling, and this has boosted the qualifications necessary for many occupations. But Japan is considerably more prosperous than Ghana, its economy growing more rapidly. Increasing numbers of Japanese are financially able as well as willing to secure advanced schooling for their children. Dore (1967:139) comments:

> The vast expansion in university education (in 1940 there were twelve, and in 1959 fifty-five, university students per 10,000 population) has not been induced by public provision and state scholarship aid but as a private enterprise response to an effective economic demand.

In 1959, he continues, 64 percent of the students were at unsubsidized private universities and the majority of those at public universities, whose fees are smaller, received no scholarship aid.

Because the examinations which determine the students' futures stress factual information more than innate ability, the active help of the family in preparing for exams is considered essential to success. Dore (1967:141) comments that reluctance "to acknowledge the importance of innate ability in determining academic or any other kind of success" is a traditional element institutionally supported in the schools. He continues:

> Determined application, it is thought, can compensate for most natural deficiencies. It is significant that intelligence tests have never been popular in Japan. They were introduced for university and high school selection after the last war, but by 1955 they were almost everywhere abandoned in favor of tests of academic achievement which the persistent can take year after year until they succeed (Dore 1967:141).

In securing employment after schooling, personal relationships are also important. It is considered a responsibility of the school to assist students in occupational placement, which ties the school system to the economy still more directly than does its function in establishing qualifications. In the lower schools, teachers work with government employment offices to guide those leaving school into appropriate positions (Singleton 1967:40, 50).

> Some elementary school teachers spend weeks of each school year touring factories—preferably those whose owner or manager is a native of their district —to arrange employment for the children about to leave school, or at least to arrange that they be allowed to take the manual aptitude and intelligence tests by which the firm selects its employees. When the textile workers union tries to enforce wage agreements it is to school teachers (through the teachers union) that it sends circulars warning against sending children to firms which underpay (Dore 1967:126)

At the university level, connections are more intricate. While universities are ranked by quality and by the access they allow to the most valued occupations and positions, many also specialize in the economic sector to which they have the closest links. For example, in the late fifties, the two leading private universities, Keio and Waseda, had dominant influence in insurance compa-

nies and department stores (Keio) and in certain newspapers and the construction industry (Waseda) (Passin 1965:294). Degrees and examination scores
serve as the baseline of qualification. Among a score or more of equally
competent applicants, which is given closer scrutiny may depend on more
personal factors, especially *kone* and *batsu* ties.

Kone (personal connection) involves introduction and guarantee; it is the
latter which makes *kone* of special interest to prospective employers. A personal guarantor links his own honor and reputation with the behavior of the
individual guaranteed, ensuring his good behavior. Not only do employers
usually require a personal guarantor of applicants, according to Dore, but such
people "may be sued successfully if the guaranteed employee absconds with
the firm's funds, provided the employer . . . [has sent] the guarantor regular
annual reports on his protege's conduct" (Dore 1967:127). *Batsu* are cliques,
informal and intimate groups based upon personal loyalties. Those formed by
graduates of the same university are of wide ranging significance in economic
and political life. The universities' role in forging *batsu* ties extends from the
placement services it provides, to the network of alumni links assiduously
maintained within the organizations employing graduates. Having been aided
by the university's connections, the new employee is obligated to provide
reciprocal assistance to fellow alumni and to support loyally other *batsu*
members within the organization.

Many observers have commented on the degree to which Japanese society
is composed of tightly knit groups and on the nature of the commitment
individuals feel toward the groups to which they belong, be they family, clique,
or firm. First of all, this principle of organization entails a set of reciprocal
obligations. For example, an individual's loyalty and fidelity to the firm by
which he or she is employed is reciprocated by a lifelong and inclusive responsibility of the firm to the employee. Not all firms and other occupational
groupings are so structured, but the largest and most stable generally are,
especially with respect to the white collar segment of the labor force. Second,
within any such group, interpersonal competition is carefully controlled.
Among strangers, competitiveness is accepted as natural, as on entrance examinations. Once admitted, however, loyalty and friendship are expected to
prevail.

> Once a child is admitted to a school, grades are not given great importance,
> and there is a strong feeling of group solidarity which serves to inhibit competi-
> tiveness between the students. Once in the firm, one's success has been assured,
> and rivalry is kept in bounds by the primacy of seniority which is non-competi-
> tive and the common interest in the success of the firm. Since schools and firms
> do not drop members for poor achievement records, there is no feeling that one's
> remaining in the group depends on another's leaving (Vogel 1968:66).[14]

Batsu within occupational organizations of this type are subject to the constraints of dual commitments. When *batsu* loyalties conflict with the goals of
the whole organization, they are less likely to take precedence.

Singleton (1967) reports on the way in which teachers in an urban middle school related to two occupational groups that claimed their loyalties: their employer (the Ministry of Education) and the Japan Teachers Union (JTU). To the school itself as their main organizational context, teachers displayed considerable dedication. They were expected to be available at any time if called upon to carry out their wide ranging duties, even during their free hours and vacation time. Both the Ministry of Education and the JTU are national organizations, though the latter is represented by a local branch, and the teachers felt notably distant from both. There seemed to be a fairly general feeling that the Ministry, left unchallenged, might attempt to assert excessive control over affairs within the school, such as the content of particular courses. At the same time the JTU, which supposedly represented the teachers in occupational matters as a collective advocate, was seen by many as not representative of their own opinions and as dominated by an aggressive, radical minority.

Some of the misgivings teachers expressed about the JTU reflected a reluctance to align themselves with a trade union; these teachers would have preferred a more professional organization, independent of the trade union movement. The JTU tried to be both. It sponsored an annual, nationwide research meeting for teacher members and financed its own research organization, the People's Education Research Institute. In both these areas, the Ministry established similar, competing activities. Further, the Ministry pressured principals and head teachers to withdraw from the JTU, with mixed success. Although some 90 percent of Japan's elementary and middle school teachers belong to the JTU, the union serves more as a brake on decisions by the Ministry than as a powerful counterforce representing the teachers' interests and perspectives.[15]

Yet the behavioral loyalty the JTU engenders locally is remarkable, considering the fundamental disagreements and even distinct opposition which so many teachers at this school feel toward it. The key seems to lie in the teachers' definition of the local JTU as "their" organization, the group to which they and their colleagues belong. This was the collectivity which most closely symbolized their mutual commitment as a work group. Quitting would have meant disaffiliation from this group, and a risk of losing the mutual support which the group provided.

The implications of schooling and *batsu* ties are perhaps clearest in politics. While the school system is the main channel for access to position and influence, relatively unschooled politicians can gain considerable support from less schooled constituencies or constituents estranged from the establishment. Thus in 1962, 74 percent of the right wing Liberal-Democratic Party members of the Diet (Parliament) were university educated versus 52 percent of the left wing Japan Socialist Party Diet members.

Within the framework of the party, the various batsu had to compete among themselves and make effective coalitions to carry on the practical work of politics, and here the bureaucratic element, with its school-based batsu, played a very important part (Passin 1965:301).

Not only are these *batsu* the basis of intraparty struggles, but they also crosscut party lines. In fact, Passin suggests, they may prevent political polarization from becoming irreconcilable by the implicit strength with which they bind fellow *batsu* members, no matter how divergent their positions.

The higher the formal level of political power, the more significant school-based *batsu* become. At the highest levels, moreover, the more homogeneous they become. For the early 1960s with a conservative government in power, Passin (1965:302–3) gives the following figures:

House of Representatives, February 1962:

> 64.6% of the Representatives had some university education;
> 61.8% had completed university education;
> 37.3% had degrees from the high ranking Government Universities;
> 26.4% had degrees from top ranking Tokyo University.

Cabinet, July 1960:

> Of the twenty members, 70% were alumni of the Government Universities, 65% alumni of the top three universities.
> One member (5%) was a middle school graduate.

Cabinet, July 1962:

> Of the twenty members, 60% were alumni of the Government Universities, 55% alumni of the top three universities.
> Two members were middle school graduates.

The high proportion of alumni from the top three universities in top government posts is more meaningful when we consider another statistic. During the year 1958 (as an example) the top three universities accommodated only 3.2 percent of the total population of universities and colleges (Passin 1965:292). *Batsu,* Passin (1965:292) comments,

> span many fields from the university into business, the professional world, government and politics. A person without a batsu faces Japanese society unsupported, with no one to support him or to help him out in times of crisis. It is one's batsu that opens the closed doors.

In Japan, the school system not only is a selection mechanism for the allocation of social rank and occupation, but it also establishes many direct personal links between participants in the system and participants in other sectors. These links are essential to the operation of the system. Within the framework of a meritocratic academic structure, each individual aspirant is dependent on a network of personal ties for achieving academic goals and the desired rewards with which they are associated. To a degree this is also true in Ghana, but that system is not predicated explicitly on group involvement in each student's scholastic and future occupational career. The continued weight of school-based ties, particularly at the upper levels of academic achievement, is likewise not absent in Ghana. However, the cultural emphasis on loyalty to one's work group and *batsu*, a central feature of Japanese social organization with wide ranging structural consequences, is not paralleled in Ghana (cf. Nakane 1970, Ishida 1971, and Hsu 1975 for further discussion of this aspect of Japanese social structure).

The sociocultural context of the Ghanaian school system, as I have emphasized, must be understood in light of its cultural diversity and the historical conflicts which this diversity has promoted. Ghana's colonial experience and its struggles to create a viable nation despite the economic and political dilemmas it inherited at independence are central to this.

The interrelationship between the Ghanaian school system and opportunities in the economic sector is clear to Ghanaians and outside observers alike. What may be less apparent but more crucial for the future is the inherent conflict between an expanding academic system and a very slow rate of economic growth. As of 1960, only 21+ percent of the employed labor force were paid employees versus 78+ percent characterized as employers, self-employed, or "family workers." In terms of occupations, 4.5 percent were in professional, administrative, technical, or clerical positions, 13 percent in small-scale trading activities, and over 60 percent in farming, fishing, forestry, or hunting. Of the jobs which school graduates tend to seek, probably nearly 60 percent are in the government bureaucracy or in government assisted institutions. As we might expect, given the Ghanaian attitudes delineated above, teachers are paid commensurate with academic qualifications. Primary and middle school teachers who may have no more than normal school training (and in some cases less) are paid relatively poorly and have rather low prestige. Secondary school and university teachers are paid relatively well and have considerably greater prestige. Those teaching in government supported or aided schools are paid better than those in private schools—correlating both with the higher rank accorded government schools and with the overall pattern of competitive remuneration in government employment, a practice established by the colonial government (Foster 1965b).

Before independence, an alternative avenue for the ambitious was in politics, a sphere in which both schooled and unschooled people might acquire influence. Since then students have seemed to be less interested in politics (and in law as a profession). The occupations represented by Africans in the colonial era were, of course, a function of the niches encouraged by the colonial governments. Those occupations of which the British had no need—whether technicians or engineers or chemists—did not therefore constitute available options for aspiring Africans; doctors or lawyers on the other hand could make a living handily. In the postindependence era, in contrast, lawyers particularly not only were less in demand, but they were in fact "in some disrepute precisely because of the[ir] prestigious role in the colonial era" (Wallerstein 1964: 141–2).

This change in aspirations also seems to reflect changes in the nature of politics in the course of securing national independence. To some extent, political activity since independence has become far more institutionalized; the opportunities it represents weighed against its costs (including a decided lack of security) may not be as attractive. In addition, militant nationalist politics just prior to independence involved strata of the population largely ignored in the nationalist efforts of an earlier school-educated elite. Increasingly, support was drawn from the new lower-middle class, peasants, workers, and market women. The political party (Congress People's Party, or CPP) in whose name independence was finally secured did not need intellectuals, either to build the party or to govern the country and made this rather clear. "Thus rejected," Wallerstein (1964:62) comments, "this younger generation [of intellectuals] went either into political withdrawal or into the Opposition; but they were effectively kept, and in turn kept themselves, out of power."

Politics and schooling are necessarily interconnected in that the school system is dependent on government subsidy. The structure, administration, and financing of the system thus is potentially subject to political debate. Particularly in a heterogeneous society in which many different groups seek to protect their respective interests, the schools, as the main source of social and economic mobility, are an obvious focus of widespread scrutiny. In Ghana, the historic differences in the availability of schooling, combined with ethnic rivalries, created a natural basis for the suspicion of discriminatory practices. Similarly, the early concentration of administration and commerce on the coast, which encouraged concentration of services in the southern part of the country, contributed to persistent inequities against which politicians work on behalf of their constituents.

To some extent, possible bases for conflict have been reduced by using state examinations to select students for futher schooling, and by placing priority on the expansion of the system to ensure students equal access to school places. Even so, controversies over those examinations, over curricula, over requirements for each level of schooling, and over long-term priorities continue to rage. The case of the University of Ghana exemplifies the types of problems that can arise.

As organized by its first administrative head, David Balme, the University College of the Gold Coast (as it then was known) was run by a system of internal government patterned after that of the University of Cambridge.

Within the college the experiment was successful. It had one surpassing merit: it involved every member of the academic staff, once he had reached a modest level of seniority, in the affairs of the college. . . . Both among Africans and among expatriate staff (most of whom had no administrative experience in British universities) this pattern of government evoked loyalty to the idea of university autonomy and responsibility for maintaining it (Ashby 1966:309).

Unfortunately this organizational scheme bypassed the college council, a predominantly lay board which originally had been mandated to govern. In so doing the college also sacrificed the reciprocal function of the council: that of translating and defending the work of the college to the public, providing the public relations necessary to root the college in public good will.

In 1957, Balme's successor proposed a new system of governance that divided authority between a predominantly lay council and a predominantly professorial senate, and reduced the influence of nonprofessorial staff members. After stormy debates with the academic staff, most of whom preferred the earlier system, he revised the proposal and submitted it to the government for approval. It was rejected. In its place a scheme was sent to the Parliament by the Prime Minister. This plan diversified control in a new way, while providing a framework within which substantial internal university autonomy could be preserved. The measure called for a governing body composed of four academic members from the university (two below professorial rank), one from an African university outside Ghana, and one from a non-African university, plus seven members (filling various roles) all of whom were to be appointed or approved by the University Chancellor, and, finally, the Chancellor himself. The key element was that the Prime Minister was to be the University Chancellor.

The new constitution took effect in 1961, but it had been preceded, and perhaps to a degree precipitated, by earlier skirmishes between the government and the university administration. At root, the difficulty lay in the clash between the complex needs of a nation struggling to achieve national unity and autonomy, and the cloistered, privileged position assumed by the university staff to be essential to a center of higher learning. The traditions of academic freedom and academic autonomy are deeply embedded in Western culture, though sometimes observed in their breach. Their utility for the growth of knowledge and the effective expansion of human intellectual limits often has been cited. Yet an argument can be made that a nation may be unable to afford this luxury, in spite of the earlier acceptance of corollary values from colonial culture. The abrogations of university autonomy that ensued can be seen simply as the acts of an aggressive, shortsighted dictator, but that would be to ignore the complexity of the task which confronted the Ghanaian government on behalf of their newly independent country, a nation by fiat.

Three examples of government interference are cited by Ashby (1966:329–330): (1) dictation of lowered entrance standards for students, including the abolition of English as a compulsory language; (2) appointment by the government, independent of university approval, of new faculty members and of change of rank for incumbent faculty; and (3) transfer of one of the departments from the University of Ghana in Accra to the Kwame Nkrumah University of Science and Technology at Kumasi. In the first case, the government argued that since there then were more places at the university than could be filled by available students, there was no justification for the stringent selection process represented by university entrance examination. Given the urgency with which young people were seeking schooling at all levels, the political import of this decision is obvious. The symbolic significance of Western-style schooling always had included the idea of access to the foundations of economic success and power, for it clearly underwrote the European monopoly in those domains. While African insistence on European standards for African schooling in the colonial era was critical to securing respect for their equality, in the era of emergent nationhood other considerations became relevant. The African government had to demonstrate its own independence from the "colonial mentality" afflicting many African intellectuals of an earlier era. It had to demonstrate that it was more responsive to the needs of the people. And it had to develop a sense of unity and national commitment in a population with diverse cultures and rankling rivalries. Although English might serve as a common language that favored no single group, it also was the symbol of the colonial yoke so recently shed. Finally, while the British standards of quality for university admission were effective in developing superior scholars, it can be questioned whether this was a high priority need for a nation struggling with the elemental problems of political and economic survival. As Wallerstein (1964:143) has pointed out, the expansion of academic opportunities often provokes complaints by members of school-educated classes about the deterioration of quality in the school system.

> This complaint . . . heard wherever education spread . . . was part of a reflex of rank perpetuation among the educated. It was to some extent a true evaluation. It was ultimately a question of weighing social priorities. Or as Abdoulaye Wade said, "The problem of education in Black Africa [was] not scholastic, it [was] political."

In the second case cited, that of appointment independent of university approval, two factors seem of particular importance. One is that the severity of the "offense" as perceived by the university was related directly to the assumption of its staff that they had a privileged status as an intellectual elite. Their cloistered disregard of the lay council was one demonstration of this, from the lay point of view. The other is that the appointments made were efforts to increase Africanization of the university faculty, again an important symbolic statement as well as an attempt to divert resources and influence into African rather than expatriate European hands.

In the third case, the transfer of the agriculture department from Accra to Kumasi had several pragmatic advantages. Most importantly, it helped decentralize school services, and it established a school of agriculture in the heart of agricultural country rather than on the commercial and urban coast. Historically, all services had been concentrated on the coast, particularly in the vicinity of Accra. By moving this department from the capital, the government both pursued its policy of parity in the distribution of academic access and acknowledged the importance of regions beyond Accra. Again it helped in the development of national unity.

The overall wisdom of these actions may be disputed. But to do so we must understand their context and their implications for the participants. By placing this particular example against the backdrop of the larger society, we can see more clearly the complexity of interrelations between this school system and the society of which it is a part.

The two school systems we have discussed have many structural similarities. Both are organized as an integrated sequence of stages, based upon a state-supervised curriculum and marked by objective, universalistic criteria of successful attainment in the form of examinations. Both are designed to encourage mobility, both within the system and in the larger society, on grounds of individual scholastic achievement rather than family class status, ethnic heritage, or other ascribed criteria. Neither is fully successful in this, but active attempts have been made in both societies to maximize the equality of access. In both systems, alternative routes have been built into the system, some leading to termination at medial levels, others proceeding to advanced schooling. Nonacademic forms of schooling seem to be more developed in Japan than in Ghana, although this disparity may change as Ghana achieves a stronger, more diversified economy.

In both cases, foreign models have been adapted to indigenous conditions. It is these conditions and the strategies that have been used to cope with them that account for the major differences between the two. We know far too little about the conditions that influenced the development of the Poro system of schooling to analyze it in this way, but available evidence suggests that it was probably an outgrowth of the Poro elite's increasing power, used in large measure as a means of maintaining the sociocultural order. The new Japanese school system was intended to serve this purpose in that, with industrialization, it constituted a set of adaptive strategies designed to counter imminent foreign domination and secure Japan's autonomy as a nation. Thus the conditions to which it was adapted included the international environment with which Japanese society had to deal. The conditions within Japan which influenced its development and modification, included at its inception a highly stratified social order, a major change in political regimes, the simultaneous development of a new type of economy, and a complex of traditional beliefs, ideas, and values. While conditions later changed in unanticipated ways, especially with Japan's defeat in World War II and the subsequent American occupation, the original introduction of the system was marked by far-sighted planning and deliberate integration into the existing sociocultural context. Many features of the contemporary system, such as the nature and function of *batsu* ties and the pervasive significance of social rank, reflect deeply rooted patterns of the larger society and thus continuity with the past.

The contemporary Ghanaian school system did not result from planning of this kind, nor was it at inception an indigenous outgrowth of the societies which comprised the Gold Coast. Rather, it was a tool of foreign cultural, political, and economic domination. The course of development which led to the modern system, however, was influenced strongly by the strategies adopted by Africans to cope with the changing conditions brought about by colonial domination. As a union of many diverse societies, Ghana has had to develop programs for scholastic development that would unify its peoples into a viable and stable nation, by minimizing ethnic and class privilege within the school system. But at the same time, it has had to deal with such problems as language, ethnic, and class rivalries, disparities in the distribution of scholastic institutions, and inadequate financial resources, which were its inheritance upon independence. Whereas Japan was able, in large measure, to protect its cultural heritage and national autonomy by anticipating domination and building an economic base that insured its relative independence, the peoples of the Gold Coast could counter domination only by adopting the system of the foreign elite in a more literal form than that elite was prepared initially to accept.[16] Following independence it became possible to adapt the system more directly to the exigencies of Ghanaian sociocultural conditions, as we have seen in the example of the university.

In the societies discussed in this chapter, as in all others, educational transmission is not effected exclusively through schooling or other formally structured institutions. Interpersonal relationships outside of such institutional settings and mass media, for example, are important adjuncts which may reinforce or modify learning which takes place within settings explicitly recognized as educational. In the case of Japan, socialization patterns within many families, according to Kiefer (1970), are highly congruent with patterns characteristic within schools. Moreover, the intense family involvement in student careers closely intertwines students' school and home experience. Kiefer argues further that schools bridge the educational activity of the family and that of the bureaucratic peer groups into which university-educated adults move upon graduation. Others (e.g., Ishida 1971) have argued that there is severe discontinuity between studenthood and postschool experience, in that the values characteristic of each realm are distinctive. That both positions are correct in some respects simply points up the complexity of the relationship between the two spheres. The congruence or lack of it between schools and subsequent work life as contexts of individual experience depend on the types of school and worklife involved. Middle class professionals or white collar employees, for instance, are likely to differ in this respect from blue collar employees or self-employed artisans. At the same time, we might expect mass media, widely available and widely used in Japan, to counter this differentiating tendency. We need to ask to what extent people of different strata and occupational niches occupy common "media worlds" and to what extent differences in their experiences apart from mass media affect their perception and interpretation of these common events. Education in workplaces, both formal apprenticeship and on-the-job training in white collar jobs, must be compared with that provided in schools and families (cf. DeVos 1975a, Rohlen 1974), and these with education in other groups from voluntary associations to institutions such as hospitals and prisons. A full analysis of the educational system in a community or society would require that we take all of these and their interaction into account.

In the next chapter a range of educational forms in addition to schools will be examined. Our focus will be on process rather than systemic structure, but in each case either analytic angle can be applied.

notes

1. On the community level, Barker and Wright (1955) attempted part of this by mapping the total set of learning environments of a child in a midwestern town.

2. As John Singleton (personal communication) points out, certain types of knowledge may be transferred through formal instruction outside the family, not because parents are themselves insufficiently informed but because they are not considered *appropriate* as teachers of the skills/ knowledge in question. In Japan, he notes, tatami mat makers do not instruct their own children in the trade, for parents, it is believed, cannot be severe enough with their children to be good teachers. The children are sent to learn the trade from another mat maker and then return to work in the family business. A similar assumption prevailed in Poro schooling, to be discussed shortly. Sex education in U.S. schools is an example of the variable of propriety as well, but less clear cut in its articulation. Incorporating sex education in the school curriculum has been advocated as a response to its frequent absence from the family educational curriculum. Many parents contend, on the other hand, that *schools* are inappropriate agencies of transmission as well. One of the underlying disagreements, of course, is whether sex itself *should* be a topic of education, of deliberate, systematic transmission; related to this is the question of whether the "information" exchanged in a child's peer group constitutes education in this sense.

3. Cohen (1971) argues that the development of schools correlates with the development of state-organized societies, that "schools do not emerge historically prior to the creation of states" (Cohen 1971:39). His position rests on a very different definition of schooling than mine: "an institution with specialized personnel, permanent physical structures, special apparatus (of which texts are an important part), formal and stereotyped means of instruction, a curriculum, and rationally defined manifest objectives." This definition obviously orients analysis and explanation in rather specific directions, different from those to which my definition leads.

4. Researchers in the 1930s and 1940s were told that Poro schooling at that time generally lasted from several months to three years depending on the district, and that formerly it had lasted about three to eight years.

5. The brief summary of early Gold Coast history presented here simplifies a rather complex period. A major factor in the early development of trade was European exchange of manufactured goods, including guns, for African slaves, captured by coastal societies from inland communities.

For a useful discussion of the impact of this feature of European-African trade relations on the growth of European domination in West Africa, see Carnoy (1974:113–141). Robinson and others (1961) is also useful for tracing the evolution of European attitudes toward Africa.

6. With the official abolition of the slave trade early in the 1800s, Britain's economic interest in West Africa was reduced, but the prospect of this region as a continuing market for British goods sustained mercantile involvement. Missionaries earlier had come to *persuade* Africans to become Christian and "westernized" (in the mold of free-trade capitalists). In the face of armed resistance from Africans, both missionaries and traders called on Britain for military aid in support of their respective endeavors, thus drawing Britain more actively into territorial domination and sanctioning the role of both missionaries and traders as agents of colonial power (Carnoy 1974).

7. It is pertinent to note that although these transformations were dominated by the Europeans, they were by no means solely responsible for them. Cocoa, for instance, was introduced in 1879 by an African laborer from Fernando Po and gradually spread throughout the inland forest region. Because Europeans presented a market for cocoa, it was adopted fairly widely by local farmers as a cash crop. Ashanti, a society in the heart of the cocoa region, had a long commercial tradition with corollary emphases on individual achievement, profit, and differential privilege; thus Western commercial culture was not especially alien to members of this society, and they took advantage of the new opportunities more readily than members of other groups less comfortable with European ways. At the same time, Ashanti strongly and successfully resisted European attempts at establishing trade relations for several decades, until rather late in the 1800s. Thus Ashanti accommodation was based partly on cultural factors and partly on the loss of its former socio-political autonomy (cf. Foster 1965:126–127).

8. Resistance to European incursion and occupation had been widespread earlier (Crowder 1971), but it was not mobilized as "nationalist" resistance prior to the development of a European-educated elite who acted as "translators" and coordinators (Carnoy 1974:143).

9. See Carnoy (1974:123–132) for a somewhat different perspective on this.

10. In 1869 when the new regime began, Tokyo was the sole university. Passin (1965) provides the following table of university growth, indicating total enrollment as well.

	Schools	Students
1887	1	235
1892	1	563
1897	2	1,974
1907	3	6,272
1917	4	7,291
1927	37	34,633
1937	45	49,546
1947	49	87,898
1948	64	(no information)
1952	220	399,513
1957	231	564,454
1960	245	626,421

(Revised from Passin 1965:284)

11. Rohlen (1977:46) indicates that high school entrance procedures vary locally. Some cities such as Tokyo have attempted to introduce reforms which would effectively reduce hierarchical ranking among public high schools, by randomly assigning students to schools within their residential district. This adds to examination performance new factors in high school entrance. Also, of course, *admission* must be complemented by financial ability to manage resulting fees and expenses.

12. Narita (1975) points out that the expansion of university places over the last century has been largely through diversification of *types* of training available at the university level. The first modern public universities provided and still provide personnel for the top level positions in any profession. Expansion of the university system near the turn of the century and in the early 1900s was a response to the increasing demand for second rank professionals. The most recent expansion is largely growth in provision for a third rank. As Rohlen (1977) says, Japanese stratification tends not toward the development of self-conscious classes but toward "wafer thin social strata." The universities, of course, are but one component of the school system's contribution to this pattern.

13. For a discussion of change and obstacles to change at the university level, see I. Hall (1975).

14. In a footnote Vogel adds:

This pattern appears to begin at an early age. Miss Kazuko Yoshinaga who taught in middle-class kindergartens in both Japan and the United States reported that in kindergartens American children are much more openly competitive than Japanese children. Even about matters of age and size, Japanese kindergarten children rarely engage in comparisons and are less interested in who is bigger and older (Vogel 1968:66n).

15. Rohlen (1977) indicates that the JTU, many local teachers, and public school officials, at least in Tokyo, have a common interest in the reforms cited earlier. This may reflect a change over time or simply a difference in locale.

16. Ishida (1971) points out that Japan was able to mediate foreign influences in part by translating foreign publications into Japanese. Today translation of publications from Europe and North America is extremely rapid. Japanese versions of newly published foreign works are often available within a few months of their original publication abroad. Ghana, on the other hand, was and is faced with a multiplicity of indigenous languages among its population. Because of British domination, the postindependence need for national integration, and its continued dependency on other nations (cf. Carnoy 1974), Ghana has lacked a similar source of continuing identity as a nation.

SIX

EDUCATION AS PROCESS

The study of educational process as outlined in the fourth chapter has three main analytic components: cognitive maps and strategies, social identities and roles of participants, and communication. Intimately interconnected in the actual course of educational transactions, these components have been distinguished conceptually in order to clarify the kinds of factors that affect such transactions.

Cultural ideas about knowledge, knowledge transmission, participants in the transmission process, and their mutual role-relationships contribute directly to the patterns of educational transaction characteristic of a particular community. Interpretation of past experiences and present events and anticipation of future ones are influenced by cultural schemes of understanding. These are equally important to the behavioral strategies participants utilize. The degree of congruence between the interpretive schemes of participants thus has important consequences for the process of knowledge transmission.

Whether effected directly through face-to-face interaction or through the mediation of objects and secondary forms of communication such as printing, film, and electronic devices, educative communication is embedded in an historical and sociocultural context. Tutelage, formal or informal, always takes place within a more encompassing social structure and complex of events that serve to frame the educational transaction itself. They may reinforce transmissions by congruence with lessons learned in other settings, or they may modify, discredit, or limit the relevance of transmissions through incongruence with lessons learned elsewhere.

In our examination of educational process, we will use a succession of vantage points, focusing on particular aspects of transmission transactions. In this way the significance of the components and their mutual interplay will become clear. The scope of analysis in each case will be limited by data available, but it will indicate the kinds of data necessary for fuller understanding of educational process. Let us begin with teaching and learning as cultural categories and behavioral strategies.

teaching and learning

Instructional strategies are predicated on conceptions of knowledge and of the nature of learners and learning, as well as on objectives to be achieved. As noted earlier, both instructional and learning strategies may favor particular sensory modes and cognitive orientations. Among the Abelam people of New Guinea, our first example, graphic art is highly valued and distinctively elaborated. Painting (i.e., two-dimensional use of color and form) has special ritual meaning, so that it is a particularly important area of knowledge transmission. Painting is a sacred activity, done only by men and only within the ceremonial context of the men's ritual organization. We will take up later how painting as an activity is learned; for the present we are concerned with how children learn the conventions of Abelam aesthetics and the symbolic meanings of painting designs, knowledge needed for full participation in adult life.

According to Forge (1970), two channels of knowledge transmission are central to learning "how to see" Abelam art. One is the observable environment of daily life; the other is the sequence of male initiation ceremonies which extend in phases from early childhood through the next twenty or thirty years of life.

Everyone can see the brightly painted facades of a ceremonial house. With its foreground, this is the center of an Abelam hamlet as well as the focal point of ceremonial activity. Against the dull ground and grey thatch sides of nearby houses, it is vibrantly noteworthy and noticed. One of the main stylistic features of Abelam painting is the use of several polychrome lines to outline all the principal designs. Although the painting is supposed to be secret, restricted to ceremonial contexts and fully initiated men, children playing outside adult supervision displayed this outlining style in their doodles in the dust. This much was learned from simple observation. The children did not attempt to reproduce the designs or motifs depicted on the facade. When given paper and paint by the researcher, they readily produced polychromatic designs multiply outlined; they much preferred white paper because the colors showed up better. Real artists, in contrast, were unable to use white paper, for their technique involved the subtler principle of outlining the whole design in white against a ground of black or grey. The children had picked up bits of the conventional ways of seeing form in two dimensions but they had not yet acquired the full graphic code. Despite their familiarity with graphic, two-dimensional design, even Abelam adults were unable to discern the forms we see in photographs without formal instruction or without having the form framed with dark outlines. Forge argues that their visual perception differs from ours in that "they have very definite and limited expectations about what they will see on any two-dimensional surface made to be looked at," expectations which differ markedly from ours (Forge 1970:287).

In addition to this informal learning of the graphic code of two-dimensional design, boys learn early in life to regard painted objects "as of great and mysterious importance" (Forge 1967:288). Display of these objects is the focus of successive initiation ceremonies, and just before they are presented to the boys' view, the boys are beaten. Thus each viewing is preceded by a painful ordeal. No verbal interpretations of the painted objects are ever given the initiates beyond naming the designs. Indeed it seems that no direct verbal translation of the visual code is possible. Rather the design elements "are assembled into harmonious compositions, which appear to act directly on the beholder without having to be named" (Forge 1967:290). Varying interpretations of compositions are possible and equally legitimate. "Abelam art is about relationships, not things." By repeated exposures of males to quantities of graphic art in the course of a lengthy sequence of initiation ceremonies, young men are taught to see the art effectively: "not so that [they] may consciously interpret it but so that [they are] directly affected by it" as a powerful ritual statement (Forge 1967:290).

This instructional strategy relies predominantly on nonverbal modes of instruction and learning. To a considerable extent, instruction in artistic production is also nonverbal in mode, though it may be accompanied by verbal exchanges and commentary. While adherence to the aesthetic code is expected and required for ritual efficacy, it is acknowledged that artists have recognizable styles. Thus a limited degree of innovation is acceptable within the framework of the formal conventions.

Among the Kpelle of Liberia, nonverbal and verbal modes are combined to effect the transmission of highly valued knowledge. Instruction emphasizes the transmission of conventional wisdom and discourages question or challenge. Gay and Cole (1967:16) remark:

> The child must never question those older than himself. If he is told to do a chore in a certain way, he must do it in that way and no other. If he asks "why?" or acts in a manner unsanctioned by tradition, he is likely to be beaten.

In everyday activities, Gay and Cole observed, children receive little direct instruction; rather they are "expected to watch, learning by imitation and repetition" (Gay and Cole 1967:16). In Poro schools, while much instruction was direct, it was even more heavily buttressed by the unquestioned authority of the elders. Even in Western-style schools, rote learning seems to be the typical instructional objective. Acquisition of specific information takes precedence over instruction in general principles capable of flexible application. General principles, insofar as they are learned, must be inferred by the individual learner. According to the researchers, learning associated with one context tends not to be used spontaneously in another context, particularly where learning content has no clear connection to the daily experience of Kpelle life. Mathematics, the main example with which Gay and Cole were concerned, is learned by children largely as a set of ritual phrases (like "three times eight is twenty-four") of use only in pleasing the teacher. Little or no understanding of reasons underlying the memorized information is imparted or received.

In village schools of Upper Burma, Nash found similar instructional strategies in use. As he (1970:161) comments:

> The method of teaching is fitted to its tasks: to stuff the mind, to train the memory, and to inculcate a respect for received wisdom. Students are rewarded for feats of memory, for long letter-perfect recitations, for knowing the pat answers to standard questions.

This type of instruction is better suited to the preservation of sociocultural continuity than to the encouragement of innovation. More importantly it raises the question of which domains of cultural knowledge are defined as subject to systematic transmission and the place of such domains in the larger cultural repertoire. Humans could not function effectively within their complex living conditions were their knowledge totally constrained by conventional wisdom.

Everywhere some types of knowledge are subject to more systematic inculcation than others; some types are more valued than others. Often, though not always, these are the same. Abelam sacred art is knowledge of this sort, for not only is it central in ritual organization but the ritual organization is an important feature of all males' lives, demanding their involvement from their earliest years. Though less dramatic in form than Abelam initiation, Kpelle and Burmese educational strategies are similarly congruent with dominant values. The most important aspects of cultural knowledge in both societies may be summed up as "precedents," in much the same sense as we use the term in Western legal practice.

Among the Kpelle, what is most important is that children learn the proper relationships among community members: males and females, young and old, clients and specialists, subjects and authorities. Technical skills are learned informally:

> The child spends all his days watching until at some point he is told to join in the activity. If he makes a mistake he is simply told to try again. He is not

punished for mistakes unless he willfully rebels against the traditional procedure, or if the error is very costly (Gay and Cole 1967:16).

The most important realm of knowledge is that of the abstract principles of social behavior and of the organization of the natural world. While this realm is built on assumptions quite different from our own, given these premises, certain courses of action logically follow. A good deal of Kpelle social life is regulated by the collective wisdom of the elders who are most competent in the body of cultural knowledge crystallized in precedents. Individual knowledgeability is associated with the highly valued attributes of verbal skill and talent in argument.

In court cases, this type of knowledge is especially noticeable. Presided over by a chief and council of elders, the court hears from each party a case supporting his or her own actions and condemning the actions of the opponent. Drawing on precedents, each party attempts to present his or her case as an exemplar of "proper" Kpelle behavior, in contrast to that of the other party. The chief listens, questions, and comments on the proceedings. In the end, as the Kpelle view it, the person who wins the case will be the one who can outwit the other in producing an argument in accord with tradition and unanswerable by the other in terms of appropriate precedents.

Definitions of appropriate characteristics of teachers and learners are closely tied to definitions of appropriate content of transmission, and both affect the strategies developed by participants to cope with transmission processes. Since knowledge of various types always is transmitted selectively to selected types of learners, assumptions about differences in their appropriate nexus warrant careful attention. Age is one obvious differentiating attribute which is associated with types of knowledge appropriately transferred, favored forms of transmissions, and strategies utilized by both instructors and learners.[1] Gender is another (cf. for example Draper 1975, Nihlen 1975). Among the rural Guajiro of Venezuela, adolescent girls are isolated and instructed in weaving and womanhood. The teacher must be a mature married woman, of impeccable social reputation; her social identity must include acknowledged credentials both as "a perfect hostess and wife" and as an excellent weaver. Acquisition of these skills, particularly in weaving, is important to the student's future social identity and security. Weaving constitutes not just an economically valuable skill in Guajiro society but also a special, highly valued domain of knowledge available only to women. The productive skills learned by males, in contrast, may also be performed by women (Watson-Franke 1976). Abelam art represents an exclusively male domain equivalent in many ways to Guajiro weaving. Kpelle rhetorical skills, while displayed predominantly by men, are accessible as a domain of cultural knowledge to both males and females. In Japan, the academic education of women is generally much lower in priority than that of men; very few women are represented at the higher levels of the school hierarchy.[2]

In Puluwat, a seafaring Micronesian society, the most highly valued realm of knowledge and skills is that of navigation, followed by boat building. Both domains are open only to males. Puluwat presents an interesting contrast to Kpelle and Upper Burma, for it has been exceptionally receptive to innovations of various kinds. While Puluwatans value the integrity of their culture and their way of life, they readily modify particular practices when experiment shows them preferable alternatives.[3]

In a population of about 400 people, only a half-dozen men are considered master navigators. Any male may choose to apprentice himself, though most often those who do are sons or relatives of navigators. Aspirants judged unlikely to succeed are often discouraged from trying. Even so, of those who do enter training, less than half complete the course and achieve eventual recognition as master navigators. Some complete training but never acquire the skill and precision necessary to make long trips alone.

As a systematic body of knowledge, navigation includes both theory and techniques. The corpus is precise, specific, and conservative; a navigator cannot afford to take unnecessary risks. It is also very extensive, requiring a long-term mutual commitment by teacher and student. Training has three stages. First, from their earliest years children play on boats and every man travels on canoes. Every aspirant therefore will bring a great deal of informal learning to his apprenticeship (cf. Gladwin 1970:128). Second, formal instruction begins on the land with schooling under the tutelage of a senior navigator. Finally, after mastery of this phase has been demonstrated to the teacher's satisfaction, further instruction takes place at sea as well as on land.

Classes, often located in the boathouse, are taught to one or several students of varying ages. Some subsystems of the full corpus of professional knowledge have separate names and are taught as discrete courses in the larger curriculum, while others are considered more general knowledge and are taught wherever they happen to fit in. In either case

> great masses of factual information must be committed to memory. This information is detailed, specific, and potentially of life-or-death importance (Gladwin 1970:128–29).

Fundamental to the whole system are the stars, "specifically the points or directions where certain stars rise and set around the horizon" (Gladwin 1970:130). These are taught with the aid of diagrams drawn with pebbles on the ground. This learned, the student proceeds to memorize star courses to be used to sail from one island to another. For commonly made journeys alone, this entails at least 55 one-way courses (110 round-trip). To satisfy his tutor, a student must be able to start with any island in the known ocean and rattle off the appropriate sequence of stars from there to all other islands. These are not memorized simply as mnemonic chains, for a navigator will be able to add

substantial additional information about sailing on that route while he indicates the star course.

After the star courses have been learned, or even at the same time, the
student is taught about special conditions affecting travel on each of the routes,
the system for keeping track of distance traveled, how to read waves, navigation in storms and upwind, techniques for finding hidden passes through the
reefs, weather forecasting, and sea life (an aid in location determination).
Again all of this must be committed to memory, although some of the information is used rarely, if ever, by any given navigator. The masters thus know star
courses for islands to which they have never sailed, and to which no one may
have sailed for the past several generations.

After the first stages of intensive learning, instruction is given both at sea
and on land, for many principles and skills can be learned only when on a
voyage. While some skills are relatively easy for people born to a seafaring life,
others are difficult, particularly judging direction and speed, skills upon which
accuracy of navigation depends. When the student has demonstrated his competence to his tutor's satisfaction, he will be considered a full-fledged navigator. Only after he has acquired both experience and seniority may he be
admitted to the ranks of the masters, the most prestigious role in Puluwat
society.

Canoe building, a craft often mastered also by navigators, is taught by
apprenticeship alone.[4] The early stages are not as systematically structured as
navigation schooling.

> A young man who wishes to learn asks one of the active canoe-builders for
> instruction. If the latter is willing and the pupil apt they work together until the
> young man is ready to start building canoes on his own. This may take several
> years. Often the apprenticeship begins with the younger man watching the older
> at work, asking questions, helping at first only with routine chores and then
> gradually with tasks which require increasing degrees of skill (Gladwin 1970:71).

The informal relationship between student and teacher becomes formalized
when the apprentice begins to construct his first sailing canoe under the
supervision of the master. The most important test here is the shaping of the
hull, for it is the hull that ultimately determines how the boat will move
through the water and how it will handle. Rigging and other secondary structures are seen as fairly standardized and modifiable after a canoe is in use. If
the student's work is approved, he becomes a master in his own right and may
build boats without further instruction or supervision. Scarcely one man in
five, however, achieves mastery.

> Every aspect of a canoe's performance is determined in the last analysis by the
> contour of the hull. Yet the distinctions are too fine and the various contours too
> complexly interrelated for them to be taught in any other way than by example,

or learned except by observation and experience. Not everyone is equal to this challenge (Gladwin 1970:79).

While the corpus of knowledge involved in navigation and boat building is conservative, it is not closed. When experimentation or newly available items make improvements possible, these are incorporated. Until traditional knowledge is proved useless or wrong, however, it is retained, for successful navigation may require every possible aid under difficult weather conditions.

Instructional strategies are related closely to concepts of types of knowledge and the relationship of that knowledge to the larger sociocultural context. They also are related to conceptions of learners and teachers and their mutual roles. As we noted earlier, the authoritarian tutorial role endured by Jewish *shtetl* students acquiring the rudiments of Hebraic literacy is transformed at later levels to the role of fellow scholar and guide. Instructional strategies likewise change, reflecting changes in the definition and evaluation of the knowledge being transmitted. Literacy is acquired through rote recitation. While prerequisite to further studies, it is not itself of high cultural value. Intensive study of the Torah and commentaries is the most highly valued activity in the community, and the relationship between more experienced and less experienced scholars is one of mutual respect. Authority is not to be challenged lightly, but no scholar's interpretation is immune to reasoned counterargument.

On Puluwat the role-relationship between navigator and apprentice also is one of mutual respect. Effective teachers must have the ability and patience to transfer and test repeatedly the student's grasp of a sizable system of knowledge. Successful students must have the memory, observational, and motor skills to diagnose accurately and to respond to a wide range of navigational circumstances. Successful canoe builders must have exceptional dexterity and manual precision, and accurate visual judgment and extensive knowledge of the forces which water will exert on the hull, in order to shape it into its proper contours. Students who do not complete training do not lose respect, but they lose the opportunity for the extra prestige of master navigators and builders. Failure is never discussed publicly nor is reference made to any individual having failed.

Kiefer (1970) describes the role of Japanese teachers as very similar to that of Japanese mothers: both serve as facilitators of student academic achievement through supportive but insistent prodding and assistance. Neither serves directly as an evaluator of student success, although in both cases student performance on qualifying examinations reflects on the effectiveness of their instructional roles.

Among the Kpelle, as we have noted, teachers are authorities to be obeyed by students without question or challenge, because of their superior wisdom and knowledge. A similar role-relationship in Upper Burma has been described by Nash. The Burmese cultural definition differs in many ways from that of Kpelle, but structurally it is much the same. Most village schools are run by Buddhist monks who teach elementary reading and writing, bits of canon and the life of Buddha, and proper conduct. The goal of these schools and their advanced counterparts is proselytism and the preparation of students for salvation. The role of teacher is one accorded great respect and even veneration, particularly since the teachings in monk-run schools are themselves sacred knowledge. Knowledge is conceived of by both teachers and students

> as a fixed, finite body of information. The teacher is the repository of this knowledge, and the student is an empty vessel waiting to be filled by association with the teacher. The role is to lead the student forward into knowledge (Nash 1970:160).

This is true also in state secular schools. In fact the role-relationship of teacher and student is just one of a number of senior-junior relationships calling for respect and obedience by the juniors. Students are expected to perform personal services for a teacher, to consult with him on matters of deep personal concern, and to learn what is taught with letter-perfect precision and unquestioning acceptance. Indeed, Nash (1970:160) asserts, "it is a cultural impossibility for a Burmese student to question, doubt or disbelieve his teacher." Although such doubt may arise at higher levels of schooling, the value of *anade* would prevent the student from openly challenging the teacher.

> *Anade* is a feeling of internal restraint at violating the status relations between seniors and juniors, and it is also a feeling of shame and inadequacy at not being able to play one's role properly. *Anade* operates all throughout Burmese personal relations, and it is highly visible in the school situation. And from the [primary level] to the University, Burmese education is marked by a lack of questioning, challenging curiosity (Nash 1970:161).

In the abstract, schooling is highly valued and a school-educated person has high prestige. However, this is true only within the domain of traditional knowledge. Thus the teacher-monk is the epitome both of moral virtue and of schooled knowledgeability in the eyes of villagers. Secular teachers, while status-superiors respected for such attributes as economic success or the ability to command people and resources, are not honored as men of learning and knowledge. What secular teachers have to teach, beyond the rudiments of literacy, is not of interest to the villagers and not worth their time and resources. This differential respect accorded to teachers of different bodies of knowledge is reminiscent in some respects of the markedly disparate statuses in Jewish *shtetl* communities of secular, paid tutors in Hebraic literacy and revered, unpaid scholars who guide study of the corpus of sacred writings. In the latter case, however, interpretations of the corpus are not constrained by the weight of precedent and rabbinical authority.[5]

Among the Cherokee, as we observed in the fourth chapter, cultural definitions of teacher-student role relationships are distinctively different from the cases cited thus far. Cultural values of emotional and behavioral restraint in dealing with others, respect for psychic and physical autonomy and the privacy of others, and patient industry in pursuing a harmonious social order all condition the appropriate attributes of learning situations and interpersonal learning relationships. As Dickeman (1971:147) remarks, Cherokee learning is initiated always by the learner, not the teacher.

> A task is begun by a novice only when he feels competent to perform the whole process; consequently, the novice learns theory and practice simultaneously. . . . Guidance, when given, is offered as opinion.

The learner retains the option to ignore or pay heed. A vivid example of Cherokee instructional strategy and teacher-learner role relationships is the instruction in reading conducted in Cherokee Baptist churches, generally attended by adults over thirty years of age. Using the Cherokee translation of the New Testament as the text, the preacher selects a passage and calls on each member of the group in turn to read aloud. An individual who is illiterate or faltering is assisted spontaneously by prompting neighbors, but never rushed or passed over. Guidance is offered in the form of supportive, cooperative assistance, within a context of acknowledged individual autonomy and worth. Learning is not, as Dickeman (1971:148) puts it, imposed from above: "The essential respect for the autonomy of others decrees that the learner shall determine the quantity and quality of his education." In Western-style schools, as we would expect, Cherokee students do not respond with the same learning strategies or definition of the teacher-student role-relationship as Kpelle or Burmese students do. Rather, they seek to establish a learning "team" or community with their peers, using the teacher as a resource and treating her or him as an autonomous equal in the self-generated quest to acquire knowledge. They do not seek to establish individual student-teacher relationships as Anglo children do, nor do they seek to compete with one another for teacher approval or prestige. As the students grow older, they interact in a progressively lesser degree with the teacher, establishing a communal social system exclusive of the teacher. The Anglo teacher is perceived as an unwelcome and discourteous intruder, making irrelevant demands.

Anglo teachers in the northeast Oklahoma school classrooms Dickeman observed, define their own role as that of an authoritative source of rules and right answers, to be learned by students under their dictation.[6] Even in classrooms less rigidly structured, the teacher's emphasis is on individual achievement and public demonstration of individual competence. In the upper grades,

teachers increasingly discourage cooperative behavior and even mutual sup-
portiveness among peers.

> [Students] are expected . . . to compete and to invidiously compare, to judge and
> be judged not on the basis of their total personalities, nor their sensitivity to
> others' feelings, but on the basis of their ability to perform allotted tasks in
> allotted periods of time. Older students experience a loss of autonomy as the
> teacher assumes an ever more authoritarian role, engaging in more ordering,
> direct questioning and testing, all of which demand an individual response
> (Dickeman 1971:161).

Within the Cherokee social system of the classroom, teaching is provided as
guidance and assistance from older to younger or more adept to less adept. The
Anglo teacher may be unable to tap the real learning accomplished in this
context because of his or her mode of instruction and requirements for demonstrating competence.

The apparent student indifference perceived by teachers, the unwilling-
ness or inability (for the teacher cannot know which) of students to respond
to queries or probes is in fact the continuing strategy of the students to preserve
their personal integrity as Cherokees in the face of culturally untenable demands. The least cooperative students, usually those least oriented to achievement in Anglo society, "pursue a consistent policy of nonresponse, rarely
answering even those questions directly pertaining to materials on which they
are prepared" (Dickeman 1971:173). Others respond minimally to questions
concerning assignments but refuse to answer the rhetorical questions which
their silence tends to evoke from the frustrated Anglo teacher—questions they
regard as irrelevant. Likewise, they refuse to answer questions that appear to
violate their emotional privacy by referring to feelings or personal thoughts.
Comments Dickeman (1971:174), "each student has come to perceive which
interrogations he must honor in order to maintain the minimal academic status
acceptable to him, and to avoid open conflict with white authority." The
acceptable limits of compromise differ for Cherokee and Anglo students; Cherokees refuse beyond a certain minimal point to compromise between emotional
honesty (which for them includes passive resistance to intrusion and pressure)
and the behaviors required by Anglo teachers. The only strategy available to
them is to maneuver the teacher toward a mode of participation that meets
their standards, by not responding to unacceptable demands.[7]

When the teacher is sensitive and responsive to the distinctive values and
expectations of the students, even if he or she is not willing to abide fully by
them, Cherokee students respond supportively to the attempt to build mutually a viable learning environment. Dumont and Wax (1969) label this as an
"intercultural classroom": one in which teacher and students "are able to enter
into a real intercultural exchange." Inevitably conflicts in cultural expectations
occur, but structured devices for reducing them emerge.

> For instance . . . the Cherokee students urge forward one of their members—
> not always the same person—to mediate and harmonize. Then if the teacher, by
> an unconscious presumption, disrupts the harmonious flow of class activity, it
> is the mediator whose deft maneuver reduces the intensity of the tension and
> relaxes the participants. In a sense what the mediator does is to restore parity
> between teacher and students by removing the nimbus of authority from the
> teacher, thus allowing the students to work out with the teacher a compromise
> which redirects class activities and so permits them to regain their proper tempo
> (Dumont and Wax 1969:223).

As the teacher grows more attuned to the students' frame of reference, the mediating role becomes less necessary to reduce tension. But mediation still helps to adapt the tasks designed by the teacher to the needs and values of the students. If the teacher insists on retaining the prerogatives of an Anglo-style teacher or on maintaining an authoritarian role, mediation becomes difficult, if all the more necessary. Because intercultural classrooms are few in Cherokee school experience, it is not surprising, as Dickeman (1971:178) concludes, that, in spite of the students' desire for knowledge and for the social flexibility which a diploma can grant, few choose to continue their schooling beyond the age at which they are legally obliged to. Dropping out of school is a Cherokee student's final strategic defense of his or her own integrity.

We may say that Cherokee culture does not recognize a role of "teacher" as an individual transmitter of a bounded corpus of knowledge, but only as a "guide" or "assistant" in the individual acquisition of knowledge. This also was somewhat the case with Jewish *shtetl* scholars. After the initial foundations of Hebraic literacy and habits of scholarship had been laid, the teacher became strictly a guide, albeit a highly respected one. If he gave an assignment from the Talmud for class study, it generally would be

> some difficult and contradictory problem, which the students [had] to work
> out, making use of different commentators and discussing the problem among
> themselves by way of rehearsal for classwork. The recitation period [would] be
> a discussion of the problem between students and teacher, an exercise in which
> the teacher as well as the student [would] try to excel (Zborowski 1955:128).

Because no absolute (human) authority was recognized, however, each student strove independently toward a new and original interpretation which was more powerful than those offered in the previous centuries of scholarship. Because all teachers were students by definition—for the study of Torah is unending: "Torah has no bottom"—the relationship of scholars must be ultimately one of equals striving toward similar goals, regardless of the stage to which their independent studies had progressed.

A somewhat different definition of the teacher-as-guide seems to characterize discussions of esoteric philosophies, such as Zen Buddhism, or of apprenticeships in quest of esoteric knowledge, such as Castaneda's (1968, 1971) description of his tutelage by a Yaqui Indian shaman. In these cases, while some concrete information may be transferred, the key component of the teacher role appears to be to awaken the intrinsic awareness and receptivity of the student which will enable learning to become an autonomous enterprise. The goal of these teacher-guides, then, is to bring the student to relinquish conceptions of knowledge as a bounded transferable corpus and of a teacher as a source of answers, and to transform the student's definition of knowledge to one that focuses on reconstituting the frameworks of knowing.

Processes of teaching and learning involve both cognitive frameworks and behavioral strategies used by participants to realize their goals. Assumptions made by the participants about transmission events as interpersonal transactions and about their respective roles in the transaction, provide fundamental routine grounds for the processes which emerge. Systematic knowledge transmission in any society builds on implicit or explicit theories of learning, theories which underlie instructional strategies. The presumed capacity of learners, their qualifications by virtue of such attributes as age, gender, class, affiliation, and the like, and prerogatives "earned" in the course of encounters by demeanor and other learner strategies all influence instructional strategies and the evaluation of instructional effectiveness. Always, the knowledge intentionally and focally taught is embedded in a dense network of implicit assumptions and expectations (cf. Dreeben 1968).

The environment in which learning takes place is always more encompassing than that of specific instructional events. A Guajiro girl, isolated from all social contact other than that with her instructor, still brings to the educative transactions her prior experience in Guajiro society and expectations about the relevance of her training to her future life back in the community. So all learners interpret instructional events in light of the larger world of which they are part. Learners' definition of teachers, their standards of appropriate instructor behavior, their evaluation of teacher social identities in the larger sociocultural world, their interpretation of teacher behavior and of the relevance of knowledge presented, all influence their own strategies in educative transactions.

The cognitive frameworks with which participants enter into educational transactions may be amplified by the acquisition of facts or principles or new cognitive strategies. This is true for both teachers and learners. Neophyte teachers or teachers encountering students of an unfamiliar type may evolve new interpretive schemes to account for their behavior (cf. Smith 1975). Cognitive frameworks may be transformed, as in the case of spiritual instruction cited earlier or in the case of teachers who recognize and adapt to radically different cultural frameworks of their students. The processes of cognitive change are a function in large part of the processes of communication which comprise transaction. While instruction may emphasize particular channels of communication, other channels also come into play, if only by framing the dominant transactional mode. Cherokee students communicate by silence as well as by words, by the ways in which they spontaneously organize their own learning activity. By these means, Dumont and Wax (1969) argue, they attempt to instruct Anglo teachers. Anglo teachers who do not learn emphasize verbal, directive communication and tacitly convey their lack of acknowledgement of Cherokee student integrity and values. Cherokee and Cherokee-oriented teacher-guides provide information about the topic of instruction, as do their Anglo counterparts, and also communicate support and respect for learners in their instructional strategies.

identities and identity change

The spectrum of communication which comes into play in educational process has important consequences, not only for the systematic transmission of valued knowledge but also for the subtler learning of personal and social identities. Roles involve a cultural definition of the behavior appropriate to types of participants in specified types of situations such as educational settings. Roles are sets of expectations that pertain regardless of the individuals performing those roles. Identity, in contrast, refers to the categories used by the participants to define an individual with respect to the group or the categories used by an individual to define himself or herself. Identities of teachers and students may be affected by the roles they are expected to play in educational transactions, but their identities are not synonymous with these roles. Identities may be situation-specific, but often they are broader in scope, extending beyond educational settings. In either case they are important to the way in which roles as expected patterns actually are performed.

The relationship between identity and role is illustrated in the Anglo-Cherokee classrooms studied by Dickeman. Anglo teachers unfamiliar with Cherokee cultural frameworks were inclined to view students as indifferent to learning if not incapable of it, because of their behavior within the student role expected by the teachers. This constituted part of the social identities accorded Cherokee students by their Anglo teachers. Cherokee students also differed among themselves in the degree of response they were willing to provide within teacher-student transactions. Those whose personal identity was exclusively Cherokee were the least willing to fulfill Anglo role expectations, while others whose personal identity definitions were inclined toward achievement in Anglo society attempted some degree of compromise between Anglo and Cherokee role expectations.

Japan provides a good example of the distinction between the teacher's role and his or her identity. As we noted in the last chapter, Japanese teachers in middle and secondary schools perform many tasks besides teaching, as part of their occupational role. Not only are they expected to maintain their pedagogical and professional qualifications outside of formal working hours, but they also are on call to provide services to students at any time of day or year and to put in obligatory appearances at various social events in the school's public relations activities. These role expectations affect the social identities they are accorded by parents, by the Ministry of Education, by students, by colleagues, and so forth. These attributed social identities vary. The identity accorded teachers by the Ministry of Education not only differs from but conflicts with that accorded by the Japan Teachers Union. For some teachers, such as those studied by Singleton, this conflict of social identities was complemented by ambivalence about personal identity. While not completely accepting the Ministry identity, they tended to prefer an identity less proletarian than that offered by the labor market-oriented JTU. They expressed a preference for a professional organization with a less politically contentious or militant stance.

Identities also are pertinent to the study of education because education is an institutionalized means of effecting identity change. Typically we think of this change as a shift from ignorance to knowledgeability, often a shift in status from child to adult. A change in the context in which acquired knowledge is to be applied may itself call for radical identity change, as in the case of neophyte professional teachers who must relinquish long-held student identities in favor of identities as full-fledged teachers (cf. Eddy 1969, Wolcott 1973 for discussion of this process in U.S. schools).[8] This identity shift is accomplished through a variety of communicative transactions with colleagues, supervisors, and students. Smith (1975) analyzes one of these types of transaction in which neophytes learn to differentiate between themselves as teachers and their students, by means of divergent causal interpretations of student behavior and teacher behavior. Others have described similar transitions in "professionalization" of identity in various occupations (e.g., Becker and others 1961, Khleif 1975).

Identity change can be more subtle, however. For an individual it may be negative personally and socially, it may entail conflict between identities within and outside of specific educational settings, and it may constrict or expand available alternative courses of action. While identity change is commonly a result of educational attainment, it also may be an adjunct to the educational process that modifies relationships among the participants and their strategies. Identity changes resulting from other sociocultural processes may cause distinctive changes in education.

In a study of the University of Allahabad in northeastern India, Di Bona (1970) found just such changes affecting traditional role definitions and socially acknowledged identities within the school institution. The model of traditional teaching was the Brahmin guru patiently imparting his knowledge of the sacred Vedic writings to a select group of students. These students became virtually part of his family, bound by a tie second in importance only to that of kinship. With personally and intellectually respectful dependence, students provided him services of all kinds; indeed their respectful subordination in response to the guru's selfless and virtuous devotion was a lifelong commitment. Today the formal signs of respect and deference are still required of students, but the personal relationship formerly associated with those forms is less often a reality.[9] Increasingly the teacher-student relationship is one of distance more alienated than respectful.

The structure and cultural orientation of contemporary Indian academia reflects its dual British colonial and Indian heritage. Before independence the university was a highly selective, elite institution whose graduates expected and found career positions in the colonial bureaucracy or affiliated with it. Faculty held secure, respected positions within the university hierarchy; the prerogatives of rank and avenues of mobility were commonly understood and accepted. With the changes brought about by national independence, including expanded enrollment, shifts in popular values with respect to traditional academic culture, and the newly politicized outlook of many participants, dramatic changes also occurred within the institution.

At the time of Di Bona's research, 90 percent of the teachers at Allahabad were former students. To obtain faculty positions, both scholarly merit and "other factors," such as the support of high-ranking faculty or administrators were important. Participants perceived the "other factors" to weigh most heavily. This meant that aspirants had to follow carefully the rules of appropriate behavior expected by senior members of the institution. Once achieved, formal entrance provided the new teacher a position at the bottom of a rigid hierarchy based on seniority. To rise to the top, the individual had to outlive everyone hired before him. For all considerations before attaining seniority, such as the scheduling of classes and promotion within junior ranks, junior faculty were dependent on the support of their senior former teachers. In return they continued to offer their services to these patrons whenever called upon. This was the system characteristic before independence, and it has continued in considerable measure since, but alternative routes of upward mobility and advancement of self-interest also have opened.

Particularly important has been the development of factional groupings which cut across older lines of authority based on seniority. Even traditionally oriented teachers feel forced to become loyal members of such a faction. The strategies used by these groups are essentially political, often bypassing the local university administration to achieve desired ends, through judicial court cases or alliance with political parties. Also eroding traditional identities are government efforts to raise scholastic qualifications for employment and advancement. Most Allahabad faculty members have only a master's degree, since that was considered adequate when they finished school. In recent years, junior members with more advanced degrees have become increasingly impatient with the advancement of those they perceive as less qualified, though more senior than themselves. In some cases they have instituted court actions against the heads of their own departments.

Social identities attributed to teachers by nonacademics also are changing. The university has incurred increasing hostility from state politicians who represent the majority rural population in the area. They look upon the teachers with their Western-style attire, English speech, and British mannerisms as out of step with postcolonial, democratic times. Teachers are accorded disparate social identities by traditionally oriented faculty, newly politicized, aggressive junior faculty, and nonacademics in the surrounding society. In Di Bona's view, they represent the conflicting pressures of a system in flux.

> The faculty are slowly moving toward a closer resemblance to the dominant intellectual type in the state and as such will blend more with others around them. But as the teacher tries to give up his colonial image he finds it difficult to recapture the aura of the virtuous *guru*. The result is a tarnished image with no place to go (Di Bona 1970:181).

Student identities, too, have changed. Before the national movement for independence, students were docile and hard working, anticipating a prestigious and lucrative position as a reward for their academic labors. They considered their courses relevant to their future careers in the colonial structure and saw the administrative forms as an embodiment of rational justice. Today academic failures are high, few good jobs are available even for those who pass, and the university bureaucracy is perceived as a source of unremitting exploitation of student powerlessness. Students tend to believe that favoritism, nepotism, and caste are the principal elements in administrative decisions.

For many students, the university is their first experience with impersonal, bureaucratic organizations, and often their first encounter with social inferiors toward whom particular behaviors and attitudes must be learned. Within the academic structure students constitute a distinct class, subordinate to faculty, and superior to the clerical and maintenance staff. Yet they have little recourse against even their supposed inferiors in clerical positions, in the event of recording errors or misplaced documents. Even among fellow students, seniority is the basis of relationships and prerogatives. The only counterforce is the student union, a protective organization which serves as an advocate of student interests. Like faculty factions, the union crosscuts the seniority structure; the union presidency is the only student position not based on seniority. Indeed the main prerequisite for this office seems to be demonstrated militancy. Students, no longer willing to accept the traditional identities accorded them by faculty and staff, are choosing leaders who can press effectively for change, through any available channels. Public sympathy for students in India has been based on a traditional identity that no longer is valid.

Therefore, as Di Bona (1970:185) points out, as the change in student identity becomes more generally recognized, the responses of others are likely to shift as well.

> In 1964 at Allahabad the first criminal case in the history of India was instituted against students. The sentences were light, but it marked a milestone in the long history of the guru-student relationship in India.

The case of Allahabad illustrates identity changes that are not themselves directly caused by the institutional educational process. Rather they result from interacting processes within and outside the institution. To understand them, our scope of analysis must include the sociocultural environment of the university. The same is true in our next two examples, those of Sioux Indian and Chicano students in the U.S. Because both groups tend to be subordinate in the larger society as well as in school, identity is a particularly appropriate focus of analysis. Conflict and congruence between personal identity and socially accorded identities are important factors in their respective adaptations to schooling. Members of both groups frequently are labeled by professional educators and other representatives of the larger society as "culturally deprived," inadequately prepared, and failure prone. Both groups typically perform poorly in the school context and thus are doomed to strictly limited opportunities for economic advancement. In some ways, though not all, the cultures are also similar. In important ways, however, their situations and adaptations are different.

Considering only male students (since most of the research thus far concentrates on them), Sioux boys on the Pine Ridge reservation are raised to be "physically reckless and impetuous. . . . proud and feisty and are expected to resent public censure" (Wax 1967:29). While they have some obligations to relatives, most of their time from the age of seven or eight is spent without adult supervision in the company of peers. Within the group, intense loyalty and highly efficient discipline prevail, coordinated with a well-defined status hierarchy. Within the reservation elementary school, the peer group is an active force in structuring the classroom society. In response to demands they will not accept, members of the peer group can mobilize effectively a range of tactics that defend their self-defined identities from intrusion. Wax (1967:31) cites as examples "unanimous inattention, refusal to go to the board, writing on the board in letters less than an inch high, inarticulate responses, . . . whispered or pantomine teasing of victims called on to recite" and in some seventh and eighth grade classes, total withdrawal into silence for hours on end.

In contrast to Cherokee students, "most Sioux children insist that they like school, and most Sioux parents corroborate this" (Wax 1967:31). Unpleasant regulations can be tolerated or evaded, bullies can be rejected by the peer group, and "mean" teachers can be made ineffective.

Identities are accorded students in classrooms both by teachers and by other students. The significance and sanctioning power of peer judgment is widely recognized, but it also represents a dimension of cultural contrast. For Sioux students within and outside classrooms, their peer group is of central daily relevance; teachers run a poor second. Most descriptions of middle income Anglo students and teachers suggest that, while peer relationships may dominate student relevance schemes in general (e.g., Cusick 1973), within the classroom the teacher is acknowledged as the dominant pivot of interaction (cf. e.g., Philips 1972, Henry 1963).[10]

By the time he has finished eighth grade, the reservation Sioux boy has established a culturally approved personal identity of physically reckless and impetuous courage, pride, curiosity, sensibility to human relationships, and intense group loyalty and integrity. He has not, however, acquired the traits valued by school authorities: respect for regulations, school property, routine diligence, and "discipline" (in the sense of not smoking in the toilets, not cutting classes, and not getting drunk). His school identity as seen by high school authorities off the reservation is not the same as his personal identity or the identity accorded by his peer group. Unskilled in making short-term, superficial adjustments to strangers, he cannot adjust easily to the school's demand for individualistic, competitive achievement in a large boarding school dormitory which allows no individual privacy. Finally, his English is not yet fluent, and is inadequate for scholastic competition with native speakers of English. The transition to high school, which requires leaving the reservation and transferring to a boarding school in town, is fraught with hazards.

Not surprisingly, many drop out very early: Wax reports a 35 percent dropout rate in the ninth grade alone during the year of her study. Those who remain longer are those who find friends with whom they can ally to cope with the exploitation of senior boarders and the maze of regulations. Coping includes defiance and daring deeds, for it would be unmanly not to be regarded as a hellion in school. Needless to say, school staff members label this behavior differently.

> Clearly the activities school administrators and teachers denounce as imma-
> ture and delinquent are regarded as part of youthful daring, excitement, manly
> honor, and contests of skill and wits by Sioux young men and many of their elders
> (Wax 1967:38).

The one "legitimate" activity which inspires equal ardor is competitive sports: indeed for some it is the main reason they keep going to school. Dropout rates remain high throughout high school despite the belief of both parents and students that the completion of high school is essential for even modest economic opportunities. Wax argues this is largely because the school does not allow students to become whole persons; in other words, it does not allow

Sioux students to develop acceptable Sioux identities within its context. Sioux young people, Wax (1967:42) concludes, "leave high school because they are too vital and independent to submit to a dehumanizing situation."

In the reservation school, an Anglo enclave in a Sioux environment, Pine Ridge Sioux boys encounter an alien set of expectations and values. Both their aggressive cultural strategies and the prevailing values of the surrounding sociocultural environment secure their personal identities against the divergent attributions of Anglo school personnel. Off the reservation in an Anglo-dominated context, these strategies are less effective. Here Sioux boys' behavior leads to social identities with an increasingly heavy price. Sustaining the Sioux male identities personally and socially valued within the Sioux community, locks students into negatively valued identities in the dominant Anglo community.[11] The consequences for the schooling process are indicated by the dropout and failure rate. If, as some commentators contend, academic lessons in Anglo-oriented schooling are but vehicles for the transmission of major cultural values, then the Sioux students described and the schools they attend fail, because the students refuse to relinquish their own cultural orientation. If the academic lessons themselves were presented within a framework built around Sioux values, would there be greater achievement in academic skills? The Cherokee case suggests that there would. One result might be the development of different, but equally positive, social identities in a young Sioux's repertoire, including identities approved within his community and identities as skilled participants within the dominant Anglo community.

The resilience of Sioux personal identities appears to be enhanced by their early schooling experience in reservation schools. Chicano students, in contrast, usually encounter greater cultural diversity from their first years in school. Not only adults but also many peers have different cultural expectations and values, often conflicting with those of Chicano fellow students. Ramírez and Castañeda (1974) summarize the values and expectations generally held by Chicanos that are the main source of conflict with Anglo-oriented schooling. First, individuals identify closely with their family and ethnic group.

> The needs and interests of the individual are considered secondary to those of the family and the individual is expected to defend his family whenever its honor is threatened, to help other members of the family whenever they are in need, and always to be cognizant of the fact that his actions and accomplishments reflect on his family, enhancing its status or hurting its reputation in the community (Ramírez and Castañeda 1974:42).

As an extension of the family, the ethnic group also is subject to loyalty and pride in membership. In the school context, teachers and administrators consider unacceptable an orientation that does not set school attendance and school work above all other family concerns. Identification with an ethnic group is discouraged in favor of an "American" identity.

Second, relationships tend to be "personalized," even outside the family. The relationship has priority over other instrumental goals. Relationships which commit participants to mutual dependence and cooperative achievement contribute to the sense of group membership referred to above. As we might expect, emphasis also is placed on the individual's development of sensitivity and skill in responding to the feelings and needs of others. This conflicts with the value for individual competitive achievement characteristic of the school. Nelson and Kagan (1972:91) contrast the competitive behavior of Mexican and Anglo children in rather vivid terms:

> Anglo-American children are not only irrationally competitive, they are almost sadistically rivalrous. Given a choice, Anglo-American children took toys away from their peers 78% of the trials even when they could not keep the toys for themselves. . . . Anglo-American children often were willing to make sacrifices in order to reduce the rewards of their peers. . . . Results indicated that with age, an Anglo-American child, significantly more so than a Mexican child, is willing to reduce his own reward in order to reduce the reward of a peer.

If the results of their research are valid, it suggests that the classroom strategies of Anglo and Mexican children are likely to be distinctly different. Instructional and evaluative strategies that emphasize individualistic and competitive student behavior will favor children who have acquired this orientation.

The third cluster of values characteristic of Chicano culture revolves around the importance of age, gender, and respect as bases of social status. Older people in general and parents in particular are the objects of esteem, deference, and obedience. Children's status depends on how well they fulfill responsibilities given them by adults and how well they behave socially. This is related closely to the individual's close identification with his or her family described above. Although the bases of male and female status are changing (cf., e.g., Rendon 1971), men tend to have higher status in business and political activities, while women tend to have higher status in the areas of child rearing, health care, and religion. These values together encourage the young to act in accordance with the expectations of respected adults with whom they have a direct personal relationship. In a study conducted in Houston, Texas, of fourth grade children and their mothers, Chicano children expressed a greater need than did Anglo-American children "for guidance, direction, and support from authority figures" (Ramírez and Castañeda 1974:45). The increasingly impersonal and formalized relationships that many Chicano children encounter as they progress through school thus violate the expectations cultivated in their home milieu.

With the added handicaps of unfamiliarity with classroom practices which many Anglo children take for granted, lesser skills in English, awareness of negative ethnic stereotypes that may be held by adults or other children, and knowledge that older siblings and other Chicanos experienced ridicule and defeat in school, the Chicano child understandably encounters schooling with much fear and confusion. If a child's own experience matches that of her or his elders, involvement in school dwindles and classroom performance declines.

> As a young child in class with Anglos or with an Anglo (or anglicized) teacher, the Chicano begins to receive abundant evidence of what he takes to be his general ineptness with the tasks assigned. . . . In assessing his own future performance, measuring his own aspirations, it becomes a habit to expect that someone else will do it better. It will not be a random someone who will do, and be, better —it will always be a member of that demonstrably superior group, the Anglo majority culture. The school, in effect, begins to provide rapidly accumulating experiences by which the Chicano child learns that the Anglo child will always be his superior (Bachelor 1970:50–51).

The effect on such a child's personal identity is likely to be an unfortunate match between the social identity accorded him by Anglo superiors (as low achiever, culturally deprived, and unpromising) and his personal identity. As Bachelor (1970:51) puts it, "It becomes much easier to live up to the stereotype than to compete in a contest that seems to be held only to prove the Chicano's unworthiness."

For male students, an alternative means to a positive identity lies in the peer group and in pursuing the values of manliness and personal honor accepted in Chicano culture. Like the Sioux, these young people thereby validate the expectations of their Anglo observers—expectations of irresponsibility, delinquency, and so forth. In both cases, however, it is a means of countering the damage to their personal identities sustained in their schooling experience.

In the course of their school career, students acquire social identities which may critically affect the personal identities they formulate. Insofar as educational transmission is used as a rite of passage for identity change, identities imputed by peers or superiors may direct individuals toward particular sets of options. Social identities may be interpreted by those controlling the transition process as fixed criteria for routing students along alternative paths toward adult identities. When student personal identities diverge from the social identities accorded them by their superiors in the school system, the greater power and authority of school personnel frequently override the students' attempts to alter the route expected of them.

Spindler (1963c) cites such a case in his description of the interaction between a teacher-counselor and the eighth grade students whom he was directing toward available high school programs. Twenty-four of the thirty-five students were Chicano. Consistently the counselor referred positively to the valued avenue of development (college), then "shut [the gates to it] in the children's faces," by reminding them that they were not qualified. He offered no suggestion of an equally dignified and worthy alternative. Moreover, he implicitly denied the possibility of a student acquiring necessary qualifications by personal effort. Consider the following excerpt from the transaction (Spindler 1963c:153–54):

Counselor: "Now you have to decide whether you want to take Algebra or not. You have to take math all the way through high school if you want to be an engineer. Now, if you've gotten B's and C's all the way through eighth grade, what are your chances of doing well in ninth grade Algebra?. . . . That's right! Not so good! So what can you do?"

Student: "Try to raise your grade."

Counselor: "Yes."

Student: "Work harder."

Counselor: "That's one thing. But what else?. . . . Do like I did when I wanted to be a singer but found I couldn't sing. What did I do? Yes . . . that's right; I changed my plans . . ."

Middle class Anglo students are not immune to the channeling effects of social identities, as Cicourel and Kitsuse (1963) have shown. Their case study of the function and activities of counselors in a mainly upper-middle class high school underscores the differential relevance of social identities accorded students by school personnel and by nonparticipants in the academic system. They found that parents usually knew nothing about college entrance requirements and simply assumed that their children were college bound. Parents assumed this regardless of their children's elementary school grades and tested scholastic aptitude. Because the student's choice of courses as a freshman largely determines the chances of her or his fulfilling college entrance requirements upon graduation, however, the initial choice of curriculum critically affects future options. In principle, each student had a right to choose a college preparatory or nonpreparatory curriculum regardless of her or his past performance, tested capability, and personal or social characteristics. In practice, these factors and their interpretation by high school admissions personnel were at least as important as the student's personal choice, for entrance into college preparatory courses was by assignment, not request.

The counselor's initial assignment of students to the available alternative programs virtually decided which of them would be eligible for college. We may ask, as Cicourel and Kitsuse did, how such decisions were made. The researchers demonstrate that the assignment of students could not be accounted for on the basis of entering grades or test scores alone, and then examine how the counselors and other student placement personnel made these decisions. Every student at the high school was assigned to a counselor with access to his or her school records, including academic, social, medical, psychological, and personal information. At the end of each grading period, the counselor reviewed the student's academic progress, primarily by comparing his or her grades with his or her aptitude test scores. Any inconsistency between the two called for investigation and interpretation. Significantly, "the characteristic interpretations made by counselors and other school personnel of [such] discrepancies [was] that students perform below or above their tested ability as a consequence of motivational, personal, and social 'problems' "; almost no references were made to possible inadequacies, defects, or failures of the system itself, even with respect to test validity or teaching effectiveness (Cicourel and Kitsuse 1963:62–63; cf. Ogbu 1974:191–204).

Most important in constructing student academic identities was the use (by both teaching and counseling personnel) of "achievement type" categories for classifying students. These were (1) "excellent student," (2) "average achiever," (3) "underachiever" (one whose grades are lower than her or his tested aptitudes warrant), (4) "overachiever" (one whose grades are higher than the aptitude test scores warrant, with the implication that the student compulsively overworks to compensate for her or his limited ability), and (5) "opportunity student" (a euphemism for the student with both low achievement and low tested aptitude scores). These categories were not simply descriptive labels, but further implied that all but types (1) and (2) have "problems." The criteria by which these "problems" were diagnosed and how they became a part of the student's academic identity are dealt with in some depth by the researchers. What is important here is that the student's progress in the transitions necessary to upward mobility within the school system

> is contingent upon the interpretations, judgments, and action of school personnel vis-à-vis the student's biography, social and personal "adjustment," appearance and demeanor, social class, and "social type," as well as his demonstrated ability and performance (Cicourel and Kitsuse 1963:136).

This affected not simply whether or not the student was identified as college bound, but also for which colleges he or she was considered eligible. Through their placement in the high school organization and through the counselors' interviews with students and parents and their recommendations to colleges and universities, the students' identities and their opportunities for further schooling were controlled. The discretionary decisions of school personnel were not subject to dispute or even to inspection by their clients.[12]

Identities are always susceptible to reformulation. Within an educational system, certain types of identity change may be actively sought, such as a change from nonliterate to literate, ignorant to knowledgeable, unskilled to skilled. The criteria by which transformation is judged successful may be less explicit than the goals themselves, but in most systems of knowledge transmission, identity change is a matter of social acknowledgment. Change is seen as accomplished when the student has met criteria set by the transmitter or the group the transmitter represents. This is an important element in the power of those engaged in the systematic transmission of knowledge. Acquiring identities valued by educational personnel tends to have a far-reaching effect on a student's future identities outside educational contexts.

Systematic education always occurs within a larger network of sociocultural relationships, accompanied by other processes of knowledge transmission. The degree of congruence among the many transmissions is highly variable. Transfer of knowledge within a given set of relationships, such as a school, is influenced greatly by transmissions in other contexts such as family life, peer group interaction, workplace, and media worlds. While case studies of the sort summarized here hint at the consequences of knowledge transmission in one context for knowledge transmission in others, we still know little about the processes by which this mediating effect occurs. The two groups of variables already examined would seem to be central, but they are not the only relevant factors.

The first variables dealt with concern the content of cultural knowledge transmitted in given contexts and the degree of congruence or redundancy across contexts and over time. Knowledge transferred in daily life on the Pine Ridge Sioux reservation is incongruent in many ways with that transmitted in Anglo-oriented schools on and off the reservation. Knowledge transferred in daily life in middle class Anglo families and peer groups, in contrast, tends to be more congruent with that transmitted in Anglo-oriented schools. Cognitive styles and strategies, orientations toward experience, values and ideas, all contribute to the level of congruence experienced by participants in educational transactions. Perceptions of congruence, like the decoding of messages received from others, are dependent on the interpretive frameworks through which individuals cognitively organize their experience. The more varied the cultural repertoires of the participants, the more complex the problems of knowledge transfer will be.

These variables are linked closely to those of social relationships and identities. My analytic focus on role-relationships and identities is based on the premise that in important ways these tend to epitomize the relationships of participants to the larger society, and on the assumption that they are central factors in the organization of interaction and communication within educational transactions. Congruence is pertinent to constituent social relationships and identities, as well as to transmission content. First, to what degree are role-relationships between knowledge transmitters and receivers congruent across educational contexts? In the fourth chapter we noted that middle class Anglo teachers in the U.S. frequently are described as "parental" in their classroom interaction style, yet Ramírez and Castañeda argue that such teachers are perceived by Chicano children as formal and impersonal compared to parents and other adults in their ethnic community. Clearly there is no single interactional style characteristic of all middle class Anglo teachers, even among those who shared a general conception of the teacher-student role-relationship. But the variation we would expect may be complemented by cultural patterns sufficiently distinctive that the range of teacher styles falls outside of the range of styles exhibited by other educators with whom a student interacts. These styles, in turn, are constrained by the role-definitions which educators in each context use to organize their transmission activity. We also may examine the congruence of role-relationships over time. Incongruence may reflect sociocultural change, as at the University of Allahabad. It also may reflect changes in student identities with age and level of knowledge. In U.S. classrooms, parent-like role definitions of teachers appear to be more common in the lower grades, giving way to more formal and impersonal role definitions at the higher levels. Analogous changes may occur in other educational contexts as well, thus complicating the analysis of congruence and its effects.

Another aspect of congruence is that between roles and identities in educational contexts, and roles and identities in other domains of individual experience. Academic identities attributing academic ineptness, cultural inferiority, and social unacceptability to non-Anglo students, for instance, may echo identities accorded them in interactions with representatives of a predominantly Anglo society outside the school context. The changing role definition of Jewish *shtetl* students correlated with increasing prestige and independence in their relationships outside of classroom. Poro schools prevented the intrusion of incongruence in identities across contexts by segregating students from their kin. It was expected that kin would offer indulgent support incongruent with the rigorous discipline imposed within the school. In multicultural societies, marked incongruence of identities and roles is particularly likely between culturally distinct domains. Insofar as Sioux, for example, conduct their lives mainly within the Sioux community, they seem to maintain role-definitions and identities inconsistent with those which prevail in Anglo-controlled contexts such as school (cf. also Sindell 1974, Wintrob 1968).

The importance of congruence is in part a function of the differential distribution of power and influence in a society. This includes not only the authority commonly exercised by knowledge transmitters over receivers but also the relative power and influence of educators across the spectrum of educational contexts. The West African Poro educational system exemplifies a pattern of distribution in which the greatest power was in the hands of the Poro elite and school personnel. The goals of schooling included the objective of realigning student loyalties from kin to the Poro organization. Poro control over schooling and other activities was not subject to challenge. Even a student's death under Poro tutelage did not need to be justified to the community or to the student's own kin.

In the U.S., the relative power of academic and nonacademic educators varies. Among the clearest sources of this variation are the goals of clients (students, parents, communities) and the relative pressure these clients and other interest groups can bring to bear on each educational sector. To the extent that schools, for instance, control access to valued goals such as specific types of knowledge and skill, economic opportunity, and social status, the potential power of academic educators is high. To the extent that valued goals are not under their control, their relative power is less. In the U.S., academic education is increasingly a prerequisite to most economic pursuits and to many other common activities. Families control access to relatively few of these valued goals. Historically, the pressure that interest groups in the U.S. have applied successfully to academic institutions has been correlated with their socioeconomic status. This has increased the influence of middle class and upper class interest groups relative to that of the socioeconomically disadvantaged. With the growing politicization of socially stigmatized ethnic groups and their increasingly militant demands for community control of schooling, this balance appears to be changing (cf. Foley 1976 for an example of this process in a predominantly Chicano community).

Academic educators are not the sole objects of such pressure. Families also have been the object of scrutiny by other educators. There has been much research on the nature of educational transmission within this context, particularly to determine factors which encourage and inhibit achievement in the academic sector. The pressures resulting from this research range from advice directed to parents in their educational roles, to proposals that children of "culturally disadvantaged," poor families be removed from their family milieus and thereby protected from the supposedly negative influence of family educational processes (Banfield 1970:229–231; cf. also Leichter 1971, 1974). Mass media too receive pressure from other educators, notably families and academic educators, as to the content, accessibility, and consequences of their transmissions. Examination of the interplay among these agencies of knowledge transmission and the contexts each controls leads us into an analysis of the social organization of the society as a whole.

In thus expanding our scope of analysis, we approach the limits of our conceptual distinction between structural systems and processes, for at this level neither can be analyzed without a simultaneous consideration of the other. Ultimately this is true whatever our level of analysis, since contextual factors are relevant at all levels. Yet for specific purposes it is possible to concentrate on constituent processes in educational transactions, such as the nature of communication in a multicultural classroom, without taking full account of the total system of relationships in which these transactions are enmeshed. In the same way we can examine the role of media in educational process with a narrow, fine-grained focus or in increasingly inclusive and general terms of systemic relations.

media in educational process

In an analysis of educational process, we must consider not only cultural and social factors but also the media through which learning is effected. To understand the relationship between the content of knowledge transmission and the strategies used in its transfer, we must examine the forms in which that content is presented and the communicative channels used.

The media of transmission both structure information through form and specify communicative channels. Books, for instance, provide primarily visual information in the forms of pictures, diagrams, and visual transcriptions of verbal language. The content of a book is of central importance insofar as it enters into the educational transaction being studied; but content is not always distinct from its medium. A book may provide additional information to its user, depending on her or his cultural (or idiosyncratic) assumptions. The belief that what is in print must be "true" or the belief that owning or touching a book provides a kind of protection or validation is as important a part of the mediated transmission as the content of the book.

The importance of media in human education is related to the nature of cognitive process and our capacity for symbolic communication. We process information through a variety of modes, not solely verbal, and organize that information within several symbolic codes. Not all of the information apprehended in one mode (or organized in one code) is totally translatable into another (Gross 1974). Just as symbolic communication multiplies the kinds and quantities of knowledge which may be conveyed, so does the use of media as vehicles for transmission. In the broadest sense, media include language, movement, and proxemics as symbolic codes as well as objects and secondary vehicles for communication such as print, electronic audio and video transmission, and cinematic film. As vehicles for knowledge transfer, media are also interpreted symbolically. The choice of medium, the organization of information so transmitted, and interpretation of the messages transferred by its use all are culturally influenced. Understanding the role of media in educational process therefore requires that we examine the cultural schemes which underlie their use by both transmitting agents and receiving learners. The first two examples which follow illustrate some uses of media in educational transactions between cocultural teachers and learners.

The master canoe builder of Puluwat has no external means of measuring his hull contour. He has only his knowledge of how water will flow along the canoe's surface, his experienced eye which not only can gauge the exact contour but also can anticipate its interaction with sea waves, and his skilled precision with his tools that allows him to shave exactly the right amount of wood away to match the goal he has in mind. To convey the fundamentals of this complex knowledge to an apprentice, the canoe builder cannot merely draw in the dust, shape a rough contour with his hands in the air, or discuss hull construction verbally. Transmitting this knowledge requires the medium of the hull itself, displayed in the lengthy process of shaping to the inquiring eye and hand and mind of the apprentice.

In the same way, Abelam artists teach aspirants the basics of their artistry. By observing the artist at work and his products, by gradually mastering the skills through practice under his supervision, the student learns what the master can teach. For painting this instruction is readily accessible, for all men share in painting as a ceremonial activity. An artist preparing for an initiation display will direct and supervise the assistants who follow the design he has laid out. Remarks Forge (1967:76), "An artist at work on painting usually keeps from eight to ten men more or less busy while still maintaining complete control over the design and its execution." An aspiring artist who shows aptitude will be encouraged to perform more and more difficult tasks under supervision, which his teacher will correct, taking over now and then when difficulties occur. Guidance and instruction thus take place through the shared medium, aided by the formal prescriptions shared by artists in the community.

Carving is more difficult to learn, though it is a necessary skill if an artist is to acquire prestige. Carving is an individual, solitary activity.

> The artist does not welcome company or conversation, and spends a good deal of time sitting in silence and looking at his work—this in great contrast to normal Abelam activity, and especially to painting, where speed, movement, and noise are predominant. . . . Young men who cheerfully help in the painting do not always care to spend days in silence and inactivity doing occasional minor tasks, and it is only the minority who persist and start to acquire carving skills (Forge 1967:80).

Those who do, tackle progressively more difficult parts of the work until they try some small simple object on their own, showing it to the master carver at each stage and relying on his finishing touches. Again, although the instruction appears to be less systematized than that of painting, it centers on the object through which they exchange information. The teacher demonstrates the skill to the student, who in turn attempts to duplicate it. In so doing he communicates the success of that phase of instruction, and the teacher corrects the displayed result. The shared labors of student and teacher symbolize their relationship and the transmission of knowledge in which they are engaged. When the student produces a piece of his own that is accepted for ceremonial display, the apprenticeship phase is coming to an end; his identity as student gives way to that of artist. In time he may become an acknowledged master with great prestige.

Both Puluwat canoe builders and Abelam artists use media of instruction which are essentially the same as the objects with which successful "graduates" will work. Learning is not vicarious in the sense that students are provided replicas or instruction detached from immediate application. Novice canoe builders do not begin their course of study by whittling toy boats, nor do they learn a body of theory before they become directly involved in the building process. Novice navigators, in contrast, study a detached corpus of navigational knowledge, mediated by verbal and visual diagrammatic descriptions, before they actively apprentice on boats. Informal learning precedes systematic instruction in all three cases. Abelam boys are familiar with much of the aesthetic code of painting and carving before participating in its creation. Puluwat aspirants likewise bring to navigational and canoe building instruction substantial experience on boats.

Let us consider a third case in which instruction is mediated through television. The scope of transmission in this instance is enlarged, both by the infinite number of learners who may be reached by the transmitter and by the message complexity to which the medium's technology lends itself. "Sesame Street," designed as an educational program for children, has become part of the environment of most U.S. preschoolers.[13] This program's objective is to use special dramatic and technical effects to teach its viewers the alphabet, numbers and simple arithmetical operations, and basic concepts relating to common social patterns. It is a highly successful agent of enculturation in such areas of cultural knowledge as family relations, occupational, age and gender roles, economic pursuits such as buying and selling and going to work, health practices, and many consumer activities. The format, intentionally that of commercial advertising, uses conventions of television program construction such as sustained variation of image and action and artfully interrupted dramatic sequences. In her analysis, Goldsen (1976) points out that the most powerful lessons of "Sesame Street" are those which enculturate its viewers in the medium of commercial television itself. While providing cultural instruction useful in academic schooling, the program omits reference to the medium most closely associated with the other agency, i.e., printed books.[14]

> The children are entertained by animations; by commercials and billboards; by pratfalls, yuk-yuks and one–liners; by rock music and light shows; by guest stars and production numbers—but never by anything that involves books! . . . The daily dramas on the street or in the Plaza never feature anyone absorbed in a book, laughing or crying over a book, so gripped by a book that he cannot bring himself to set it aside. . . . The incessant "commercials" sing the praises of letters and numbers, but never of books and reading. The set itself, the familiar scene in the Plaza, doesn't even give the children a chance to see books: Don Ramon's store sells everything but books . . . (Goldsen 1976:210–11).

What viewing children are being taught to read is not books, but television. Nearly all the cultural information being transmitted matches that broadcast by other commercial programming, including adventure series like "Batman and Robin," variety shows, and commercial messages encouraging consumer acquisitiveness. All experience is depicted in compressed, fast-paced, action sequences, embellished by exciting visual and aural displays. "Sesame Street" provides a powerful cultural package, through both its sophisticated production and its congruence with other television transmissions. The effect of this enculturating experience on others such as school and family life, deserves intensive study. Particularly for those children whose cultural background differs from that advocated in such television transmissions, what arc the consequences of the resulting cultural disjunction? Given the ubiquity of televisions in U.S. households, we might expect an increasing tendency toward cultural homogenization. But we know relatively little about how such media transmissions are themselves mediated by family interaction and experiences in other contexts.

Both the form and content of educational media may be foreign to a student's previous experience. Hobart and Brant (1965) found this to be the case in Canadian Eskimo schools. At the time of their research, curriculum materials in these schools consisted largely of printed textbooks, a medium unfamiliar in Eskimo homes. Virtually no Canadian Eskimo literature besides an Eskimo translation of the New Testament exists or is likely to be written, since instruction in written Eskimo is available only through sparsely attended classes held by the church. Moreover, the content of school text materials was oriented to southern Eurocanadian children, bearing very little relationship to Eskimo life in the western Canadian Arctic.

In Greenland, textbook materials in Eskimo schools were designed specially to reflect Greenlandic Eskimo life, written in their language, and appropriately illustrated. At the time of Hobart's and Brant's study, several dozen Greenlandic books had been prepared, covering many fields such as reading, history, geography, arithmetic, music, and religion. We will examine the reasons for these different educational strategies in the next chapter. However, it should be noted here that the place of Greenlandic study in the school curriculum has encouraged the development of a written literature in the larger community and Greenlandic language transmissions on electronic media. This not only has increased congruence across educational contexts but also has created additional agencies of knowledge transmission. In the Canadian town of Frobisher Bay, the Honigmanns (1965) found very little radio programming in or for Eskimo, although Eskimo constituted a substantial portion of the population. Radios were played a great deal by Eskimo for music and entertainment, and movies were quite popular. The latter particularly, the researchers found, were a medium of instruction in English and Eurocanadian culture as well as a source of entertainment. Yet for many, insufficient mastery of English limited the educational utility of these media. Eskimo preferred "fast action films . . . in which the activity carries the story, obviating reliance on long dialogue scenes" which most people found hard to follow (Honigmann and Honigmann 1965:217).

The central position of language in many educational transactions creates special problems when the language of instruction is not the same as the language used by students outside that context. Given the ambiguity inherent in any communicative exchange, the instructional use of symbolic codes in which learners are not fluent increases the likelihood of miscommunication. This danger is still greater when participants do not recognize that the codes they are using differ. Gay and Cole (1967) discovered this in Kpelle Western-style schools. Before they began school, Kpelle children knew little English, the official language of instruction. More importantly, the variety of English which they did know (and which they identified as English) was a Liberian pidgin, synthesized from both English and Liberian dialects. Teachers unfamiliar with the dialect berated children for their "bad English." Teachers who spoke it themselves also tended to identify it with standard English. Because the meanings of certain words in each language often were different, insoluble confusion entered the process of information transfer. Gay and Cole (1967:32) cite this example:

> A first grade class we observed, taught by a good teacher, using a good textbook, a copy of which was in the hands of each pupil, failed completely to understand the concept "as many as." But there was a reason. In . . . Liberian-English, to say that there are more boys than girls, one may say that the boys are "many than" the girls. "Many than" is the closest phrase in Liberian-English to "as many as," therefore the child identifies the two. Naturally, he is totally confused when the teacher tells him that a set of five boys is "as many as" a set of five girls. . . . The teacher who failed to grasp the situation, was baffled and impotent.

In situations of this sort, particularly when the two languages in use by participants are similar in many respects, students often are stigmatized as incompetent in the language in use, and their own language is dismissed as an incorrect version of the language of instruction. Analogous hazards in communication and identity attribution are common in many U.S. classrooms for students whose native tongue is Black English Vernacular (BEV). Although it has much of the same vocabulary and grammar as Standard American English, BEV differs syntactically in important ways. Teachers who are unaware that BEV is a separate, independent dialect of English (cf. Labov 1972) are hampered in their attempts to teach its speakers the second dialect, Standard American English, as well as other subjects for which it is the medium. Students, in turn, are confronted with the fact that the language in which they are fluent is unacceptable as a vehicle for communication with teachers and that their language is considered inferior.

Educational strategies also are affected by cultural differences in the organization, interpretation, and use of various media. Styles of verbal transmission, the value accorded a speaker's facility, the domains of experience subject to verbal report all are culturally influenced. Cherokee students in

Anglo-oriented classrooms often are caught between conflicting cultural orientations of this sort. An example cited earlier showed that instructional strategies designed to facilitate learning by asking students for their thoughts and feelings, are interpreted by Cherokee as distinct invasions of privacy. They did not consider those thoughts and feelings appropriate topics for public verbal report, particularly in the presence of adults.

Both (a) the assumptions and expectations associated with a medium and (b) how the content it conveys is organized relate directly to the cognitive strategies used in interpretation. The importance of cultural differences in organizing media content is illustrated by the experiments of Worth and Adair (1972). Interested in cultural factors in visual and film communication, they taught six Navajo young adults the technical rudiments of using cameras and editing film footage. Compared to Anglo graduate students whom the researchers were accustomed to teaching, the Navajo learned these operations and developed professional skills in many areas extremely rapidly.[15] The films they made were very different from those made by either amateur or professional Anglo filmmakers.

The goal of all six Navajo filmmakers was to convey information, to teach something; in only one case, that of an art student somewhat more removed from traditional Navajo culture than the other five, did personal expression have a part in the film's production. In all cases, the filmmakers thought about what they wanted to film and how it would be structured before they began to run the camera. Their footage and subsequent editing of that footage showed a systematic execution of the conceptual design with which they had begun. This is not an ability Anglos can take for granted. Worth and Adair (1972:195) point out that the sophisticated facility demonstrated by their Navajo students commonly takes years of experience for Anglo university students. The latter have difficulty "visualiz[ing] specific images in a [complex] sequence." This is an ability common to Navajo craftspeople, who visualize complex design plans before they begin working.

The structure of Navajo films is marked by a visual code different from that of Anglos. First, the treatment of motion in the films and in the filmmakers' discussions of their work reflects its conceptual importance in Navajo language and thought. Certain kinds of motion are precisely portrayed, with a skill in editing very difficult for Anglos to match (cf., e.g., Worth and Adair 1972:99–100, 203). Yet in depicting other types of motion in which Anglos would value continuity, the Navajos allowed visual breaks in the motion through jump cuts. Almost all of the films devoted a great deal of footage to the portrayal of someone walking. In three ten-to-twenty minute long films, close to three-quarters of the footage was of walking. While for Anglo filmmakers cinematic depiction of walking tends to be a transition device, for the Navajo it was "an important event in and of itself" (Worth and Adair 1972:147). Walking is both a part of the conceptualization of event and a means of punctuating separate activities. It is a convention of Navajo narrative code, "a necessary element to a Navajo telling a story about Navajos" (Worth and Adair 1972:147). The films depicted facets of the Navajo world, often traditional activities such as weaving or sandpainting or silversmithing. The subject matter called for traditional treatment. In the two films which treated nontraditional topics, these conventions were less fully observed. The Navajo audience's reaction to these two was not as favorable as to the other films. When asked about the nontraditional films, audience members replied that they didn't understand them because they were "in English."

Second, while the filmmakers used various focal lengths and camera angles to achieve their purposes, they usually avoided taking close-up shots of people's faces. The exceptions were brief images of craftspeople looking up slightly, a stance understood to signify thinking about the design being executed, or brief shots of people looking away from the camera. In Navajo daily life and in filming, direct eye contact and staring are transgressions of Navajo social etiquette. Unless obviously done for humorous effect, they are invasions of privacy and potential insults. To look someone in the eye without blinking is very insulting (Worth and Adair 1972:156). Typically both adults and children react to full-face closeups on television or in films by giggling, smiling, or looking away.

Third, the filmmakers were bound by Navajo conceptions of property rights and intrusion. They were extremely careful to choose family members and family-owned objects as subjects of their filming, unless they secured formal permission to film others' possessions. Their attitude toward photographing an animal or a house was similar to what Anglos would think of as "borrowing." They also restricted themselves to the reservation, to their own territory.

Fourth, the way the filmmakers cut up and organized the flow of events was culturally patterned. They made very different assumptions about the proper relationship of the film event to the actual event and about the import of film images and segments than Anglo filmmakers would. For one film, Worth and Adair compared three vantage points: that of the Navajo filmmaker filming her mother weaving, that of the researchers as Anglo filmmakers, and that of an accomplished Anglo weaver. The Anglo filmmakers and the Anglo weaver mostly agreed about what should be included in a film about weaving, but the Navajo filmmaker made other choices. For example:

> The warp is strung by passing the wool over the top and bottom supports of the loom, tying a knot at the top for each pass. Since the warp is composed of several hundred threads, it is a highly repetitive job. [The Anglo weaver] noted the type of knot used and then simply waited for the next step. [The Navajo filmmaker], however, made thirty-seven [shots] of this process, paying particular attention to the motions of her mother's hands as she passed the ball of wool over

the wooden supports in a sort of flipping hand-over-hand motion with the ball
of wool passing from one hand to the other. There were many close–ups of the
number of knots tied and the exact way they were done. The sequence in the final
film showed the entire warp being put on with all the knots shown clearly and
often (Worth and Adair 1972:126).

While in this case the filmmaker gave more detailed or "literal" treatment than
her Anglo observers would have chosen, in other instances, continuity necessary by Anglo standards was ignored as unnecessary by the Navajo. The
choices made by the filmmakers were rooted in cultural knowledge shared by
their Navajo audience. Those films that were organized by a Navajo symbolic
code were appreciated and understood by the audience. Those films that
violated the Navajo conventions were seen as being "in English"; they did not
communicate successfully.

The viability of media as educational tools depends not only on the format
of organization but also on the implications of each medium within a particular
culture. Perhaps because of their cultural emphasis on motion, Navajo are
extremely receptive to the medium of cinematic film. Some cultures, on the
other hand, do not include visual codes that render film or photographic
images intelligible. Forge (1970) observed that the Abelam did not easily
distinguish people in photographs, unless they were distinctly framed either by
a solid background or by thick lines similar to those which outline forms in
their graphic art. They had particular difficulty when the person was not facing
the camera. Houses and objects were picked out more readily, although specific
identification still was difficult. Because he needed specific identifications from
photographs of various events, Forge trained some Abelam boys to "read"
photographs in the Western manner: "they learnt to do this after a few hours
of concentrated looking and discussions on both sides" (Forge 1970:288).
Ward (1977) argues that the extensive spread of Chinese culture to previously
heterogeneous ethnic groups was due in great measure to the performing arts
of theater and storytelling. In conjunction with colonization by Chinese settlers and administrators, theatrical performances associated with religious
festivals became a powerful educative force. The importance of popular theater
as a medium for knowledge transmission, recognized by several earlier Chinese
governments, is acknowledged also in China today, where it has become a
prominent educative tool.

Other cultural values can influence the use of media in educational transmission. The practical experience of apprentice canoe builders on Puluwat
includes first-hand participation in construction. In this society, canoe building
and navigation are the two most esteemed professions. At the University of
Allahabad, Di Bona found very different strategies for acquiring knowledge
and skills. Here, education is associated with a rigid system of stratification in
which each participant's status is linked with specific privileges and obligations. While subordinate to faculty, students are superordinate to the clerical,

technical, and domestic staff. The last are servants and subordinate to everyone else. To preserve their superior status, faculty and students pass menial tasks or tasks which require physical exertion down the status hierarchy to servants and other low status assistants. Under these circumstances, Di Bona asserts (1970:194):

> Student and teacher alike are prevented from coming to grips with empirical problems. In the photography class, for example, chemicals are often prepared by the assistant, thus giving the students little but theoretical awareness of the technical problems involved. During an agricultural experiment, one master's student not owning any work clothes sent the [servant] into the field to check on the progress of his plants. In zoology an animal catcher is employed because the students are never able to seek out animals and thus learn something of their habits. It would be considered most degrading to perform the work of this menial. . . .

Bypassing the "labor" of the laboratory, Di Bona indicates, seriously compromises the educational experience in empirical disciplines. Whether Di Bona's contention is correct requires further evidence. Is it a cultural assumption or a demonstrable fact that competence in zoology requires an intimate familiarity with animals in their natural habitat? The answer requires that we first specify what competence means in terms of the goals of knowledge acquisition. The educational strategies described by Di Bona would not be especially limiting in systems oriented to perpetuating authoritative traditions of knowledge. However it is not clear that they preclude empirical innovation in knowledge, if empirical information is transferred from assistants to their status superiors. Di Bona remarks that inferiors may not ask questions of superiors, but superiors may ask questions of inferiors. Whatever the nature of knowledge transmission at the University of Allahabad, it would be hazardous to assume that the rigid division of labor described, with its selective distribution of access to various media, inherently prohibits the development of empirical knowledge.

Consider a hypothetical question: could automobile mechanics be taught effectively without any manual experience during their instruction? The answer may depend on the student's learning strategies. Learning strategies in many American Indian cultures, as we have noted, are characterized by patient, detailed observation of others' activities. Only after they have mastered cognitively the details of the instructor's actions, do learners attempt to duplicate the activity, and they usually do so successfully on their first attempt. This facility is part of a culturally valued emphasis on acute visual discernment. Collier (1967) found that Navajos could identify and interpret details in photographs of familiar scenes that he was unable to detect without a magnifying glass.

Study of the symbolic codes and interpretive schemes applied to media form and content must be complemented by careful analysis of the sociocultural factors that influence the utilization of a particular medium. What little we know about these topics is based largely on Western experience. McLuhan and others have argued that the revolutions in communications wrought first by the printing press and more recently by the electronics industry have changed irrevocably the perception and orientation of all people touched by them. Masland and Masland (1975) argue that the acceptance of any technology carries with it a substratum of values and categories for organizing experience. Analyzing educational change in Samoa, they observe that "the use of tools carries with it . . . the idea of constructing a complex structure from simpler parts." There are also values inherent in the choice of one technological mode over another. Nail fastenings imply the value of permance and rigidity, whereas bound fastenings imply the value of flexibility and responsiveness to natural forces. Television, as they note, is a more complex tool than hammer and nail, but equally value-laden (Masland and Masland 1975:191). The ways in which the values implicit in a medium will affect prevailing modes of organizing experience cannot be predicted fully, for adopted technologies are also intepreted and adapted by those who make use of them. As little as we know about the ways in which Euroamericans process newer mass modes of communication or older forms, we know still less about how they are defined and understood by people with different cultural repertoires. The research of Worth and Adair is an important contribution to our understanding of these phenomena.

Media may be more than just the tools of educational transmission. They also may become alternative or competing agencies (cf. Gerbner 1974). Many schools in the U.S. use television programming as a part of classroom instruction. They also seek in some cases to counter its effect, competing with difficulty for student attention and credence against the powerful, multisensory appeal of television.[16] Books remain the chief instructional media, in spite of arguments that the cultural impact of printed media has diminished among young people because of their immersion in a pervasively electronic media environment (cf. Parker 1974, Carroll 1974). Printed materials, like electronic media, are used selectively; printed media not valued or even unacceptable to academic educators are also potential competitors with the transmissions they control. An interesting instance of competition within the academic context is cited by Dickeman (1971). Cherokee students who had effectively withdrawn from educational transactions initiated by the teacher, defined books in the classroom library as an alternative resource. In their free time they read these avidly.

The availability of educational media within and outside specific educational contexts is partly a function of patterns of media control, which in turn relates to the distribution of financial and material resources. Some educational media include objects freely available. Art and craft production may capitalize on discarded items or objects of little value as resources. Dyes, wood, clay, and fibers may be gathered readily from lands shared by the community. Diagrams etched in the dust, conversation, dance, and some forms of music require only human energy to become instructional media. But access to many educational media, like the knowledge required to use them, is bought at a price. In the U.S., access to scientific, electronic, and other types of manufactured equipment commonly used in school instruction, varies widely with funding levels. In financially weak schools, school library collections may be minimal, and even textbooks and other supplies for graphic communication may be in short supply and of poor quality. Distribution of media resources in other educational sectors also varies, partly because of the distribution of wealth and partly because of differences in prevailing values among participants.

Control over access is complemented by control over media content. All systematic education entails control over the content of transmission and over the media selected to convey that content. The content of mass media, however, is controlled by production agencies, which may or may not be responsive to pressure from other interest groups. When we speak of media as educational agencies analogous to schools, families, peer groups, and other such agencies of knowledge transmission, we refer to organizations producing simultaneous communications to populations, groups not differentiated as individuals. These communications may be described as secondary, in that they are not person-to-person but rather mass information transfers to classes of receivers. Media agencies may compete or cooperate as organizations, and their educational transmissions may exhibit varying degrees of mutual congruence. Insofar as the information they convey is controlled by similar interest groups, it may be analytically useful to consider them together. In societies like the U.S. in which mass-produced communications ranging from radio, television, and cinematic film, to consumer goods, are present in nearly all the environments of daily life, we may ask whether media agencies effectively dominate the society's educational system, as Gerbner (1974) has argued.

The role of interest groups in regulating the content of media transmission is important in analysing the interplay among educational agencies. In some societies, the state controlled content of radio and television transmission renders programming a tool of national proselytism, serving the goals of interest groups which most directly underwrite the government in power. Arnove (1975:6) reports that

> In multiethnic, multilingual societies using [educational television], I have not found a case where members of minority or nondominant social and cultural groups have actively participated in curriculum planning and development. For the most part, members of the urban elite have joined forces with the excolonial or trust power, to plan and develop curricula.

Curricula, not surprisingly, are often "mere transplants, with some trimming and pruning, of the standard curricula of the metropolitan country" (Arnove

1975:6). "Pirate" and "underground" broadcasters sometimes attempt to establish competitive channels of information transmission, with varying success. However, state control does not necessarily mean a monopoly of the content of transmission. In Scandinavia, regulatory councils are mandated to guarantee diversity in programming and representation by competing interest groups in that programming.[17] Nevertheless to some degree, both political and fiscal strength are prerequisite to significant influence over mass media of all kinds.

In distinctly multicultural societies (and increasingly there are no other kinds), the control of media transmission is of particular interest. As in schools, transmission content frequently reflects the cultural perspective of the controlling agency or dominant group. Media often establish and sustain definitions of sociocultural context which affect individual interpretations of the information conveyed. In the U.S. mass media are generally dominated by representatives of middle class Anglo culture, both as their controlling agents and as subjects of depiction. With the recent mobilization of minority populations into effective pressure groups with both economic and political influence, the content of transmissions has become somewhat more eclectic in its cultural orientation. Twenty years ago, black Americans found only grotesque stereotypes of themselves in radio, television, and cinema productions, along with the message that middle class Anglo culture was the only acceptable and prestigious one. Today a somewhat greater selection of black and other minority life styles is represented by the media.

This increased acknowledgement of minority groups as full-fledged members of the society, through more positive and accurate depictions, is part of the sociocultural context of other educational transactions. This is why the educational system of any society includes all the educational agencies engaged in knowledge transmission. For each agency, the others are part of its context and thus influence the specific educational transactions each controls. The availability of printed material and radio programs in Greenlandic, for example, conveys not only particular content but also a contextual message about Eskimo in relation to the multicultural society in which they live. The absence of Eskimo-language media transmissions in the Canadian Arctic carries equally significant information. In each case interpretation of these messages is influenced by the level of redundancy or inconsistency across contexts of individual experience.

Processes of knowledge transmission in specific educational contexts are important in their own right. Intensive studies of such processes in situ are essential, if we are to understand the actual dynamics of human learning. Adequate analysis must also take into account their sociocultural contexts. We cannot understand the underlying message exchange in classroom (family, peer group, and so forth) interaction without knowing the cultural repertoires of participants. The significance of role-relationships and identities prevailing in one educational context is not comprehended until they are analyzed in relation to those in other contexts of participant experience. Neither can the structural characteristics and operation of educational systems be fathomed without considering the interpersonal and group processes which generate, maintain and change them.

In the next chapter the dual types of analysis will be brought together. Looking at education as an agent both of sociocultural continuity and of sociocultural change, we will examine the interplay of structure and process in the organization of knowledge transmission.

notes

1. The controversy about sex education in U.S. schools is a useful illustration of differing assumptions about the age at which such knowledge should be transferred, the form this transfer should take, and instructional strategies appropriate to the task. The development of adult education programs in the U.S. likewise first had to modify the popular assumption that schooling was appropriate only to children or preadults. The differences in learning strategies used by children and more widely experienced adults is an important consideration for those responsible for organizing adult education programs. Many such efforts (e.g., in literacy training) have been hampered by the direct transfer of instructional strategies and materials effective with children to adult learners.

2. As Watson-Franke (1976) points out, relatively little cross-cultural research has been devoted to transmission of "female" domains of knowledge beyond skills of housekeeping. In large measure this may be attributed to the gender and gender-orientation of researchers. As E. Ardener (1975) has observed, even female researchers, because they have been trained in male-dominated disciplines, have tended to take the analytic vantage point of males. See further S. Ardener (1975) and Reiter (1975).

3. Relative innovativeness in various groups can be assessed adequately only when the domains compared are equivalent. Gladwin (1970) suggests that Puluwatans are experimental in orientation, but it is not clear from his treatment to what extent this characterizes other areas of Puluwat life. We would need to ask, for example, whether Kpelle farming is as convention-oriented as Kpelle social relations, to properly contrast the two approaches to knowledge.

4. An interesting comparison with Puluwat canoe building might be made with canoe building among the Warao of Venezuela, described by Wilbert (1976b). As in Puluwat, canoe building is a male occupation requiring long apprenticeship; mastery is achieved only by an artisan elite.

5. The Chassidic movement, which began as a revolt of the unlearned against the scholasticism of *shtetl* culture, developed a rabbinical tradition different from that described here. At first the knowledge of respected leaders was seen as inspired rather than scholastic; later it was viewed as being based on book learning. However the Chassidim remain "the only group of Jews for whom the religious leader represents absolute and indisputable authority" (Zborowski 1955:137).

6. Ward (1971) found a somewhat similar divergence between middle income Anglo parents and low income black parents in a rural community near New Orleans. Anglo parents systematically teach their children language by engaging them in conversation, expanding and correcting their utterances, and focusing on utterance form as much as or more than utterance content. The black mothers she studied did not attempt to instruct their children deliberately in language use, nor did they converse much with them. Children in this community nevertheless developed communicative competence in the language of the community at the same rate as Anglo children do. Thus differing cultural assumptions about the nature of learners and learning do not in themselves necessarily hamper learning process, so long as learner and instructor *share* congruent or complementary strategies for coping with the transmission process.

7. Wolcott (1967, 1974b), in his study of a Kwakiutl classroom, reports not only a conspiracy of silence but also of equally effective strategies for thwarting Anglo teachers' instructional efforts. In contrast to the successful compromises on which "intercultural" Cherokee-Anglo classrooms are based, Kwakiutl students, Wolcott found, both disliked school and strongly resisted any attempt to modify it. (Cf also King 1967.)

8. The interplay between teacher role and identity in U.S. schools is considerable. What a teacher is supposed to *do* in that role (e.g., instruct, model, evaluate, consult) is distinguishable from what a teacher is supposed to *be*. Yet the style in which these tasks are performed, contributes a great deal to social identities accorded by peers, superiors, and students. Further, a teacher's personal identity may affect that person's definition and performance of a teacher role (cf. Lightfoot 1973).

9. Di Bona (1970) comments that superiors may ask questions of inferiors but that inferiors may not put questions to superiors. While he refers to this in the context of relations between faculty and staff, the implication is that this is (or was) also true of teacher-student relations. The apparent similarity to the Burmese and Kpelle patterns calls for more intensive study of the nature of knowledge transmission where student/novice questions are strictly proscribed.

10. See Colletta (1976) for a description of peer group control of elementary school classroom transactions on Ponape (Micronesia).

11. For discussion of the similar conflict between student identity and male identity among U.S middle income Anglos, see Sexton (1969) and Hartley (1959).

12. Ogbu (1974) describes the gatekeeping functions of school counselors in a school in a low income neighborhood in similar terms. He adds that these children, largely black and Chicano, receive little counseling, partly because counselors themselves are overloaded with clients and administrative tasks. In general, the students, who have few independent sources of information about academic requirements necessary to reach long-range scholastic and occupational goals, are channeled into "dead end" courses of neither long term utility nor immediate intrinsic interest.

13. It is also rapidly becoming a part of the environment of many preschoolers elsewhere in the world. According to Goldsen (1976), versions of "Sesame Street" modified for language differences are now being shown in sixty-nine countries to better than forty million children. In addition, the English-language version has been purchased for broadcast in more than fifty countries, including Japan, Curaçao, Poland, and Yugoslavia. The producers of "Sesame Street" assert "that it is adaptable with only slight modifications to almost any social system" (Goldsen 1976:204). Not all countries have accepted the argument. Goldsen (1976:204–205n) points out that "Sesame Street" was rejected in England by the BBC, although they purchased "The Electric Company" in 1975; Britain's Independent Television Authority, on the other hand, did buy "Sesame Street." Rejection by the Peruvian Ministry of Education and the Soviet Union, and critical comments elsewhere (e.g., the Mexican journal *Siempre,* August 1973), are all based "on the claim that the programs project a particular set of values appropriate to a particular set of social relations in a particular social system."

14. "The Electric Company," also produced by Children's Television Workshop, *does* represent books and libraries. Since both are transmitted in the U.S. by the Public Broadcasting System, the reason for the difference between the two (insofar as it continues to hold) is not clear.

15. Worth and Adair (1972:85) note in this regard a conversation they had several weeks later with the former treasurer of the Navajo Tribe. When they told him how quickly the Navajo mastered filmmaking, he replied that they had also shown marked facility in learning to use IBM equipment bought recently by the tribe, and added with a smile,

Maybe you didn't tell them it was hard and they couldn't do it. Maybe they didn't know making movies was supposed to be a tough job.

16. Gerbner (1974) reports the results of content analyses of U.S. mass media depictions of teachers, students, and schools. As of the mid 1960s, he found teachers typically depicted as weak, ineffectual, neurotic, tyrannical, and generally unsuccessful. Depictions of scholars were disproportionately small, compared to their representation in the population at large; more interesting is the finding that portrayal of a teacher nearly always signalled a comedy. While the 1970s

witnessed some improvement in this, U.S. teachers clearly have not risen to the status of social heros, and schools as major segments of every individual's life experience tend to be notably underrepresented in mass media transmission in the U.S. Moreover, nearly all of the positive representations have been of male teachers. See Lightfoot (1977) for a discussion of teacher and mother images in U.S. elementary education.

17. Uniformity in mass media transmissions does not necessarily indicate central control. For the case of Japan, see Ishida's (1971:83–93) brief overview and Thayer's (1975) case study of Japanese newspapers.

SEVEN

EDUCATION AND SOCIOCULTURAL CHANGE

Basic to systematic knowledge transmission is the goal of perpetuating knowledge, whether through conveying new knowledge or through modifying earlier beliefs. Education is a means of conserving cultural knowledge over generations and also a tool for changing it. As the preceding chapters have emphasized, knowledge transmission is a social enterprise. The complex relationships between educational transactions and other facets of social life, among educational agencies, and between educational systems and the societies they serve, all make education equally relevant to continuity and change in social systems. In the sections that follow we will explore the role of education as an agent of sociocultural continuity and sociocultural change from various angles, using the analytic frameworks developed earlier.

education and the conservation of tradition

The relationship between education and the conservation of culture is implied in our definition of education as a deliberate and systematic attempt to transmit cultural knowledge and attitudes. We also have noted that sources of incomplete or modified transmission are found in every society. Since individuals within a society differ in their cultural repertoires, and since the communication process itself mediates between an instructor's intentions and the messages a student receives, culture is never transferred intact from one generation to the next. Nevertheless cultural knowledge can be and often is substantially shared from generation to generation.

Forge (1967) provides an interesting example of this among Abelam artists. Artistic styles and types of production vary among Abelam villages, and aspiring artists may seek instruction from a variety of tutors. Still, all artists work within fairly narrow stylistic limits. Since all their products are intended for ceremonial use, they must meet the accepted criteria for ritual effectiveness. While the artists themselves are interested in aesthetic criteria of evaluation, their larger public judges art products only by their correctness and effectiveness.

When two artists painting the facade of a new ceremonial house introduced a very narrow band of decoration slightly different from a traditional form, public reaction was at first dubious, with outright opposition by some older men. The artists, both of whom were renowned, and their helpers were adamant about retaining the design elements. The neighboring villages much admired the innovations and the ceremonial house even gained special prestige. Had the yam crop, which then was harvested, been of lesser quality than usual, however, the artistic innovation might have received some of the blame.

That stylistic change is actually endemic is demonstrated in a comparison of old and new carvings. Yet Abelam artists claim a continuity of tradition.

> Normally ... the stylistic difference does not worry anyone; it is simply ignored. ... [After the ethnographer confronted artists with the obvious differences, however,] artists ... speculated on the change in style, wondering whether their style or the old style is the right one, ending by saying that anyhow they know how to carve only in their present style and could not recreate the old style if they wanted to (Forge 1967:83).

This gradual change shows the creative approach of Abelam artists. They never copy one another or a model; rather they study and internalize the essential features of traditional forms and reproduce them from their own vision. But this change is not radical. In response to contact with the Australian colonial administration and missions, Abelam art has become still more conservative, for it now serves as a symbol of Abelam culture in its encounter with colonialism.

Puluwat navigators, as we noted earlier, also are conservative, though experimental. Unless their knowledge proves inaccurate or ineffective, they are inclined to retain it as part of the professional corpus, even if they have never used it. New knowledge is eagerly accepted if it can be adapted to their working repertoire. For instance, Gladwin (1970) found that magnetic compasses had become standard equipment on may Puluwat canoes, but they were not used primarily as navigational tools. For this, the traditional system of reckoning by the stars was preferred. Although navigators were aware of the relationships between star readings and compass readings, and could make the necessary calculations to translate compass readings for their navigational schemes, it simply was an unnecessary and cumbersome addition to their traditional reckonings. Magnetic compasses, therefore, were used as complements to that system, increasing its effectiveness. They were used principally to maintain a course reckoned by the stars or to keep track of direction when a canoe was caught in a heavy storm.

In both the Abelam and Puluwat cases, the cultural tradition being transmitted is valued as the accumulated wisdom of previous generations. Both as a valued cultural heritage and as a valued set of skills, this knowledge is taught carefully. The student is freed from the tutor's supervision when he demonstrates mastery of that knowledge to the tutor's satisfaction. On Puluwat, Gladwin reports, even a master navigator may return to the tutorial relationship with his still more experienced teacher when in doubt about a detail of that knowledge. In an essay on French primary schooling, Jean Boorsch (1958–59) remarks on one of the sources of cultural continuity in that society: the very slow rate of change in curriculum, teaching methods, and textbooks. Certain readers have been used for at least half a century. We may discern in these examples an abiding sense of cultural continuity in the participants as well as mechanisms which promote it.

As these cases illustrate, conservation of tradition generally is a matter of degree. By what criteria are we to assess relative continuity? Abelam artists see themselves as more culturally conservative than does Forge, their foreign observer. This conservative image seems to be related to the Abelam definition of knowledge in the domain of art and its associated values. The ritual efficacy of artistic productions depends on their fidelity to a traditional code. Innovation, when it occurs, is subject to pragmatic test, but it is a risky proposition. Puluwat navigators, too, see innovation as risky, but their corpus of knowledge is not conceived as closed.

There are several issues involved in the concept of cultural continuity. First, in which domains of knowledge is continuity valued and sought? Is the conservation of cultural tradition a general value or is it associated only with particular types of knowledge? Because cultural knowledge is not a fully consistent and organized system, people may value continuity in some types of knowledge regardless of its congruence with other types . For this reason continuity, such as Boorsch reports in French schooling traditions, may not reflect continuity in the knowledge used in other areas of daily life. Second, what is the relationship between cultural conceptions of continuity and the degree of continuity perceived by an outside observer? Both of these questions are important for documenting continuity and its relationship to education. Many of the societies studied by anthropologists have been characterized as conserving of tradition, but it is not always clear to what extent this conservatism is selective and to what extent it represents an expressed value that masks historical change. Finally, whose tradition is conserved? While this is of greatest importance in multicultural societies, the control which educative agencies in any society exert over the knowledge transmitted implies selective conservation by each agency. The teachings in Poro schools were not fully congruent with knowledge and attitudes learned within the family. Children's play groups in many societies are repositories of knowledge not transmitted by any other agency. Yet often knowledge gathered in such groups does not survive in the repertoires of adults (cf. Opie and Opie 1960). Incongruence of transmissions by various agencies frequently is coupled with variation in the value or credence accorded each set of transmissions in the course of an individual's life.

In the U.S., Illich (e.g., 1971a) and others have argued, schools teach children, explicitly and implicitly, a view of "the way life really is" which is a distorted picture of reality. Both the selection of intellectual knowledge incorporated in the curriculum and the organization of school life itself, it is said, effectively communicate a view of society that ignores the fundamental conflicts, cultural and social, which are present in "real life." This view, as Apple (1975:353) puts it,

> often supports political and intellectual quiescence rather than conflict and serious questioning by students. . . . Assumptions of consensus—both intellectual and normative—seem to dominate the knowledge itself.

While in some ways this is so, it can also be argued that students are taught very realistic lessons in school: they are taught implicitly, for instance, how bureaucratic structures work, the nature of power, and the relevance of behavioral style and personal characteristics to evaluation of their objective performance. It is not so much that children in schools are presented a simplistic, idealized view of the sociocultural system (although this is largely the case), as that they are taught to see the system from the point of view of a single segment of the population, that segment economically and politically dominant. Carnoy (1974) labels this the "colonizing" function of schools.[1] Belief in meritocracy, in equality of academic opportunity and access to valued goods (e.g., occupation, income, status) on the basis of academic credentials, is encouraged both in schools and outside them. Credence given to this premise, however, varies; members of subordinate minorities faced with the realities of occupational access do not always learn this lesson.[2]

In analyzing the content of knowledge transmission within a given organization or context, such as schools, we must ask how the transmissions (both formal and informal) reflect the interests and orientations of those who disseminate them, how they compare with transmissions to the same learners by other agencies, and what value is placed by transmitters and learners on the transmissions and the traditions they represent. To analyze the processes of transmission in schools, Apple (1975:355) suggests three areas of investigation:

> (1) how the basic day-to-day regularities of schools contribute to these ideologies; (2) how the specific forms of curricular knowledge reflect these configurations; and (3) how these ideologies are reflected in the fundamental perspectives educators themselves employ to order, guide, and give meaning to their own activity.

We also must determine to what degree the corpus of knowledge transmitted is the same among schools. For instance, is the content of transmission the same in a wealthy Chicago suburban school and a southside black ghetto school?[3] Even within predominantly middle class Anglo schools, there are other influences on the effective transmission of such traditions. Unless we include the decoding and interpretive strategies used by the receivers, we cannot establish the significance of instructional continuities for the perpetuation of such cultural ideas as Apple describes. To assess the role of U.S. schools in conserving cultural tradition, we must also investigate messages received by students and the ways in which this information is interpreted in light of their experiences in other contexts.

The question was asked earlier: whose tradition is conserved? To this we need to add a corollary question: by whom is a body of knowledge carried on? Abelam artistry and Puluwat navigational expertise are transmitted fully only to men. Certain domains of knowledge controlled by Poro organizations were available exclusively to progeny of the Poro elite. Cultural continuity, in other words, cannot be analyzed without considering the distribution of knowledge in society and its relationship to social structure. As an agent of sociocultural continuity, education is effective insofar as it perpetuates that distribution and the underlying structure of social relationships.

In the historical Poro schools of West Africa, students were instructed in various kinds of knowledge, including the hierarchical organization of social relations. Students learned to respect authority and to obey the demands of those higher in status. They learned that knowledge was power and that to secure power, they had to secure the favor of the established elite. Sociopolitical mobility and even social acceptance depended on conformity with the traditions and standards represented by the establishment. Cultural innovation that threatened its hegemony was largely thwarted until a combination of social forces, including colonial rule, undermined their power base. At the same time, among the Kpelle (whose grandparents knew more of the Poro tradition than contemporary Kpelle do), conservatism as an ideological principle of the culture seems to persist, supported by other educational experiences which have taken over the central role of the full-fledged Poro schools.

In preindustrial England, sociocultural continuity was effected in part by providing different types of schooling to different groups. In his study of British elite schooling, Wilkinson (1964:95) asserts:

> Admittedly, the Victorian public schools did their bit to create unequal opportunity: by helping to crystallize an "Establishment" style and accent, they made it all the harder for a working-class person without that style and accent to be accepted in the top circles of power. Likewise the emphasis on classics, however nobly viewed, provided the schools with a neat formula for offering free and reduced-fee scholarships and still excluding the lower-class boy. The formula worked because, at primary school level, Latin and Greek were a virtual monopoly of private education—the "prep" school and family tutor. By stressing Latin, public school entrance examinations deterred working-class families from even seeking entry to these schools.

By providing only catechetical instruction to farmers, vocational training to the working class, training in the classics and professions to the prosperous middle class and upper class, with little chance of transfer between the separate schooling tracks, it was theoretically possible to maintain the stability of the social system and the prevailing allocation of roles, rights, and material benefits.

Conservation of sociocultural continuity depends on the effectiveness of control over the distribution of knowledge and over the traditional structure of social relationships. Changing conditions in a society, however, may lessen the effectiveness of education as an agent of conservation. This is apparent in Di Bona's study of the University of Allahabad. While the goals of the institution's administration remained conservative, the milieu in which the university operated was changing. To a degree, the university remains an effective agent of tradition. Much of the knowledge transmitted concerns the relationship between types of persons: subordinates to superordinates, students to teachers, students to clerks, students to domestics, junior faculty to senior faculty, and so forth. All "factual" learning takes place within this intricate social structure and is affected by it, as in the separation of manual and intellectual work within scientific disciplines. This helps to perpetuate the hierarchical system of stratification characteristic of Indian social structure.

In the colonial era, university education, as in preindustrial England, was a direct route to a prestigious and remunerative socio-occupational position. Since then access to university training has broadened, allowing entry to students with more diverse socioeconomic backgrounds, and the certainty of desirable employment has decreased. The traditional hierarchy within the university is increasingly crosscut by factional interest groups, traditional values supporting that hierarchy are changing, and the respected, privileged status of academic participants in the larger society is no longer secure. These changes, largely resulting from events outside the university, have diminished its effectiveness as an agent of sociocultural conservation.

Education can contribute to sociocultural continuity even when it is designed to eradicate existing traditional barriers to valued knowledge and prerogatives.[4] In the school system introduced by the French revolutionaries, a policy of equal academic opportunity was supported by using scholastic merit as the sole criterion of academic mobility. This was intended as a mechanism for creating a society in which individual merit, rather than social status ascribed by birth into privileged classes, would be the basis of upward mobility. Yet academic merit was and is influenced by factors inherent in the existing social structure. Social structural bases of differential individual or group mobility are not necessarily eradicated by the formal elimination of social criteria of admission and advancement within academic institutions. A similar situation is found in the U.S. As in France, the U.S. system of academic education is based on the concept of equal opportunity. What sociocultural factors affect the achievement of such a goal and how does schooling, in turn, help to maintain prevailing sociocultural conditions?[5]

The network of social relationships and the distribution of valued knowledge, material wealth, power, and access to them which together make up social structure, also establish environments for knowledge transmission. The greater the differentiation in distribution of these elements, the more the learning environments of privileged groups or social sectors will differ from those of the less privileged. In the U.S., we find differences in such features as (a) the various types of role models available within an individual's personal community or sphere of personal acquaintances and within the group or social sector with which an individual most closely identifies (e.g., the scarcity of women, blacks, and other less privileged populations in top administrative positions); (b) available media depictions of the sociocultural reality experienced by individuals in different sectors and of the valued options open to them; (c) access to a diversity of learning resources, especially those which promote types of learning valued by academic transmission agencies; (d) access to high quality instruction and instructional materials in school; (e) cultural congruence between instructors and learners, and between learners and curriculum in academic contexts; (f) congruence across contexts of knowledge transmission. Each of these may affect the processes of knowledge transmission and acknowledged achievement within the academic context. In part they do so through their cumulative effect on the social and personal identities individuals acquire. In part they enter into the interpretive and adaptive strategies that individuals develop to deal with their schooling experiences. And in part they filter the types of knowledge available to individuals during their schooling, with direct consequences for their future options within the society as a whole.

Coupled with these differences in learning environments are differences in the patterns of knowledge use in the society. Types of knowledge tend to be associated with types of economic and social roles. Acquiring particular types of knowledge opens particular options to learners, but it also may close off other options, as choosing either a college preparatory or vocational high school curriculum. From patterns of differential distribution of valued prerogatives and perquisites, the society's members receive information about their own probable futures. If access routes through academic mobility are perceived by students as limited or effectively closed, much of the academic curriculum and even schooling itself may be perceived as a meaningless exercise. This is particularly probable if transmissions of other agencies, such as media, families, and peer groups, confirm these perceptions. In other words, both real and expected barriers to upward mobility may reduce students' efforts to meet academic criteria for advancement by acquiring academic knowledge.

Social structure is perpetuated partly through the power of dominant groups in controlling access to valued goods such as wealth, status, influence, and knowledge. But cultural beliefs can also be an important conservative force. In Japan, as we have seen, a widely shared belief that academic opportunity is not related to class and that socioeconomic mobility is a function of individual merit, helps to perpetuate a highly stratified system. In the U.S. an ideology of equal opportunity is also shared by many. The system of public schools and compulsory attendance has been designed in part to help establish equal opportunity as a reality. But cultural beliefs associated with the equality ideal, as in Japan, hinder its achievement. These beliefs shape the decisions of those assessing academic merit within schools and those controlling access to valued prerogatives in other sectors of the society. One such belief, widely held, is that people "naturally" have different aptitudes. "Discovery" of these aptitudes is one function of academic educators, who thereby assist in allocating people to various occupational niches. In principle, this selection and allocation process is based on aptitude and achievement. By what criteria are these two characteristics assessed? As the studies cited in earlier chapters indicate, determination of aptitude is by no means a straightforward procedure. "Objective" tests of aptitude are problematic in that the strategies and cultural orientations of those tested are rarely considered in designing and administering such tests. Moreover, as Cicourel and Kitsuse (1963) have documented, test results are colored further by the evaluators' subjective interpretations. Achievement, too, represents a judgment which is made according to particular cultural standards, generally standards congruent with the values of the dominant or elite social sector which effectively controls both the academic domain and access to privilege in the larger society. Those who meet the standards most closely are selected for elite roles and access to privilege. Clearly there are more opportunities for those whose other educative experiences have provided them with the most appropriate adaptive strategies, and fewer opportunities for those with a differing background.

At the same time, the principle of equal opportunity is widely assumed to prevail. That it does is demonstrated by reference to Those Who Made It; that a black child in Harlem grows up and becomes a respected author is evidence that the principle works. Together these beliefs influence the assessment of individual merit. The assumption of the "natural" inferiority of some individuals or groups is readily extended to those whose culture is not the same as that of the dominant group and the educative agency they control. Enlightened perspectives, disavowing genetic or racial explanations of these differences, may explain them as results of "cultural deprivation." Either way, the source of inferiority is attributed to the less privileged group, not to the system of classification used and to the manipulation of opportunity by representatives of the dominant social class.

Academic education helps to conserve the existing social structure and the dominant culture (a) by establishing criteria for prestige and advancement consonant with the values of dominant sociocultural groups; (b) by categorizing students and assigning them to alternative curriculum channels, thereby ensuring differential preparation and allocation to roles; (c) by training students to accept the identities established for them by the educational decision makers and, for many, to accept the reduced autonomy and low aspirations deemed appropriate to their "types"; and (d) by training students to adjust to a bureaucratic system.[6] Because this educative agency, like others in the society, is susceptible to pressure from other interest groups, the organization of schooling tends to reflect the interests of the most influential of these groups (cf. Tyack 1974). The history of education in the U.S. indicates that educational reform has nearly always been an innovation of privileged groups, aimed first at improving conditions for their own children. The expansion and improvement of educational facilities has not been primarily an effort to equalize access to the valued goods of the society. Compulsory schooling, for instance, was established to control entry into the labor market. The upgrading of minimum educational qualifications for employment reflects this, as well as employers' concerns for enhanced skills in the occupations they control (cf. Berg 1970).

At the same time, continuity in both academic and nonacademic realms is relative; change is occurring in both. The causes of both conservation and change are complex and have not been investigated adequately. Those discussed above represent a few of the most apparent contributions of U.S. academic education to sociocultural conservation. Another angle from which to examine this topic is through analysis of the internal organization of educative agencies, concentrating on those features which tend to minimize change and maintain established traditions.

Studies of successful and unsuccessful innovations in U.S. school systems have indicated that certain types of innovation succeed more readily than others, notably changes in curricula content, in specific activities added to or subtracted from the school routine, and in vocabularies used to describe what happens in school. Less apt to change have been the organization of role responsibilities in the school and in the larger school system, the way in which administrators relate to classroom teachers, the way in which teachers relate to students, and patterns of classroom interaction and basic educational processes. As Sarason (1971) argues, attempts at innovation in schools typically have ignored the cultural and structural traditions of the school as a sociocultural system or have assumed the nature of these traditions from the attributes of an ideal model built into the theory being applied. Aspiring innovators, usually outsiders to the school, rarely study the particular features of the school(s) in which they intend to initiate change, before designing and introducing the new scheme.

In an earlier chapter we observed that social structure and culture are adaptive responses to environmental conditions broadly defined. Because those conditions are never constant through time, all groups which manage to survive thereby demonstrate some capacity for adjusting to environmental changes. Cumulative adjustments can lead to marked alterations in the group's social or cultural organization. At the same time, because experience, including participants' perceptions of environmental conditions, is filtered through cultural frames of reference, new information tends to be assimilated into the corpus of knowledge in terms of familiar categories and traditional assumptions. However receptive to change a particular group or society may be (by virtue of cultural attitudes or modes of social organization), there is always a dialectic relationship between change and continuity. Schools are like other human groups in these respects.

The actual social structure of a school does not necessarily match its model. The relationships among participants reflect many conditions specific to the external and internal environment of that school, the history of those relationships, and the evolved culture of the school society. How the school works as a social system depends in large measure on how role relationships are conceived by participants, for these assumptions underlie the alternatives each participant sees as available to her or him within the system. Beliefs about how the system works vary with role vantage points, such as those of teacher, principal, parent, student, and outside consultant. The culture of the school society includes such diverse beliefs as these as well as beliefs and attitudes held in common by all participants.

In the organizational charter of the school system, the principal is given a rather vaguely defined set of supervisory and administrative responsibilities. As an official in a more inclusive bureaucracy, he or she must answer both to system superiors and to the public the school serves. As the designated manager of activities within the school, the principal must also develop strategies to secure desired behavior from other active participants in the school society.[7] The way in which a given individual actually performs the principal's role in this context varies, depending on her or his beliefs about what the principal's responsibilities and functions should be, beliefs about how much leeway the system will allow a principal in fulfilling these responsibilities, and so forth. As Sarason (1971), Vidich and McReynolds (1971), and Wolcott (1973, 1974a) have all pointed out, those who become principals are usually those who have adjusted best to the sociocultural traditions of the school; as such they are not likely to be very innovative. Nor do the criteria of qualification used in recruiting principals include innovative leadership. Because some principals do test the limits of their authority vis-à-vis the school system or the community, we can see that those limits are in fact negotiable, and that many alternatives are potentially available.[8] The belief that alternatives are few and fixed, however, prevents many principals from deviating from traditional paths, and from testing apparent limits. The widespread belief that change is "positive" and "progressive" pressures other principals to encourage some types of innovation in order to demonstrate their enlightened approach to school management (cf. Wolcott 1973:307–309).

Teachers, too, often feel boxed in by beliefs of this sort. Their beliefs about what the principal should do, what they themselves as teachers should do, what children should do, are complicated by their beliefs about what principals, parents, and other teachers expect of them and of the students they teach, and about the likely consequences should they choose a nonroutine alternative. Fuchs (1969) documents the socialization of new teachers into the system of the school, a process which helps to establish these beliefs. Like the principal, teachers are confronted with impossible tasks; what they and others feel *should* be accomplished in the classroom or the school cannot be achieved. Teachers know they are unable to do justice to the academic and personal needs of each child. As Sarason (1971:155) says, "Within the limits of time and capability the teacher may try to reach and help each child, but these attempts are rarely sufficient to enable the teacher to maintain the myth that she [or he] is indeed helping each child." Moreover, teachers often feel that the difficulties of their role are not appreciated by parents, children, or principal; yet they tend simultaneously to share others' negative appraisals of their own inabilities to achieve their classroom goals. While principals often lament the reluctance of some teachers to deviate from traditional curricula and modes of instruction, teachers in the same schools often believe that they *must* not deviate, that the constraints are external to them. As with principals, such beliefs are often sufficient to prevent experiment. The power of these traditions is based on several unquestioned assumptions constituting the cultural core of school society. Particularly important is the value placed on objective measures of productivity.

Within most U.S. elementary and secondary schools, instruction is influenced by the following conditions. First, in each grade, students are expected to acquire specific academic skills measurable by achievement tests.

This is one of the teacher's primary responsibilities: to ensure that all or most of the students in his or her class meet objective (i.e., external) standards of achievement. Teachers believe, with good reason, that they themselves are evaluated largely by the accomplishments of their students—by their superiors, by their fellow teachers, and by parents. Second, this learning must be achieved within the limited time period of the school year. The students must "get through" the material whatever the cost to other promising kinds of learning. Third, the students must be ranked relative to one another and relative to their presumed ability. This involves two issues, graded classroom levels and individual grade reports. Like the open classroom concept in the school studied by Goetz (1975), upgraded schools usually are new labels for unchanged classroom organization (cf. McLoughlin 1968). Even when students move through grade levels in different subjects at varying paces, the grade levels themselves remain important as "public," "objective," "measurable" criteria of student evaluation. The elimination of letter grades in favor of conferences also changes neither the emphasis on measurable student achievement nor the recording of related evaluations. Fourth, student achievement levels both within classes and through the graded class sequence are a major determinant of student prestige. The better the academic performance and the more advanced the grade level, the more worthwhile the student is considered by teachers, the principal, and other students. Teachers, too, gain prestige as they rise in the grade sequence with a marked jump from elementary school (with a general curriculum) to high school (with specialized courses).

The first two conditions, the requirement that students be prepared to demonstrate specific types of learning in a limited period of time, limit the teacher's experimentation. This is true particularly if the teachers have not been consulted in designing intended innovations, have not been convinced of the understanding support of those evaluating the outcomes of any experiments, and have not been told clearly the goals, probable timetable, and overall strategies of the proposed change.[9] Sarason (1971:221–222) rightly emphasizes the importance of history in this regard. Part of the background knowledge school participants use in interpreting new attempts to introduce change is the memory of past attempts. Past failures and the reasons for them do not help engender cooperative enthusiasm for a new version of an old idea. Change in some areas may be valued and/or expected, while in others change may be resisted. In either case, the identity of the innovation's "source" will affect its interpretation by participants (Gallaher 1965). If change is introduced from outside the school, as is often the case, the principal and teachers may view it suspiciously both because outsiders typically do not know the facts of daily life in the particular school, and because change implies previous inadequacy, which threatens the educators' self-esteem. Moreover, practitioners faced with classroom realities in implementing curricular innovation often find themselves handicapped by the absence of complementary teaching materials for achieving the ideal objectives of researcher-theorists.

As Sarason points out, substantive changes in school organization or in classroom life cannot be made by following a master formula that is not adapted to the particular school society. Neither can they be achieved without important kinds of unlearning and relearning by those responsible for the status quo. Such relearning can take place when teachers are enlisted as active colleagues in the innovation process, and when they are granted the support and leeway necessary to allow risk-taking. When intended changes go against ingrained cultural values and beliefs, these values and beliefs must be clarified and reassessed before change can be made in some derivative behavior.

Neither can we assume that students are simply passive recipients of other participants' decisions. Students, too, filter encounters with the school through interpretive schemes that affect their perception of alternatives and choice of strategies. Because the cultural emphases on "objective achievement" and "right answers" have been learned so thoroughly, students learn to resist alternative kinds of learning. The tendency of teachers to be the center of classroom interactions, "orchestrat[ing] the contributions and responses of students around his or her own periods of lecture" (Scrupski 1975:150), reinforces the idea of the teacher as the source of information, answers, and achievement evaluation. In an analysis of videotaped first, sixth, and eleventh grade classroom interactions, Adams and Biddle (1970:39–40) found not only that the entire class was in one teacher-centered group 75 percent of the time and that the teacher was principal actor 84 percent of the time, but also that 65 percent of the time was spent simply in disseminating information, while only 20 percent of the time was spent on intellectual processes such as reasoning, deducing, and expressing opinion. Sarason (1971:74) cites research on questioning in the classroom which sheds additional light on the origin of student conservatism.

1. Across the different studies the range of rate of teacher questions per half-hour is from 45–150.

2. When asked, educators as well as other groups vastly underestimate the rate of teacher questions, the estimated range being 12–20 per half hour.

3. From 67 to 95 percent of all teacher questions require "straight recall" from the student.

4. Children ask *fewer* than two questions per half hour. . . .

5. The greater the tendency for a teacher to ask straight recall questions the fewer the questions initiated by children. This does not mean that children do not have time to ask questions. They do have time.

. . . .

7. The rate of questions by children does not seem to vary with IQ level or with social-class background.

Students learn well that questions have answers, that there is one correct solution to a problem, that learning means the retention of information and that the demonstration of learning means the regurgitation of this information. When told that there may be no "right" answers to a question posed by a teacher, or that there are alternative solutions to a problem, when asked to "think creatively" about material rather than simply to organize and reproduce it, students so trained become bewildered, anxious, or angry. Certainly many will not support such innovation by an experimental teacher; their skepticism and resistance would have to be overcome before such an innovation could succeed (cf. Wolcott 1967).

Finally we must look at the organizational structure of the school as a source of conservatism. Four elements of this structure are particularly relevant. First, the teachers, especially those in elementary schools, are largely isolated from contact with other adults, whether fellow teachers or administrative superiors. Moreover, like students, they are almost never alone. Second, the interpersonal adult relationships within the school that teachers do have, are typically with other teachers. McPherson (1972:73, 81) comments about the small town school she studied:

> The congruence of one teacher's attitudes and behaviors with the other teachers was increased by her contact with them. As she listened to the comments about pupils and the experiences of others, she found justification as well as standards.
>
> . . . .
>
> The barriers between upstairs and downstairs, old guard and new, regular and special, primary and intermediate teachers were all important, but all of those became somewhat less important to the teacher than her unity with her colleagues when she was face to face with . . . the pupil, the parent, or the administration.

Third, in most schools the structure is hierarchical. Principal-teacher interactions are analogous to teacher-student interactions in that communication tends to be in one direction, from superior to subordinate. In this structure, teachers rarely initiate conversation with the principal; rather the principal talks and teachers listen. Participants' perceptions of this hierarchy and its implications for their own action, encourages their assigning ultimate responsibility "elsewhere" in the system. To be acceptable, responsibility requires access to resources and autonomous authority; without these an individual cannot meet the associated obligations. Even principals often lack these requirements for responsibility and effectiveness and so must refer responsibility "up" to their system superiors. Because principals (like teachers) are primary evaluators of their subordinates, teachers often feel compelled to maintain personal distance and distrust toward them. If the principal takes a laissez-faire or hands-off stance toward what happens in the classroom, and if the principal shows respect for the teacher's activities and role performance, more relaxed relations and greater cooperation in a principal-supported program of innovation are likely to follow.

Schools and other educational institutions are subject to the conservative weight of sociocultural traditions taken for granted by the participants, but they are also complex organizations susceptible to adjustment and change. Participants in U.S. schools face day-to-day contingencies and requirements that discourage serious innovation, as well as biographical and social-historical factors that condition their expectations of innovative schemes. Change generated within the school usually is minor, largely because of the selection process which initiates new teachers, rewarding those who adapt to existing conditions, and the relative isolation of roles, which minimizes consultation and cooperation among student, teacher, parent, and principal. Change introduced from the outside is rarely formulated to meet the specific conditions of the institution and more rarely still takes into account the human factors in successful change.

Sociocultural conservation and change are inherent in human social life, but the relative weight of each and the domains each characterizes differ across societies. Their relationship to educational systems is illustrated by Hobart and Brant's (1965) comparison of Eskimo schooling in two distinctly different sociocultural contexts, Danish Greenland and the Canadian Arctic, based on both fieldwork and historical research. While neither case represents an indigenous system of education in that the development of academic schooling resulted from colonial intervention, they reflect very different colonial policies.

The Canadian policy has been one of "cultural replacement," attempting to replace traditional Eskimo culture with "modern" (i.e., Canadian) attitudes, organizational forms, and technological skills. The Danish policy has been one of "cultural continuity," attempting to allow all the basic features of the culture to persist intact, with a recent policy shift to "cultural synthesis," a planned, gradual introduction of change that allows for cultural reformulation under the direction and by the choice of the Eskimo themselves. As Hobart and Brant point out, Danish policies were designed to protect Greenlanders from "disruptively rapid acculturation." Economic transactions, channelled through the Royal Greenland Trading Company, were organized on a "break-even" rather than a profit-making basis. Access to the colony[10] was limited to those individuals who were serving it in some respect, thereby minimizing the introduction of new diseases and uncontrolled European settlement. Administrative policy, particularly in judicial matters, drew heavily on Eskimo values and sanctions.

Fostering the continuation of Eskimo culture in all major respects except religion (having introduced Lutheranism), the Danes established a wide network of local schools, with teachers recruited from the local population. Usually these were individuals trained as Lutheran catechists. The language of instruction and of textbooks was Eskimo, as was the content of the curriculum, to a considerable extent. Book learning was supplemented by practical training in traditional skills and crafts, to help the people use local resources and established techniques in making their living in an isolated Eskimo society.

As a result, illiteracy was abolished a century ago, and facilities for secondary and continuation schools have been expanding for the past several decades. Trained leadership has been developed locally: until 1955, all teachers were Greenlanders, and Greenlanders currently head the school system as well as other public facilities. Following World War II and the postwar change in status from colony to province of Denmark, Greenland's school system changed significantly, mostly as a result of Greenlanders' demands.

During World War II when Denmark was occupied by German forces, the Danish ambassador in Washington, D.C. concluded on Denmark's behalf an agreement with the U.S. with respect to Greenland. The agreement was

> that America should take Greenland under her protection and in return be permitted to establish her military bases there "for the duration of the present situation" i.e., Nazi Germany policy of conquest. But "present situations" have a habit of lasting more or less indefinitely (Lauring 1968:255).

The status of the American military base has been under intermittent negotiation since; the extent to which it drew or draws on local population for personnel is unclear, but it may account in part for the Eskimos' expanded awareness of new technological and economic opportunities. After the war, through a constitutional amendment, Greenland was given the status of a Danish province (county) rather than that of colony. With this a program of modernization was begun to bring schools, hospitals, trades, and local administration up to the standards in the rest of Denmark. The resulting changes, brought about at first by the importation of Danish technical personnel, created a socioeconomic class division between Danes and Greenlanders, a consequence considered by the Danish government as a problem to be solved.

These changes caused others in the schooling curriculum, particularly a greater emphasis on transmission of two bodies of cultural knowledge. Both Danish and Eskimo languages are taught; more curricular materials on Denmark have been included, though primary emphasis on Greenlandic literature, history, geography, art and music continues; instruction in European-derived practical skills, increasingly relevant in Greenlandic life, has been added; and diversification and expansion of advanced schooling opportunities, including study in Denmark, have been instituted.

The curricular reforms were supplemented by importing many Danish teachers. These newcomers have made a marked effort to be integrated into the local Greenlandic community, residentially, economically, and socially. Separated most by linguistic barriers (for relatively few Greenlanders know Danish well and few Danish teachers are fluent in Greenlandic), many Danish teachers have taken advantage of free language lessons in their desire to interact more meaningfully with the Greenlanders. Although there is a growing demand for more thorough instruction in Danish, especially from better-schooled Greenlanders, Hobart and Brant (1965:52) found "no discernible tendency for Greenlanders at any social level to downgrade their image of the mother tongue nor to anticipate its replacement as the language of daily life." The vitality of Greenlandic, as noted earlier, is enhanced by its use in radio transmissions and by the development of a body of literature in written Greenlandic.

Both a substantial part of the curriculum and the ambience of many schools is thoroughly Greenlandic. Hobart and Brant found this to be true even in the boarding schools established for gifted children ten years of age or older. Altogether, they report (1965:52) "a high degree of maintenance of feelings of group esteem and a positive valuation of most aspects of traditional culture," whether technology, attitudes, or social behavior. This was particularly evident in the less acculturated districts, but elsewhere as well they "found evidences of considerable independence of outlook, and of overt resistance when Danish teachers or other officials were regarded as tactless or overbearing in their behaviour." At the same time, the bicultural curriculum and community have contributed to the continuity-with-gradual-change envisioned by Danish planners in their policy of "cultural synthesis." One symbol of the emerging synthesis, remark Hobart and Brant (1965:52), has been the growing "insistence by many on the usage 'Greenlander" rather than the disjunctive labels 'Eskimo' and 'Dane'."

In spite of these indications of a fairly successful perpetuation of Eskimo culture in changing sociocultural conditions, the addition of substantial numbers of Danish teachers to the schooling system has jeopardized the original goal of Eskimo-controlled cultural transmission and reformulation. In the first place, although immigrant teachers have integrated into Greenlandic life to a great degree, Hobart and Brant found that about 60 percent of them stayed only for their two-year contract. Such a high turnover rate means that in any given year, many of the Danish teachers are culturally unprepared to teach Greenlanders. Unfamiliar with Greenlandic culture, many fall back on teaching strategies and lesson content expected in Danish schools. Pupils confronted by illustrative examples drawn from an unfamiliar world, by an authoritarian and distant teacher, and by threat of punishment as an inducement to learning move from initial bewilderment at this kind of treatment to alienation. Yet such teachers are themselves in a bind. Establishing relationships with Eskimo

community members, relationships through which teachers might acculturate more rapidly to Eskimo ways, takes a long time. By the time many teachers have acquired the necessary understanding, they return to Denmark. Novice teachers who are unsure of themselves are most likely to fall back on an authoritarian manner to conceal their own bewilderment. Since the least experienced usually are sent to the smallest and most remote settlements, students and parents who have had the least previous exposure to Danes often have to deal with teachers who are least sophisticated in Greenlandic culture and have little access to needed advice. In such cases teachers and students rapidly become mired in cultural misunderstanding with little hope of effective rescue.

The second major problem results from the practice of placing a young Danish teacher, commonly a novice like those just described, in a position of authority over the native teacher who has taught in the community for several decades. In theory the Danish teacher has the most "advanced" pedagogical training as well as more thorough academic qualifications; in practice the Dane is professionally inexperienced. For the native teacher, the impact on his identities, both personal and social, can be devastating. As teacher and cate-chist, he has been one of the most respected members of the community, until he is suddenly subordinate to a young stranger half his age. The policies and procedures of the experienced teacher are usually modified by the newcomer, implying that the veteran is incompetent.

> Inevitably the native teacher's morale and self-respect suffer drastically. In a number of communities we heard of native teachers who in this circumstance had become listless, uncaring, and often increasingly given to alcoholism. There were stories of native teachers who sat reading magazines while the class was left to its own devices, teachers who were drunk on the job—and in most cases these men had been good, effective teachers, as measured by the prevailing standards, before their sudden subordination (Hobart and Brant 1965:55).

For the students as well as their parents, the implication is that it is the Danish origin and white skin which justify the superordination of the Dane and the subordination of the Greenlander.

This might have been avoided had the Danes expended the money and effort on upgrading the native teachers' preparation so that they could teach the new curriculum[11] instead of bringing Danish teachers to Greenland. The program formulated in 1965 to improve the school system, however, simply aggravated the problems already created. As in so many colonized lands, the best-schooled Greenlanders, in their quest for social and cultural parity, in-sisted on making the qualifications for Greenlandic teachers exactly the same as those for Danish teachers in Denmark. Danish certification requires fluency in English and a reading knowledge of German. Greenlanders seeking certifi-cation thus would have to be fluent in Greenlandic, Danish, and English, with a reading knowledge of German. Such a policy, as Hobart and Brant point out, is likely to increase the proportion of teachers in Greenland who are Danish, increase thereby the tendency for Danes to have high status jobs while Greenlanders held low status ones, impede the scholastic mobility of Greenlanders by the heavier requirements of academic qualification, and increase polarization between a prosperous and powerful Danish-oriented group and a relatively powerless, impoverished, apathetic group, more traditionally Greenlandic.

The Greenlandic school curriculum does hold out the possibility of viable cultural alternatives and synthesis. In terms of language, attitudes, and skills, both Greenlandic and Danish bodies of cultural knowledge are presented with equal weight. The goal has been and remains to make available to students a viable choice among alternatives and among cultural identities. Further research is necessary to determine how real these alternatives are outside the academic domain. That prosperity and impoverishment, power and powerlessness, seem to be associated, respectively, with Danish and traditional cultural orientations suggests that the alternatives are not as equal as the school curriculum implies. If Danish language facility, cultural knowledge, and organizational forms are in fact prerequisite for access to prerogatives and influence in the larger multicultural society, then the choice of traditional identities and orientations may well be a choice of reduced autonomy, influence, and access to valued goods. To what degree will Greenlandic remain the language of daily life? To what degree will the emerging Danish-oriented Eskimo elite favor the continued conservation of Eskimo culture in educative transmissions? In what ways will the cultural synthesis affect Greenlandic social structure and the options available to members of that society?

That such questions are irrelevant in the Canadian Arctic underscores the differences between the two cases. In Canada, no systematic provision for Eskimo schooling was made until 1959, long after unregulated access to the Arctic territories had wreaked havoc with Arctic ecology and Eskimo life. At first under missionary auspices and later under government supervision, Canadian Eskimo schooling has been characterized by the exclusive use of English language instruction, Eurocanadian teachers, and Eurocanadian curriculum materials, in addition to a heavy use of boarding schools rather than local facilities.

Unlike the Danes in Greenland, Hobart and Brant report, Canadian teachers in the Arctic lead an insulated life which affords little extra-classroom contact with Eskimo.[12] Professional credentials are primary in teacher selection, with preference given to teachers experienced in southern schools. Many have no training for teaching elementary school students (the bulk of their Arctic clientele). Transience further reduces their potential effectiveness. Southern teachers sign two-year contracts for Arctic positions; many leave before the term is up and very few[13] spend more than two years there. With no preparation for the particular problems in teaching children of this culture and no on-site source of appropriate information, teachers often vent their frustrations, born of culture shock and isolation in a trying environment, in harsh reactions to their students. In one remote community, Eskimo parents still were visibly shocked in reporting that two years before a teacher frequently had shouted or screamed at the children. Such incidents reduce the appeal of school, despite the high esteem in which schooling is held.

The exclusive use of English as the language of instruction by teachers who know nothing of Eskimo language naturally does little to enhance the speed with which students master either English or other academic subject matter.[14] With the first year or two given over almost entirely to the teaching of English, Eskimo students fall behind their peers in other Canadian schools and never catch up. The use of Eskimo even among the students themselves is discouraged, especially in boarding schools, with the aim of increasing their facility in English. With few exceptions, text materials reflect objects and concepts familiar to Eurocanadian children in the south but irrelevant and alien to Arctic children. Distinctive aspects of Eskimo life and culture find little place in the school curriculum.[15]

The significance of this for the identities of Eskimo students is not difficult to predict. Since adult Eskimo consider schooling important, the fact that things Eskimo are completely ignored in it suggests to their children that there is nothing in the native tradition worth learning. Moreover, the virtually total separation of home life and school life creates, in Eskimo students, a very compartmentalized perspective. Hobart and Brant (1965:60) cite an example:

> When children past grade three are instructed in school to draw a house, they portray a two-storey house, surrounded by trees, with a flagstone walk leading up to the door; in short, a "schoolbook" house which they have never directly seen and which is unrelated to the houses they know.

Finally, when children are absent from the Eskimo community for some seven or eight years, receiving instruction devoid of Eskimo influence, the result is that they are culturally incompetent as Eskimo, ignorant of the values and skills prerequisite to living in the Eskimo community (cf. Sindell 1974). In a comparative study of the effects of boarding school on children from rural Eskimo communities and from Anglo-oriented wage earning families in towns, Hobart (1970b) found a marked difference. In the former case (one of maximum environmental and cultural disjunction), he found far more disruptive changes in outlook, behavioral strategies, and physiological adaptations than in town-reared children.[16] Both the school itself and the surrounding sociocultural environment induced these changes. For town-reared children, there was greater continuity in preschool and school experience, as well as greater congruence between school expectations of future life paths and those toward which the students and their parents were themselves oriented.

Canadian policy explicitly includes the goal of replacing Eskimo culture with Eurocanadian culture, as noted earlier. Without delving into the merits of the official rationale for this policy, we may note that it is a high risk program, reckless in its potential damage to the unconsulted victims. Numerous studies have shown the effects of such policies among Arctic peoples in Canada and elsewhere. Many, alienated from Eskimo ways and unable to adapt to Eurocanadian patterns, drift through towns and through their lives, labeled as drunkards, vagrants, thieves, and troublemakers. Weaned from the warm and attentive support of families at the age of six or seven and thrust into the impersonal embrace of a large boarding school, many fail to develop the internal controls and coherent identities necessary for successful adaptation in either the Eskimo or the Eurocanadian world (cf. Hobart 1968, Honigmann and Honigmann 1965).

Some do adapt successfully; these seem to be individuals who have adopted a largely Eurocanadian cultural orientation. Honigmann and Honigmann (1965) suggest that this receptivity to changed cultural circumstances may reflect the security and confidence engendered by Eskimo child rearing practices, but this consideration would not apply to most children raised in Eurocanadian boarding schools.[17] The Honigmanns' research focused on the town of Frobisher Bay and thus on Eskimo who had chosen to live in urban circumstances. The schools here, while Eurocanadian in content and structure, are day schools; nevertheless, Eskimo participation is relatively limited. Even with compulsory attendance, many children start school late, sometimes as late as ten years of age. Absenteeism is a chronic problem, dropping out begins after age eleven, and class participation by Eskimo children is slight. Teachers attribute this lack of participation to shyness.

Even with schooling, however, and the desire to secure a niche in Eurocanadian society, Eskimo often have difficulty finding employment and respect within that society. It is here that the official and widely echoed policy of "bringing the Eskimo into the modern world" rings most like hollow rhetoric. Successful entrants into the mainstream society usually are individuals sponsored by Eurocanadians, rewarding those who conform to Eurocanadian cultural standards and values.

The schooling of Canadian Eskimo represents one part of a deliberate program of sociocultural change directed toward one segment of the society by another. It serves equally as a program of conservation and perpetuation of the sociocultural order favored by the dominant group, in that it allows few viable alternatives to Eskimo who do not adapt to Eurocanadian ways. This contrasts with the systematic attempt in Greenlandic schooling to provide bicultural education and complementary efforts in that society to develop a truly integrated social system, based on equal status for both Eskimo and Danish identities. While Greenlandic social reality may not match fully the guiding vision of its planners, both Eskimo and Danish, the schooling policy represents a deliberate effort to allow for cultural continuity, change chosen and directed by Eskimo themselves, and a positive, respected status for the cultural heritage of all members of the society.

education and sociocultural change

As the previous examples indicate, continuity and change are never completely separable. But it can be useful to focus on each separately to clarify the factors which affect it. The use of education as a deliberate tool for change, as for conservation, involves a complex cluster of assumptions, values, goals, and strategies which affect the results achieved. One important variable in such programs is the relationship of the controlling agency to the target population.

In the following section, we will examine three types of educational programs designed to substitute knowledge valued by an intervening change agent for knowledge valued indigenously by members of the target group. While there are significant differences among these three types, general characteristics of externally-directed change may be discerned through their comparison.

MISSIONARY EDUCATION

The category "missionary education" refers primarily to the educational efforts made by mission groups in the pursuit of religious conversion or heightened religious commitment. Christianity and Islam, far more than other religions, have been characterized by active proselytism among societies other than those in which the religion arose. By and large, Islam spread in recent times independently of the cultural-political expansion of its parent societies. The spread of Christian missions in the last two centuries, however, was closely paralleled by the political-economic expansion of European colonial powers.

Islamic proselytism has a much longer history in the non-Western world than does Christian. In West Africa, for example, Islamic influence was evident as early as the thirteenth century. Rulers of the great West African empires of the next three centuries recognized Islam, propagated by merchants on the Sudan trade routes, as a useful unifying force and developed a network of Muslim schools and colleges. By the sixteenth century, these institutions were of such renowned quality that they attracted divines and scholars from throughout the Islamic world (Oliver and Fage 1966:86–91). In more recent times Islamic proselytism has proceeded largely through the offices of local learned men who adapted Muslim prescripts to the local culture. Unlike most Christian missionary policies, Muslim missionaries encouraged conversion by stages. That is, indigenous religious beliefs were not prohibited but rather were subordinated to those of Islam and relatively few changes in social practice were required (Greenberg 1941). Islam's educational requirement for conversion was sufficient literacy in Arabic to read the Koran.

Christian missionaries, too, sought first to develop literacy skills sufficient to read and understand the New Testament, in some cases through developing a written form of the local vernacular, in other cases through instruction in the European language of the mission group. However, their requirements for conversion involved greater cultural and social changes. To illustrate this, let us consider missionary education in Ghana before independence. As in Great Britain at that time, early Gold Coast school facilities were mainly due to the efforts of voluntary agencies. As the colony government took on increased responsibility for the distribution and subsidy of schooling, a dual set of facilities developed, one under government aegis, the other under the missionaries. Two main missionary organizations operated in the Gold Coast: the Wesleyans and the Basel Mission. Their educational strategies were distinctive. The Wesleyans, concentrating their efforts on the coast, used only English as the language of instruction. The Basel Mission preferred to work in the hinterlands, away from the corrupting influences of the urban coast, and to use vernacular languages as the medium of instruction. The Basel Mission favored boarding schools as a means of cutting students off from traditional settings and practices, thus facilitating the replacement of traditional ways with Christian habits of living, whereas the Wesleyans used day schools. Both favored elementary academic education with emphasis on vocational training, although the Basel Mission was by far the most vocationally oriented.[18] As noted in the fifth chapter, this orientation on the part of European educators seriously conflicted with African aspirations. More importantly, it suggests the inextricable connections between the missionaries' religious goals, their cultural ethnocentrism, and the political and economic aspects of colonialism.

Graham (1971:62–66) points out that the attempts to develop agricultural schools and "model farms" as a major part of their educational facilities were partly a response to the missions' need for local subsidy and England's desire for a source of cotton other than the United States. Both missionaries and administrators considered it imperative to teach

> habits of steady industry through training in manual work [without which] true "civilisation" could never be achieved. Soil-tilling by organised labour on a big scale and selling its products was placed alongside Christianity as an instrument of civilisation. And in this context, "civilisation" meant visible results, rather than the ideas that would produce them (Graham 1971:65–66).

While educators made some effort to adapt curricula to the African context, it was a context viewed almost exclusively through European cultural assumptions and points of view. While the interests of missionaries and administrators did not always match, their common investment in the success of the colony as an economic and political jewel in the imperial coffers and their shared cultural orientation intertwined their respective courses of action.

This is not to deny the very real contributions of the missionaries to the development of schooling in Ghana. Not only was the eventual establishment of a full-scale academic educational system built largely on mission foundations, but missionaries also were responsible for most of the research necessary to write grammars, dictionaries, and translations of local African languages. The schooled elite which secured Ghana's independence had, in fact, acquired their conceptual arsenal partly in mission schools.

In the case of Ghana it becomes difficult to distinguish clearly between missionary and colonial education, because so much of the responsibility for provision of schooling was left to mission organizations. Moreover, the goals of administrators and missionaries were not generally in conflict.[19] Although government policies might be thought to have been pragmatic in contrast to the moral concerns of missionaries, European colonial governments also claimed, with the missionaries, the burden of changing those features of colonized societies most offensive by European cultural standards.

Many imperial powers, notably France, Belgium, and Portugal, followed policies of "assimilation" similar to the Canadian policy of cultural replacement. Under these policies, academic mobility meant acquiring the colonial power's cultural knowledge, with the promise of full citizenship to those who completed the re-enculturation process. Mission policies in these countries tended also to reflect this orientation: French Roman Catholic missions, for example, emphasized the twofold goal of conversion and the development of "love for France" (cf. Clignet 1970).

COLONIAL EDUCATION

Not all colonial education was connected with missionary education. Two examples will illustrate this. Truk, an atoll in the island chain which includes Puluwat, was occupied and administered as a Japanese colony between the two World Wars, from about 1924 to 1939. During this time, the Japanese established a district school system that provided first three years of elementary schooling, then two additional years, with further vocational education available in carpentry, agriculture, and surveying. Because schools were centrally located to serve several communities, many students had to leave their home community to attend, and had to obtain lodging and meals from distant clan relatives or family friends in the host community. Only the first three years were compulsory; the two succeeding stages of schooling were open only to selected graduates of the previous level. Access to carpentry school, the earliest vocational training center instituted and the most popular among the Trukese, was further restricted, even for those eligible, for it was located on Palau, a thousand miles to the west.

According to Fischer (1961), the purposes of the Japanese colonial administration were twofold: to "civilize" the Trukese and to integrate them politically and economically into the empire, by making them loyal, economically useful citizens. The first goal was to be achieved by developing a small, semischooled, native elite that then would help to change Trukese society, with government support. This policy was complemented by administration-introduced changes such as the election of local officials and technological innovations such as Japanese carpentry techniques. The second goal was to produce a supply of general and skilled laborers and domestic servants who understood the Japanese language. The administration had no apparent interest in providing more advanced academic training, and the Trukese did not indicate a desire for it.

The Trukese goals with respect to schooling were to acquire skills useful in dealing with Japanese officials, traders, and employers, and to acquire culturally valued technological skills. Carpentry was a highly respected craft and Japanese carpentry was admired for its technical superiority as well as for its association with the ruling group. Agricultural training in the second stage of elementary schooling, which entailed cultivating vegetables in the Japanese teacher's garden, was not regarded as education by Trukese students. (In fact, Fischer [1961:85] comments, "the average Trukese . . . does not regard green vegetables as fit for human consumption.")

The school curriculum was heavily weighted toward Japanese language study, with secondary emphasis on simple arithmetic. Training in written Trukese, if learned at all, was available only from Western missionaries who had translated parts of the Bible, hymns, and other religious writings. The official emphasis on Japanese coincided with the Trukese interest in acquiring the necessary verbal facility to express their desire for certain changes, to resist disliked changes, to manipulate individual Japanese into acting contrary to government policy, and to monitor administrative activity. The strategic importance of Japanese language skills was considerable.

> The interpreters, jailers, and assistant policemen employed by the Japanese government consisted almost entirely of public school graduates chosen for their ability to speak some Japanese. . . . many of them were secretly responsive to the recognized Trukese leaders in the performance of their duties as well as to their Japanese employers. It is said that they often served as spies on the government for the Trukees community, and communicated information between the community and prisoners whom the community wished to support, thus enabling witnesses and accused to fabricate consistent alibis. Education, as colonial powers have often discovered, can be a two–edged sword (Fischer 1961:88).

Nevertheless, schooling was not a pleasant experience for students. Trukese culture valued cooperation, modesty, submissiveness, and helping kinsmen, as well as unfettered childhood free of heavy demands for labor and concentrated attention. Schooling, particularly far from home, violated those values. Methods of instruction were mainly rote memorization and drill involving public recitation. Not only did these impose heavy work burdens on the students, but they also called upon children to show off their knowledge, thus exposing them to ridicule from their peers. Students often were very homesick and anxious about residing in a community with which their home community had warred before colonization. They also had to impose on the limited resources of their local hosts for food and often were expected to compensate by working for them after school. Discipline in school was harsh and much feared. As Fischer (1961:85–86) comments

> Very likely the corporal punishment experienced by the native students was more severe than would be administered to pupils in the Japanese homeland. We no doubt think of these punishments as something that would not be administered by American teachers but parallel examples could be cited from accounts of American Indians . . . describing their white teachers. The severity of the punishment in both cases can be attributed to the relatively small danger of effective protest by the children or their parents for any injury short of serious maiming, and also especially to the numerous frustrations in the teacher's job. . . . partly . . . the inherent difficulties of teaching small children in a language not their own about a culture not their own, but also because of the lack of motivation of most of the Trukese students.

There are more parallels between colonial schooling of Trukese and of Native Americans than simply harsh disciplinary measures, however, and many of these seem endemic to colonial situations. In the course of European-Indian encounters in America, Indians became pawns in the territorial and political expansion of European settlers across the continent, in the latters' aggressive exploitation of the land, and in their ideologies of racial and cultural superiority. As colonial policies of Indian extermination gradually gave way to policies of Indian confinement on reservations, an educational perspective was developed calling for the cultural assimilation of Indians. The same phenomenon as that labeled "cultural replacement" in Canada or "civilizing"in Truk and Africa, was, in the United States, the substitution of cultural genocide for the earlier policy of racial genocide.

While schooling was at first provided by mission groups, by the turn of the century, schooling had been brought under federal jurisdiction.

> Paying little attention to the multitude of linguistic and other cultural differences among Indian peoples, and ignoring the varied traditions of child rearing in preparation for adulthood in the tribal communities, the government entered the school business with a vigor that caused consternation among the Indians. The package deal that accompanied literacy in English included continuing efforts to "civilize the natives." Old abandoned army forts were converted into boarding schools, children were removed—sometimes forcibly—long distances

from their homes, the use of Indian languages by children was forbidden under threat of corporal punishment, students were boarded out to white families during vacation times, and native religions were suppressed. These practices were rationalized by the notion that the removal from the influence of home and tribe was the most effective means of preparing the Indian child to become an American (Fuchs and Havighurst 1973:6).

Indians long had recognized the desirability of schooling. In the words of one Native American scholar,

> In our contact with the whites, we have always and without fail asked for one thing. We wanted education. You can examine any treaty, any negotiations with the American whites. The first condition, specifically asked for by the Indian tribes, was education (Costo, cited by Cahn and Hearne 1969:27).

Several tribes operated and financed extensive school systems for their children, preparing many graduates for further study at white colleges. The Cherokee of the nineteenth century, who taught both Cherokee and English in their schools, had very high rates of literacy, perhaps as much as 90 percent, and had levels of general schooling greater than those of the white settlers in their area. But with the establishment of federal jurisdiction over Indian schooling, these schools, too, were closed.

The federally mandated curriculum emphasized "citizenship" and vocational training over even literacy. Academic study was included insofar as it was considered useful to "the farmer, mechanic, and housewife" (Fuchs and Havighurst 1973:9). Despite federal responsibility for the provision of schooling, however, there were never enough Indian schools to accommodate more than a fraction of the population; federal subsidies to nearby public schools supposedly covered the remainder, but these schools were given no other assistance in meeting Indian needs, had little accountability for the funds, and were not reimbursed for nonreservation Indian students. A significant portion of the school age population remained totally outside the formal educational systems. Moreover, federal educational programs were directed solely by whites and professional administrators, with no effective input from either Indians or white professional educators.

The abysmal school conditions of Native American students were improved somewhat following the appointment of John Collier as the Commissioner of Indian Affairs under Franklin Roosevelt. The Indian Reorganization Act of 1934 provided an almost revolutionary turn in Indian affairs. Among other things, it provided for increased autonomy and self–determination of Indian tribes, recognition of civil and cultural rights, and expanded opportunity for employment in the administrative structure of the Bureau of Indian Affairs and for loans to subsidize further schooling. In addition, Collier pushed to phase out boarding schools, replacing and supplementing them with community day schools. Curricula were to be bilingual, bicultural, and, when possible, taught by qualified Indian teachers. Unfortunately, these efforts met with strong opposition, eventually forcing Collier's resignation. The expressed opinion of the Congressional Indian Affairs Committee in 1944 is suggestive of the prevailing attitude.

> The Indian Bureau is tending to place too much emphasis on the day school located on the Indian reservation as compared with the opportunities afforded Indian children in off-the-reservation boarding schools where they can acquire an education in healthful and cultural surroundings without the handicap of having to spend their out-of-school hours in tepees, shacks with dirt floors, and no windows, in tents, in wickiups, in hogans, or in surroundings where English is never spoken, where there is a complete lack of furniture, and where there is sometimes an active antagonism or an abysmal indifference to the virtues of an education (Cited in Fuchs and Havighurst 1973:13).

Although attitudes within the academic community have changed over the last thirty years, partly in response to calls by Native American groups for recognition of their dignity, integrity, and rich cultural heritage, programs for revamped Indian schooling have yet to be implemented on a large scale. As Fuchs and Havighurst (1973:220) remark, schooling for Native Americans generally has drawn on a curriculum designed for non-Indians. Where the effort at schooling has failed, fault has been attributed to the Native American student rather than to the inappropriate curriculum and pedagogic strategies.

Missionary education, whatever the faith of its representatives, involves an ideology that differentiates between the truth value and moral worth of alternative systems of cultural knowledge. In the conviction that the corpus offered is inherently superior or preferable to the corpus currently held by the group approached, missionaries seek through various strategies to replace this with the more highly valued corpus they bring or to modify the indigenous corpus so that it comes to resemble their own more closely. Missionaries vary widely in their respect, both personal and cultural, for those they seek to convert; many are humane and tolerant people. Nevertheless, their commitment to a specific knowledge system and to the dissemination of that knowledge system is essential to their educational endeavors.

Missionary groups, at least theoretically, may meet target groups as equals, acting as "merchants of ideas," the value of which they hope to demonstrate to their potential "buyers." Colonialism, however subtle, involves hierarchy and subordination of one group to another; colonial education is based on this political-economic relationship. Whatever the rhetoric which publicly justifies or explains the changes in political relations which render one group feal to another, it still is a form of domination dependent on the collective power of the colonialists over the colonized, and on the benefits derived by the colonialists from their control over the colony. Economic benefits nearly always predominate, augmented by various political benefits. When the colonial relationship is ratified by reference to cultural beliefs and values which proclaim the genetic or cultural superiority of the superordinate group,[20] as is often the case, definite educational consequences tend to follow.

Although beliefs about genetic versus cultural superiority/inferiority are sometimes difficult to disentangle from one another, particularly since each may be taken for granted to varying degrees within the dominant group, beliefs about genetic differences in cognitive capacity or learning aptitudes are especially likely to lead to a vocationalist educational orientation. In such cases we find a concern for adapting scholastic content and opportunities to the presumed aptitudes of the target population. The vocations encouraged under programs of this type usually are those considered useful to the dominant group. Teaching individuals these skills, then, provides an economic benefit to the colonialists.

Beliefs about cultural superiority/inferiority, often associated with an evolutionist concept of cultural differences,[21] tend to give rise to "civilizing" goals for education. Since "civilizing" in this context means, essentially, "making them more like us," its educational aims depend on two processes: at least partial de-culturation of the target group and enculturation in some version of the dominant group's culture. To become competent in the new corpus of cultural knowledge and skills, it is assumed, the old corpus (or those elements conflicting with the new) must be eliminated. Even those who favor cultural autonomy for the subject group often argue that some degree of re-culturation is necessary if the colonized group is to "enter the modern world" (i.e., the political-economic world dominated by the industrial superpowers). The reasonableness of this position is undermined, however, by the unchanged assumption of cultural replacement as the basis of "modernization." That an awareness of cultural difference need not result in a policy of cultural replacement, is illustrated by programs providing bicultural schooling and the option of cultural synthesis, such as that of the Danish administration in Greenland.[22]

Programs for formal education require decisions not only about fundamental aims but also about the structure of access. Schooling established by the dominant group can have spiraling political, social, and economic consequences, as many observers, both colonialist and non-colonialist, have pointed out. Literacy training was forbidden to slaves in the U.S. for this reason, and the effects of such education when acquired despite the proscription often bore out the fears of its opponents. In Ghana the development of a European-educated African elite accelerated the African push for increased academic facilities and the eventual demand for independence from colonial rule. The availability of formal schooling under colonial aegis may create or widen divisions in the colonized society by differential historical access (as in Ghana), or by differential success within the academic system. Some colonial powers have attempted to avoid disruptive consequences by providing very limited opportunities to the colonized. In practice, this policy was followed by Japan on Truk and by Belgium in the Congo.

Finally, schooling for "civilizing" purposes often is provided initially to a select portion of the subordinate group, individuals chosen as a vanguard of reculturation and as an agency of more extensive efforts to transform the colonized population as a whole into loyal, productive citizens. This schooled elite, as a result of its privileges, usually identifies with the dominant group, both socially and culturally. Often they acquire the dominant group's ethnocentrist attitudes toward the culture of the colonized. However, when their upward mobility within the dominant social system is thwarted, by the artifical ceiling of color, birth, or colonized status, they may become outspoken opponents of colonial domination.

Both missionary and colonial uses of schooling as a tool of sociocultural change indicate the importance of such issues as whose tradition is being conserved, in what respects, and by whom. The aim of reculturation programs is not only change for the target population but also conservation through knowledge propagation by the change agents. Insofar as these programs restrict instruction to certain areas of cultural knowledge and skills, however, they do not provide full access to the sociocultural systems those agents represent. Rather they are designed to prepare students to enter that sector of the larger system in which they will best serve the interests of the dominant group and threaten least the existing distribution of valued prerogatives and opportunity. That, as Fischer phrases it, "education is a two-edged sword," simply underscores the complex processes which such programs can set in motion.

Missionary education often is designed to achieve fairly limited goals of cultural reformulation. In these cases, agents of re-education must provide incentives to attract the target population. Medical services, training in literacy skills, access to new opportunities for upward mobility, and information about dominant groups are among those commonly offered. When missionary efforts are complemented by colonial domination, as is often the case, schooling in the sociocultural system represented by the dominant group becomes a valuable commodity to many. Adaptive strategies of both individuals and communities then may include efforts to maximize their skills in accommodating to and manipulating the new status quo.

The responses of target populations to educational programs introduced by the dominant group reflect in part their interpretations of the utility of such education. Another factor of considerable importance is the degree of congruence among educative agencies. In the Gold Coast and on Truk, the dominant group comprised a relatively small contingent of expatriate representatives. While their power was apparent, and the effect of their intervention on local social structure marked, their influence was not sufficiently pervasive to dominate the majority of educative transmissions. Native Americans and Canadian

Eskimos, in contrast, found themselves not only subordinate to but surrounded as well by a far more numerous dominant group. In neither of the first two cases was the traditional economic base of the target population so thoroughly undermined; for the latter this change increased the pressure to reculturate as an adaptive strategy. In the first two cases, while the cultural inferiority of the target populations was taken for granted, cultural replacement was not intended to be complete. Rather, those cultural domains considered most important by colonial standards of morality and self-interest were the particular targets of reformulation. In the latter two cases, cultural replacement was intended to be total, perhaps largely because of the minority status of these populations in an enveloping society.

American Samoa is interesting, for it blends certain features of both missionary and colonial education. Acquired as an "unincorporated territory" in 1899, American Samoa was administered first by the U.S. Navy and subsequently by the U.S. Department of the Interior. Administration of the school system introduced was rather laissez-faire until the early 1960s. In 1962, the South Pacific Commission announced plans to hold its annual conference in Pago Pago, the capital. U.S. officials, who were concerned about their image in Southeast Asia, launched efforts "to make the Samoan territory a showcase for the benefits of American influence" (Masland and Masland 1975:180).

Before the reforms, the school system somewhat resembled its American model and administrative policy stressed English language instruction. Because instruction at the primary level was by Samoan teachers, and because there was little centralized control over instruction, the system allowed considerable leeway for local adaptation. In 1960 the outgoing Samoan-born governor defined the official policy as including conservation of "the best of Samoan culture," while guiding Samoans "in developing changes which are to their advantage" (Coleman 1961:42, cited by Masland and Masland 1975:181).

The new governor, appointed in 1961, initiated a distinctly different program for school development. The school system was expanded through a large-scale construction program, the curriculum was modified to match more closely U.S. standards and content, with greater stress on English language proficiency, and centralized control over instruction was greatly increased. Educational television was introduced as the core of instruction at both the primary and secondary levels. By the end of the 1960s, the television studio in Pago Pago was producing "as many as 200 class programs a week for all primary and secondary grades" (Masland and Masland 1975:182). Local classroom teachers (Samoan) "supervised by an American principal, facilitated and complemented the TV lessons by following the lesson plans" provided by the central production studio (Masland and Masland 1975:183).

None of the personnel centrally involved in curriculum development and lesson formulation were Samoan. Although some effort was made to adapt materials to Samoan culture,[23] the bulk of the content, its organization, and the instructional strategies used were based on Anglo assumptions and values. Central features of Samoan social organization and fundamental Samoan values were ignored in the reculturating scholastic transmissions. As in other colonial systems, the pervading theme was the inferiority of the indigenous culture to that of the colonial power. The stated aim of the reformed system "was to rapidly acculturate [Samoans] to the American language and patterns of life" (Masland and Masland 1975:186).

When the reform first was proposed it was supported by the Samoan senate, which granted the governor a free hand in reorganizing the system. In that respect, the initial venture seems to have been a voluntary transaction similar to that of missionary education. By 1969, however, Samoan support was considerably less avid. Universal compulsory schooling, marked by the "indiscriminate introduction of American ideas" was bringing about undesired changes in the Samoan way of life.

> Most Samoans were indeed willing, even eager, to learn English and the American way of doing things in order to have the contacts with Europeans that increased their well-being and prestige—but as a foreign language and as a foreign way of doing things. The Samoans rapidly adopted such American ways of doing things as suited them; otherwise, they preferred their language, their patterns, their culture. . . . By resisting the compulsory training in English and the American viewpoint, the Samoans were resisting the reshaping of their culture and the imposition of another (Masland and Masland 1975:186, 187).

By the mid-1970s both U.S. participants and Samoans agreed that the institutionalized reform was in need of substantial modification. In 1973 Samoans were appointed to high level, decision making positions, including the office of Director of Education, and the number of high level U.S. personnel simultaneously was reduced. Television transmissions were cut back, especially to secondary schools, and teachers were permitted greater leeway in using them. During the next year, the virtually exclusive emphasis on English language proficiency was replaced with a renewed emphasis on Samoan, with English introduced as a foreign language at the elementary level. Not until the secondary level does English become the primary language of instruction. While regaining control of their social system, Samoans are reexamining instructional policies and priorities and their effects upon Samoan children. They are looking to the experiences of neighboring South Pacific countries as a guide to the creation of a more appropriate strategy for academic development, adapted to their desired cultural independence (Masland and Masland 1975: 196-198).

To see these approaches to cultural transmission in perspective, let us turn to a related phenomenon in the U.S. frequently labeled as "remedial education."

REMEDIAL EDUCATION

Remedial education is education designed either to provide supplementary assistance to less successful students to bring them up to some external performance standard, or to provide alternative schooling to students deemed incapable of learning a standard curriculum. In the U.S., a disproportionate number of students in remedial classes are members of low income and ethnic minority groups. One widely accepted explanation for this is based on the concept of "cultural deprivation."

As an explanatory concept, "cultural deprivation" is used in two ways. In its most popular usage, it implies that its victims, through their home life in impoverished circumstances under the care of poorly educated kin, have been deprived of culture. This notion, echoing the 1944 Congressional Indian Affairs Committee's opinion quoted earlier, is based on a naïve understanding of culture. The absence of visible signs of middle class Anglo culture is taken to indicate the absence of any culture whatsoever, or the absence of "civilized" culture. In its more technical usage, "cultural deprivation" refers to a supposed deficiency in the victim's home environment of certain types of content, a deficiency which cripples the child's capacity for learning.

The idea of cultural deprivation is closely related to two others, "stimulus deprivation" and "the culture of poverty." "The culture of poverty" concept was developed by Oscar Lewis (1966) to label what he contended were distinctive beliefs and practices of people in impoverished circumstances, whatever their ethnic heritage. He argued that these were the result of adaptive responses to similar environmental conditions. Once established, they were perpetuated by force of cultural tradition and were resistant to change even in the presence of improved circumstances. Among the characteristics he attributed to poverty culture was an impoverishment *of* culture, a "thinness" unlike the usual intricacy and density of other cultures around the world. Critics of Lewis have pointed out that "poverty culture" is not necessarily as he portrayed it. The cultures of the poor are complex and various, although the alternatives available to them are restricted by their position at the bottom of social, economic, and political hierarchies. The cultures of the poor represent pragmatic responses to the world as they experience it, rather than entrenched cultural habits invulnerable to change. While arguing that the poor have been backed into their cultural cul-de-sac by the oppressive forces of an unjust political and economic system, Lewis asserted that change would require generations because of that cultural entrenchment. By this he was thought to mean that the poor were ultimately responsible for their own predicament, including their failures in schooling: their academic failures reflected inadequacies in their culture rather than in their schooling.

Stimulus deprivation is a concept derived from psychological research on the cognitive and emotional effects of isolation from sensory stimuli of any kind. One result of this research has been to establish the biological necessity of adequate levels of sensory stimulation for the development of a child's ability to learn cognitive and social skills. Together with the supposed impoverishment of the cultural environments of the poor, this concept has reinforced the idea that the children of the poor are handicapped by backgrounds which are inferior in content and complexity to those of middle income children.

It is usually true that the home environments of children of impoverished families are different in many ways from those of more prosperous children, for poverty does impose limitations, just as the identities and aspirations encouraged by the school do. At issue is the interpretation of this difference, its causes, and solutions to the problems it poses for successful schooling. One interpretation has been labeled the "vacuum ideology," because it assumes that the child on entering school has had no previous learning. As Wax and Wax (1971) remark, this ideology effectively insulates schools from responsibility for a "victim's" failure to learn, while it assigns all responsibility for the child's achievements to the school's intervention. Because a child from a "deprived" home enters the school, in this view, as a blank slate, "presumed deficient in almost every realm of experience" (Wax and Wax 1971:132), virtually anything done by teachers is considered "educative." And because the child's home and community environments are seen as culturally impoverished, the school is justified in remaining isolated and insulated from the community whose children it ostensibly serves.

Another interpretation, the ideology of cultural deficiency, assumes that the problems reside not in an absence of culture but in its inadequacy as a foundation for abstract thought, conceptual learning, and academic curricula. Baratz and Baratz (1970), in a critique of Head Start programs and their theoretical rationale, summarize several examples of this ideology as it has been applied to black Americans' home experience and language skills. Ignoring the distinctive cultural matrix of low income black families, investigators attribute the children's academic difficulties to either genetic or environmental deficiencies. In the latter case, because Head Start programs failed to "fill" the supposed cultural deficit with which such children entered school, advocates have argued for earlier and earlier intervention in family life, in order to fend off the intellectual "damage" black mothers ostensibly inflict by "incompetent" child rearing practices. The goal has become, in effect, to destroy black culture, replacing it with "healthy," middle class Anglo patterns.

Closely related to this is the ideology of cultural inferiority which asserts that the corpus of knowledge of the child's group is simply wrong or worthless, as when the speech of a ghetto black child is labelled "bad English," rather than a variant form of English, equally systematic with its own syntactic rules. Castro (1971), employed as a specialist in speech improvement and speech arts in a Brooklyn elementary school, reports that when she began work, she had been led to believe that the children were linguistically incompetent. Their impoverished vocabularies and lack of verbal skills were attributed to deficiencies in their home environments. Yet when she turned for a few days from highly structured lessons designed to correct students' "improper usage" and "enrich their vocabulary" to ask them about games they knew, she found impressive vocabulary and communication skills. Moreover, when she pursued the topic with her students, it became apparent that they placed great value on accurate reproduction of the language, gestures, and rhythms of these games. "It was evident," she remarks, "that there was a wealth of vocabulary, descriptive phrases, ideas and fluency here" (Castro 1971:83). Thus a fourth interpretation is suggested: the ideology of cultural diversity. In this view, children may bring to school a cultural repertoire different from the teacher's and thus unrecognized. If there is respect for the students' knowledge, this experience may be tapped as a vital learning resource and as an index of cognitive development.

The two predominant measures used to document cultural adequacy or advantage are language skills and IQ. As earlier noted, the cross-cultural testing of cognitive capacity is fraught with hazards; differences in performance do not necessarily indicate differences in the capacities being tested. Within our society, IQ tests, long the principal tools for evaluating individual and group differences,[24] are still in active use in many schools and still serve as a basis for speculative theorizing (cf. Jensen 1969, Herrnstein 1973). Tests of intelligence used in schools are primarily verbal; performance level depends on linguistic competence in the language of the test. They also are designed to tap specific kinds of knowledge and skills, originally selected because they correlated with school performance. Thus IQ tests refer not to an individual's overall cognitive ability or mental aptitude, but to an individual's probability of success in middle class Anglo oriented schools. Drucker (1971:48) has described the use of such tests as "a sort of cultural litmus test" which screens for individuals who are adept at a particular intellectual and behavioral style, that style favored by the academic system. The selection accomplished by this type of evaluation procedure channels students who display the favored style into the "success-oriented" tracks and programs in the school system. Students whose style does not conform are shunted into programs that label their participants as academically inferior and effectively reduce future opportunities. Despite the many studies which claim to have "demonstrated" different levels of learning potential among low income, "deprived" and middle income, "advantaged" children, research which controls for cultural factors has indicated no such difference.

Poverty can affect learning and cognition through nutritional deficits, unhealthy physical surroundings, and so forth. Pasamanick (1969), for example, has documented the effects of inadequate diet on attention, alertness, attendance and other school-relevant variables, and the changes produced by nutritional improvement. Certain kinds of stimulation and experience common in middle income homes may be rare or absent in low income homes, just as certain kinds of stimulation and experience common in low income homes may be rare or absent in middle income homes. In the same way, home experience may differ among Chicano, Native American, Anglo, and black families whatever their economic status, as it may (and does) vary within an ethnic group. When tapped, however, the experience has proved rich enough to be a basis for school learning. Research by Witkin and his associates on cognitive style indicates that schools and middle class homes both may encourage the development of verbal comprehension and social communication skills, but that development of personal and cognitive autonomy

> is more under the influence of the quality of relations with critical persons (as in the family) early in life. Given the necessary interpersonal relations, these important attributes of any autonomous person may apparently develop even under conditions of so-called cultural deprivation (Witkin 1967:248).

It is essential, as John (1971) has argued, to distinguish between language as a communicative process and language as a medium of cognitive process. It is the former which is systematically taught in "typical" middle class homes and in schools. Language is socially acquired and practiced. When teachers deny children speaking a nonstandard form of English a receptive and rewarding audience—by derogating the speech forms as "incorrect" or "stupid"—children lose a necessary component of speech development. Many observers have concurred with Kohl's (1967) observation that disadvantaged children will not speak in class because they cannot trust their audience. They are not thereby isolated from learning, verbal or otherwise; but the classroom often ceases to be one of their learning environments.

Remedial education in schools is based on diagnosis of student test scores and classroom performance levels. For reasons now clear, these bases for evaluation reflect many factors unrelated to intelligence and aptitude for scholastic learning. This is why the exploration by Rosenthal and Jacobson (1968a, 1968b), Brophy and Good (1970), and Rist (1970) of the "Pygmalion effect" of teacher expectancies is so illuminating. By showing that student classroom and test performance were affected by teacher expectations, the researchers broadened the question of why students fail. Studies of counselors, such as those carried out by Cicourel and Kitsuse (1963) and Armor (1969), provide additional insight into the process of student differentiation and allocation to distinct echelons of the society.

Much of the remedial education directed toward ethnic minorities and low income groups resembles colonial education. First, it is designed to replace the less valued knowledge and orientations of the target population with those of the dominant segment of the population. Second, it usually allows only selective access to occupational and other roles in U.S. society. The "Pygmalion effect" is complemented by the "Matthew effect": "To him who hath shall be given, from him who hath not shall be taken, even that which he hath" (Merton 1968).

To change the U.S. system of schooling so that the goal of equal academic opportunity is realized, is not impossible nor even unfeasible. Indeed, such programs already have been launched. Their success requires, first and foremost, recognition of the bases of our current problems and failures. Commitment to the values of cultural autonomy and self-formulated cultural synthesis is a prerequisite, for the U.S. always has been a multicultural society. Because the U.S. is also a socioculturally stratified society, with economic and political dominance the prerogative largely of middle and upper class Anglos, schooling designed to convey both the dominant cultural knowledge and that of less powerful groups is necessary. Bicultural schooling can establish real options for students and provide skills required for dealing with their multicultural environment.[25]

Because schools are only one of the educative agencies involved in knowledge transmission, effective programs also must take into account the other agencies such as families, peer groups and media. Identification and use of resources available in the various contexts of knowledge transmission would require active consultation and cooperation with these other agencies. This, in turn, would require modification of the prevailing conceptions of schooling goals. Schooling as a system of enculturation has been guided in the U.S. by the academic educators' belief that they were best able to determine the appropriate content of knowledge transmission in the school context. Insofar as they have represented the dominant sociocultural group, their decisions have reflected these interests. Active consultation with other client groups not only would facilitate the development of schooling programs better suited to their goals, but also would redefine the role of academic educators as agents of cultural self-determination.[26]

How such programs would affect the equalization of opportunity in the larger social system cannot be predicted fully. Arnove (1976) and others have shown neither qualitative nor quantitative improvements in school systems necessarily lead to greater individual opportunity or social benefit. Certainly economic and political change are not produced directly by expanded schooling. Jencks and others (1972) have argued similarly that improvements in the quality of U.S. schools do not by themselves affect the existing system of inequality. Educators control few of the avenues of access to valued goods in the larger society. But many academic skills do remain prerequisites of access, if not sufficient in and of themselves. Improving the cultural fit of academic education with the knowledge students acquire in other contexts, would ease the acquisition of academic skills. For example, bilingual instruction in Spanish or Black English and Standard American English would help students for whom SAE is not native to learn it and to use it effectively in acquiring other skills. Using instructional strategies oriented to the cultural styles of students, such as Dumont and Wax (1969) describe in the "intercultural" Cherokee-Anglo classroom, would reduce the frustration and attrition of learning now common in many classrooms.

The interrelationship of schools with other sectors of society is relevant not only to the results of such programs but also to their establishment. In Colorado, for instance, legislators tried to pass a bill providing for bicultural and bilingual education in schools with a significant non-Anglo enrollment, but it met with staunch opposition. According to B. Hall (1976:519), many parents and legislators express

> fears that teaching in other languages and about other cultures will somehow "de-Americanize" innocent schoolchildren, that it is merely one more unwanted educational expense, that it is neither proper nor necessary for the majority to make special allowances for minorities.

The original bill required that bilingual and bicultural education be made available in every public school with twenty students, or more than five percent of the student body, whose first language is not English. It would be run by both local school boards and parent advisory committees. They would share in staff selection and decisions about the programs. In 1975, the law in its final form applied only to the first four grades (kindergarten through third grade) in schools with fifty students, or ten percent of their student body, whose first language is not English. Parents, while part of the program, do not have the power in choosing staff and content proposed in the original bill. The funding allowed by the legislature also has been reduced. Despite problems of organization and implementation, by the fall of 1976, sixty-one school districts had established these programs.

While some school administrators resented the intrusion of the state on their domain, the new programs have been received enthusiastically by many teachers. The path had been carved by federally funded, experimental programs in several Colorado schools, and these had demonstrated that the concept could work. In Fort Lupton's three-year-old program,

> The number of Spanish–speaking children who have to be kept back at the end of the year has dropped drastically over the past three years. In the three years before the program began, the retention rate had been as high as 53 per cent; in the first year of the program, it dropped to 20 per cent and [in 1975] was 9 per cent. And test scores also show that the Spanish–speaking children are performing better (B. Hall 1976:520).

Proponents of the new design for minority schooling argue that bilingual education in only the early grades is inadequate to their goals, although it can serve as a testing ground for the scheme. Because continued funding depends on demonstrated results, those involved with the programs are under considerable pressure. Both the law itself and those who control financial resources require that success or failure be evaluated in statistical terms. Yet many of the benefits to be derived from such programs, like positive personal and social identities, may not show up quantitatively. Moreover, because demonstrable results of innovative programs often are demanded after a year or two by wary legislators or funding agencies (as in Colorado), such programs can little afford to emphasize long-term or gradual change.

We can set this problem in perspective by considering one last example of attempted change. This is from a country far less prosperous than the U.S., one in which long-range planning and careful implementation of those plans are essential to its economic survival.

education and sociocultural change in tanzania

Mainland Tanzania, known as Tanganyika before independence and its subsequent union with Zanzibar, is a large, impoverished country. Like Ghana, Tanzania is unevenly populated and unevenly developed. Historically the coastal area reaped the benefits of trade and greater intercultural contact. Like Ghana, it is a nation formed from many smaller societies. Tanganyika's colonial experience differed, however, from that of the Gold Coast. It was brought under German colonial rule in 1887, but for two decades the German regime was unable to pacify the African population. Afterwards, it established an administrative system of direct rule, working through local agents, Swahili-speaking Muslims from the coast.

In its long history of cosmopolitan contacts, the Tanganyikan coast had harbored traders of many societies. Among the most successful and wide ranging were the Arabs, who spread not only their material goods of trade, but also Islam and the Bantu-Arabic language of Swahili as a common vernacular for intercultural communication. The German administration used Swahili-speaking intermediaries for its own political purposes. In order to staff their administrative machinery at least partly from local resources (a far cheaper strategy than importing all functionaries from Europe), the Germans were forced to create a school system to train clerical, technical, and lower level administrative personnel, and teachers. For these limited purposes, it was a sound system. Faithful to colonial pattern, it was concerned both with utilitarian and "civilizing" goals. More importantly, it was a centralized system, Swahili was used as the medium of instruction, with German also taught, and the system was established independently of the Christian mission schools proliferating in the interior of the country. In addition, much administrative business was conducted in Swahili, and the government put out a periodical Swahili-language paper which contained news, announcements, letters to the editor, and Swahili poetry.

During the First World War, Tanganyika became a battlefield. School facilities and administrative personnel were requisitioned, and many Africans lost their lives. Yet during this time, Africans kept many local schools in session.

Following Germany's defeat in 1918, Tanganyika became a British Mandated Territory under the supervision of the League of Nations. While in effect a colony in the British Empire, Tanganyika's status as a mandate and later as a trust territory under United Nations auspices, had a distinct effect on its colonial experience. By 1925, British administrative policy took shape. As in Ghana, the colonial administration was designed to work as much as possible through local political institutions and leaders (in contrast to the German policy of direct rule), but the caretaker role assigned Great Britain in its mandate responsibilities lent a somewhat different cast to the application of policy in Tanganyika. Although the German school system had been decimated by the war, the schools maintained by the Africans, the schools provided by mission organizations, and the schools serving the small Asian and European populations, all were assisted financially. Unfortunately, in the wake of postwar reconstruction, the worldwide depression severely weakened the colony's economy. Since British colonial policy at this time was based on the fiscal self-sufficiency of each colony, whatever surplus could be mustered for social services, including schooling, had to be squeezed from meager local sources. Tanganyika differed from the Gold Coast in that it lacked resources that could be exploited profitably by Europeans.

In 1938, at its last meeting, the Permanent Mandates Commission severely criticized Great Britain for its excessively small expenditure on African schooling in the mandate. Between 1939 and 1945, with financial aid from Great Britain, the colonial government more than doubled its schooling budget; much of this was invested in establishing government schools, supplementing those already being run by missions and local Native Authority boards (composed of Africans). Nevertheless, until after the Second World War international pressure was mostly unheeded; still less was consideration given to the goals and concerns of the African population. Policy for African schooling was developed by colonial administrators in response to pressures from London and from local European and Asian communities. These two groups represented mainly officials in the colonial administration, missionaries, and business entrepreneurs.

By 1945 all primary schools used Swahili as the medium of instruction, including mission-run schools that formerly had opposed its use. English was used in postprimary instruction. The government school system was intended to provide adequate education to develop an African elite for local administration. Missionary schools, in contrast, sought to maximize the availability of primary catechetical education as a strategy of evangelization. Opportunities for either government or missionary schooling were distributed unevenly among the African population. Because the government-run schools were intended to develop "leaders" who could carry out colonial policy at local and regional levels, children and close relatives of those in recognized positions of authority were given preference in admission. Students therefore generally represented the elite sectors of African societies, their status further enhanced by their access to European-style schooling and their subsequent roles in the new colonial power structure. Christian missionary schools, concentrated inland where Muslim influence had not penetrated, were most numerous in those areas most receptive to proselytism.

Following World War II, the United Nations Trusteeship Council took over the responsibilities of the Permanent Mandates Commission, and a new era began for the Tanganyika Trust Territory. Not only did the UN oversee more vigorously the administration of the trust territories, but the unequivocal confidence of Europeans in their own superiority and the institution of colonialism also had been shaken. There were growing doubts about the moral basis of colonialism, and more questioning of the appropriateness and viability of the political and economic goals which had led to the growth of empires. As a result, British administration in Tanganyika reflected a growing emphasis on compromise, adaptation to African needs and aspirations, and on deliberate planning for developmental goals, both political and economic, in preparation for self-government. Financial subsidy from Great Britain was augmented by aid provided by UN specialized agencies and in the late 1950s by additional funds from British and American philanthropic foundations.

In 1947 the first full-scale development plan was put into effect. Covering all aspects of development, this ten-year plan allocated one-quarter of the total budget to schooling. Two features of the educational policy involved are particularly important. First, it consolidated the school system, increasing central control. At the same time, the local Native Authority school committees were granted greater advisory and budgetary authority for all primary schooling, including that offered by the missions. Needless to say, this policy was resisted, albeit without success, by the missionaries. Second, the development program was geared toward a deliberate pacing of postprimary school expansion so as to avoid producing graduates which the predominantly agricultural economy could not absorb. This policy reflected recognition of the need for a highly trained cadre of administrators and other professionals, technicians, and teachers; the results included the allocation of elite status to this highly schooled group. As Morrison (1976:57) points out,

Africans who became teachers, medical assistants, and clerks were not as privileged as members of the European elite or many Asians, but they had many more social and material advantages than people who lived at the level of near–subsistence.... Moreover, access to economic and political influence assured their own children a much better chance than most of securing [scarce] school places.

The administration of this development plan was supervised to some degree by the UN Trusteeship Council. Every three years (in 1948, 1951, and 1954), a Visiting Mission arrived to receive testimony and grievances from the administration and the people. The resulting reports and international pressure, partly through the UN General Assembly, were pushing Great Britain to complete preparations for Tanganyika's self-government at a much more rapid pace.

In 1955 consultation was initiated at every level, canvassing the people for ideas, desires, and suggestions. While the government could not afford all that was proposed, even for schooling, the information collected was considered in the resulting formulation of long-range goals and a more limited Five Year Development Plan. Two main objectives at this stage were to increase late primary and secondary school opportunities and to upgrade the quality of the primary facilities expanded during the previous plan. This was to be accomplished partly by upgrading the teacher training programs and by strengthening the supervision of schools. The importance of developing trade schools also was emphasized. Financing was a continuing problem, for costs were increasing without a matching increase in economic production. Native Authority commissions were given greater financial responsibility for both the capital and recurrent costs of primary schooling, but major expenses remained. In any event the plan was never implemented fully, for Tanganyikan independence overtook it.

Several criticisms were made of this plan by the increasingly vocal public. One was its "excessive" vocational emphasis. Throughout the previous decade, efforts had been made to adapt curricula to local needs, and to the brute fact that most of those who completed primary schooling (not to speak of earlier school leavers and the more than half of the school age population not attending at all) would be unable to secure places at the secondary level. For this reason, all primary schools were to have model farms attached where children would learn improved farming techniques. Parents tolerated this inclusion of agriculture in the curriculum as the price of schooling, just as many had previously tolerated missionary proselytism. But schooling was viewed as a route out of the harsh poverty of subsistence farming, not as an adornment of it. At the same time, the mobility which primary schooling once had offered an able student no longer was possible. Thus a demand arose for more advanced places and more chances for primary schooling, with a greater emphasis on the academic subjects which would lead to the desired mobility. Just as in Ghana, Africans suspected attempts to provide nonacademic schooling of being strategies for keeping the Africans down. Another criticism was that the main administrative posts all were filled by expatriate Europeans. People also objected to the continued government subsidy of separate schools for the Asian and European minorities. Although less than one percent of the population, they were allotted about one-sixth of the school budget.

Throughout the colonial period, African access to formal schooling was distinctly limited, relative to that available for children of the European and Asian minorities. For the latter groups, there were always available school places. But disparities also existed within the African population. Since most school facilities were provided by Christian voluntary agencies, places in the Western-style schools available to Muslims were relatively few. This was aggravated further by the opposition of many local Muslim leaders to Christian-dominated schooling. As a result, although Muslims outnumbered Christians in the African population by a margin of three to two, the number of Christians enrolled in primary schools as late as 1956, exceeded the number of Muslims by a ratio of three to one. In addition, the preferential access given earlier to children of traditional political authorities and the concentration of mission schools in particular inland areas contributed to the uneven distribution of academic opportunity (cf. Morrison 1976:53–57).

Independence was achieved in 1961, with Julius Nyerere, leader of the independence movement, as Prime Minister of the British-style government. Before assessing the changes that have been planned, implemented, and unexpectedly encountered by independent Tanzania, we should consider several events. First, Nyerere was a school teacher, educated in the United Kingdom at the University of Edinburgh. TANU (Tanganyika African National Union), the political organization he and other nationalists built, was, like the Congress People's Party (CPP) in Ghana, a grass roots party. Unlike the CPP, however, TANU also welcomed the services of the African elite. Before and after independence, Nyerere used TANU as an agency for educating the people about the basic issues of independence and self-determination. Indeed, Nyerere is known by the Swahili title for teacher, Mwalimu. Six weeks after taking office as Prime Minister, Nyerere resigned, startling the world. Returning to the task of educating the people, he toured the countryside, explaining the problems and goals that lay ahead, explaining the newly formulated Three Year Development Plan, and attempting to elicit the active participation of the masses in these great undertakings. The following year, when Tanganyika and the island of Zanzibar joined in the Republic of Tanzania, he was elected President, a post that by popular acclaim he continues to hold.

Second, upon independence, mainland Tanzania became a one-party state. This was necessary for the uphill effort to unite a nation of many cultural groups, spread over a large territory with only inadequate lines of communication to join them. Committed to democracy, Nyerere set up a commission to examine how such a political system could be made as democratic as possible. A report followed in 1965, advising that party membership be open to all to avoid elitism, and that alternative candidates always be offered for each elected post, so that voters would have a real choice. This style of openly drafting problems, seeking a range of opinions, and developing an appropriate, often experimental, position on that basis has been characteristic of Tanzanian political process (Svendsen 1966).

Third, the first development plan which followed independence, a three year plan had, according to Cameron and Dodd (1970:171), "a degree of sophistication not possessed by previous plans." Even the UN Economic Commission for Africa hailed it as altogether superior. Partly, as Cameron and Dodd (1970:171) rightly point out, this was so because "it was both the object of international support and interest, and the product of a time when highly integrated planning was coming into its own." Partly it was so because it was the outgrowth of a distinct vision of society, the achievement of which would require specific strategies, realistically conceived and rigorously implemented. As Svendsen (1966:50) states, planning has the important consequence of forcing a country's politician-planners to take positions on a number of important questions. Whereas the British "caretakers" had sought to assist Tanganyika in developing along lines familiar to them, Tanzania's own development goals diverged necessarily from those earlier expectations. Whatever the eventual success of Tanzania in achieving its goal of a democratic, self-reliant, socialist society, the goal itself serves as a framework against which progress can be measured, new objectives assessed, and appropriate strategies laid out.

At the time of its independence, Tanzania was one of the most underdeveloped countries in East Africa. The cream of the small schooled cadre had been skimmed off to form the government itself, and rapid economic development also required the highly skilled. The first Three Year Development Plan (1961–1964), therefore, gave highest priority to meeting national needs for formally educated personnel. Only through economic growth could Tanzania hope to achieve the self-reliance and independence central to their long-term goals; only through economic growth could it provide the schooling and community improvement the people so desperately craved. Efforts were directed first toward increasing the number of secondary school places and college facilities, increasing teacher training, and extending primary schooling to the full eight-(later seven-) year course. The European and Asian school systems gradually were integrated into the African system, and fees were abolished in government subsidized secondary schools on the grounds that they discriminated against the children of poor (always African) parents. Nearly total authority for primary education was delegated to the local councils. Limited authority for secondary schools and teacher-training colleges was delegated to boards of governors, pending evaluation of results of this decentralization. A unified teacher service was begun, establishing uniform standards, a "code of professional conduct," and a pension plan for teachers in all schools, mission, government, and local.

Schooling-as-economic-investment demanded close attention to the effectiveness of the curricula in use. All schooling at the primary level was now in Swahili, although English as a second language was begun in the third grade. The content of history, geography, and citizenship courses needed to be localized. The latest improvements in teaching language, science, and math were required. Curriculum reform is problematic when it calls for radical changes alien to a teacher's own educational background. Teachers trained in a British-oriented curriculum and imbued with the colonial ethos of individualism, academic elitism, and authoritarian tutelage in facts rather than in critical analysis, had predictable difficulty in adapting to these revisions. Curriculum content itself posed serious problems, largely because of the absence of adequate supportive materials in Swahili. Part of the difficulty lay in retraining teachers to transmit the new content competently.

Sarason (1971:33–48) has described the difficulties of introducing the "new math" as a curricular reform in a U.S. school system. As in Tanzania, the impetus for this change was external to the schools themselves, and the teachers involved in carrying out the revised program had not participated in design or implementation decisions. Moreover, the content of the new mathematics curriculum was not merely supplementary to their previous training but in many respects was antithetical to it. In order to prepare teachers for classroom use of the new material in the fall, intensive, five-week workshops were conducted during the preceding summer. Reports Sarason (1971:42):

> The summer workshop took place in an atmosphere of tension and pressure. . . . There was little sensitivity to the plight of the teachers—they were being asked to learn procedures, vocabulary, and concepts that were not only new but likely to conflict with highly overlearned attitudes and ways of thinking.

Much of the tension felt by teacher-participants stemmed from the prospect of teaching students in several weeks, material of which they had only the shakiest grasp.

In Tanzania, this process was complicated still further by language. Not only were materials in Swahili unsatisfactory or nonexistent, but many teachers were insufficiently fluent in English to learn from English sources and then teach concepts for which there were no accurate Swahili translations (Cameron and Dodd 1970:194).

Curriculum reform also required reconsideration of the ethos and social values transmitted in schools. As Morrison (1976:226) points out, the lack of suitable curriculum materials was not the only obstacle. Equally significant was "the culture of a school community as expressed in the norms and values that guide behaviour within it." Carnoy (1974) has commented on the contradiction between egalitarian ideology and hierarchical structure in schools, and between the transmission of knowledge sanctioned by authority and the development of independent, critical thought. While the schools had helped to establish a sense of Tanzanian national identity, they had not succeeded in developing either the creative analytic skills or the socialist attitudes necessary to achievement of national goals. A survey conducted in 1966, a few years after the initial curriculum reform began, revealed that there were few statistically significant differences between political attitudes of school children in Tanzania and those of neighboring Kenya, which had an essentially capitalist and less coherently planned scheme for development (Koff and Von der Muhll 1967). The authors of this survey report only one difference between the two student populations that relates clearly to national ethos: Tanzanians tended to express slightly more egalitarian and less elitist values than their Kenyan counterparts, and this difference held only at the secondary school level. To encourage a sense of national unity and shared commitment to nation-building, self-help schemes were introduced in the schools, and attempts were made to associate them more closely with the surrounding communities. TANU Youth League groups were started in schools to increase the students' political awareness of their place in the collective struggle to create an equitable social order. The effectiveness of these proposed reforms varied widely.

These attempted changes were costly, both in money and in human effort. Although fees had been and continued to be charged for primary schooling, local resources were insufficient to cover the increased expenses, and government subsidies did not make up the difference. Cameron and Dodd (1970:195) assert that "the teachers seem[ed] to be expected to implement great changes without the material and textbooks to support them." Still more gravely, they charge (1970:195):

> Those initiating changes at the top, by outrunning the ability of the educational system to keep up with them, . . . increasingly tended to assume that what they want[ed] to happen [was] in fact happening. Those at the receiving end, the teachers [were] having their enthusiasm blunted by a growing suspicion that the initiators [did] not appreciate what the real state of affairs in the classroom [was]. Curriculum reform [had] thus become for many teachers a depressant, not a stimulant. In particular the Primary School Inspectors, who are the go-betweens and the translators of policy into action in the primary schools [were] carrying a great burden.

Policies intended to integrate efforts on the local and centralized levels were critical in the program for society-wide change. In 1964 development commissions were established at village, district, and regional levels to design and implement plans for furthering national objectives locally. Self-help schemes of many kinds were encouraged vigorously, though not all succeeded. The new Five Year Plan of 1964–69 was formulated on this foundation.

The Five Year Plan was well constructed. But it nearly foundered because of unpredictable natural and human factors. Overestimating anticipated domestic production and fiscal resources available from abroad, underestimating population increase and rises in costs, the plan was beleaguered by problems endemic to societal planning. Added were the hazards of planning for an agricultural economy acutely vulnerable to natural and market calamities. In 1965 a disastrous drought affected both food and cash crops and in the same year, world prices for cash crops fell. Although the administrative machinery for implementing and monitoring the plan had been created, this structure was not yet well coordinated, and its personnel lacked experience in its use. This hampered the effective channeling of available money into appropriate development schemes. In addition, sizable expenditures were made that bypassed the plan altogether. Primary education, now under local control, expanded far more than had been intended,[27] thus widening the gap between primary school graduates and secondary school openings. This enhanced the frustration of the "losers" and the elitist attitudes of the "winners" in the academic competition. At the same time, salaries of teachers, army, and police were raised, despite the spirit of self-discipline and restraint asked of citizens as a prerequisite for successful development. The climax came in 1966 when legislation was drafted requiring students who had been educated at the government's expense to repay the nation with two years of national service. After many months of discussion, and vocal protests by students at "having been singled out for conscription and subjected to financial sacrifices which they considered unjust," nearly four hundred students staged a formal demonstration against the bill (Resnick 1968b:10). President Nyerere replied by ordering them to leave their colleges and return home. Most were readmitted a year later if they could show that they had been engaged in useful work since their suspension.

At the root of this confrontation was a conflict between two antithetical sets of values. At one pole were the values exhorted by TANU, Nyerere, and the development plans that called for mutually supportive, cooperative endeavor toward achievement of a cohesive democratic society, a society in which none would be deprived to support the aggrandizement of a few. Opposing these were the values, in part a legacy of the colonial era, which linked schooling with privilege and freedom from the drudgery of subsistence labor. The emphasis on schooling as an economic investment and the systematic training of those selected few who were to provide skills critical in the development process, was in itself sufficient to elicit in them a sense of elite identity. This was further reinforced by providing them salaries and fringe benefits "commensurate" with the value of their services to the nation. Although in the colonial era highly skilled Europeans had been well paid and the Africans who took over their positions naturally sought equivalent recompense, this pattern was no longer appropriate in the post-Independence era, with the vast bulk of the population so desperately poor and national resources so thinly stretched.

As Nyerere (1967) underscored in his manifesto, *Education for Self-Reliance,* much of this elitist attitude was a product of the schooling system. Colonial schooling

> emphasized and encouraged the individualistic instincts of mankind instead of his co-operative instincts. It led to the possession of individual material wealth being the major criterion of social merit and worth.

This meant that colonial education induced attitudes of human inequality, and
in practice underpinned the domination of the weak by the strong, especially in
the economic field. . . . (Nyerere 1967:51).

This was the system inherited, and "it takes years for a change in education
to have its effect" (Nyerere 1967:52). The system continued to fail to instill the
values needed in the new kind of society Tanzania was trying to build. Nyerere
cited several reasons for this. First, the system of schooling was thoroughly
oriented to the tiny minority of students who actually continue up the academic ladder, providing relatively little of value to those who study for a
limited period of time. This emphasized the supposed intellectual superiority
of those who succeeded and induced the growth of elitist class structure.
Second, the school world was effectively separate from the larger community,
both because the curriculum was not very relevant to subsistence activities, and
because parents themselves encouraged a sense of distinctive identity in their
student children. School "is a place children go to . . . which they and their
parents hope will make it unnecessary for them to become farmers and continue living in the villages" (Nyerere 1967:57).[28] Third, the school encouraged
students in the idea that all worthwhile knowledge is acquired from books or
other schooled people. This was suggested partly by the intensive selection
process, which was based on performance on examinations testing information
retention. Because curriculum reform had never effectively substituted training
in analytic skills for the older emphasis on facts, students saw little relationship
between their school learning and the experiential learning of their unschooled
fellows. This undervaluation of informally acquired knowledge and experience
extended throughout the whole administrative system.

If a man has [specified academic] qualifications we assume he can fill a post;
we do not wait to find out about his attitudes, his character, or any other ability
except the ability to pass examinations. If a man does not have these qualifications we assume he cannot do a job; we ignore his knowledge and experience.
For example, I recently visited a very good tobacco-producing peasant. But if
I tried to take him into government as a Tobacco Extension Officer, I would run
up against the system because he has no formal education (Nyerere 1967:58).

There was also a subtle contradiction between ideological principles and
prevailing values in the allocation of funds for general education. The Five
Year Plan provided for the formal school system under the Ministry of Education, vocational school and in-service training contributed by other Ministries,
and both formal and informal education directed at the rural adult population.
Despite the importance theoretically accorded to the latter and the ambitious
hopes for it, the whole adult education program received about four percent
of the total funding allocated to the Ministry of Education. That some gains
were made in rural adult education was due in part to the dedication of
participants in the program, in part to the foundations laid before independence.

Materials written in Swahili and vernacular languages had been published by missionaries and the German administration as early as the turn of the century. Under British rule, newspapers multiplied, British publishing firms brought out Swahili-language books, and a publishing bureau serving all of East Africa began in Nairobi, Kenya. This publishing house brought out cheap, well made editions (many by African authors) and increased distribution by circulating portable "book-box" libraries. By the late 1940s, radio broadcasting was accessible even in the hinterlands, and the listening public grew rapidly. At independence these media were available, but needed sufficient funds to be used.

Radio, in particular, facilitated the spread of Swahili, making it a truly national language. As part of community development programs, both radio transmissions and inexpensive written materials circulated new information and helped to develop appropriate attitudes. Radio broadcasts to schools helped upgrade both curriculum content and teacher qualifications through special background programs.

Ultimately, however, TANU itself was the prime educative agency for the common people, both before and after independence. Through their participation in planning and decision making at local party levels, through communal self-help schemes and cooperative enterprises in which they were encouraged by TANU representatives, the common people learned the pragmatic meaning of the revolutionary ideology guiding Tanzania's development. If there had been more consistency between that ideology and the actual social structure of Tanzania, however, the lessons might have been more convincing.

Directing sociocultural change is a complex endeavor. Values, ideas, and attitudes can obstruct or facilitate the change process. The human factor in socioeconomic change is critical and no amount of careful planning can outweigh its influence. At independence the new Tanzanian government

> believed that to transform the situation we had only to replace expatriate administrators and policy–makers with local people, to expand the provision of public service, and to make the people aware that the Government now consisted of TANU members. In other words, we thought to energise the system we knew, and to reverse certain policies to which we had always been opposed (Nyerere 1974:4).

The Tanzanian planners gave priority to both the economic motor of development and the educational fuels which would enable it to run. Their realism and target orientation contributed to a distinctly utilitarian scheme. The expansion of schooling beyond the primary level was controlled, to match exactly the projected need for school-educated personnel. Academic specialization itself was planned around the nation's most pressing requirements. Since nearly all advanced schooling was government-financed, assistance was given only to students qualified for the most needed courses of study, mainly science and mathematics. This specialized schooling, however, lacked an effective enculturative component, necessary to produce not just the skills but the attitudes required to achieve the long-range goals. As Nyerere (1967) has declared, colonial schooling was a revolutionary affair, designed to re-culturate those who passed through it. To achieve the Tanzanian goals required an analogous revolution.

Tanzanian planners have not been unwilling to challenge assumptions long held by educators and others. When the policy of instrumentally controlled access to advanced schooling first was proposed, it was not well received by most educators. Thomas (1968:113) remarks:

> It was cited as dictatorial, described as "directed" or "controlled" . . . implying that young people were being forced to accept scholarships and 'required' to pursue a course of study other than the one they would have chosen under other circumstances. Dire warnings were uttered of the catastrophic results which might be expected of "forcing young people into careers not of their own choosing and for which they have no special aptitude."

Describing the objections to the policy as "arrant twaddle," Thomas describes the rationale behind the plan. Free choice of specialization was tried first, with dismal results. Left to their own devices, students tend to opt for liberal arts degrees (in Tanzania and elsewhere) which would not equip them to meet national needs. Concluding his argument on behalf of the planners' decision, Thomas (1968:114) observes:

> Strangely enough no anguished wails have ever been directed to the situation of the lower [secondary school] . . . leaver. . . . the majority are faced with exactly the same kind of choice under the manpower programme as the prospective university candidate. . . . The [lower secondary school leaver] . . . can take a course to become a Grade A teacher, an agricultural technician, a veterinarian, a medical or engineering technician, and that is about all. This situation predated the university programme by many years. As far as is known, not a single voice has ever been raised to describe it as dictatorial, cruel and unusual or as a policy "forcing young people into careers not of their own choosing and for which they have no special aptitude."

A latter battle began when the Ministry of Education proposed major capital outlays for new schools in the formulation of the 1964–69 Five Year Plan. Briefly, the Ministry of Development Planning pointed out that secondary school plants were wholly unused for 25 percent of the year (vacations and holidays), and that they were mostly unused for half of the daylight hours throughout the school year. It would be more economical to operate the existing plant at full capacity with two shifts and add housing for extra teachers and boarding students. The Ministry of Education replied that this would be both organizátionally unworkable and pedagogically unsound, but the Ministry of Development Planning refuted this argument, referring to other socialist countries in which many secondary schools had two shifts. As Thomas (1968:120) phrases it,

> The Ministry of Education's response, loosely translated, suggested they still found the proposal immoral, illegal and fattening and would have nothing to do with it.

The stalemate was resolved by compromise at the Cabinet level. After the first angry reactions against the violation of territorial dominion, the educators even assisted in making the scheme workable.

The assumptions surrounding education as a process have not been tackled so directly. Two are especially crucial. First is the presumed significance of academic learning for the personal and intellectual worth of the learner. Although Nyerere has emphasized that schooled skills, while critical to development, are simply skills like any other, most Tanzanians do not appear to agree. Resnick (1968a) points out that the overvaluation of formal education has held back development by ignoring other pools of talent and alternative ways of producing necessary skills. But the largest rewards still go to the schooled. Second, despite the innovative programs of extrascholastic education designed to serve school leavers and the unschooled, education is defined rather narrowly. Only those transmissions of knowledge intended as educative have been considered systematically by the planners. The context of those intentional transmissions has only recently come to be seen as part of the lesson. Yet we know that context and unintended communication are often more voluble than the intended message.

To effectively "revolutionize" or reculturate the citizenry of Tanzania, the entire social system must be understood as a powerful educative statement. The specific objectives put forth by TANU include the following: "equality and respect for human dignity; sharing of the resources which are produced by our efforts; and work by everyone and exploitation by none" (Nyerere 1967:53). No matter how inspiring the rhetoric or how thoughtful the curricular design, the perceived realities of social life will dispel the intended value change, if they run counter to the ideology propounded. Radical change in the values and attitudes of the people requires that the visible structures of inequality, elitism, and privilege be brought into congruence with the favored ideology. This is not simply another way of phrasing the "legislation of equality." Rather I am suggesting the following: first, that change in values depends on the perception that the new value is realistic, that it is adaptive or beneficial to hold. If the value is seen as a rhetorical defense of someone else's interests at the expense of one's own, it will not be adopted. Second, that the privileged will tend not to activate egalitarian values that significantly reduce their own privileges unless forced to do so by (a) ideological commitment or (b) the sanction of higher authority or strong group pressure. And finally, that the disappearance or massive reduction of these symbols of outmoded values and their tangible benefits will facilitate the reconstruction of new values among the formerly privileged and the acceptance by the formerly less privileged of the adaptive merit of the new value.

That this also represents President Nyerere's position is suggested by a series of events following the student discontent of 1966. Nyerere

> saw the students' rejection of National Service, under which they were required to perform some short–term quasi–military service and were expected to fill certain jobs after graduation, largely as teachers, as a rejection of commitment to the nation which had financed the students through the educational system. He saw the emergence of an educated elite cut off from its rural roots and without an ethic of service to the nation (Bienen 1970:427).

In response to the student complaint that they alone were the targets of government austerity, Nyerere announced that he was taking a permanent twenty-percent cut in pay. Cabinet members followed suit, while lower ranking officials and party leaders took ten- to fifteen-percent pay cuts. Members of Parliament took no salary cuts but were denied further increases. Various fringe benefits which had been perquisites of high office were eliminated. Associated with these changes was a new series of policy formulations put out by the National Executive Committee of TANU, known as the Arusha Declaration. This manifesto and the subsequent Five Year Development Plan demanded that leaders at all levels exemplify socialist principles of equitable distribution of wealth and nonexploitative relations with others. Leaders had to give up investments, rental properties, and other evidences of personal gain through public service. Some resigned rather than do so; elected officials guilty of such self-aggrandizement often were defeated in the next election. At the regional and national levels, in any event, the pressure for conformity was strong, and considerable popular support was shown by the election results.

The second Five Year Plan (1970–74) also reflected a shift in orientation. It was projected that by 1980, the wage sector would be saturated with secondary school graduates. Therefore the new priority was to be primary school education. Primary school education was to be redesigned as a full scholastic education in itself, integrated into the life of the surrounding community and preparing students to return to agrarian life. An ethic of social service was to be instilled at all levels and students were to be judged by their service as well as by their academic accomplishments. The relative proportion of primary school-age children served was to increase, with the longer-term goal of universal, seven-year primary schooling by 1989. Accomplishing the changes in the academic ethos and community attitudes toward schools has not been easy. At the secondary level, teachers who are themselves products of an elitist system may be less than effective transmitters of a new socialist ethos. Primary school teachers who have had less training in the academic system are more likely to be sympathetic to these changes. Many teachers lack training in the newly required agrarian skills, and the aspirations of parents and children are not redirected so readily.

The strict control maintained over the growth of postprimary schooling has paid off in some respects. Bienefeld (1972:174–5, cited in Morrison 1976:273) observes that

> Tanzania has been able to build up an educational system that is meeting its manpower needs consistently with the [national goal of achieving] self-sufficiency in high and middle level manpower by 1980 and without creating future over capacity in institutions of higher education or producing large numbers with expensive skills who will find themselves unable to use such skills.

However, controlled access to advanced, specialized schooling has reinforced its elitist character within the schooling system and the expectation of occupational rewards by those securing it.

Among the strategies devised to counter this has been the extension of Swahili as the sole medium of instruction into the secondary schools, although the lack of suitable curriculum materials has hampered realization of this goal. The use of English in postprimary instruction was both creating an additional symbol of status distinction between those with and without further schooling and promoting a sense of remoteness in academic instruction from the problems of the masses.

Another strategy planned which has yet to be implemented systematically is reform of the system of academic examinations and promotion. At the primary level, according to Morrison (1976:274), evaluation of student service and "socialist" attitude has not yet become an important criterion in selection for further study;

> the traditional criteria—performance in written theory papers, tempered by often class-biased evaluations of academic ability and conduct by headteachers —continue to dominate.

The same is true at postprimary levels. Although in 1971 Tanzania, like Ghana, ceased to participate in the Cambridge-accredited examination system, "it did not lead to a departure from the historically-entrenched examinations syndrome" (Morrison 1976:274).

Efforts at equalizing academic opportunity both regionally and throughout the social strata of the population also have not been fully successful. Both urban children and children from privileged classes seem to retain the advantage in access to postprimary schooling. Based on national statistics from 1969, Morrison (1976:278) concludes:

We have no firm evidence to support the hypothesis that class is an important factor in selection for publicly-assisted secondary schools. However the number of private institutions has steadily grown and high fees . . . place entrance to these schools out of reach for most Tanzanian children. Some idea of the extent of this aspect of class privilege is apparent in . . . that 21 per cent of all secondary students were enrolled in private schools. . . .

Adult education, on the other hand, has been given substantially greater priority than under previous plans, particularly with respect to the goal of universal literacy. On the assumption that literacy is crucial to effective transmission of attitudes and skills necessary for successful development, and for a sound grasp of the principles of Tanzanian socialism, extensive literacy drives have been carried out. Supplementing these campaigns, TANU has expanded its programs for adult political education, and the curriculum for teacher trainees has been revised to include more ideological training.

The anticipated results of this last strategy have not yet been realized. It is reasonable to expect that a minimum of several years would be necessary for significant effects to be discerned in the school system, as former trainees take up active teaching posts. Even then, their effects as individuals are likely to be diluted by those of colleagues trained in an earlier system. Morrison (1976:279) notes a "tendency of teachers at all levels to accept Western values rather uncritically." It is unreasonable to expect teachers to represent the height of ideological clarity. First, teachers at the primary levels have had relatively little exposure to advanced schooling. Second, those teachers who do secure advanced academic instruction confront a curriculum and an educational context which has not yet fully integrated the ideologically favored ethos into other curricular subjects. Contributing to this are the use of English in much of the advanced instruction and the continued emphasis on examinations of factual knowledge rather than on systematic evaluation of analytic skills. Both, as we noted earlier, hamper acquisition of a perspective linking academic learning with the specific problems of development encountered by the masses in the countryside. As Morrison (1976:287–288) comments,

the failure thus far to integrate agricultural and political education effectively into the broader curriculum has meant that these subjects, while given great emphasis, have been taught in an isolated and fragmented way. Moreover, as Dr. Mbilinyi reports, ". . . 'self-reliance' activities are treated as something separate from the rest of school work, as extra-curricular.". . . .

The divorce of politics, agriculture and productive labor from the rest of the school experience and often from the wider political and economic context, certainly lessens the potential for cultivating the socialist and self-reliant attitudes desired by the Tanzanian leadership.

Pilot projects using a fully integrated syllabus were launched in several primary schools in 1973, but the extent of this experiment, whatever its potential

results, has been severely restricted by limited personnel and financial resources.

A third obstacle to effective transmission of a well-grounded socialist
ethos within the classroom may well be the selection process for teaching
personnel. In his survey of educators, Morrison (1976:281, 300–302) found
that many teachers, especially at the primary level, expressed discontent with
their salaries. Indeed, primary teachers have been among the lowest paid
public employees. Many teachers, especially at postprimary levels, expressed
the belief that their status had declined since independence. Although many
felt that it had risen because of the growing value placed on schooling, those
who perceived a decline may have been responding, in part, to increased
challenges of their professional prerogatives in controlling the content and
strategies of academic transmission. While not universal, this discontent may
reflect a growing perception of teaching as a less preferred occupation. If this
is so, we might expect many to enter the teaching force who fail in the stiff
competition for more specialized and better rewarded professional training.

Fourth, many academic administrators, Morrison (1976:282) reports,
believe that schooling is properly the preserve of educators, not politicians,
local communities, or students. Thus they oppose the involvement of national
or local planners in school reform. Community participation is minimized, and
students are expected to be passive recipients of knowledge. These administrators view "politicized" curricular content as inappropriate to high quality
schooling. They favor the use of formal, British-style examinations and academic standards for determining occupational qualifications. As administrators, they have considerable influence over the educational process in the
schools they supervise and thus over potential change in the academic system.
Expanding the number of local supervisory posts under the second Five Year
Plan has diminished this obstacle to change. Yet the promotion of young,
well-qualified teachers to these posts also has removed some of the best talent
from primary and secondary school teaching.

The new plan's educational objectives were complemented by a reorganization of economic priorities. This shift reflects both a new phase of economic development and a heightened awareness of the importance of the
socioeconomic context in validating the new academic emphases. The addition
of economic productivity to the school's goals, a strategy aimed at bringing
academic institutions into greater congruence with the life of the masses, also
created an exercise in self-reliance. In the nonacademic sector, the aggregate
growth and capital-intensive strategies emphasized under the previous plans
gave way to the immediate objective of raising the quality of rural life. This
was to be accomplished by increasing available food for consumption and
improving social and agricultural extension services in rural areas. Both local
self-help improvement projects for which minimal financial or technical assistance would be necessary, and the mobilization of local leadership received

increased stress. Accompanying this emphasis on local leadership was the larger objective of strengthening TANU organization at local and district levels. Self-reliance was the keynote. At the same time, certain responsibilities had been taken out of local hands, weakening local influence in favor of regional administrations. Schooling was among these. Before the government's reabsorption of authority in this area, many district councils had experienced severe financial difficulties; by 1969, following the unplanned florescence of primary facilities, several were all but bankrupt.

The structure of TANU itself was called into question by the move to eliminate self-aggrandizers from official and party ranks. The planners have continued to depend on the educational functions of TANU, particularly on the local level; the more stringent requirements established for TANU membership and leadership roles may well represent an application of the educational principle of modeling desired behavior, as well as a more general organizational strategy. Local TANU leaders have played a crucial part in communicating national objectives and measures, and in reorienting people's thinking to accord with them. This has been marked, inevitably, by a diversity of actual interpretations. Ideas disseminated from the center undergo transformation in transmission to the more distant reaches of the society. This diversity is both recognized and accepted by Nyerere as desirable leeway in local interpretation of general principles. Not all Tanzanian administrators agree with this, nor does all government action reflect it. Bienen (1970:461) remarks in this regard,

> Despite the general acclamation of President Nyerere and his statements in Tanzania, . . . it cannot be taken for granted that support exists throughout the country or at all levels of the leadership for all the policies, or even the general goals, that the Arusha Declaration states or implies. However, in Tanzania a relatively unified political culture is available which both masses and elites share, so that communication is possible between them.

As our discussion thus far indicates, "relatively unified" is an apt description, for unanimity, especially across classes and interest groups, remains a rather distant goal.

The ideological concepts of equality, cooperation, and nonexploitation have been lent empirical significance at the local level by the continuing travels and extensive personal contact of Nyerere. Traveling throughout the country, he has consistently encouraged individuals to come forward at mass meetings with grievances and complaints. A Permanent Commission on Enquiry also travels throughout the country receiving complaints and serving as a "collective ombudsman." Neither TANU nor government officials are allowed to be present when complaints are heard. Some cases are settled on the spot, the rest at Commission headquarters in the capital.

Other measures are also necessary, yet each carries potential costs and

risks. Strategies to raise the standard of living in rural areas must be complemented by enforcing ceilings on the wage and salary levels of urbanites and
professionals, until the relatively wide gap between them narrows to more
equitable proportions. Yet, despite the substantial support the government
now holds in the rural areas, it cannot afford massive disaffection among the
politically articulate elite.

"Careerism and elitism," Morrison (1976:290) observes, "remains as
powerful motive forces among most students in the University and other
institutions of higher education." This is not easily changed. As Bienefeld
(1972:180, cited in Morrison 1976:290) concludes,

> Attempts to eliminate the pervasive elitism of the highly educated are all but
> hopeless in the face of the social exclusiveness of life in present boarding schools
> and the university, the general social attitude to education, the students' exposure
> to the competitive selectiveness of the educational process and to the authoritari-
> anism of the institutions, and the fact that education still is the gateway to high
> incomes, status, and power.

Solutions are being sought that take into account the interconnection of these
and other factors. Recently, for example, the government embarked on a crash
program of primary school expansion aimed at achieving universal primary
schooling by November 1977. Secondary school students who have completed
the final form are now required to spend time living and working in the
community. Subsequent university admission will be based on the recommen-
dation of the TANU branches. These two strategies may help to reduce the
perceived gap in experience and status between the highly schooled and the
majority of the population. The evaluation of demonstrated commitment to
the common cause as a criterion for access to advanced academic education
—a privilege subsidized since independence by the population as a whole—
may also have an effect on the attitudes of those who achieve it.

The probable costs of such strategies must not be underestimated. Morrison (1976:307) points out that

> a rapid rise in the output of elementary schools may well contribute, at least
> in the short-run, to increases in urban employment and rural underemployment
> and [thereby] to social and political tensions that can divert the allocation of
> resources away from their most productive use.

This is likely because the Tanzanian economy cannot expand rapidly enough
to sustain a high level of wage employment. On the other hand, expansion of
primary schooling opportunities in concert with well-designed and properly
implemented curricula can conceivably counter some of the unrealizable expectations of wage employment that schooling has tended to carry. This is

possible if other socioeconomic goals are simultaneously realized. As Morrison (1976:312) notes,

> making use of the socializing potential of schools to reorient attitudes towards rural life and to give youths the incentive to undertake modern farming, can be effective only in the context of more farreaching policies for stimulating agricultural production and improving living conditions in the countryside.

De-emphasis of examination scores and formal academic criteria for access to advanced schooling, in favor of assessments of service could make access to schooling susceptible to personal influence and literal or figurative nepotism. Even in conjunction with appropriate academic curricula and supportive materials, community service may not radically reduce the elitist attitudes of the privileged. Critical too is the degree of congruence between these experiences and those influenced by other educative agencies such as family, peer group, church, voluntary organizations, and the social structure of which these are part.

The key issue for us, and to a considerable degree also for Tanzania, is the part that education can play in facilitating desired change. Foster (1965a, 1969) has argued that schools are so thoroughly entrenched within existing social structures that they can be agents only of conservation, not of sociocultural change. Illich (1971a) contends that the very structure of schooling inherently impedes radical change. There is evidence to support both theses, but they suffer from oversimplification. Neither takes into account the full range of alternatives possible in the formulation of systematic education or the intricate dialectical relationship among agencies of transmission and between these agencies and their sociocultural context (cf. Mwingira 1969).

It is this dialectic which Tanzanian planners are taking increasingly into account. The initial decisions to treat schooling as a source of technical skills, for example, were later modified in light of evidence that other goals were being simultaneously thwarted. As in other societies, the formal educational system of Tanzania is embedded in a larger sociocultural context. Tanzanian planners have begun to recognize the variety of channels through which education in the broad sense can and does take place. Recognizing them, they have striven to use them systematically to convey the new culture they seek to build. The constraints on the strategies available to planners and participants alike are many. Material poverty and limited natural resources other than land, a predominantly agricultural economy, and a commitment to economic self-reliance as a nation all contribute to the hard reality of marginal fiscal resources. At the same time, fulfillment of the people's most basic needs, from improved agricultural production to medical care and schooling, requires substantial financial outlay. The culturally heterogeneous population, their colonial heritage, and their vulnerability to international pressure (such as the recent invasion by Uganda) also create problems which must influence their decisions.

It would be a serious mistake to view the Tanzanian educational strategies from only one vantage point, whether it be economic, political, or scholastic in the narrow sense. Economic development, it is true, requires the dissemination of new skills and orientations among the populace. Political integration and national autonomy likewise depend on the development of sociopolitical awareness and commitment to shared interests among diverse groups. But these goals are part of a more encompassing aim, that of sociocultural transformation. This larger goal demands more than economic growth, political strength and stability, and an informed literate citizenry. It also requires the reformulation of basic attitudes across the spectrum of the Tanzanian population and a redistribution of knowledge and privilege throughout the society. It is in this respect that Tanzania provides a useful test case for our understanding of knowledge transmission and its significance for conservation and change.

Nyerere especially has "consistently understood socialism primarily as an attitude of mind" (Bienen 1970:460). Given this, his unequivocal conviction that education is the key is understood easily. Education is communication: multichannel, contextual, transactional, and negotiable. That education has been accorded so important a role in Tanzania's strategies and that it has come to be conceived so broadly provide some pragmatic confirmation of the theoretical position advocated in this book.

The pace of progress which Tanzania has been able to maintain toward its national goals is impressive in view of the many obstacles along the route. The scope of its achievement, limited though it has been with respect to its long-range goals, suggests the significance of the overall strategy developed: a combination of systematic and detailed planning to achieve specified goals, vigilant monitoring of the realities of Tanzanian life, and reassessment of the plans in light of these facts. If we compare the Tanzanian experiment with that which Colorado has undertaken in multicultural schooling, we find they differ in several ways. First, the Colorado experiment is much narrower in scope, for it involves a program of change within a single educative agency (public schools) rather than a coordinated plan for change across multiple domains of social life. Second, it represents goals which have garnered enough public support to allow the passage of the necessary legislation, but it in no way reflects goals shared even rhetorically across the communities involved. Third, although many of its proponents are oriented to long-term goals, political compromise has forced the experiment to be instituted in a restricted form and its effectiveness is to be evaluated in terms only of short-term, readily quantified goals such as relative dropout rates. If the Colorado experiment were seen as a means to social or cultural transformation, it is unlikely that even limited funding of the program would be continued.

Tanzania, in contrast, while it can ill afford the fiscal and temporal waste of poorly designed experiments, seems to accept the risk of partial failure as part of its long-range strategy for developing viable solutions and desired change. Monitoring programs as they are put into operation, in combination with a fairly coherent set of shared goals for such programs, enables Tanzanian planners to modify program design without abandoning the program as a whole. Partly this is because responsibility for effecting change, even within the academic system itself, is spread among representatives of many sectors of the society. In the Colorado experiment, some diffusion of responsibility was attempted in the plan as originally formulated. Parents, particularly, were given an active role in the administrative structure of the academic experiment. As instituted, they retained only a minor role, with most of the responsibility back in the hands of professional educators. Participation from outside the academic sector is now confined largely to the watchful eye of fiscally–oriented legislators and the nebulous domain of public opinion.

A more appropriate and far-reaching comparison would require analysis of other nations that have attempted to effect sociocultural transformations on an equivalent scale, such as Cuba, Israel, the Soviet Union, and the People's Republic of China. In each case, the transformation attempted has been constrained by a variety of historical and contemporary factors, but the experiments all have involved radical change in educational systems and processes. We also need to examine the forms of educational change that have characterized less revolutionary societies which have utilized strategies of long-term planning for directed change, such as those of Scandinavia. In more prosperous societies, less beset by insufficiency of skilled specialists and analysts, what have been the results of deliberate planning for desired change?

To make such comparisons here would lengthen this book inordinately and go well beyond its stated goals. More importantly, effective comparison requires data of wide scope and depth, data not yet available in sufficient quantity. We need not only careful analysis of existing literature but also intensive field studies of these educational systems in operation, to determine the relationships between knowledge transmission and sociocultural conservation and change. We need data appropriate to all the analytic levels discussed in the preceding chapters, data reflecting not simply the structural features of educational systems but also the processes by which knowledge transmission is effected. We need to examine the dialectic relationships among the various agencies of transmission characteristic of each society, not simply their schools. And we need to consider carefully the effects on our analyses of the theoretical orientations we choose to apply.

notes

1. Carnoy (1974:365) asserts that

   all children in school learn to evaluate society on grounds favorable to the rich and powerful. Children are taught that those in power are necessarily the best judges of good and bad, and are generally right because they have access to more information than the rest of the electorate. . . . the abstract reality developed by [the] knowledge [imparted in schools] is made more *legitimate* than people's day-to-day experiences.

2. Ogbu (1974), for instance, found ambivalence on this issue expressed by parents in the low income neighborhood he studied. While many urged their children to get an education in order to get ahead, they also acknowledged that chances of getting ahead were not as good if you were black as if you were white (see also Lewis 1967). For documentation of the meritocratic fallacy see Michelson (1969) and Blair (1972). Blair shows that schooling as an economic investment has differential payoffs for Chicanos and whites. Chicanos get a much higher rate of return on that investment at non-completion (drop-out) levels than at degree levels, due to discrimination in the job market. Michelson demonstrates that minority poor must have *more* schooling than whites to reach the same income level, including minimum levels.

3. Not only do U.S. schools vary regionally and locally in official curriculum and in materials available to promote learning, but they also vary in areas such as emphasis on authority and discipline, typical teaching strategies, and scope of student participation in selecting among academic options. Similar variation, of course, exists within schools as well as among them.

4. There are numerous examples of this. See, for instance, Higgins (1976), Moore (1973), Comitas (1967).

5. Cf. Shea (1977) for a critical survey of studies on status attainment, schooling, and antecedent sociocultural factors.

6. Raskin (1971) explores this function of schooling and shows its relation to the development of identities. Schools, he argues, teach students not only to operate within a hierarchy (and to accept it as natural), and the prevailing criteria for definition of success and failure and their associated rewards and punishments, but also the importance of their "record" or "file," the accumulated judgments on their whole student career which will follow them throughout their lives.

7. See Becker (1961) for a discussion of the balance of power between teachers and principal and of their joint accomplishment of authority within the school. For commentaries on the increased pressure on principals since the advent of teachers' collective bargaining, see Vidich and McReynolds (1971) and Bradfield and Kraft (1970).

8. See Smith and Keith (1971) for a case study of an innovative principal in an innovative elementary school, especially pp. 235–278.

9. Involving teachers directly in the development of an innovative program and providing a supportive environment for their efforts does not guarantee smooth transformation, as Smith and Keith (1971) have documented.

10. Since Norwegian sealers, fishermen, and hunters had access to the eastern territories, access validated by treaty in 1924, this control probably pertains most directly to the western region which was the original Danish colony. It is noteworthy, however, that the Dano-Norwegian treaty allowed free access only to the *use* of those lands, not to their ownership (Åhman 1950).

11. Compare in this regard Early (1973) who reports on the training of local peasants to serve as literacy teachers.

12. This is particularly true in rural locales. In towns the isolation of teachers reflects the de facto residential segregation of Eskimo and white communities. Where de facto segregation does not exist, Hobart (1970b:130) indicates, "the unfamiliarity of teachers with the way of life of local native peoples is far less marked." Also, differences between the ways of life of town-oriented, wage-earning Eskimo and of whites are not as great as those between rural Eskimo and whites.

13. Hobart (1970a:60) reports on a survey of ten communities during the spring of 1969. Of the total 48 teachers, only one-fourth had spent more than two years there. Half to two-thirds of all teachers are new in any given year.

14. Hobart (1970a:65–67) describes briefly an innovative program developed in Quebec, in which the first three years of school are conducted in Eskimo, and Eskimo without traditional professional credentials are being trained and employed as teachers. Although the results appear to be promising, systematic follow-up studies are needed to evaluate the program.

15. Hobart (1970a:64–65) comments that the few northern-oriented materials available are both less attractively presented than the standard southern materials (and thus less appealing to children), and unappealing to southern-trained teachers who are accustomed to southern-oriented materials and have only a short-term commitment to their Arctic charges. A small addition also has been made to school budgets to cover the cost of including presentation of a few aspects of Eskimo culture (e.g., Eskimo storytellers, carvers, speakers might display or teach their skills), but according to Hobart this was no more than a token in practice, albeit of significant potential.

16. Rural Eskimo children returned home from boarding schools no longer adapted to a predominantly meat diet and pervasive cold; behaviorally they expressed dissatisfaction with prevailing conditions in an Eskimo community, were disrespectful of their parents who were ignorant of school-knowledge, were disobedient, uncooperative, jealous, and prone to fighting and lying, and in some cases to stealing. All of these behaviors violate Eskimo norms and values. Accustomed to the authority structure of the school, they did not take the autonomous responsibility expected of them; they had to be told what to do. Nor had they developed the skills necessary to secure a livelihood outside the wage sector.

17. Kleinfeld (1973) documents the effect of varied parental styles on Eskimo and Indian children's behavior in a study of boarding home parents.

18. Carnoy (1974:154, note 154) argues that missions other than the Basel Mission "did not push vocational education very hard" and "that missionaries felt [more] comfortable offering a curriculum based on morality and academic learning (their own educational experience) than one based on skilled trades."

19. In colonies in which a "world" religion such as Islam or Buddhism prevailed, administrators attempted to prevent active proselytization by their Christian compatriots. This was true in the Muslim areas of the Gold Coast and Nigeria.

20. Political domination and concepts of genetic inferiority are closely related in the West. Only after Europe became involved in the slave trade were non-European races commonly defined as genetically, as well as culturally, inferior. Even after abolition of the slave trade, the expansion of European colonial empires was ideologically buttressed by this dogma, justifying Caucasian hegemony over the "colored races" as the "the white man's burden."

21. The concept of cultural evolution has two rather distinct referents, one historical and the other ideological. Historically, the evolution of human culture refers to the evolution of the human species and the development of particular cultures from earliest antiquity to the present day. Ideologically, various cultures are ranked on a scale of "progress," generally progress toward some ideal state of perfection or realization of human potential. Because such a scale presupposes values about that ideal state, the criteria of "progress" generally match the characteristics of the society whose members are doing the ranking. Thus Euroamerican concepts of progress tend to involve technological complexity, industrial economy, and political centralization as key components. From this point of view, nonindustrial societies with less complex technological arsenals and less extensive politcal hegemony are "culturally inferior" to their more highly evolved counterparts.

22. For a critique of literature on bilingual education (generally a central aspect of bicultural education), see Engle (1976).

23. The Maslands (1975:185) report some attempts to adapt program content through the use of names, locales, and objects familiar to Samoan children, and through the use of a few Samoan television teachers. However, attempts at integrating Samoan culture and environment into transmission content were mostly restricted to a semi-weekly program about the Samoan way of life and insensitively presented. Where Samoan adults appeared, they were often "used . . . as a prop," following the instructions of the Anglo, and implicitly suggesting the Samoan's inferiority to his Anglo counterpart.

24. Kamin (1974) points out that the use of IQ testing in the U.S. has been affected by political-historical factors. The French Binet test from which the "science of IQ testing" derived, was designed to measure only academic aptitude, with the aim of providing assistance to those diagnosed as likely to fail in scholastic endeavors. Many U.S. scholars interpreted this test as a measure of *innate* intelligence, explicable genetically. On this basis, performance scores of lower class and immigrant minorities have been interpreted as evidence of their genetic inferiority.

25. See Gibson 1976 for a critical discussion of current approaches to multicultural education in U.S. schools. Cf. also the companion essays in Gibson, ed. (1976), Trueba (1974), Brennan and Donoghue (1974) and Rosen (1977).

26. See Aoki (1973) and Sabey (1973) for contrasting perspectives on this problem. Aoki describes a program designed to increase community control over schooling on four Canadian Indian reserves. Sabey describes a program designed to incorporate into the national curriculum acknowledgment of the many cultures comprising Canadian society, a modification in which local communities apparently play no part. The project organization involved appears to be distinctly "professional."

27. Samoff (1974) reports that in Kilimanjaro District this overexpansion was strongly encouraged by local mission groups. This echoes the conflict of interest mentioned earlier between church and state with respect to educational goals in colonial times. More importantly, the implicit sabotage of central planning efforts that do not suit mission interests seems to be an ongoing phenomenon in this district. Possibly it is occurring elsewhere as well.

28. Tessler and others (1973:61–63) point out that schooling became particularly attractive in areas where population pressure on the land was high, as in the village of Usangi. In this community, they report, parents use several strategies to maximize their children's chances of academic success. One is to send a child to primary school at the age of ten or eleven years, on the premise "that older children have a better chance to succeed." (The assumptions underlying this belief are not clear from their account.) Another, when there is an opportunity to choose among schools, is to evaluate "the level of success in examinations of students" at each school, as in Japan. A third, also reminiscent of Japan, is having one's child repeat the last grade of elementary school, in the hope that the child will achieve higher examination scores the second time and be able to continue on to secondary school. Bribery of school officials is also attempted.

CONCLUSIONS

The study of education must be an interdisciplinary endeavor. A universal feature of human societies, the systematic transmission of knowledge is affected by the full gamut of human characteristics and experience. The psychobiological underpinnings of the learning process are not fully understood, but they cannot be ignored. Both the universals of cognitive operations and the diversity of their cultural expressions are relevant, as is the interplay among physiological factors like nutrition, culturally valued or expected cognitive orientations, and culturally patterned strategies of transmission and learning. Psychological theories of cognition cannot be tested adequately within a single culture. Cross-cultural testing requires extraordinary care, precisely because individual cognitive process is inseparable from the cultural matrix which lends it form and content.

The study of nonhuman primates provides another vantage point for assessing psychobiological factors. Since learning in these species is apparently more limited than that among humans, it may be easier to isolate the biogenetic variables in the learning process through this type of research. But in this case as well, we must not discount the importance of context for the behavior of research subjects. Nor can we ignore the distortions which may be introduced in analysis by the theoretical premises of researchers. Because we do not have a way of testing our interpretations against those of primate subjects, we may fail to consider important factors influencing the behavior we observe.

Psychobiological foundations of learning are integrally related to learning contexts, with their material, historical, and sociocultural components. These constrain and direct the organization of educative processes in critical ways. One of the main contributions anthropology can make to educational research, I have argued, is to clarify the interrelationship of all these variables. The contexts of learning and knowledge transmission must be taken actively into account if we are to understand how education takes place and how it affects cognitive process.

Central to contextual analysis is the coordinate transmission of knowledge through both deliberate, explicit instruction and implicit, often unintended communication. For this reason I have given special attention to the role of communication in educational process. Effective communication itself depends on the establishment of shared codes or interpretive repertoires. In essence these repertoires are cultural, although they can be developed between persons of different cultural backgrounds. Because anthropology has focused far more than other disciplines on the analysis of cultural systems and of the impact of culture on behavior, it has an important contribution to make in this area of inquiry as well.

With an increased emphasis on the interplay of psychobiological, material, and sociocultural factors in the contexts and processes of learning, we need anthropology's comparative orientation. Though the study of human biological and sociocultural heritage around the world, anthropology serves to ground speculations about human universals in the reality of human diversity. Education is such a universal, but the organization of knowledge transmission into structured systems and the strategies used to effect it are various. In the preceding chapters, I have discussed a number of factors which contribute to this diversity. Our understanding of education in any particular society or community is enhanced by the recognition of these factors. The organization and strategies favored by a group represent both constraining circumstances and choices among alternatives. When we compare them to the range of alternatives developed by humans in other societies, the nature of these choices is clarified and their bases can be more readily discerned.

The relationship of education to social processes of conservation and change is equally both universal and diverse. It is clear that knowledge transmission is essential to the perpetuation of existing sociocultural systems. The ways in which it acts as a conservative force are not so obvious, given the sources of variation inherent in human social experience. Because we adjust continuously to changing conditions, because our interpretations are never quite the same from person to person, sociocultural conservation must be viewed as an active accomplishment rather than as an inevitable consequence of cultural transmission.

The relationship of education to sociocultural change also is problematic. First, the implementation of change through education is not always accomplished readily, as studies of multicultural classrooms have shown, and the changes effected are not always the same as the changes intended. Second, change in other domains of sociocultural life is not always accompanied by simultaneous change in educational institutions. The incongruence which can result may retard the rate of change in those other domains. To unravel the factors influencing intended and unintended sociocultural change, we must examine carefully the interplay of educational processes which occur in the various domains of social life. Intensive study of the instructional, learning, and general interpretive strategies used by participants in educational transactions can help clarify both the degree of congruence among those domains and its consequences for change. Finally, the effect of sociocultural change on the processes of knowledge transmission can be understood only if we include in analysis the encompassing patterns of social structure and cultural knowledge in which educational transactions are enmeshed.

Generalizations about the part played by education in conservation and change must derive from empirical studies of specific societies representing a broad spectrum of conditions and orientations. The role of theory in this endeavor is by no means negligible, for theories guide inquiry by focusing investigation, posing questions and hypotheses that can be studied cross-culturally, and providing clues to subtle interrelationships among variables. By such guidance, however, a theoretical framework can also narrow our vision. Thus adequate answers to global questions (such as the relationship of education to conservation and change) depend on the application of various theoretical perspectives, tempered by respect for the empirical data from which meaningful generalizations are derived.

The significance of well-wrought studies of education is difficult to overestimate. Because knowledge transmission, both systematic and informal, is universal in human societies and a pervasive feature of social life, its investigation is necessary for our understanding of sociocultural process as a whole. For particular types of change, education has been recognized as a crucial factor. Many impoverished Third World countries, for example, have found education to be a key variable in their strategies for economic development. Although education alone is far from sufficient to produce these economic transformations, its neglect imperils the best planned schemes. In part, education is requisite to the development of specific skills needed for the economic transformation itself. Equally critical are the mobilization of the populace in support of these national goals and the widespread acquisition of strategies which will facilitate their implementation. It is also clear that these same nations can ill afford to risk scarce capital on inappropriate or ineffective educational programs. For these societies, educational analysis of the sort advocated here is an urgent need.

The systems and strategies developed in the West are not always the best models for other societies to follow. While many non-Western societies have inherited Western-style educational systems from their sojourns under colonial domination, major modifications can and must be made to adapt these systems to local sociocultural needs and goals. Countries like Tanzania which actively seek alternatives may draw from other models better suited to their own circumstances, such as those of China or Cuba. But in these cases, far less information is available concerning the actual workings of the educational systems created, and in any event appropriate adaptations must be made.

The role of education in sociocultural change also has become a concern of the "post-industrial" nations. Here, too, the legacy of educational systems suited to a previous era and to earlier goals requires the adaptation of resources and strategies to meet changing conditions. Although it has been less difficult to subsidize schooling, other educative agencies, and experimental alternatives in these more prosperous nations, we still lack answers to major problems of educational change. What are the appropriate goals for schools and how may they best be achieved? What is the relationship among schools and other agencies of knowledge transmission? What role do these agencies play in adapting participants to changed and changing conditions and what roles could they play? Obviously the more heterogeneous a society, the less consensus we can expect with respect to goals and strategies. Yet the alternative to systematic consideration of these problems and quest for viable solutions is likely to be increasing incongruence between schools and other agencies and increasing waste of human and material resources.

To resolve such problems we must go beyond philosophical speculation and parochial studies. Education is a pan-human concern. It has garnered a myriad of responses, each reflecting and affecting its sociocultural context. By analyzing the constituent strategies of each such response, we can see more clearly the range of potential alternatives available. We have been hampered in this pursuit by a variety of conceptual/cultural obstacles.

Among these has been, first, the tendency to equate education with academic schooling or to view the education which occurs in academic contexts as central to inquiry. It is largely this emphasis on schooling per se which underlies the qualitative distinction commonly assumed between education in "primitive" and "civilized"/state-organized societies. Where institutions similar to Western schools appear to be absent, education is often consigned analytically to the category of informal socialization-enculturation. By then comparing these "informal" processes with schooling, the special characteristics of schooling loom as far more significant and distinctive than they actually are. From such a perspective, important differences between schools in various societies, differences at least as significant as those between academic and nonacademic educational processes, tend to be underestimated. The institutionalization of education through schooling establishes important contextual features of the educational processes occurring within school environments. It also affects the distribution of knowledge and the structural relationships among educative agencies. But educational processes which occur in schools are not necessarily different from those which occur in other settings. If we wish to assess the influence of social structure or societal "types" on education, we must compare the organization and constituent processes of educational systems, taking into account the full range of educative agencies and transmission contexts in each society.

Another obstacle has been the tendency to focus on the structure and function of educational systems. Many such analyses of education have emphasized its conservative aspects and its function as a mechanism for allocating roles and status to participants. While this is worthy of study, too often it is viewed simplistically as a system through which people pass rather than as a complex network of negotiated settings and transactions. Implicit in the former perspective is the dual assumption that structure and process are empirically distinct, and that sociocultural systems exist independent of the people who live within them. On the contrary, structure and process are analytic aspects of a single empirical phenomenon, products of the way we choose to view the behavior we observe. Sociocultural systems exist only within the acts (interpersonal and cognitive) of people who thereby create, maintain, and modify them. As members of a society, we are likely to experience sociocultural reality as existing apart from us as individual actors. This is partly because our material and social environment, which reflects decisions made by our predecessors, is an obstacle as well as a resource for our own action. Largely it is because sociocultural systems represent cumulative consequences of participants' decisions, interpretations, and actions.

I do not mean to imply here a radical distinction between individual and society nor unlimited freedom for individual action. While individual variation is a part of the human condition, so is sociocultural sharing. Most cultures do not conceive of humans as radically independent units but rather, recognize the fluid boundaries between members of a social group or community. This is an important insight, for it underscores the degree to which we are influenced by the social contexts of our experience. The concept of identity can be clarified in this light, for it is not so much a way of defining individual uniqueness as it is a way of defining one's relationship to those with whom one interacts and coexists. To focus on the individual rather than on the group, on process rather than on structure is an analytic decision based on an analytic distinction. For certain purposes such dichotomies are useful, but we must not accord them unquestioned empirical status.

We also must be wary of granting epistemological purity to the concept of "fact," for facts, as I have emphasized, always reflect cultural categories for ordering experience. The "facts" with which a scientist works similarly reflect the cultural frame of "scientific knowledge." Theoretical frameworks prescribe how we sort our experience into conceptual categories, how we allocate the status of "fact" to bits of that experience, and how we link those facts to one another in networks of causal relationship. Facts do not exist independent of the cultural or scientific theories which define them and verify their "factual" status.

The importance of this for the study of education is twofold. First, it emphasizes the importance of applying diverse analytic perspectives in research on knowledge transmission. Second, it points up the impact of participants' knowledge repertoires on educational transactions. For those engaged in transmission, especially in multicultural contexts, the content of other participants' knowledge repertoires cannot always be assumed. It is for this reason that I have accorded communication, interpretation, and strategies of learning and instruction so much importance in my discussion.

The scope of inquiry I have recommended requires intensive research into a variety of topics as yet relatively neglected. It can be best accomplished by using a range of analytic approaches, carefully examining the sociocultural premises which condition our conclusions, and by integrating the research efforts of all the disciplines concerned with human learning.

BIBLIOGRAPHY

ADAIR, JOHN 1973 *The Human Subject: the Social Psychology of the Psychological Experiment.* Boston: Little, Brown and Co., Inc.

ADAMS, RAYMOND S. and BRUCE J. BIDDLE 1970 *Realities of Teaching: Explorations with Videotape.* New York: Holt, Rinehart and Winston, Inc.

AOKI, T. 1973 "Toward devolution in the control of education on a native reserve in Alberta: the Hobbema curriculum story." *Council on Anthropology and Education Newsletter* 4(3):1–6.

APPLE, MICHAEL W. 1975 "Ivan Illich and deschooling society: the politics of slogan systems." In N. Shimahara and A. Scrupski, eds., 1975, pp. 337–360.

ARDENER, EDWIN 1972 "Belief and the problem of women." In S. Ardener, ed., 1975, pp. 1–17.

ARDENER, SHIRLEY, ed., 1975 *Perceiving Women.* New York: John Wiley and Sons, Inc.

ARMOR, DAVID J. 1969 *The American School Counselor.* New York: Russell Sage Foundation.

ARNOVE, ROBERT 1975 "Sociopolitical implications of educational television." *Journal of Communication,* vol. 25. Reprinted in R. Arnove, ed., 1976, pp. 1–21.

ARNOVE, ROBERT, ed. 1976 *Educational Television: A Policy Critique and Guide for Developing Countries.* Praeger Special Studies in International Politics and Government. New York: Praeger Publishers, Inc.

ASHBY, SIR ERIC 1966 *Universities: British, Indian, African. A Study in the Ecology of Higher Education.* Cambridge, MA: Harvard University Press.

ÅHMAN, BRITA SKOTTSBERG 1950 "Scandinavian foreign policy, past and present." In H. Friis, ed., *Scandinavia—Between East and West.* Ithaca: Cornell University Press, pp. 255–305.

BACHELOR, DAVID L. 1970 "Chicanos and the schools." In A. Vogel, J. Zepper, and D. Bachelor, eds., *Foundations of Education: A Social View.* Albuquerque: University of New Mexico Press, pp. 47–56.

BANFIELD, EDWARD C. 1970. *The Unheavenly City.* Boston: Little, Brown and Co., Inc.

BARATZ, STEPHEN S. and JOAN C. BARATZ 1970 "Early childhood intervention: the social science base of institutional racism." *Harvard Educational Review* 40(1):29–50.

BARKER, ROGER G. and LOUISE S. BARKER 1961 "Behavior units for the comparative study of culture." In B. Kaplan, ed., *Studying Personality Cross-Culturally.* Evanston, Ill.: Row, Peterson, pp. 456–476.

BARKER, ROGER G. and PAUL V. GUMP 1964 *Big School, Small School: High School Size and Student Behavior.* Stanford: Stanford University Press.

BARKER, ROGER G. and H. F. WRIGHT 1955 *Midwest and Its Children.* Evanston, Ill.: Row, Peterson.

BATESON, GREGORY 1942 "Social planning and the concept of deutero-learning." In G. Bateson, 1972, *Steps to an Ecology of Mind.* New York: Ballantine Books, Inc., pp. 159–176.

BATESON, GREGORY 1955 "A theory of play and fantasy; a report on theoretical aspects of the project for study of the role of paradoxes of abstraction in communication." *Psychiatric Research Reports* 2:39–51.

BATESON, GREGORY 1956 "The message 'this is play'." In B. Schaffner, ed., 1956, *Group Processes: Transactions of the Second Conference.* New York: Josiah Macy, Jr. Foundation.

BATESON, GREGORY and MARGARET MEAD 1942 *Balinese Character: A Photographic Analysis.* Special Publications of the New York Academy of Sciences, vol. 2. New York: New York Academy of Sciences.

BECKER, HOWARD 1961 "The teacher in the authority system of the public school." In A. Etzioni, ed., *Complex Organizations: A Sociological Reader.* New York: Holt, Rinehart and Winston, Inc. pp. 243–255.

BECKER, HOWARD, BLANCHE GEER, ANSELM STRAUSS, and EVERETT HUGHES 1961 *Boys in White: Student Culture in Medical School.* Chicago: The University of Chicago Press.

BENNETT, JOHN 1969 *Northern Plainsmen: Adaptive Strategy and Agrarian Life.* Chicago: Aldine Publishing Co.

BENNETT, JOHN 1976 "Anticipation, adaptation, and the concept of culture in anthropology." *Science* 192(4242):847–853.

BERG, IVAR 1970 *Education and Jobs: The Great Training Robbery.* New York: Frederick A. Praeger Publishers, Inc.

BERNSTEIN, BASIL 1958 "Some sociological determinants of perception. An inquiry into sub-cultural differences." *British Journal of Sociology* 9:159–174.

BERNSTEIN, B. 1959 "A public language: Some sociological implications of a linguistic form." *British Journal of Sociology* 10:311–326.

BERNSTEIN, B. 1960 "Language and social class." *British Journal of Sociology* 11:271–276.

BERNSTEIN, B. 1962a "Linguistic codes, hesitation phenomena and intelligence." *Language and Speech* 5:31–46.

BERNSTEIN, B. 1962b "Social class, linguistic codes and grammatical elements." *Language and Speech* 5:221–240.

BERNSTEIN, BASIL B. 1972 "A critique of the concept of compensatory education." In C. Cazden et al., eds., 1972, pp. 135–151.

BERRY, JOHN W. 1966 "Temne and Eskimo perceptual skills." *International Journal of Psychology* 1:207–229.

BERRY, JOHN W. 1971a "Ecological and cultural factors in spatial perceptual development." *Canadian Journal of Behavioral Science* 3:324–336.

BERRY, JOHN W. 1971b "Müller-Lyer susceptibility. Culture, ecology, or race?" *International Journal of Psychology* 6:193–197.

BIENEFELD, M. A. 1972 "Planning people." In J. F. Rweyemamu et al., eds., *Towards Socialist Planning.* Dar es Salaam: Tanzania Publishing House.

BIENEN, HENRY 1970 *Tanzania: Party Transformation and Economic Development,* revised edition. Princeton: Princeton University Press.

BIRDWHISTELL, RAY 1970 *Kinesics and Context.* Philadelphia: University of Pennsylvania Press.

BIRDWHISTELL, RAY 1971 "Kinesics: inter- and intra-channel communication." In J. Krisleva et al., eds., *Essays in Semiotics.* The Hague: Mouton, pp. 527–546.

BLUMER, HERBERT 1930 "Science without concepts." In H. Blumer, 1969, pp. 153–170.

BLUMER, HERBERT 1954 "What is wrong with social theory?" In H. Blumer, 1969, pp. 140–152.

BLUMER, HERBERT 1956 "Sociological analysis and the 'variable'." In H. Blumer, 1969, pp. 127–139.

BLUMER, HERBERT 1969 *Symbolic Interactionism: Perspective and Method.* Englewood Cliffs, N.J.: Prentice-Hall, Inc.

BOGGS, STEPHAN 1972 "The meaning of questions and narratives to Hawaiian children." In Cazden et al., eds., 1972, pp. 299–330.

BOLTON, R., C. MICHELSON, J. WILDE, and C. BOLTON 1975 "The heights of illusion: on the relationship between altitude and perception." *Ethos* 3:403–424.

BOORSCH, JEAN 1958–59 "Primary education." *Yale French Studies,* 22:17–38.

BORNSTEIN, M. H. 1973 "The psychophysiological component of cultural difference in color naming and illusion susceptibility." *Behavioral Science Notes* 8:41–101.

BOWLES, SAMUEL and HERBERT GINTIS 1976 *Schooling in Capitalist America.* New York: Basic Books, Inc.

BRADFIELD, LUTHER and LEONARD KRAFT, eds. 1970 *The Elementary School Principal in Action.* Scranton, PA: International Textbook Company.

BRENNAN, PAMELA and ANNA DONOGHUE 1974 "Biculturalism through experiential language learning." *Council on Anthropology and Education Newsletter* 5(3):15–19.

BREUNIG, ROBERT G. 1975 "Schools and the Hopi self." In J. Bennett, ed., 1975, *The New Ethnicity: Perspectives from Ethnology* (1973 Proceedings of the American Ethnological Society). St. Paul, New York, Boston, Los Angeles, San Francisco: West Publishing Company.

BRONFENBRENNER, URIE 1976 "The experimental ecology of education." *Educational Researcher* 5:5–15.

BROPHY, JERE E. and THOMAS L. Good 1970 "Teachers' communication of differential expectations for the children's classroom performance: some behavioral data." *Journal of Educational Psychology* 61(5):365–374.

BRUFORD, W. H. 1935 *Germany in the Eighteenth Century.* Cambridge: Cambridge University Press.

BRUNER, JEROME, ALISON JOLLY, and KATHY SYLVA, eds. 1976 *Play—Its Role in Development and Evolution.* New York: Basic Books, Inc.

BRUNER, JEROME, ROSE R. OLIVER, PATRICIA M. GREENFIELD, and others. 1966 *Studies of Cognitive Growth.* New York: John Wiley and Sons, Inc.

BRUYN, SEVERN 1966 *The Human Perspective in Sociology: The Methodology of Participant Observation.* Englewood Cliffs, N.J.: Prentice-Hall, Inc.

BURNETT, JACQUETTA 1969 "Ceremony, rites, and economy in the student system of an American high school." *Human Organization* 28:1–10.

BURNETT, JACQUETTA 1974 *Anthropology and Education: an Annotated Bibliographic Guide.* New Haven: Human Relations Area Files.

BYERS, PAUL and HAPPIE BYERS 1972 "Nonverbal communication and the education of children." In C. Cazden, et al., eds., 1972, pp. 3–31.

CAHN, EDGAR S. and DAVID W. HEARNE, eds. 1969 *Our Brother's Keeper: The Indian in White America.* Washington, D.C.: New Community Press.

CAMERON, J. and W. A. DODD 1970 *Society, Schools and Progress in Tanzania.* Oxford: Pergamon Press, Inc.

CAMPBELL, DONALD and JULIAN STANLEY 1963 *Experimental and Quasi-Experimental Designs for Research.* Chicago: Rand McNally College Publishing Company.

CARNOY, MARTIN 1974 *Education as Cultural Imperialism.* New York: David McKay Company, Inc.

CARNOY, MARTIN, ed. 1975 *Schooling in a Corporate Society: The Political Economy of Education in America.* New York: David McKay Company, Inc.

CARROLL, JOHN 1974 "The potentials and limits of print as a medium of instruction." In D. Olson, ed., 1974, pp. 151–179.

CASTANEDA, CARLOS 1968 *The Teachings of Don Juan: A Yaqui Way of Knowledge.* New York: Ballantine Books, Inc.

CASTANEDA, CARLOS 1971 *A Separate Reality: Further Conversations with Don Juan.* New York: Simon and Schuster, Inc.

CASTRO, JANET 1971 "Untapped verbal fluency of Black schoolchildren." In E. Leacock, ed., 1971, pp. 81–108.

CAZDEN, COURTNEY B. 1966 "Subcultural differences in child language: an interdisciplinary review." *Merrill-Palmer Quarterly of Behavior and Development,* 12:3. Reprinted in Ianni and Storey, eds., 1973, pp. 49–83.

CAZDEN, COURTNEY 1970a "The neglected situation in child language research and education." In F. Williams, ed., 1970, pp. 81–101.

CAZDEN, COURTNEY 1970b "The situation: a neglected source of social class differences in language use." *Journal of Social Issues* 26(2):35–60.

CAZDEN, COURTNEY and VERA JOHN 1971 "Learning in American Indian children." In M. Wax et al., eds., 1971, pp. 252–272.

CAZDEN, COURTNEY, VERA P. JOHN, and DELL HYMES, eds. 1972 *Functions of Language in the Classroom.* New York: Teachers College Press.

CICOUREL, AARON 1964 *Method and Measurement in Sociology.* New York: The Free Press of Glencoe.

CICOUREL, AARON 1968 *The Social Organization of Juvenile Justice.* New York: John Wiley and Sons, Inc.

CICOUREL, AARON 1974 *Cognitive Sociology. Language and Meaning in Social Interaction.* New York: The Free Press.

CICOUREL, AARON 1974 "Some basic theoretical issues in the assessment of the child's performance in testing and classroom settings." In A. Cicourel et al., eds., *Language Use and School Performance.* New York: Academic Press, Inc.

CICOUREL, AARON and JOHN I. KITSUSE 1963 *The Educational Decision-Makers.* Indianapolis: The Bobbs-Merrill Co.

CLIGNET, REMI 1970 "Inadequacies of the notion of assimilation in African education." *Journal of Modern African Studies* 8:425–444.

COHEN, ROSALIE 1968 "The relation between socio-conceptual styles and orientation to school requirements." *Sociology of Education* 41:201–220.

COHEN, ROSALIE 1969 "Conceptual styles, culture conflict, and nonverbal tests of intelligence." *American Anthropologist* 71(5):828–856.

COHEN, ROSALIE 1971 "The influence of conceptual rule-sets on measures of learning ability." In C. L. Brace, G. Gamble, and J. Bond, eds., 1971, *Race and Intelligence.* Anthropological Studies, No. 8, American Anthropological Association, pp. 41–57.

COHEN, ROSALIE, GERD FRANKEL and JOHN BREWER 1968 "The language of the hard-core poor: implications for culture conflict." *Sociological Quarterly* 10:19–28.

COHEN, YEHUDI 1971 "The shaping of men's minds: adaptations to the imperatives of culture." In M. Wax et al., eds., 1971, pp. 19–50.

COLE, MICHAEL 1975 "An ethnographic psychology of cognition." In Johnson-Laird and Wason, eds., 1976, pp. 468–482.

COLE, MICHAEL and JOHN GAY 1972 "Culture and memory." *American Anthropologist* 74:1066–1084.

COLE, MICHAEL, JOHN GAY, JOS. A. GLICK, DONALD W. SHARP 1971 *The Cultural Context of Learning and Thinking. An Exploration in Experimental Anthropology.* New York: Basic Books, Inc.

COLE, MICHAEL and SYLVIA SCRIBNER 1974 *Culture and Thought: A Psychological Introduction.* New York: John Wiley and Sons, Inc.

COLEMAN, PETER TALI 1961 *1960 Annual Report, the Governor of American Samoa to the Secretary of the Interior.* Document No. 5758120-61-7. Washington, D.C.: Department of the Interior.

COLLETTA, NAT 1976 "Cross-cultural transactions in Ponapean elementary classrooms." *Journal of Research and Development in Education* 9(4): 113–123.

COLLIER, JOHN 1967 *Visual Anthropology: Photography as a Research Method.* New York: Holt, Rinehart and Winston, Inc.

COMITAS, LAMBROS 1967 "Education and social stratification in contemporary Bolivia." In F. Ianni and E. Storey, eds., 1971, pp. 402–418.

COOMBS, L. M., R. KRON, E. COLLISTER and K. ANDERSON 1958 *The Indian Child Goes to School.* Bureau of Indian Affairs, U. S. Department of the Interior.

CRAIN, ROBERT 1977 "Racial tension in high schools: pushing the survey method closer to reality." *Anthropology and Education Quarterly* 8:142–151.

CROWDER, MICHAEL, ed. 1971 *West African Resistance.* New York: Africana Publishing Company.

CUSICK, PHILIP 1973 *Inside High School: The Student's World.* New York: Holt, Rinehart and Winston, Inc.

DASEN, P. R. 1972a "The development of conservation in aboriginal children: a replication study." *International Journal of Psychology* 7:75–85.

DASEN, P. R. 1972b "Cross-cultural Piagetan research: a summary." *Journal of Cross-Cultural Psychology* 3:23–40.

DASEN, P. R. 1974 "The influence of ecology, culture, and European contact on cognitive development in Australian aborigines." In J. W. Berry and P. R. Dasen, eds., 1974, *Culture and Cognition: Readings in Cross-cultural Psychology.* London: Methuen and Co., pp. 381–408.

DAWSON, J. L. M. 1967 "Cultural and physiological influences upon spatial and perceptual processes in West Africa." Parts I and II. *International Journal of Psychology* 2:115–128, 171–185.

DAWSON, J. L. M. 1972 "Temne-Arunta hand-eye dominance and cognitive style." *International Journal of Psychology* 7:219–233.

DE BROGLIE, LOUIS 1939 *Matter and Light: The New Physics.* New York: W. W. Norton and Co., Inc.

DEIKMAN, A. 1971 "Bimodal consciousness." *Archives of General Psychiatry* 25:481–489

DENZIN, NORMAN 1970 *The Research Act: A Theoretical Introduction to Sociological Methods.* Chicago: Aldine Publishing Co.

DEVOS, GEORGE 1975a "Apprenticeship and paternalism." In E. Vogel, ed, 1975, pp. 210–227.

DE VOS, GEORGE 1975b "Ethnic pluralism conflict and accommodation." In G. De Vos and L. Romanucci-Ross, eds., 1975 *Ethnic Identity, Cultural Continuities and Change.* Palo Alto: Mayfield Publishing Company.

DI BONA, JOSEPH 1970 "Role stability and change in an Indian university."
In J. Fischer, ed., 1970 *The Social Sciences and the Comparative Study
of Educational Systems.* Scranton, Pa.: International Textbook Co.

DICKEMAN, MILDRED 1971 "The integrity of the Cherokee student." In E.
B. Leacock, ed., 1971, pp. 140–179.

DOBBERT, MARION 1975 "Another route to a general theory of cultural
transmission." *Council on Anthropology and Education Newsletter* 4(2):
22-26.

DORE, RONALD P. 1958 *City Life in Japan. A Study of a Tokyo Ward.*
Berkeley: University of California Press.

DORE, RONALD P. 1965 *Education in Tokugawa Japan.* Berkeley: University
of California Press.

DORE, RONALD P. 1967 "Mobility, equality and individuation in modern
Japan." In R. Dore, ed., 1971, *Aspects of Social Change in Modern Japan.*
Princeton: Princeton University Press.

DRAPER, PATRICIA 1975 "Sex differences in cognitive styles: socialization and
constitutional variables." *Council on Anthropology and Education Quarterly* 6(3):3–6.

DREEBEN, ROBERT 1968 *On What is Learned in School.* Reading, MA: Addison-Wesley Publishing Co.

DRUCKER, ERNEST 1971 "Cognitive styles and class stereotypes." In E. Leacock, ed., 1971, pp. 41–62.

DUMONT, ROBT. V., JR. 1972 "Learning English and how to be silent: studies
in Sioux and Cherokee classrooms." In C. Cazden, et al., eds., 1972, pp.
344–369.

DUMONT, ROBT. V., JR. and MURRAY L. WAX 1969 "Cherokee school society
and the intercultural classroom." *Human Organization* 28(3):217–226.

DUSEK, JEROME B. 1975 "Do teachers bias children's learning?" *Review of
Educational Research* 45(4):661–684.

DUSEK, JEROME B. and E. J. O'CONNELL 1973 "Teacher expectancy effects
on the achievement test performance of elementary school children."
Journal of Educational Psychology 65:371–377.

DWYER-SCHICK, SUSAN 1976 *The Study and Teaching of Anthropology: An
Annotated Bibliography.* Anthropological Curriculum Project, Publication No. 76-1. Athens, GA: University of Georgia.

DYK, RUTH B. and HERMAN A. WITKIN 1965 "Family experiences related
to the development of differentiation in children." *Child Development*
36(1):21–55.

EARLY, JOHN 1973 "Education via radio among Guatemalan highland
Maya." *Human Organization* 32:221–230.

EDDY, ELIZABETH 1969 *Becoming a Teacher: The Passage to Professional Status.* New York: Teachers College Press.

EGGAN, DOROTHY 1956 "Instruction and affect in Hopi cultural continuity." *Southwestern Journal of Anthropology,* 12:347–365.

EKMAN, PAUL 1972 "Universals and cultural differences in facial expressions of emotion." In J. Cole, ed., 1972 *Nebraska Symposium on Motivation.* Lincoln, NE: University of Nebraska Press.

EKMAN, PAUL 1973 "Cross-cultural studies of facial expression." In P. Ekman, ed., 1973 *Darwin and Facial Expression: A Century of Research in Review.* New York: Academic Press.

EMBER, CAROL 1977 "Cross-cultural cognitive studies." *Annual Review of Anthropology* 6:33–56.

ENGLE, PATRICIA 1976 "The language debate: education in first or second language?" In P. Sanday, ed., 1976 *Anthropology and the Public Interest: Fieldwork and Theory.* New York: Academic Press, Inc., pp. 247–272.

ERICKSON, FREDERICK 1973 "What makes school ethnography 'ethnographic'?" *Council on Anthropology and Education Newsletter* 4(2):10–19.

EVERHART, ROBERT 1977 "Between stranger and friend: some consequences of 'long term' fieldwork in schools." *American Educational Research Journal* 14:1–15.

FABREGA, HORACIO, JR. 1977 "Culture, behavior, and the nervous system." *Annual Review of Anthropology* 6:419–56.

FILSTEAD, WM. J. (ed.) 1970 *Qualitative Methodology: Firsthand Involvement with the Social World.* Chicago: Markham Publishing Co.

FISCHER, J. L. 1961 "The Japanese schools for the natives of Truk, Caroline Islands." *Human Organization* 20:83–88.

FOERSTEL, LENORA 1977 "Cultural influences on perception." *Studies in the Anthropology of Visual Communication* 4(1):7–50.

FOLEY, DOUGLAS 1976 "Legalistic and personalistic adaptations to ethnic conflict in a Texas school." *Journal of Research and Development in Education* 9(4):74–82.

FORGE, ANTHONY 1967 "The Abelam artist." In M. Freedman, ed., 1967, *Social Organization: Essays Presented to Raymond Firth.* Chicago: Aldine Publishing Co.

FORGE, ANTHONY 1970 "Learning to see in New Guinea." In P. Mayer, ed., 1970, *Socialization: The Approach from Social Anthropology.* London: Tavistock Publications Ltd. pp. 269-291.

FORTES, MEYER 1938 *Social and Psychological Aspects of Education in Taleland.* Oxford: Oxford University Press.

FOSTER, PHILIP 1965a "The vocational school fallacy in development planning." In C. A. Anderson and M. J. Bowman, eds., 1965 *Education and Economic Development.* Chicago: Aldine Publishing Co.

FOSTER, PHILIP 1965b *Education and Social Change in Ghana.* Chicago: University of Chicago Press.

FOSTER, PHILIP 1969 "Education for self reliance: a critical evaluation." In R. Jolly, ed., *Education in Africa: Research and Action.* Nairobi: East African Publishing House.

FOX, RICHARD 1972 "Rationale and romance in urban anthropology." *Urban Anthropology* 1(2):205–233.

FRIEDENBERG, EDGAR Z. 1963 "The modern highschool: a profile." *Commentary* 36: 373–380. Reprinted in E. Friedenberg, *The Dignity of Youth and Other Atavisms.* Boston: The Beacon Press.

FRIEDMAN, NEIL 1967 *The Social Nature of Psychological Research.* New York: Basic Books.

FUCHS, ESTELLE 1969 *Teachers Talk: Views from Inside City Schools.* Garden City, N.Y.: Anchor Press/Doubleday and Co., Inc.

FUCHS, ESTELLE and ROBT. J. HAVIGHURST 1973 *To Live on this Earth: American Indian Education.* Garden City, N.Y.: Anchor Press/Doubleday and Co., Inc.

GALLAHER, ART, JR. 1965 "Directed change in formal organizations: the school system." In F. Ianni and E. Storey, ed., 1973, pp. 323–338.

GARFINKEL, HAROLD 1964 "Studies of the routine grounds of everyday activities." *Social Problems* 11:225-250.

GARFINKEL, HAROLD 1967 *Studies in Ethnomethodology.* Englewood Cliffs, N.J.: Prentice-Hall.

GAY, JOHN and MICHAEL COLE 1967 *The New Math and an Old Culture.* New York: Holt, Rinehart and Winston, Inc.

GEARING, FRED 1973 "Where we are and where we might go: steps toward a general theory of cultural transmission." *Council on Anthropology and Education Newsletter* 4(1):1–10.

GEARING, FRED 1975 "Overview: a cultural theory of education." *Council on Anthropology and Education Quarterly* 6(2):1–9.

GEARING, F. and B. A. TINDALL 1973 "Anthropological studies of the educational process." *Annual Review of Anthropology* 2:95–105.

GEARING, FREDERICK with A. TINDALL, A. SMITH, and T. CARROLL, 1975 "Structures of censorship, usually inadvertent: studies in a cultural theory of education." *Council on Anthropology and Education Quarterly* 6(2): 1–22.

GEERTZ, CLIFFORD 1973 *The Interpretation of Cultures.* New York: Basic Books, Inc.

GERBNER, GEORGE 1974 "Teacher image in mass culture: symbolic functions of the 'hidden curriculum'." In D. Olson, ed., 1974, pp. 470–498.

GERTH, HANS and C. WRIGHT MILLS 1954 *Character and Social Structure.* London: Routledge and Kegan Paul Ltd.

GIBBS, JAMES L., JR. 1965 "The Kpelle of Liberia." In J. Gibbs, ed., 1965, *Peoples of Africa.* New York: Holt, Rinehart and Winston, Inc.

GIBSON, MARGARET 1976 "Approaches to multicultural education in the United States: some concepts and assumptions." *Anthropology and Education Quarterly* 7(4):7–18.

GIBSON, MARGARET, ed. 1976 "Anthropological perspectives on multi-cultural education." *Anthropology and Education Quarterly* 7(4).

GLADWIN, THOMAS 1970 *East is a Big Bird. Navigation and Logic on Puluwat Atoll.* Cambridge, MA: Harvard University Press.

GLASER, BARNEY and ANSELM STRAUSS 1967 *The Discovery of Grounded Theory.* Chicago: Aldine Publishing Company.

GOETZ, JUDITH PREISSLE 1975 *Configurations in Control and Autonomy: A Microethnography of a Rural Third Grade Classroom.* Anthropology Curriculum Project, University of Georgia, Athens, Georgia.

GOFFMAN, ERVING 1956 "The nature of deference and demeanor." *American Anthropologist* 58:473–502.

GOFFMAN, ERVING 1959 *The Presentation of Self in Everyday Life.* New York: Doubleday and Company, Inc.

GOFFMAN, ERVING 1963 *Stigma: Notes on the Management of a Spoiled Identity.* Englewood Cliffs, N.J.: Prentice-Hall, Inc.

GOLDSEN, ROSE K. 1976 "Literacy without books: the case of 'Sesame Street'." In R. Arnove, ed., 1976, pp. 203–222.

GOODENOUGH, WARD 1963 *Cooperation in Change.* New York: Russell Sage Foundation.

GOODENOUGH, WARD 1965 "Rethinking status and role." In *The Relevance of Models for Social Anthropology.* Monograph No. 1. London: Tavistock Publications Ltd., pp. 1–24.

GOODENOUGH, WARD 1971 *Culture, Language, and Society.* Reading, MA: Addison-Wesley Modular Publications No. 7.

GOODENOUGH, WARD 1975 "Multiculturalism as the normal human experience." *Anthropology and Education Quarterly* 7(4):4–7.

GRAHAM, C. K. 1971 *The History of Education in Ghana, from the Earliest Times to the Declaration of Independence.* London: Frank Cass Ltd.

GREENBERG, JOSEPH 1941 "Some aspects of Negro-Mohammedan culture contact among the Hausa." *American Anthropologist* 43:51–61.

GRINDAL, BRUCE 1974 "Students' self-perceptions among the Sisala of northern Ghana: a study in continuity and change." In G. Spindler, ed., 1974, pp. 361–372.

GROSS, LARRY 1974 "Modes of communication and the acquisition of symbolic competence." In D. Olson, ed., 1974, pp. 56–80.

GUMP, PAUL with L. R. GOOD 1976 "Environments operating in open space and traditionally designed schools." *Journal of Architectural Research* 5:20–27.

GUMPERZ, JOHN and EDUARDO HERNÁNDEZ-CHAVEZ 1972 "Bilingualism, bidialectalism, and classroom interaction." In Cazden et al., eds., 1972, pp. 84–108.

HAGSTROM, WARREN 1968 "Deliberate instruction within family units." In A. Kazamias and E. Epstein, eds., *Schools in Transition: Essays in Comparative Education.* Boston: Allyn & Bacon, Inc.

HALL, BEVERLY 1976 "Colorado's lucky children: the bilingual, bicultural schools." *The Nation,* 223:519–522.

HALL, EDWARD 1959 *The Silent Language.* Garden City, N.Y.: Anchor Press/ Doubleday and Co.

HALL, EDWARD 1966 *The Hidden Dimension.* New York: Doubleday and Co.

HALL, EDWARD 1974 *Handbook for Proxemic Research.* Studies in the Anthropology of Visual Communication. (Special Issue) Washington, D.C.: Society for the Anthropology of Visual Communication.

HALL, EDWARD 1976 *Beyond Culture.* Garden City, N.Y.: Anchor Press/ Doubleday and Co.

HALL, IVAN 1975 "Organizational paralysis: the case of Todai." In E. Vogel, ed., 1975, pp. 304–330.

HANDEL, WARREN 1972 *Perception as a Constructive Process.* Unpublished Ph.D. dissertation, University of California, Santa Barbara.

HANSON, NORWOOD R. 1958 *Patterns of Discovery. An Inquiry into the Conceptual Foundations of Science.* Cambridge: Cambridge University Press.

HARLEY, GEO. W. 1941 *Notes on the Poro in Liberia.* Papers of the Peabody Museum of American Archaeology and Ethnology 19:2. Cambridge, MA: Peabody Museum of American Archaeology and Ethnology.

HARLEY, GEO. W. 1950 *Masks as Agents of Social Control in Northeast Liberia.* Papers of the Peabody Museum of American Archaeology and Ethnology 32:2. Cambridge, MA: Peabody Museum of American Archaeology and Ethnology.

HARLOW, HARRY E. 1949 "The formation of learning sets." *Psychological Review* 56:51–65.

HARRINGTON, CHARLES and JOHN WHITING 1977 "A model for psychocultural research." In P. Leiderman, S. Tulkin and A. Rosenfeld, eds., 1977, *Culture and Infancy. Variations in the Human Experience.* New York: Academic Press, Inc.

HARRISON, BENNETT 1972 "Education and underemployment in the urban ghetto." In M. Carnoy, ed., 1975, pp. 133–160.

HARTLEY, RUTH 1959 "Sex-role pressures and the socialization of the male child." *Psychological Reports* 5:457–468.

HENRY, JULES 1955 "Docility, or giving teacher what she wants." *Journal of Social Issues* 11:33–41.

HENRY, JULES 1957 "Attitude organization in elementary school classrooms." *American Journal of Orthopsychiatry* 27:117–133.

HENRY, JULES 1959 "The problem of spontaneity, initiative, and creativity in suburban classrooms." *American Journal of Orthopsychiatry* 29:266–279.

HENRY, JULES 1960 "A cross-cultural outline of education." *Current Anthropology* 1:267–305.

HENRY, JULES 1963 *Culture Against Man.* New York: Random House, Inc.

HERNDON, JAMES 1968 *The Way it Spozed to Be.* New York: Simon and Schuster, Inc.

HERON, A. 1971 "Concrete operations, 'g' and achievement in Zambian children." *Journal of Cross-Cultural Psychology* 2:325–336.

HERRNSTEIN, RICHARD J. 1973 *I.Q. in the Meritocracy.* Boston: Atlantic Monthly Press.

HERSKOVITS, MELVILLE 1947 *Man and His Works.* New York: Alfred A. Knopf, Inc.

HERSKOVITS, MELVILLE 1964 *Cultural Anthropology.* New York: Alfred A. Knopf, Inc.

HERZOG, JOHN 1974 "The socialization of juveniles in primate and foraging societies: implications for contemporary education." *Council on Anthropology and Education Quarterly* 5(1):12–17.

HIGGINS, PATRICIA 1976 "The conflict of acculturation and enculturation in suburban elementary schools of Tehran." *Journal of Research and Development in Education* 9(4):102–111.

HOBART, CHARLES 1968 "Some consequences of residential schooling." *Journal of American Indian Education* 7:7–17.

HOBART, CHARLES 1970a "Eskimo education in the Canadian Arctic." *Canadian Review of Sociology and Anthropology* 7:49–69.

HOBART, CHARLES 1970b "Some consequences of residential schooling of Eskimos in the Canadian Arctic." *Arctic Anthropologist* 6:123–135.

HOBART, CHARLES and C. S. BRANT 1965 "Eskimo education, Danish and Canadian: a comparison." *Canadian Review of Sociology and Anthropology* 3(2):47–66.

HONIGMANN, JOHN and IRMA HONIGMANN 1965 *Eskimo Townsmen.* Ottawa: Canadian Research Centre for Anthropology, University of Ottawa.

HORNER, VIVIAN and JOAN GUSSOW 1972 "John and Mary: a pilot study in linguistic ecology." In Cazden et al., eds., 1972, pp. 155–194.

HORTON, DONALD 1971 "The interplay of forces in the development of a small school system." In M. Wax et al., eds., 1971, pp. 180–194.

HOWARD, ALAN 1973 "Education in 'Aina Pumehana: The Hawaiian-American student as hero." In S. Kimball and J. Burnett, eds., 1973, pp. 115–130.

HSU, FRANCIS L. K. 1975 *Iemoto: the Heart of Japan.* Cambridge: Schenkman Publishing Company.

HYMES, DELL 1967 "Models of the interaction of languages and social settings." *Journal of Social Issues* 23:8–28.

HYMES, DELL 1972 "Introduction." In Cazden et al., eds., 1972, pp. xi–lvii.

HYMES, DELL 1974 "Ways of speaking." In R. Bayman and J. Sherzer, eds., 1974, *Explorations in the Ethnography of Speaking.* London: Cambridge University Press.

HYMES, DELL 1977 "Qualitative/quantitative research methodologies in education: a linguistic perspective." *Anthropology and Education Quarterly* 8:165–176.

IANNI, FRANCIS and EDWARD STOREY, eds., 1973 *Cultural Relevance and Educational Issues: Readings in Anthropology and Education.* Boston: Little, Brown and Company.

ILLICH, IVAN 1971a *Deschooling Society.* New York: Harper & Row Publishers, Inc.

ILLICH, IVAN 1971b "Education without school: how it can be done." *New York Review of Books* 15:25–31.

ILLICH, IVAN 1971c "The alternative to schooling." *Saturday Review* 54:44–48.

IRWIN, H. M., G. N. SCHAFER, and C. P. FEIDEN 1974 "Emic and unfamiliar category sorting of Mano farmers and U. S. undergraduates." *Journal of Cross-Cultural Psychology* 5:407–423.

ISHIDA, TAKESHI 1971 *Japanese Society.* New York: Random House, Inc.

JACKSON, PHILIP 1968 *Life in Classrooms.* New York: Holt, Rinehart and Winston, Inc.

JAHODA, GUSTAV 1971 "Retinal pigmentation, illusion susceptibility and space perception." *International Journal of Psychology* 6:199–208.

JENCKS, CHRISTOPHER, et al. 1972 *Inequality: A Reassessment of the Effect of Family and Schooling in America.* New York: Basic Books, Inc.

JENSEN, ARTHUR R. 1969 "How much can we boost I.Q. and scholastic achievement?" *Harvard Educational Review* 39(1):1–123.

JOHN, VERA P. 1971 "Language and educability." In E. Leacock, ed., 1971 pp. 63–80.

JOHNSON-LAIRD, P. N. and P. C. WASON, eds. 1977 *Thinking. Readings in Cognitive Science.* Cambridge: Cambridge University Press.

JOLLY, ALISON 1972 *The Evolution of Primate Behavior.* New York: The Macmillan Co.

KAGAN, JEROME, HOWARD MOSS and IRVING SIGEL 1963 "Psychological significance of styles of conceptualization." In J. Wright and J. Kagan, eds., 1963, *Basic Cognitive Processes in Children.* Monographs of the Society for Research in Child Development 28(2):73–112.

KAHNEMAN, D. 1973 *Attention and Effort.* Englewood Cliffs, N.J.: Prentice-Hall, Inc.

KAMIN, LEON J. 1974 "The science and politics of IQ." *Social Research* 41(3):387–415.

KAPLAN, ABRAHAM 1964 *The Conduct of Inquiry: Methodology for Behavioral Science.* Scranton, Pa.: Chandler Publishing Co.

KARMILOFF-SMITH, ANNETTE and BÄRBEL INHELDER 1974/5 "If you want to get ahead, get a theory." *Cognition* 3:195–212. Excerpted in Johnson-Laird and Wason, eds., 1977, pp. 293–306.

KATZ, MICHAEL 1971 *Class, Bureaucracy and Schools.* New York: Praeger Publishers, Inc.

KAWAI, MASAO 1965 "Newly acquired precultural behavior of the natural troop of Japanese monkeys on Koshima islet." *Primates* 6:1–30.

KELLEY, JOHN 1977 "A social anthropology of education: the case of Chiapas." *Anthropology and Education Quarterly* 8:210–220.

KHLEIF, BUD 1971 "The school as a small society." In M. Wax et al., eds., 1971, pp. 144–155.

KIEFER, CHRISTIE W. 1970 "The psychological interdependence of family, school, and bureaucracy in Japan." *American Anthropologist* 72:66–75.

KIEFER, CHRISTIE 1977 "Psychological anthropology." *Annual Review of Anthropology* 6:103–120.

KIMBALL, SOLON T. 1967 "Culture, society and educational congruency." In S. Kimball, 1974, pp. 7–24.

KIMBALL, SOLON 1974 *Culture and the Educative Process: An Anthropological Perspective.* New York: Teachers College Press.

KIMBALL, SOLON and JACQUETTA BURNETT, eds. 1973 *Learning and Culture.* Proceedings of the 1972 Annual Spring Meeting of the American Ethnological Society. Seattle: University of Washington Press.

KLEINFELD, J. S. 1973 "Characteristics of successful boarding home parents of Eskimo and Athabascan Indian students." *Human Organization* 32:191–204.

KING, RICHARD 1967 *The School at Mopass: A Problem of Identity.* New York: Holt, Rinehart and Winston, Inc.

KOFF, DAVID and GEORGE VON DER MUHLL 1967 "Political socialization in Kenya and Tanzania—a comparative analysis." *Journal of Modern African Studies* 5(1):13–51.

KOHL, HERBERT 1967 *Thirty Six Children.* New York: New American Library.

KOHL, HERBERT 1970 *The Open Classroom.* New York: New York Review/Vintage Books, Inc.

KOZOL, JONATHAN 1967 *Death at an Early Age.* Boston: Houghton Mifflin Co.

KUHN, THOMAS 1964 "A function for thought experiments." In P. Johnson-Laird and P. Wason, eds., 1977, pp. 274–292.

KUHN, THOMAS 1970 *The Structure of Scientific Revolutions,* second ed., Chicago: University of Chicago Press.

KUMMER, HANS 1971 *Primate Societies: Group Techniques of Ecological Adaptation.* Chicago: Aldine Publishing Co.

LABOV, ROGER 1969 "The logic of non-standard English." In F. Williams, ed. 1970, pp. 153–189.

LANCEY, DAVID F. 1975 "The social organization of learning: initiation rituals and public schools." *Human Organization* 34(4):371–380.

LARGEY, G. and D. WATSON 1972 "The sociology of odors." *American Journal of Sociology* 77:1021–1034.

LAURING, PALLE 1968 *A History of the Kingdom of Denmark.* Translated from Danish by David Hohnen (Danish edition 1960). Copenhagen: Høst & Son.

LAVE, JEAN 1977 "Cognitive consequences of traditional apprenticeship training in West Africa." *Anthropology and Education Quarterly* 8:177–180.

LAZARUS, R. S., M. TOMITA, E. OPTON, JR., and M. KODAMA 1966 "A cross-cultural study of stress-reaction patterns in Japan." *Journal of Personality and Social Psychology* 4:622–633.

LEACOCK, ELEANOR BURKE 1969 *Teaching and Learning in City Schools: A Comparative Study*. New York: Basic Books, Inc.

LEACOCK, ELEANOR BURKE 1972 "Abstract versus concrete speech: a false dichotomy." In Cazden et al., eds., 1972, pp. 111–134.

LEACOCK, ELEANOR BURKE, ed. 1971 *The Culture of Poverty: A Critique*. New York: Simon and Schuster, Inc.

LEE, DOROTHY 1949 "Being and value in a primitive culture." *Journal of Philosophy* 46:401–415. Reprinted in D. Lee, 1959, *Freedom and Culture*. Englewood Cliffs, N.J.: Prentice-Hall, Inc.

LEE, DOROTHY 1950 "Codifications of reality: lineal and nonlineal." *Psychosomatic Medicine,* May 1950, no. 12. Reprinted in D. Lee, 1959, *Freedom and Culture*. Englewood Cliffs, N.J.: Prentice-Hall, Inc.

LEICHTER, HOPE JENSEN 1971 "The school and parents." In D. W. Allen and E. Seifman, eds., 1971, *The Teacher's Handbook*. Glenview, Ill.: Scott, Foresman.

LEICHTER, HOPE JENSEN 1974 "Some perspectives on the family as educator." *Teachers College Record* 76(2):175–217.

LEIN, LAURA 1975 " 'You were talkin' though, oh yes, you was': Black American migrant children, their speech at home and school." *Council on Anthropology and Education Quarterly* 6(4):1–11.

LEWIS, HYLAN 1967 "The changing Negro family." In J. Roberts, ed., 1967, *School Children in the Urban Slum*. New York: Free Press, pp. 397–405.

LEWIS, OSCAR 1966 "The culture of poverty." *Scientific American* 215(4): 19–25.

LIGHTFOOT, SARA 1973 "Politics and reasoning: through the eyes of teachers and children." *Harvard Educational Review* 29(4):197–244.

LIGHTFOOT, SARA 1977 "Family-school interactions: the cultural image of mothers and teachers." *Signs: Journal of Women in Culture and Society* 3:395–408.

LITTLE, K. L. 1951 *The Mende of Sierra Leone. A West African People in Transition*. London: Routledge & Kegan Paul.

LOIZOS, CAROLINE 1967 "Play behaviour in higher primates: a review." In D. Morris, ed., 1967, *Primate Ethology*. Chicago: Aldine Publishing Company.

LURIA, A. R. 1977 *The Social History of Cognition*. Cambridge: Harvard University Press.

MAHONEY, M. J. 1976 *Scientist as Subject: the Psychological Imperative*. Cambridge, MA: Ballinger Publishing Co.

MASLAND, LYNNE and GRANT MASLAND 1975 "The Samoan ETV project: some cross-cultural implications of educational television," Parts I and II,

...cational Broadcasting, March/April and May/June 1975. Reprinted R. Arnove, ed., 1976, pp. 180–202.

...ALL, GEORGE and J. L. SIMMONS, eds. 1969 Issues in Participant Observation: A Text and Reader. Reading, MA: Addison-Wesley Publishing Co.

MCDERMOTT, R. P. 1974 "Achieving school failure: an anthropological approach to illiteracy and social stratification." In G. Spindler, ed., 1974, pp. 82–118.

MCLOUGHLIN, WILLIAM 1968 "The phantom nongraded school." Phi Delta Kappan 49:248–250.

MCPHERSON, GERTRUDE 1972 Small Town Teacher. Cambridge, MA: Harvard University Press.

MEAD, MARGARET 1939 From the South Seas. Studies of Adolescence and Sex in Primitive Society. New York: William Morrow and Co., Inc.

MEAD, MARGARET 1942 And Keep Your Powder Dry. New York: William Morrow and Co., Inc.

MEAD, MARGARET 1943 "Our educational emphasis in primitive perspective." American Journal of Sociology 48:633–639.

MERTON, ROBERT 1968 "The Matthew effect in science." Science 159(3810): 56–63.

MICHELSON, STEPHAN 1969 "Rational income decisions of Blacks and everybody else." In M. Carnoy, ed., 1975, pp. 113–132.

MILLER, DANIEL 1963 "The study of social relationships: situation, identity and social interaction." In S. Koch, ed., 1963 Psychology: A Study of a Science 5:639–737. New York: McGraw-Hill Book Co.

MILLER, R. J. 1973 "Cross-cultural research in the perception of pictorial materials." Psychological Bulletin 80:135–150.

MISHLER, ELLIOT G. 1972 "Implications of teacher strategies for language and cognition: observations in first-grade classrooms." In Cazden et al., eds., 1972, pp. 267–298.

MITCHELL-KERNAN, CLAUDIA 1972 "On the status of Black English for native speakers: an assessment of attitudes and values." In Cazden et al., eds., 1972, pp. 195–210.

MITROFF, IAN 1974 The Subjective Side of Science: A Philosophical Inquiry into the Psychology of the Apollo Moon Scientists. Amsterdam: Elsevier Scientific Publishing Company.

MOORE, G. ALEXANDER 1973 "The validation of ascribed status: gentry careers in Guatemala." In S. Kimball and J. Burnett, eds., 1972, pp. 97–114.

MORRISON, DAVID R. 1976 Education and Politics in Africa: The Tanzanian Case. London: C. Hurst and Company.

MYNATT, CLIFFORD, MICHAEL DOHERTY, and RYAN TWENEY 1977 "Confirmation bias in a simulated environment: an experimental study of scientific inference." *Quarterly Journal of Experimental Psychology* 29:85–95. Excerpted in P. Johnson-Laird and P. Wason, eds., 1977, pp. 315–325.

MWINGIRA, A. C. 1969 "Education for self-reliance: the problems of implementation." In R. Jolly, ed., *Education in Africa: Research and Action.* Nairobi: East African Publishing House.

NAKANE, CHIE 1970 *Japanese Society.* Berkeley: University of California Press.

NARITA, K. 1975 "The university in Japan." In M. Stephens and G. Roderick, eds., 1975, *Universities for a Changing World. The Role of the University in the Later Twentieth Century.* New York: Halsted Press, pp. 174–185.

NASH, MANNING 1970 "Education in Burma: an anthropological perspective." In J. Fischer, ed., 1970, *The Social Sciences and the Comparative Study of Educational Systems.* Scranton, Pa.: International Textbook, pp. 148–166.

NEEDHAM, JOSEPH 1956 "Mathematics and science in China and the West." *Science and Society* 20:320–343.

NEISSER, ULRIC 1967 *Cognitive Psychology.* New York: Appleton-Century-Crofts, Inc.

NEISSER, ULRIC 1976 *Cognition and Reality: Principles and Implications of Cognitive Psychology.* San Francisco: W. H. Freeman & Company.

NELSON, LINDEN and SPENCER KAGAN 1972 "Competition: the star-spangled scramble." *Psychology Today* 6:53–56, 90–91.

NIHLEN, ANN S. 1975 "Assumptions about female learning styles and some implications for teaching." *Council on Anthropology and Education Quarterly* 6(3):6–8.

NYERERE, JULIUS K. 1967 "Education for self-reliance." Reprinted in I. Resnick, ed., *Tanzania: Revolution by Education.* Arusha: Longmans of Tanzania, pp. 49–70.

NYERERE, JULIUS K. 1974 "From uhuru to ujamaa." *Africa Today* 21(3):3–8.

O'CONNELL, E. J., J. DUSEK, and R. A. WHEELER 1974 "A follow-up study of teacher expectancy effects." *Journal of Educational Psychology* 66:325–328.

OGBU, JOHN 1974 *The Next Generation: an Ethnography of Education in an Urban Neighborhood.* New York: Academic Press, Inc.

OKINJI, O. M. 1971 "The effects of familiarity on classification." *Journal of Cross-Cultural Psychology* 2:39–49.

OLIVER, ROLAND and J. D. FAGE 1966 *A Short History of Africa,* Second edition. London: Penguin Books Ltd.

OLSON, DAVID, ed. 1974 *Media and Symbols: The Forms of Expression, Communication and Education.* Seventy-third Yearbook, part 1, of the National Society for the Study of Education. Chicago: National Society for the Study of Education.

OPIE, PETER and IONA OPIE 1960 *The Lore and Language of School Children.* London: Oxford University Press.

ORNSTEIN, ROBERT 1972 *The Psychology of Consciousness.* San Francisco: W. H. Freeman and Company.

PAREDES, J. ANTHONY and MARCUS J. HEPBURN 1976 "The split brain and the culture-and-cognition paradox." *Current Anthropology* 17:121–127.

PARKER, HARLEY 1974 "The beholder's share and the problem of literacy." In D. Olson, ed., 1974, pp. 81–98.

PARSONS, TALCOTT 1959 "The school class as a social system: some of its functions in American society." In T. Parsons, 1964, *Social Structure and Personality.* New York: Free Press.

PASAMANICK, BENJAMIN 1969 "A tract for the times: some sociobiologic aspects of science, race, and racism." *American Journal of Orthopsychiatry* 39(1):7–15.

PASSIN, HERBERT 1964 *Society and Education in Japan.* New York: Bureau of Publications, Teachers College, Columbia University.

PASSIN, HERBERT 1965 "Japan." In J. Coleman, ed., 1965 *Education and Political Development.* Princeton: Princeton University Press, pp. 272–312.

PERKINSON, HENRY J. 1968 *The Imperfect Panacea: American Faith in Education 1865–1965.* New York: Random House, Inc.

PHILIPS, SUSAN V. 1972 "Participant structures and communicative competence: Warm Springs children in community and classroom." In C. Cazden et al., eds., 1972, pp. 370–394.

PIAGET, JEAN 1952 *Play, Dreams, and Imitation in Childhood.* New York: W. W. Norton and Co., Inc.

POIRIER, FRANK 1973 "Socialization and learning among nonhuman primates." In S. Kimball and J. Burnett, eds., 1973, pp. 3–42.

POLANYI, MICHAEL 1966 *The Tacit Dimension.* Garden City, N.Y.: Doubleday & Company, Inc.

POLLOCK, R. 1970 "Müller-Lyer illusion: effect of age, lightness, contrast, and hue." *Science* 170:93–94.

PRICE-WILLIAMS, D. R. 1962 "Abstract and concrete modes of classification in a primitive society." *British Journal of Educational Psychology* 32:50–61. Reprinted in I. Al-Issa and W. Dennis, eds., 1970, *Cross-Cultural*

Studies of Behavior. New York: Holt, Rinehart and Winston, Inc., pp. 95–110.

PRICE WILLIAMS, D. R., W. GORDON, and M. RAMIREZ, III 1969 "Skill and conservation: a study of pottery-making children." *Developmental Psychology* 1:769.

RAMIREZ, MANUEL (III) and ALFREDO CASTANEDA 1974 *Cultural Democracy, Bicognitive Development, and Education.* New York: Academic Press, Inc.

RASKIN, MARCUS 1971 "The channeling colony." In M. Carnoy, ed., 1975, pp. 25–37.

REILLY, MARY, ed. 1973 *Play as Exploratory Learning: Studies of Curiosity Behavior.* Beverly Hills: Sage Publications.

REITER, RAYNA, ed. 1975 *Toward an Anthropology of Women.* New York: Monthly Review Press.

RENDON, ARMANDO B. 1971 *Chicano Manifesto.* New York: The Macmillan Co.

RESNICK, IDRIAN 1968a "Educational barriers to Tanzania's development." In I. Resnick, ed., 1968, *Tanzania: Revolution by Education.* Arusha: Longmans of Tanzania, pp. 123–134.

RESNICK, IDRIAN 1968b "Introduction." In I. Resnick, ed., 1968 *Tanzania: Revolution by Education,* pp. 3–12. Arusha: Longmans of Tanzania.

REYNOLDS, V. 1968 "Kinship and the family in monkeys, apes, and man." *Man* n.s. 3:209–223.

RIST, RAY 1970 "Student social class and teacher expectation: the self-fulfilling prophecy in ghetto education." *Harvard Educational Review* 40:411–451.

RIST, RAY 1977 "On the relations among educational research paradigms: from disdain to detente." *Anthropology and Education Quarterly* 8:42–49.

ROBBINS, RICHARD 1973 "Identity, culture, and behavior." In J. Honigmann, ed., 1973, *Handbook of Social and Cultural Anthropology.* Chicago: Rand McNally College Publishing Company.

ROBINSON, RONALD, JOHN GALLAGHER, and ALICE DENNY 1961 *Africa and the Victorians.* New York: St. Martin's Press.

ROHLEN, THOMAS 1971 "*Seishin Kyōiku* in a Japanese Bank: a description of methods and consideration of some underlying concepts." In G. Spindler, ed., 1974, pp. 219–229.

ROHLEN, THOMAS 1977 "Is Japanese education becoming less egalitarian? Notes on high school stratification and reform." *Journal of Japanese Studies* 3:37–70.

ROHNER, RONALD P. 1965 "Factors influencing the academic performance of Kwakiutl children in Canada." *Comparative Education Review* 9:331–340.

ROSEN, DAVID 1977 "Multicultural education: an anthropological perspective." *Anthropology and Education Quarterly* 8:221–226.

ROSENTHAL, ROBERT and LENORE F. JACOBSON 1968a *Pygmalion in the Classroom: Self-Fulfilling Prophecies and Teacher Expectations.* New York: Holt, Rinehart and Winston, Inc.

ROSENTHAL, ROBERT and LENORE F. JACOBSON 1968b "Teacher expectations for the disadvantaged." *Scientific American* 218(4):19–23.

ROSIN, R. THOMAS 1973 "Gold medallions: the arithmetic calculations of an illiterate." *Council on Anthropology and Education Newsletter* 4(2):1–9.

SABEY, RALPH 1973 "The preparation of culturally sensitive curriculum material for Canadian schools: an overview." *Council on Anthropology and Education Newsletter* 4(3):7–10.

SACHS, NAHOMA 1975 Personal communication.

SAMOFF, JOEL 1974 *Tanzania: Local Politics and the Structure of Power.* Madison: University of Wisconsin Press.

SARASON, SEYMOUR B. 1971 *The Culture of the School and the Problem of Change.* Boston: Allyn and Bacon, Inc.

SCHATZMAN, L. and A. STRAUSS 1973 *Field Research: Strategies for a Natural Sociology.* Englewood Cliffs, N.J.: Prentice-Hall, Inc.

SCHEFLEN, ALBERT 1972 *Body Language and Social Order: Communication as Behavioral Control.* Englewood Cliffs, N.J.: Prentice-Hall, Inc.

SCHUTZ, ALFRED 1944 "The stranger: an essay in social psychology." *American Journal of Sociology* 49:499–507. Also in A. Schutz, 1964, pp. 91–105.

SCHUTZ, ALFRED 1953 "Common sense and scientific interpretation of human action." In A. Schutz, 1962, pp. 3–47.

SCHUTZ, ALFRED 1962 *Collected Papers I: The Problem of Social Reality.* The Hague: Martinus Nijhoff.

SCHUTZ, ALFRED 1964 *Collected Papers II: Studies in Social Theory.* The Hague: Martinus Nijhoff.

SCHUTZ, ALFRED 1970 *On Phenomenology and Social Relations.* Chicago: University of Chicago Press.

SCHWARTZ, GARY and DON MERTEN 1968 "Social identity and expressive symbols: the meaning of an initiation ritual." *American Anthropologist* 70:1117–1131.

SCRIBNER, SYLVIA 1975 "Recall of classical syllogisms: a cross-cultural investigation of error on logical problems." In R. Falmagne, ed., 1975 *Reasoning: Representation and Process.* Hillsdale, N.J.: Erlbaum.

SCRIBNER, SYLVIA 1977 "Modes of thinking and ways of speaking: culture and logic reconsidered." In P. Johnson-Laird and P. Wilson, eds., 1977, pp. 483–500.

SCRIBNER, SYLVIA and MICHAEL COLE 1973 "Cognitive consequences of formal and informal education." *Science* 182(4112):553–559.

SCRUPSKI, ADAM 1975 "The social system of the school." In N. Shimahara and A. Scrupski, eds., 1975, pp. 141–186.

SELIGMAN, C., R. TUCKER, and W. LAMBERT 1972 "The effects of speech styles and other attributes on teachers' attitudes towards pupils." *Language and Society* 1:131–142.

SEXTON, PATRICIA 1969 *The Feminized Male: Classrooms, White Collars and the Decline of Manliness.* New York: Vintage Books, Inc.

SHEA, BRENT 1977 "Schooling and its antecedents: substantive and methodological issues in the status attainment process." *Review of Educational Research* 46:463–526.

SHEPARD, PAUL 1969 "Introduction: Ecology and man—a viewpoint." In P. Shepard and D. McKinley, eds., 1969 *The Subversive Science: Essays toward an Ecology of Man.* Boston: Houghton Mifflin Co.

SHIMAHARA, NOBUO and ADAM SCRUPSKI, eds. 1975 *Social Forces and Schooling: An Anthropological and Sociological Perspective.* New York: David McKay and Co.

SHIPMAN, M. D. 1968 *Sociology of the School.* London: Longman Ltd.

SHUY, ROGER 1970 "The sociolinguist and urban language problems." In F. Williams, ed., 1970, pp. 335–350.

SIEGEL, BERNARD 1974 "Conceptual approaches to models for the analysis of the educative process in American communities." In G. Spindler, ed., 1974, pp. 39–61.

SINDELL, PETER 1974 "Some discontinuities in the enculturation of Mistassini Cree children." In G. Spindler, ed., 1974, pp. 333–341.

SINGLETON, JOHN 1967 *Nichū. A Japanese School.* New York: Holt, Rinehart and Winston, Inc.

SMITH, ALLAN 1975 "Causal ascriptions in the classroom: the varieties and uses of causal explanations for behaviors within the classroom." *Council on Anthropology and Education Quarterly* 6(2):13–16.

SMITH, LOUIS and WILLIAM GEOFFREY 1968 *Complexities of an Urban Classroom: An Analysis Toward a General Theory of Teaching.* New York: Holt, Rinehart and Winston, Inc.

SMITH, LOUIS and PAT KEITH 1967 *Social Psychological Aspects of School Building Design.* Final Report, Project No. 3–223, Bureau of Research, U.S. Office of Education.

SMITH, LOUIS and PAT KEITH 1971 *Anatomy of Educational Innovation: an Organizational Analysis of an Elementary School.* New York: John Wiley & Sons, Inc.

SOMMER, ROBERT 1969 *Personal Space: The Behavioral Basis of Design.* Englewood Cliffs, N.J.: Prentice-Hall, Inc.

SPINDLER, GEORGE 1963a "Personality, sociocultural system, and education among the Menomini." In G. Spindler, ed., 1963, *Education and Culture: Anthropological Approaches.* New York: Holt, Rinehart and Winston, Inc., pp. 351–399.

SPINDLER, GEORGE 1963b "The role of the school administrator." In G. Spindler, ed., 1963 *Education and Culture: Anthropological Approaches.* New York: Holt, Rinehart and Winston, Inc., pp. 234–258.

SPINDLER, GEORGE 1963c "The transmission of American culture." In G. Spindler, ed., 1963 *Education and Culture: Anthropological Approaches.* New York: Holt, Rinehart and Winston, Inc., pp. 148–172.

SPINDLER, GEORGE, ed. 1974 *Education and Cultural Process: Toward an Anthropology of Education.* New York: Holt, Rinehart and Winston, Inc.

SPINDLER, GEORGE and LOUISE SPINDLER 1971 *Dreamers without Power: The Menomini Indians.* New York: Holt, Rinehart, and Winston, Inc.

SPIRO, MELFORD E. 1966 "Buddhism and economic action in Burma." *American Anthropologist* 68:1163–1173.

SPRADLEY, JAMES P. 1972a "Adaptive strategies of urban nomads: the ethnoscience of tramp culture." In T. Weaver and D. White, eds., 1972 *The Anthropology of Urban Environments.* Society for Applied Anthropology Monograph No. 11.

SPRADLEY, JAMES 1972b "Foundations of cultural knowledge." In J. Spradley, ed., 1972, *Culture and Cognition: Rules, Maps, and Plans.* San Francisco: Chandler Publishing Co.

SPRADLEY, JAMES and DAVID MCCURDY, eds. 1972 *The Cultural Experience in Ethnography in Complex Society.* Chicago: Science Research Associates, Inc.

STRAUSS, ANSELM et al. 1964 *Psychiatric Ideologies and Institutions.* New York: The Free Press.

STUDSTILL, JOHN 1976a Student Attrition in Zaire: The System and the Game in the Secondary Schools of Masomo. Unpublished Ph.D. Dissertation, Indiana University, Bloomington.

STUDSTILL, JOHN 1976b "Why students fail in Masomo, Zaire." *Journal of Research and Development in Education* 9:124–136.

SUNLEY, ROBERT 1955 "Early nineteenth-century American literature on child rearing." In M. Mead and M. Wolfenstein, eds., 1955 *Childhood in*

Contemporary Cultures. Chicago: University of Chicago Press, pp. 150–167.

SVENDSEN, KNUD ERIC 1966 "Tanzania." In E. Jørgensen and J. Vedel-Petersen, eds., 1966, *Vi og Udviklingslandene.* Denmark: Fremad.

SZOMBATI-FABIAN, ILONA and J. FABIAN 1976 "Art, history, and society: popular painting in Shaba, Zaire." *Studies in the Anthropology of Visual Communication* 3(1):1–21.

TALBERT, CAROL 1970a "Interaction and adaptation in two Negro kindergartens." *Human Organization* 29:103–114.

TALBERT, CAROL 1970b "Studying education in the ghetto." In T. Weaver, ed., 1970, *To See Ourselves: Anthropology and Modern Social Issues.* Glenview, IL: Scott, Foresman and Co.

TEN HOUTEN, W., J. W. MORRISON, E. P. DURRENBERGER, S. I. KOROLEV, and J. SCHEDER 1976 "More on split-brain research, culture, and cognition." *Current Anthropology* 17:503–511.

TESSLER, MARK, WILLIAM O'BARR, and DAVID SPAIN 1973 *Tradition and Identity in Changing Africa.* New York: Harper and Row Publishers, Inc.

TEXTOR, ROBERT 1977 "Foreword." *Anthropology and Education Quarterly* 8:37–39.

THAYER, NATHANIEL 1975 "Competition and conformity: an inquiry into the structure of the Japanese newspapers." In E. Vogel, ed., 1975, pp. 284–303.

THOMAS, ROBERT L. 1968 "Problems of manpower development." In I. Resnick, ed., 1968, *Tanzania: Revolution by Education.* Arusha: Longmans of Tanzania, pp. 106–122.

TINBERGEN, NIKOLAAS 1974 "Ethology and stress diseases." *Science,* 185:20–27.

TINDALL, B. ALLAN 1976 "Theory in the study of cultural transmission." *Annual Review of Anthropology* 5:195–208.

TRUEBA, HENRY 1974 "Bilingual bicultural education for Chicanos in the southwest." *Council on Anthropology and Education Newsletter* 5(3): 8–15.

TYACK, DAVID 1974 *The One Best System: A History of American Urban Education.* Cambridge, MA: Harvard University Press.

VAUGHAN, MICHALINA and MARGARET SCOTFORD ARCHER 1971 *Social Conflict and Educational Change in England and France 1789–1848.* Cambridge: Cambridge University Press.

VIDICH, ARTHUR and CHARLES MCREYNOLDS 1971 "Rhetoric versus reality: a study of New York City high school principals." In Wax, et al., eds. 1971, pp. 195–207.

VOGEL, EZRA F. 1967 "Kinship structure, migration to the city, and modernization." In R. Dore, ed., 1971, *Aspects of Social Change in Modern Japan*. Princeton: Princeton University Press, pp. 91–111.

VOGEL, EZRA F. 1968 *Japan's New Middle Class. The Salary Man and His Family in a Tokyo Suburb*. Berkeley: University of California Press.

VOGEL, EZRA, ed. 1975 *Modern Japanese Organization and Decision-Making*. Berkeley and Los Angeles: University of California Press.

VON BERTALANFFY, LUDWIG 1968 *General Systems Theory: Foundations, Development, Applications*, Revised edition. New York: George Braziller, Inc.

WALLACE, ANTHONY 1968 "Anthropological contributions to a theory of personality." In E. Norbeck, D. Price-Williams and W. McCord, eds., 1968 *The Study of Personality: An Interdisciplinary Appraisal*. New York: Holt, Rinehart and Winston, pp. 41–53.

WALLACE, ANTHONY 1970 *Culture and Personality*. Second Edition. New York: Random House, Inc.

WALLACE, ANTHONY and RAYMOND FOGELSON 1965 "The identity struggle." In I. Boszormenyi-Nagy and J. Framo, eds., 1965 *Intensive Family Therapy*. New York: Harper and Row Publishers, Inc., pp. 365–406.

WALLERSTEIN, IMMANUEL 1964 *The Road to Independence: Ghana and the Ivory Coast*. The Hague: Mouton.

WARD, BARBARA 1977 "Readers and audiences: an exploration of the spread of traditional Chinese culture." In R. Jain, ed., 1977, *Text and Context: the Social Anthropology of Tradition*. American Society for Anthropology Essays in Social Anthropology, vol. 2. Philadelphia: Institute for the Study of Human Issues.

WARD, MARTHA 1971 *Them Children: A Study in Language Learning*. New York: Holt, Rinehart and Winston, Inc.

WARD, THOMAS 1974 "Definitions of theory in sociology." In R. Denisoff, O. Callahan, and M. Levine, eds., 1974 *Theories and Paradigms in Contemporary Sociology*. Itasca, IL: F. E. Peacock Publishers, Inc.

WASON, P. C. 1968 " 'On the failure to eliminate hypotheses . . .'—a second look." In P. Wason and P. Johnson-Laird, eds., 1968, *Thinking and Reasoning*. Harmondsworth, Middlesex: Penguin. Reprinted in P. Johnson-Laird and P. Wason, eds., 1977, pp. 307–314.

WATANABE, MASAO 1974 "The conception of nature in Japanese culture." *Science* 184:279–282. See also letters of reply and Watanabe's rejoinder, *Science* 184:849–853.

WATKINS, MARK HANNA 1943 "The West African 'bush' school." *American Journal of Sociology* 48:666–675.

WATSON-FRANKE, MARIA-BARBARA 1976 "To learn for tomorrow: enculturation of girls and its social importance among the Guajiro of Venezuela." In J. Wilbert, ed., 1976, pp. 191–212.

WAX, MURRAY, STANLEY DIAMOND, and FRED GEARING, eds. 1971 *Anthropological Perspectives on Education.* New York: Basic Books, Inc.

WAX, MURRAY, ROSALIE WAX, and ROBERT DUMONT, JR. 1964 *Formal education in an American Indian community.* (with R. Holyrock and G. Onefeather). Monograph No. 1, Society for the Study of Social Problems.

WAX, MURRAY L. and ROSALIE H. WAX 1971 "Cultural deprivation as an educational ideology." In E. Leacock, ed., 1971, pp. 127–139.

WAX, ROSALIE 1967 "The warrior dropouts." In J. Howard, ed., 1970, *Awakening Minorities: American Indians, Mexican Americans, Puerto Ricans.* Chicago: Aldine Publishing Company, pp. 27–42.

WEBB, EUGENE, DONALD CAMPBELL, RICHARD SCHWARTZ, and LEE SECHREST 1966 *Unobtrusive Measures: Nonreactive Research in the Social Sciences.* Chicago: Rand McNally College Publishing Company.

WENTZ, ROBERT 1977 "Critique." *Anthropology and Education Quarterly* 8:161–162.

WHITING, BEATRICE (ed.) 1963 *Six Cultures: Studies of Child Rearing.* New York: John Wiley and Sons, Inc.

WHITING, JOHN 1977 "A model for psychocultural research." In P. Leiderman et al., eds., 1977, *Culture and Infancy: Variations in the Human Experience.* New York: Academic Press, Inc.

WHITING, JOHN and IRVIN CHILD 1953 *Child Training and Personality: a Cross-cultural Study.* New Haven: Yale University Press.

WHORF, BENJAMIN 1941 "The relation of habitual thought and behavior to language." In L. Spier, A. I. Hallowell, and S. Newman, eds., 1960 *Language, Culture, and Personality: Essays in Memory of Edward Sapir.* Menasha, Wisc.: Sapir Memorial Publication Fund, pp. 75–93.

WILBERT, JOHANNES, ed. 1976a *Enculturation in Latin America: an Anthology.* Latin American Studies, vol. 37. Los Angeles: University of California Latin American Center.

WILBERT, JOHANNES 1976b "To become a maker of canoes: an essay in Warao enculturation." In J. Wilbert, ed., 1976, pp. 303–358.

WILKINSON, RUPERT 1964 *Gentlemanly Power: British Leadership and the Public School Tradition, A Comparative Study in Making of Rulers.* London: Oxford University Press.

WILLIAMS, FREDERICK 1970 "Language, attitude and social change." In F. Williams, ed., 1970, pp. 380–399.

WILLIAMS, FREDERICK, ed. 1970 *Language and Poverty: Perspectives on a Theme.* Chicago: Markham Publishing Company.

WILSON, STEPHEN 1977 "The use of ethnographic techniques in educational research." *Review of Educational Research* 47:245–265.

WINTROB, RONALD 1968 "Acculturation, identification, and psychopathology among Cree Indian youth." In N. Chance, ed., 1968, *Conflict in Culture.* Ottawa: Canadian Research Centre for Anthropology, University of Ottawa.

WITKIN, HERMAN 1963 "Discussion." In J. Wright and J. Kagan, eds., 1963, *Basic Cognitive Processes in Children.* Monographs of the Society for Research in Child Development 28(2):118–122.

WITKIN, HERMAN 1967 "A cognitive-style approach to cross-cultural research." *International Journal of Psychology* 2(4):233–250.

WITKIN, HERMAN and J. BERRY 1975 "Psychological differentiation in cross-cultural perspective." *Journal of Cross-cultural Psychology* 6:5–87.

WITKIN, HERMAN, R. B. DYK, H. F. FATERSON, D. R. GOODENOUGH, and S. A. KARP 1962 *Psychological Differentiation.* New York: John Wiley and Sons, Inc.

WITKIN, HERMAN, HANNA F. FATERSON, DONALD R. GOODENOUGH, and JUDITH BIRNBAUM 1966 "Cognitive patterning in mildly retarded boys." *Child Development* 37(2):301–316.

WOLCOTT, HARRY 1967 *A Kwakiutl Village and School.* New York: Holt, Rinehart and Winston, Inc.

WOLCOTT, HARRY F. 1973 *The Man in the Principal's Office: An Ethnography.* New York: Holt, Rinehart and Winston, Inc.

WOLCOTT, HARRY 1974 "The elementary school principal: notes from a field study." In G. Spindler, ed., 1974, pp. 176–204.

WOLCOTT, HARRY 1974 "The teacher as an enemy." In G. Spindler, ed., 1974, pp. 411–425.

WOLCOTT, HARRY 1975 *Ethnographic Approaches to Research in Education. A Bibliography on Method.* Anthropology Curriculum Project, Publication No. 75-1. Athens, GA: University of Georgia.

WORTH, SOL 1969 "The development of a semiotic of film." *Semiotica* 1:282–321.

WORTH, SOL and JOHN ADAIR 1972 *Through Navajo Eyes. An Exploration in Film Communication and Anthropology.* Bloomington: Indiana University Press.

WYLIE, LAURENCE 1964 *Village in the Vaucluse,* Second edition, revised. Cambridge: Harvard University Press.

ZBOROWSKI, MARK 1955 "The place of book-learning in traditional Jewish culture." In M. Mead and H. Wolfenstein, eds., 1960 *Childhood in Contemporary Cultures.* Chicago: University of Chicago Press, pp. 118–141.

ZETTERBERG, HANS 1965 *On Theory and Verification in Sociology,* Third edition. New York: The Bedminster Press, Incorporated.

INDEX

Early, J. 238
Eastern European *shtetl* 32, 33, 35, 36, 38, 40, 78, 144, 145, 147, 161, 175
ecological analysis (*see* analysis, ecological)
Eddy, E. 150
education, definition of 28, 39, 244
education, remedial 210–14
educational institutions, change in 65, 79, 107–10, 118, 190, 192, 214–16, 221–23, 225–28, 231, 235, 238, 243
educational process 2, 30, 63, 68, 77, 78
educational system 1, 2, 9, 63, 64, 66–68, 101–10, 221–36, 244, 245
egalitarianism 37, 222–25, 228, 233
Eggan, D. 78
Ekman, P. 87
Ember, C. 22
enculturation 22, 26–28, 70, 101, 214
England (*see also* Great Britain) 17, 34, 107–10, 112, 113, 182
Erickson, F. 59
Eskimo, Canadian 166, 174, 192, 196–98, 238, 239
Eskimo, Greenlandic 166, 174, 192, 193–96, 198, 199, 206
ethnographic method 48, 53, 54, 58, 59, 105
Everhart, R. 58
explanation, scientific 47–49, 52, 56, 58, 61, 62, 64, 107

Fabrega, H. 6, 7
facts 38, 42, 43, 45, 53, 57, 245, 246
Filstead, W. 50, 59
Fischer, J. 202, 203
Foerstel, L. 5
Foley, D. 162
Forge, A. 5, 137, 138, 164, 170, 179, 180
Fortes, M. 78
Foster, P. 112, 113, 120, 121, 127, 134, 235
Fox, R. 69
France 35, 38, 44, 107–10, 119, 180, 184, 201
Friedenberg, E. 37, 38, 65
Friedman, N. 55
Fuchs, E. 79, 188, 204, 205
functional analysis (*see* analysis, functional)

Gallaher, A. 189
Garfinkel, H. 8, 52, 56, 59
Gay, J. 15, 138–40, 167
Gearing, F. 29, 30, 87, 89, 93
Gerbner, G. 172, 173, 176
Germany 33, 34, 216, 217
Gerth, H. 39
Ghana 111–14, 119–22, 127–35, 200, 201, 206, 207, 216, 217, 219, 220, 230
Ghana, University of 120, 128–31
Gibbs, J. 104, 105
Gladwin, T. 141–43, 175, 179, 180
Glaser, B. 44, 52
Goetz, J. 40, 58, 65, 79, 82, 95, 189
Goffman, E. 75, 100
Gold Coast (*see* Ghana)
Goldsen, R. 165, 176
Goodenough, W. 3, 39, 100
Great Britain (*see also* England) 111, 112, 119, 134, 151, 183, 217, 219

Grindal, B. 121
Gross, L. 163
Guajiro 140, 148
Gump, P. 66, 68, 69
Gumperz, J. 92, 93

Hagstrom, W. 102
Hall, B. 215
Hall, E. 5, 8, 22, 87
Hall, I. 135
Handel, W. 6
Hanson, N. 42
Harley, G. 104, 105
Harlow, H. 9
Harrington, C. 49
Hartley, R. 176
Hawaiian-American 90, 94
Henry, J. 38, 76, 77, 79, 97, 100, 102, 154
Herndon, J. 78
Heron, A. 14
Herskovitz, M. 27, 39
Herzog, J. 11, 22
Higgins, P. 238
Hobart, C. 73, 166, 192–98, 238, 239
Honigmann, J. 166, 198
Hopi 78
Horner, V. 100
Horton, D. 67
Howard, A. 90
Hsu, F. 127
Hymes, D. 23, 30, 41, 88

identity 28, *70–77*, 80, 81, 88, 93, 94, 96, 100, 124, 125, 136, 140, 144, 148–50, 152–55, 157–61, 164, 176, 195–98, 238, 245
Illich, I. 181, 235
India 150–53, 161, 170, 171, 177, 183
information processing, cognition as 5–7, 19, 22, 163
information processing, modes of (*see* cognition, modes of)
innovation, educational (*see* educational institutions, change in)
innovation, primate 11
instructional strategies 10, 29, 35, 73, 78, 81–83, 89–93, 97, 137–43, 145–49, 156, 163, 164, 167, 170, 171, 175, 188, 194, 195, 197, 205, 215, 238, 241, 242, 246
intelligence quotient (*see* cognitive skills, testing of)
interpretation 3, 4, 8, 16, 18, 21, 26, 28, 43, 47, 55, 57, 58, 64, 67, 69, 70, 79, 80, 85, 88, 89, 98–100, 136, 158–60, 172, 174, 182, 184, 242, 246
interpretive frameworks (*see* interpretation)
interpretive process (*see* interpretation)
Irwin, H. 13
Ishida, T. 127, 132, 135, 177
Ivory Coast 119

Jackson, P. 65, 96
Jahoda, G. 22
Japan 86, 110–19, 122–27, 131–35, 140, 143, 149, 150, 185, 201–3, 207, 240
Japanese-American 71, 72
Jencks, C. 214

socialization 21, 26, 27, 49, 61, 70, 80, 88, 99, 191, 132, 235
sociopsychological analysis (*see* analysis, sociopsychological)
Sommer, R. 65
space, use of (*see also* proxemics) 65, 94, 95
Spindler, G. 36, 37, 62, 63, 157, 158
Spiro, M. 7
Spradley, J. 7, 8
Standard American English 93, 94, 167, 214
Strauss, A. 44, 52, 59, 100
structural-functional analysis (*see* analysis, functional)
structure and process as analytic focus 49, 77, 98, 109, 110, 162, 174, 175, 245
Studstill, J. 48, 49
Sunley, R. 78
Svendsen, K. 220
systems, analysis of social 61–64, 99, 106
systems analysis 30

Talbert, C. 76
Tallensi 78
Tanganyika (*see* Tanzania)
Tanzania 216–37, 240
teachers (*see also* roles; identities) 33, 66, 67, 73–76, 78, 79, 89–91, 94, 116, 117, 125, 177, 188–91, 194–97, 222, 232
teachers, parental character of 76, 97, 98, 160, 161
teachers, socialization of 79, 150
television, educational 165, 166, 172, 173, 176, 177, 208, 209, 239
ten Houten, W. 7
Tessler, M. 240
Textor, R. 41
Thayer, N. 177
theories, scientific 43–46, 57, 243, 245
thinking (*see* cognition; cognitive maps; cognitive strategies)
Tinbergen, N. 63
Tindall, B. 30
Tokyo University 115, 117
triangulation 53, 54, 56
Trobrianders 15
Trueba, H. 240
Truk 201–3, 207
Tyack, D. 186

University College of the Gold Coast (*see* Ghana, University of)
University of Allahabad (*see* Allahabad, University of)
University of Ghana (*see* Ghana, University of)
University, Tokyo (*see* Tokyo University)

U.S. (*see also* Anglo-American; Black American; Cherokee; Chicano; Hawaiian-American; Hopi; Japanese-American; Menomini; Native American; Navajo; Puerto Rican; Sioux; Warm Springs Indian) 8, 19, 23, 28–30, 37, 38, 40, 48, 60–100, 118, 150, 153–55, 161, 162, 176, 181, 182, 184–92, 206, 210–16, 236, 237

Vai 103
validity 49–52, 54–56
values 35, 57, 69, 70–72, 79, 81, 83, 88, 91, 101, 114, 118, 123, 131, 144, 145, 153, 155, 156, 180, 202, 209, 222, 223, 228, 229, 232, 234, 239, 241
Vaughan, M. 107–9
Venezuela (*see* Guajiro; Warao)
verification 50, 52
Vidich, A. 188, 238
Vogel, E. 111, 116, 119, 135
von Bertalanffy, L. 99

Wallace, A. 4, 21, 29, 50
Wallerstein, I. 113, 119, 128, 130
Warao 175
Ward, B. 170
Ward, M. 100, 175
Warm Springs Indian 91, 92
Wason, P. 22, 45
Watanabe, M. 21
Watkins, M. 105
Watson-Franke, M. 140, 175
Wax, M. 73, 211
Wax, R. 153–55
Webb, E. 54
Wentz, R. 56
Western society and culture 15, 39
Whiting, B. 49
Whiting, J. 49
Wilbert, J. 175
Wilkinson, R. 183
Williams, F. 88
Wilson, S. 41
Wintrob, R. 161
Witkin, H. 21, 23, 213
Wolcott, H. 54, 58, 62, 63, 76, 89, 150, 176, 188, 191
Worth, S. 5, 168–70, 172, 176
Wylie, L. 35

Zaire 48, 207
Zambia 30
Zborowski, M. 33, 36, 40, 78, 147, 175